VMware vSphere 6.5 Host Resources Deep Dive

VMware vSphere 6.5 Host Resources Deep Dive

International Standard Book Number: ISBN 9781540873064

Version: 1.0

ABOUT THE AUTHORS

Frank Denneman is a Senior Staff Architect at VMware R&D focusing on VMware Cloud on AWS. Frank is a VCDX (29) and co-author of the bestselling vSphere Clustering Deep Dive series. Frank presents on a regular basis at global virtualization events and has been a VMworld Top 10 speaker for five consecutive years. You can find his articles at **www.frankdenneman.nl**. Follow Frank on Twitter @frankdenneman.

Niels Hagoort is a freelance Virtualization Architect with more than 15 years of experience. Niels has extensive knowledge in the field of designing, building and implementing complex enterprise IT infrastructures. Niels presents on a regular basis at global virtualization events and is a VCDX (212). You can find his articles at **www.cloudfix.nl**. Follow Niels on Twitter @NHagoort.

ACKNOWLEDGEMENTS

If you want to go fast go alone.
If you want to go far go together.

This African proverb resonated strongly with us. Although we have spent countless of hours of writing, editing, rewriting, deleting and rewriting again, this book wouldn't be in its current shape with the help of the following people.

We would like to thank Kit Colbert for providing us an amazing foreword. Pat Gelsinger, Carl Waldspurger, Christos Karamanolis and Andrew Lambeth for sharing their thoughts on the state of the industry and how new and future services require a refocus on host design.

We want to extend our gratitude towards Myles Gray, Marco van Baggum, Duncan Epping, Rutger Kosters and Anthony Spiteri for reviewing the book from an administrator and architect point of view. Jane Rimmer did her utmost best to educate us on the finesse of the English grammar.

Despite the lab providing us immense value, presenting us a test bed to create and destroy many workloads, we stood on the shoulders of many giants by distilling their research work and academic papers.

Although reverse engineering helps you grasp the finer details of the product we would extend our gratitude to Chris Gianos (Intel) and VMware employees; Valentin Bondzio, Haoqiang Zheng, Richard Lu, Duncan Epping, Cormac Hogan, Paudie O'Riordan and Pete Koehler to help us stay honest and review the content from a technical perspective. External to VMware, Ed van Hout, Joop Carels and Rosa Martinez Perallon for providing ideas on various network related content and help with test setups.

And last but not least, thanks for supporting this book within VMware: Charu Chaubal, Kristine Anderson, Michael Adams and Mark Lohmeyer.

FOREWORD

When Frank and Niels approached me to write the foreword for their latest book, I jumped at the opportunity. Obviously both of them are titans within the virtualization and cloud computing community, so it was an honor just to be asked. But what really got me excited was their purpose behind writing the book. Both Frank and Niels are strong, passionate technologists, never content for only a surface-level understanding of the systems they build and use. Instead they always are digging deeper, looking to learn more and more. This book is the fruit of that passion. It's about getting back to basics, gaining deep insight into the systems we run and how to maximize their value and performance.

Stepping back, the general direction of the IT industry is toward lightweight, distributed applications, sometimes called 'microservices'. The simultaneous advent of containers has brought a new approach to 'build once, run anywhere.' Applications are now bundled in containers, designed to be scaled out, and can then be run on the cloud of the user's choice. Need to support more load? Simply increase the number of application instances and presto, problem solved. In this model, one might assume that the specifics of the underlying infrastructure don't matter. It's been abstracted away by higher level APIs. In fact, solutions around 'functions as a service' (FaaS) have taken to be called 'serverless'. Of course, we all know that this code has to run somewhere, but the point is that the user doesn't need to know or care. Thus, we can consider this paradigm as effectively 'serverless.' Yet the notion that infrastructure details don't matter is simply false.

To be clear, I'm a big fan of all these technologies. The cloud-native revolution that's happening - with the associated technologies and approaches of containers, FaaS, and microservice architectures - is undeniably yielding tremendous benefits and allowing us as an industry to do things we couldn't have imagined before.

At the same time, this doesn't mean that we don't need to care about what's happening under the covers. The reality is that infrastructure matters. Infrastructure configuration matters. Hardware matters. All the software layers we add on top of that hardware also matter. Whether It is virtualization, orchestration, cloud, or even the operating system itself, all of these affect performance and potentially correctness of any solution.

Take one simple example: virtualization versus 'bare metal' performance. Many assume that virtualized workloads are always slower than those running on 'bare metal'. But what those people fail to realize is that the application is not running directly on 'bare metal', but indeed on top of an OS. And this operating system can also introduce its own overheads. One particularly interesting example of this is with memory-bound workloads, such as big data or AI type workloads. What we've found is that running these workloads on VMware vSphere actually outperforms Linux 'bare metal' systems by around 5% in some scenarios. How can this be, given that vSphere has some virtualization overhead (even as minimal as it is these days)? Well it turns out that VMware ESXi has far superior NUMA scheduling capabilities than Linux and because of that memory access latencies are lower with VMware ESXi, giving it a slight performance advantage. (Of course, this book delves quite deeply into NUMA architecture!)

Details matter. Knowing your systems inside and out is the only way to be sure you've properly handled those details. It's about having a passion for these details. It's about loving the systems we build. It's about understanding them end-to-end. This is the philosophy of Frank and Niels and this is why I'm so excited to be writing this foreword!

To some degree, It is about appreciating the beauty and complexity of all the systems around us. I'm particularly passionate about operating systems. I studied them in college and when I first came to VMware, I was a developer on the VMkernel team. (The VMkernel is the core part of the VMware ESXi OS.) I think operating systems are amazingly cool because they create all the fundamental mechanisms we take for granted. For example: threading.
We all understand threading at a high level, but it is up to the operating

system to actually implement it. I remember in the advanced operating systems class at my university, we actually had to implement a function called swtch(). swtch() was a mind-blowing function: you called it from the context of one thread and when it returned, you were now in a different thread! Isn't that crazy - when the function returned, you were somehow (magically?) in a different thread. How did that work? What needed to happen for this thread switch to occur? These were questions we had to answer and understand well enough to code. Thread switching seems like a random thing to bring up, but it literally happens trillions of times a day across the world. If we could somehow make swtch() (or more correctly its modern-day equivalents) even 0.001% faster, how much more computing could we get done across the world?

During my time as a VMkernel engineer, I would always want to be sure interview candidates had a strong understanding of the systems they were going to work on. Specifically, I would ask them to describe, in as much detail as they could, what happens when one types 'l' then 's' then '<enter>' in a terminal on a Linux system.

The simple answer is of course that the current directory's contents are listed. But that really misses the point. What's happening within the system in order for the contents of the current directory to be listed? How does it work? If a candidate couldn't talk for least fifteen minutes about what happens, then, for me, he or she didn't understand operating systems well enough to work on the VMkernel team.

The reality is that it can easily take hours to go into just the basics of what happens when typing 'ls<enter>'. You could start with what happens within the physical keyboard when you depress those keys. How does the keyboard know which key is pressed and how is it encoding that information? How does it send the fact that a key was just pressed back to the Linux host? Is the keyboard physically connected or wireless? If It is wireless, how does that work? (A discussion of Bluetooth protocols alone could easily span hours!) Once the key press arrives at the host, how does the host handle it? How do interrupts work? How does the operating system do process switching (back to the swtch() question)? What happens in the top half versus bottom half of an interrupt handler? Why is there even a top and bottom half? How is locking handled? You can go in so many directions here, diving down into the details of how the physical CPU works, getting into the specifics of virtual memory and how It is implemented, or maybe even what it looks like if this guest OS is actually running inside a VM (another multi-hour detour!). Then there's the question of how those key presses are 'delivered' to the terminal application. How does Linux even know to send them to that app versus another one? Assuming you get as far as the '<enter>' part, what happens then? How does Linux know where the binary executable for the 'ls' command is on-disk (it does have to load it from somewhere!)? What happens when it 'execs' that process?

So as you can see, fifteen minutes only allows you to scratch the surface. I don't even claim to fully understand all aspects of what happens when you type 'ls<enter>'! But nevertheless all these things happen, constantly throughout the day on all the computers all over the world. The level of complexity is daunting, but rather than scaring us off, we crave to learn more. We see this as an opportunity to gain deeper insight and appreciation for our systems and then use that knowledge to make them better, to optimize them further.

As I read through proof copies of this book, I was just astounded at the number of design decisions that go into building any system and the massive effect on performance it can have. Just focusing on CPU and memory for a second (as I'm most familiar with them), do you assume you can put any sized VMs on any ESX host? Have you considered how those VMs map down to the NUMA nodes on those ESX hosts? If the VM has more memory than a single NUMA node, then necessarily some of its memory accesses will hit remote NUMA nodes, degrading performance. Furthermore, questions regarding whether to enable Hyper-threading or not or how to configure power management in the BIOS can have a large effect on performance. How much should you overcommit CPUs (i.e. vCPU to pCPU ratio)?

What data are you using to know you're not missing big on a higher consolidation ratio that wouldn't sacrifice performance? Have you considered the type of memory in your system and how its throughput relates to the needs of the applications running on it? Are you using large pages? Is there a good reason you're not, as not doing so has dramatic performance consequences. Are you probably accounting for both host and VM memory overhead in your memory consolidation ratios?

As you can see, like the seemingly simple question of 'explain what happens when you type 'ls<enter>'', the question of workload performance on vSphere explodes into a constellation of considerations, ranging from the physical hardware to the vSphere software layer. I hope that you can start to appreciate that, as I mentioned at the beginning, while the IT industry is moving to a 'build once, run anywhere' mentality, the reality is that specifics of the infrastructure matter. Details matter.

This book shows that we can fundamentally and materially improve the systems we're building. Application not running fast enough? We don't always need to adhere to the knee-jerk reaction to add more application instances! (Such an infrastructure-agnostic solution!) We can make the currently running ones faster by deeply understanding and optimizing our systems. That's the point of this book. We know we can always do better.

So how well do you understand your systems? I can guarantee you that after reading this book, you'll understand them much more deeply! Have fun!

Kit Colbert
San Francisco, CA
May 2017

Kit Colbert is the VP & CTO of the Cloud Platform Business Unit at VMware. At the start of his career, Kit was the technical lead for the creation, development, and delivery of the vMotion and Storage vMotion features in vSphere.

PREFACE

First of all, we would like to thank you for obtaining this book. Writing a book is a great experience, but the reward comes when people, like you, read our book.

We set out writing this book to refocus on the fundamental component of the virtual datacenter, the ESXi host. We noticed that a lot of today's focus is on advanced distributed platforms such as vSAN and NSX. These topics are exciting and take IT to the next level, but we also understand that proper host design and management fabricates the foundation for success.

The introduction of these new overlay services presents new consumers of host resources. Correct selection and configuration of these physical components lead to creating a platform that performs consistently. This platform is the foundation for the higher-level services and increased consolidation ratios.

The book contains four parts, CPU, memory, storage, and networking. Within each section, we create a foundation by focusing on the physical elements first, before moving on to the virtual layer of the VMkernel and VM configurations.

Our goal is to provide you with an in-depth view of the four primary host resources. Instead of showing you where to click to achieve a particular configuration, we explain the inner-workings of these components and how various physical and virtual constructs interact with each other.

We believe that this method provides a basis – a foundation on its own - that helps you to design and build the best possible architecture that aligns with the customer requirements each and every time.
The one thing we ask from you is to approach all content with an open mind. Through experience, we all learned a lot. Experience we use every

day to build and manage complex virtual infrastructures. We use recommendations presented by community experts. Some recommendations made in the past are still used today. Typically, these experiences and recommendations are based on the limitations of the technical stack at that particular time.

Fortunately, both software and hardware improved over the years. Some improvements have been evolutionary, some improvements revolutionary. With this in mind, older recommendations can be outdated, and some lessons learned might not be applicable anymore. Therefore, it is key to consume the content in an unbiased way allowing you to rediscover the fascinating world of host resource technology.

Before you begin your journey through this book, we would like to emphasize that this technical deep dive is to explore the boundaries of the technology in your datacenter. It can help to clear the shrouds when travelling uncharted land. This book should not be seen as a manual to get vSphere working. vSphere is extremely easy to use. We have been working with the product for over ten years and it still amazes us what it can do straight out of the box. It provides a stable, consistent, properly performing platform for 95% of the workloads.

This book helps you to understand the finesse of system architecture. To help you to get the most out of the platform you run. Customization breeds complexity! It's up to you how far you want to push the envelope.

Frank and Niels

P1

CPU RESOURCES

PROLOGUE

Having worked on microprocessors for almost 30 years, they have always had a special allure as the 'center' of the system, where it all comes together: the application runs there, storage and networking subsystems are called upon and memory feeds the beast.

The integration of other subsystems which began in earnest with my beloved 80486 taking on the Cache and floating point has and will continue unabated now taking memory control, security, networking, fabric, graphics and fpga functions along with them.

The multi-core transition we began in the last decade likewise has continued unabated with today's CPU's at a mind bogging 24 cores with more to come. This trend, more than any other, has created the potential for incredible workload density per socket.

While the ascent of Moore's is moderating a bit it is far from over. These trends, combined with virtualization and distributed systems enable a cloud infrastructure that is tackling unimaginable breakthroughs in AI, Machine Learning, analytics and IOT that will keep our system design work alive and well for decades to come. The magic of technology is alive and very well.

Pat Gelsinger

Pat Gelsinger is the CEO of VMware. Before joining VMware, Pat led EMC's Information Infrastructure Products business as president and COO. A respected IT industry veteran, he was at Intel for 30 years becoming the company's first CTO and driving the creation of key industry technologies including USB and Wi-Fi. He led Intel to be the dominant supplier of the microprocessor – while in the significant role as the architect of the original 80486 processor.

01

CPU ARCHITECTURE

At his previous employer, Frank had access to telemetry data of many VMware customers worldwide. At the end of 2015, Frank published the research results of the CPU and memory configuration of ESXi hosts. Recent studies showed that these numbers have not skewed in the last year.

Insights into ESXi Host Configurations

The study focused on the distribution of CPU socket configurations. After analyzing the dataset, it is clear that dual socket CPU configurations are the most popular setup in modern datacenters. Four-socket systems are not as popular as they used to be. Starting in 2005, we deployed Quad-CPU four-socket servers to host the virtualized workload. With each passing year, core density increased. Compare those systems with the current Xeon version; the 'mid-range' E5-2683 v4 provides the same number of cores as the entire system back then.

CPU Density increase, licensing cost coupled with risk-mitigation (smaller failure domains) typically drive the decision towards scale-out (more smaller server) than scale-up (fewer big servers).

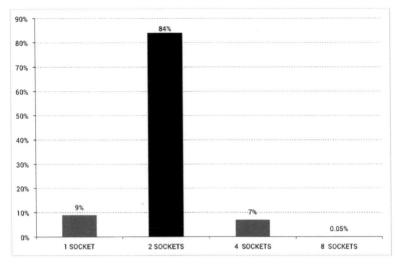

Figure 1: Number of CPU Sockets in ESXi Hosts

CPU Core Density per ESXi Host

The 16 CPU cores per ESXi host is the most popular core density configuration. With the availability of the E5-2600 v4 (Broadwell) and the upcoming Skylake release this year, it is expected to see ESXi hosts with a CPU count that is between 40 to 50 cores.

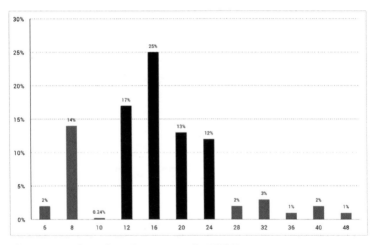

Figure 2: Total Number of CPU Cores in ESXi Hosts

Core Distribution of Dual CPU ESXi Hosts

When zooming into the dataset of a dual CPU ESXi host, it becomes apparent that eight core CPU's are the most popular. Compared with an earlier dataset, quad and six core systems are slowly reducing popularity. Six core CPU's were introduced in 2010, assumable most will be up for renewal end 2016 begin 2017, a perfect time to publish a book about ESXi host resources. ;) Chapter two and three zoom into the CPU microarchitecture and the Uncore to provide detailed insight why particular CPU packages provide more value than core count alone.

Memory Configuration

Getting insights into memory configuration of the servers provides us a clear picture of the overall compute power of these systems. What is the most popular memory configuration of a dual socket server? As it turns out, the most popular configurations are systems containing 256 GB or 384 GB of memory.

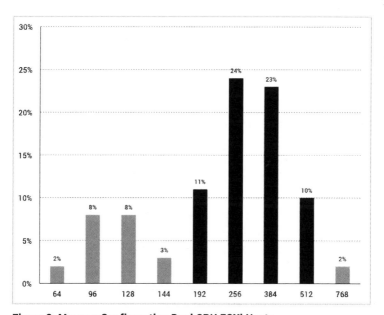

Figure 3: Memory Configuration Dual CPU ESXi Hosts

384 GB is an interesting memory configuration in a modern dual socket system. Discovering this configuration triggered the idea of writing about optimal CPU and memory configurations of modern ESXi systems. Part 2 covers memory configuration in detail.

One thing to note is that more than 95% of the servers use Intel microprocessors. Due to these numbers, we focus ourselves on exploring the intricacies of Intel processors deployed in dual socket systems. Most of the content applies to large-scale servers. However, we have not invested time into analyzing potential caveats when using those systems.

Nehalem microarchitecture (2008) introduced *Non-uniform memory access* (NUMA) architecture to the virtual infrastructure. Although Part 1 focuses on CPU architecture, we mostly dive into this shared memory architecture and examine its close relationship with CPU scheduling.

Non-Uniform Memory Access

NUMA is a shared memory architecture used in today's multiprocessing systems. Each CPU is assigned its local memory and can access memory from other CPUs in the system. Local memory access provides the best performance; it provides low latency and high bandwidth. Accessing memory that is owned by the other CPU has a performance penalty, higher latency, and lower bandwidth.

Modern applications and operating systems such as ESXi support NUMA by default. Yet to provide the best performance, *Virtual Machine* (VM) configuration should be done with the NUMA architecture in mind. If incorrectly designed, inconsistent behavior or overall performance degradation occurs. It can happen for that particular VM, or in the worst-case scenario, for all VMs running on that ESXi host.

But before we arrive at modern CPU architectures, it is helpful to review the history of shared-memory multiprocessor architectures to understand why we are using NUMA systems today.

From UMA to NUMA

It seems that an architecture called Uniform Memory Access would be a better fit when designing a consistent, low latency, high bandwidth platform. Modern system architectures will restrict it from being truly uniform. To understand the reason behind this we need to go back in history to identify the key drivers of parallel computing.

With the introduction of relational databases in the early seventies, the need for systems that could service multiple concurrent user operations and excessive data generation became mainstream.

Despite the impressive rate of uniprocessor performance, multiprocessor systems were better equipped to handle these workloads. To provide a cost-effective system, shared memory address space became the focus of R&D labs.
Early on, systems using a crossbar switch were advocated, however with this design complexity scaled along with the increase of processors, which made the bus-based system more attractive. Processors in a bus system are allowed to access the entire memory space by sending requests on the bus, a cost effective way to use the available memory as optimally as possible.

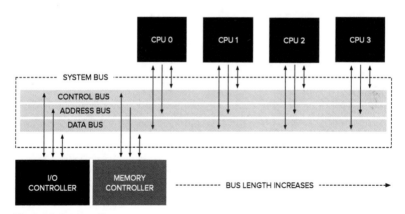

Figure 4: System Bus

However, bus-based systems have their scalability problems. The main issue is the limited amount of bandwidth. It restricts the number of processors the bus can accommodate. Adding CPUs to the system introduces two major areas of concern. Adding a CPU:

- Decreases the available bandwidth per node
- Increases the bus length, thereby increasing latency

The performance growth of CPU, particularly the speed gap between the processor and the memory performance was, and still is, devastating for multiprocessors. Since the speed gap between processor and memory was expected to increase, a lot of effort went into developing effective strategies to manage the memory systems. One of these strategies was adding memory cache, which introduced a multitude of challenges. Solving these problems is still the primary focus of today for CPU design teams, a lot of research is happening on caching structures and sophisticated algorithms to avoid cache misses.

Caching Snoop Protocols

Attaching a cache to each CPU increases performance in many ways. Bringing memory closer to the CPU reduces the average memory access time and the bandwidth load on the memory bus. The challenge with adding cache to each CPU in a shared-memory architecture is that it allows multiple copies of a memory block to exist. This is referred to as the cache-coherency problem.

Caching Snoop protocols were invented to create a model that provides the correct data while not eating up all the bandwidth on the bus.

The most popular protocol, write-invalidate, erases all other copies of data before writing the local cache. Any subsequent read of this data by other processors will detect a cache miss in their local cache and is serviced from the cache of another CPU containing the most recently modified data. This model saved a lot of bus bandwidth and allowed for Uniform Memory Access systems to emerge in the early 1990s.

Uniform Memory Access Architecture

Processors of Bus-based multiprocessors that experience the same - uniform - access time to any memory module in the system are referred to as *Uniform Memory Access* (UMA) systems.

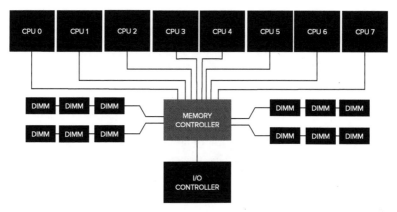

Figure 5: UMA Architecture

With UMA systems, the CPUs connect via a system bus (Front-Side Bus) to the northbridge. The northbridge contains the memory controller and all communication to and from memory must pass through the northbridge. The I/O controller, responsible for managing I/O to all devices, is connected to the northbridge. Therefore, every I/O has to go through the northbridge to reach the CPU.

Multiple busses and memory channels are used to double the available bandwidth and reduce the bottleneck of the northbridge. To increase the memory bandwidth even further some systems connected external memory controllers to the northbridge, improving bandwidth and support of more memory. However, due to the internal bandwidth of the chip and the broadcasting nature of early Snoopy cache protocols, UMA was considered to have a limited scalability. With today's use of high-speed flash devices, pushing hundreds of thousands of IO's per second, they were right that this architecture would not scale for future workloads.

29

Non-Uniform Memory Access Architecture

To improve scalability and performance, three critical changes were made to the shared-memory multiprocessors architecture:

- Non-Uniform Memory Access organization
- Point-to-Point Interconnect topology
- Scalable cache coherence solutions

Non-Uniform Memory Access Organization

NUMA moves away from a centralized pool of memory and introduces topological properties. By classifying memory location based on the signal path length from the processor to the memory, latency and bandwidth bottlenecks are avoided. Redesigning the whole system of the processor and chipset does this. NUMA architectures gained popularity at the end of the 90's by SGI supercomputers using it on systems such as the Cray Origin 2000. NUMA helped to identify the location of the memory. In the case of these systems, they had to determine which memory region in which chassis held the memory bits.

In the first half of the millennial decade, AMD brought NUMA to the enterprise landscape where UMA systems reigned supreme. In 2003, the AMD Opteron family was introduced, featuring Integrated Memory Controllers with each CPU owning designated memory banks. Each CPU has now its own memory address space.

A NUMA optimized OS such as ESXi allows workload to consume memory from both memory address spaces while optimizing for local memory access. Let's use an example of a two CPU system to clarify the distinction between local and remote memory access within a single system.

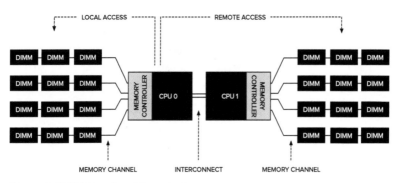

Figure 6: NUMA Local and Remote Access

The memory connected to the memory controller of the CPU 0 is considered local memory. Memory connected to another CPU socket (CPU 1) is deemed to be remote for CPU 0. Remote memory access has an additional latency overhead compared to local memory access, as it has to traverse the point-to-point link (Interconnect) and connect to the remote memory controller. As a result of the different memory locations and distances, this system experiences 'non-uniform' memory access time.

Point-to-Point Interconnect

AMD introduced their point-to-point connection HyperTransport with the AMD Opteron microarchitecture. Intel moved away from their dual independent bus architecture in 2007 by incorporating the QuickPath Architecture in their Nehalem processor family design.

The Intel Nehalem architecture was a significant design change within the Intel microarchitecture and is considered the first true generation of the Intel Core series. The current Broadwell architecture is the 4th generation of the Intel Core brand (Intel Xeon E5 v4), the last section in this chapter contains more information on the microarchitecture generations. Within the QuickPath architecture, the memory controllers moved to the CPU and introduced the *QuickPath Point-to-point Interconnect* (QPI) as data links between CPUs in the system.

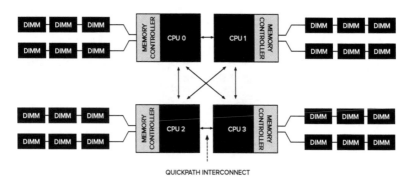

QUICKPATH INTERCONNECT

Figure 7: QuickPath Interconnect Architecture

The Nehalem microarchitecture not only replaced the legacy front-side bus but also reorganized the entire sub-system into a modular design for server CPU. This modular design was introduced as the Uncore, and it creates the building blocks for caching, and QuickPath Interconnect speeds.

Removing the front-side bus improves bandwidth scalability issues. Yet intra- and inter-processor communications have to be considered when dealing with enormous amounts of memory capacity and bandwidth. Both the Integrated Memory Controller and the QuickPath Interconnects are a part of the Uncore and are *Model Specific Registers* (MSR). They connect to a MSR that provides the intra- and inter-processor communication.

The modularity of the Uncore architecture allows Intel to provide different QPI speeds. At the time of writing the Intel Broadwell-EP microarchitecture (2016) offers 6.4 *Giga-transfers per second* (GT/s), 8.0 GT/s and 9.6 GT/s, respectively providing a theoretical maximum bandwidth of 25.6 GB/s, 32 GB/s and 38.4 GB/s between the CPUs.

The front-side bus provided 1.6 GT/s or 12.8 GB/s of platform bandwidth to put the QPI performance into perspective. When introducing Sandy Bridge Intel rebranded Uncore into System Agent, yet the current documentation still sports the term Uncore. You can find more about QuickPath and the Uncore in chapter 2.

Scalable Cache Coherence

Each core has a private path to the LLC. Each path consists of a thousand wires, and you can imagine this doesn't scale well if you want to keep on decreasing the transistor die manufacturing process size (currently 14 nanometers) while also increasing the number of cores that require cache access.

To be able to scale, the Sandy Bridge architecture moved the LLC out of the Uncore and introduced the scalable ring on-die Interconnect. It allowed Intel to partition and distribute the LLC in equal slices. This architecture provides higher bandwidth and associativity, each slice is 2.5 MB, and a slice associates with a single core.

The ring allows each core to access every other slice. Pictured on the next page is the die configuration of a *Low Core Count* (LCC) Xeon CPU of the E5-2600 v4 (Broadwell) (2016).

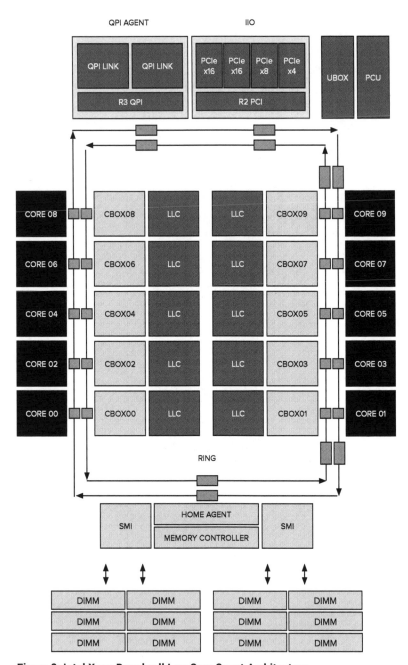

Figure 8: Intel Xeon Broadwell Low Core Count Architecture

This caching architecture requires a Snooping protocol that incorporates both distributed local cache as well as the other processors in the system to ensure cache coherency. As core count scales in the system, the amount of Snoop traffic grows, since each core has its steady stream of cache misses. This affects the consumption of the QPI links and last level caches, requiring ongoing development in Snoop coherency protocols. Chapter 3 includes an in-depth view of the Uncore, scalable ring on-die interconnect and the importance of caching Snoop protocols on NUMA performance.

Sufficiently Uniform Memory Architecture

Physical memory is distributed across the motherboard. However, the system can provide a single memory address space by interleaving the memory between the two NUMA nodes. This process is called Node-interleaving (Chapter 2 covers this setting). When node interleaving is enabled, the system becomes a *Sufficiently Uniform Memory Architecture* (SUMA).

Instead of disclosing the topology information, the system breaks down the entire memory range into 4 KB addressable regions. It maps them in a round robin fashion from each node. This process provides an 'interleaved' memory structure where the memory address space is distributed across the nodes.

When ESXi assigns memory to VMs it allocates physical memory located at two different nodes. When the physical CPU located in Node 0 needs to fetch the memory from Node 1, the data will traverse the QPI links.

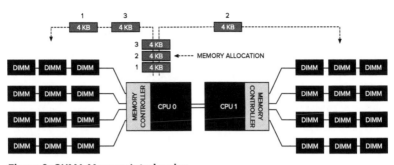

Figure 9: SUMA Memory Interleaving

The interesting thing is that the SUMA system provides a uniform memory access time. Only not the most optimal one! It heavily depends on contention levels in the QPI architecture. *Intel Memory Latency Checker* was used to demonstrate the differences between NUMA and SUMA configuration on a dual socket Intel Xeon E5 2630 v4 system.

This test measures the idle latencies (in nanoseconds) from each socket to the other socket in the system. The latency of memory node 0 reported by socket 0 is local memory access. Memory access of memory node 1 by socket 0 is remote memory access in the system configured as NUMA.

NUMA	MEMORY NODE 0	MEMORY NODE 1
Socket 0	75.7	132.0
Socket 1	131.9	75.8

SUMA	MEMORY NODE 0	MEMORY NODE 1
Socket 0	105.0	106.4
Socket 1	106.0	104.6

Table 1: NUMA and SUMA Latencies

The question arises, how does SUMA manage to provide a uniform memory access time? Although the access time difference between NUMA and SUMA is a physical characteristic due to the number of hops between cores and memory banks, it is all about the law of averages. Some memory will be super quick and some not, as the requested memory location is at a greater distance.

Using the data of table 1: Socket 0 - memory 0 = 75.7, memory 1 = 132.0 (memory 0 is local, 1 is remote) 75.7 + 132.0 = 207.7 / 2 == 103.85 close to the SUMA score of 105.5 and 106.4.

The test of loaded latencies provides a good insight on how the system performs under normal load. During the test, the load injection delays are automatically changed every two seconds. Both the bandwidth and the corresponding latency are measured at that level. This test uses 100% read traffic. The NUMA test results are displayed in figure 10, SUMA test results are displayed in figure 11.

```
Measuring Loaded Latencies for the system
Using all the threads from each core if Hyper-threading is enabled
Using Read-only traffic type
Inject  Latency Bandwidth
Delay   (ns)    MB/sec
========================
 00000  185.58  113083.7
 00002  185.87  112884.8
 00008  185.26  113111.4
 00015  186.11  113034.6
 00050  183.58  113029.8
 00100  122.92   99408.9
 00200  102.24   55891.9
 00300   93.07   38191.1
 00400   89.69   29032.2
 00500   88.05   23541.1
 00700   85.45   17160.6
 01000   82.93   12318.5
 01300   81.63    9689.6
 01700   80.36    7619.5
 02500   79.27    5456.5
 03500   78.57    4138.9
 05000   78.10    3148.7
 09000   77.50    2120.9
 20000   77.21    1412.2
```

Figure 10: NUMA Loaded Latencies Test Results

The reported bandwidth for the SUMA system is lower while experiencing a higher latency than the system configured as NUMA. Therefore, the focus should be on optimizing the VM size to leverage the NUMA characteristics of the system.

```
Measuring Loaded Latencies for the system
Using all the threads from each core if Hyper-threading is enabled
Using Read-only traffic type
Inject  Latency Bandwidth
Delay   (ns)    MB/sec
============================
 00000  237.05   92409.7
 00002  236.75   92665.0
 00008  235.69   92711.9
 00015  235.23   92763.6
 00050  226.35   92989.1
 00100  170.99   92309.9
 00200  127.43   55652.6
 00300  119.45   38017.2
 00400  116.09   28854.3
 00500  114.01   23370.6
 00700  112.23   16978.5
 01000  110.62   12123.8
 01300  109.66    9488.6
 01700  108.90    7412.9
 02500  108.40    5238.6
 03500  108.24    3915.9
 05000  108.15    2909.7
 09000  108.07    1885.9
 20000  108.04    1175.6
```

Figure 11: SUMA Loaded Latencies Test Results

CPU Microarchitecture Overview

With the introduction of the Intel Nehalem microarchitecture in 2008, Intel moved away from the NetBurst architecture and introduced NUMA. Along the years, Intel introduced new microarchitectures and optimizations, according to its famous Tick-Tock model.

The Tick-Tock development methodology of Intel consists of two major efforts, the manufacturing process (Tick) and the microarchitecture design (Tock). A full cycle completes when the new microarchitecture design is combined with a new smaller die area.

With the first step, Intel updates its fabrication plants and the manufacturing process to produce a smaller die. This occurs at a cadence of roughly every 36 months. When introducing a new CPU generation based on the new die-size, it leverages the previous microarchitecture. Typically, the core count is increased, and some incremental improvements are introduced with this release.

While the manufacturing process matures, Intel produces a new microarchitecture. This is typically the release that provides the most improvements. It provides an increased feature set as well as yielding a higher *Instruction Per Cycle* (IPC) rate.

Three Phase Cadence

Last year after the introduction of Broadwell Intel announced that it no longer follows the Tick-Tock strategy but is moving to a three-phase cadence. PAO stands for Process, Architecture, and Optimize. This model introduces a new phase called optimization and follows the process and architecture phase. As a result, the 14-nm node introduced with the Broadwell generation will be used by the newer microarchitecture Skylake and in turn will be optimized by the Kaby Lake generation.

Even though Intel provides a consistent branding model since 2012, people tend to use Intel architecture codenames to discuss the CPU generations. Even the vSphere Cluster EVC baselines list these internal Intel codenames. Both branding names and architecture codenames are used throughout the book:

GENERATION	BRANDING	YEAR	PROCESS	CADENCE	MAX CORES
Nehalem	X5500	2008	45nm		4
Westmere	X5600	2010	32nm	Tick	6
Sandy Bridge	E5-2600-v1	2012	32nm	Tock	8
Ivy Bridge	E5-2600-v2	2013	22nm	Tick	12
Haswell	E5-2600-v3	2014	22nm	Tock	18
Broadwell	E5-2600-v4	2016	14nm	Tick-Progress	22
Skylake	2P	2017	14nm	Architecture	28

Table 2: CPU Microarchitecture Overview

Skylake is expected to be released in summer 2017. Intel is moving away from the E5 and E7 naming scheme. The rumored names are 2P for CPU packages supporting dual socket configurations (was E5-2x). The E7 name (4 CPU) is likely to be replaced by Xeon Gold and Xeon Platinum.

02

SYSTEM ARCHITECTURE

Reviewing the physical layers helps to understand the behavior of the CPU scheduler of the VMkernel. This helps to select a physical configuration that is optimized for performance. This chapter covers the Intel Xeon microarchitecture and zooms in on the Uncore.

Terminology

There are a lot of different names used for something that is apparently the same thing. Let's review the terminology of the physical CPU and the NUMA architecture.

The CPU package is the device you hold in your hand, it contains the CPU die and is installed in the CPU socket on the motherboard. The CPU die contains the CPU cores, multiple levels of cache and the Uncore. More information about the Uncore can be found in the paragraph CPU System Architecture within this chapter. A CPU core is an independent execution unit and can present two virtual cores to run *Simultaneous MultiThreading* (SMT).

Intel's' proprietary SMT implementation is called *Hyper-Threading* Technology (HT). Both SMT threads share the components such as the various cache layers and access to other components of the CPU package.

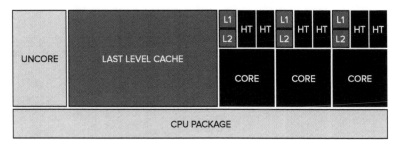

Figure 12: CPU Package Overview

Interesting entomology; the word 'die' is the singular of dice. Elements such as processing units are produced on a large round silicon wafer. The wafer is cut 'diced' into many pieces. Each of these pieces is called a die.

NUMA Architecture

In the following scenario, the system contains two CPUs, Intel 2630 v4 each containing ten cores (20 HT threads). The Intel 2630 v4 is based on the Broadwell microarchitecture and contains four memory channels, with a maximum of three DIMMs per channel.

Each channel is filled with a single 16 GB DDR4 RAM DIMM. 64 GB of memory is available per CPU package with a total of 128 GB in the system. The system reports two NUMA nodes. Each NUMA node, sometimes called a NUMA domain contains ten cores and 64 GB.

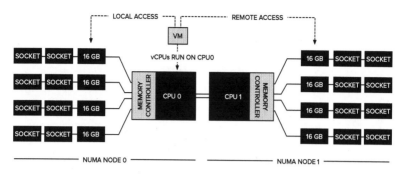

Figure 13: VM NUMA Local Access and Remote Access

Consuming NUMA

The CPU can access both its local memory and the memory controlled by the other CPUs in the system. Memory capacity managed by other CPUs is considered remote memory and is accessed through the QPI.

The CPU and NUMA schedulers of the ESXi kernel handle the allocation of memory to a VM. The goal of the NUMA scheduler is to maximize local memory access and attempts to distribute the workload as efficiently as possible. This depends on the VM CPU and memory configuration and the physical core count and memory configuration.

A more detailed look into the behavior of the ESXi CPU and NUMA scheduler is done in chapter 4, how to size and configure your VMs is discussed in chapter 6. This part focuses on the low-level configuration of a modern dual-CPU socket system. Esxtop reports 130961 MB (PMEM /MB) and displays the NUMA nodes with its local memory count.

```
5:48:41am up 3 min, 795 worlds, 0 VMs, 0 vCPUs; MEM overcommit avg: 0.00, 0.00, 0.00
PMEM  /MB: 130961   total: 2508     vmk,110 other, 128341 free
VMKMEM/MB: 130575 managed:  1920 minfree,  7466 rsvd, 123109 ursvd,  high state
NUMA  /MB: 65423 (64019), 65536 (63938)
```

Figure 14: Esxtop Host NUMA Memory Overview

Each core can address up to 128 GB of memory. As described earlier the NUMA scheduler of the ESXi kernel attempts to place and distribute *virtual CPUs* (vCPU) as optimally as possible, allocating as much local memory to the CPU workload as is available.

When the number of vCPUs of a VM exceeds the core count of a physical CPU, the ESXi server distributes the vCPUs evenly across the minimal number of physical CPUs. Additionally, it exposes the physical NUMA layout to the VM OS. Allowing the NUMA-aware OS and/or application to schedule their processes as optimal as possible.

> **To ensure the physical NUMA layout is exposed, ensure the BIOS is set to 'NUMA enabled' or 'Node Interleaving disabled'.**

In this example, a 12 vCPU VM is running on the dual Intel 2630 v4 system, each containing 10 cores. MS-CoreInfo informs us that six vCPUs are running on NUMA node 0 and six vCPUs are running on NUMA node 1.

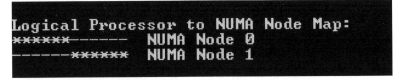

```
Logical Processor to NUMA Node Map:
******-----     NUMA Node 0
-----******     NUMA Node 1
```

Figure 15: MS-CoreInfo Logical Processor to NUMA Node Map

BIOS Setting: Node Interleaving

There seems to be a lot of confusion about this BIOS setting, we receive lots of questions on whether to enable or disable Node Interleaving. It seems the term 'enable' makes people think it is some sort of performance enhancement. Unfortunately, the opposite is true and it is strongly recommended to keep the default setting and keep Node Interleaving disabled.

Node Interleaving Disabled: NUMA

By using the default setting of Node Interleaving (disabled), the ACPI 'BIOS' will build a *System Resource Allocation Table* (SRAT). Within this SRAT, the physical configuration and CPU memory architecture are presented, i.e. which CPU and memory ranges belong to a single NUMA node.

It proceeds to map the memory of each node into a single sequential block of memory address space. ESXi uses the SRAT to understand which memory bank is local to a physical CPU and attempts to allocate local memory to each vCPU of the VM.

Node Interleaving Enabled: SUMA

One question that is asked a lot is how to turn off NUMA. You can turn off NUMA, but remember your system is not a transformer that can change your CPU and memory layout from a point-to-point-connection architecture to a bus system. Therefore, when enabling Node Interleaving the system will not become a traditional UMA system, it becomes a SUMA system.

BIOS Setting: ACPI SLIT Preferences

The ACPI *System Locality Information Table* (SLIT) provides a matrix that describes the relative distance (i.e. memory latency) between the NUMA nodes. Often a NUMA node is referred to as a proximity domain, especially in documentation covering SLIT. In the past, a system could experience a larger latency from Node 0 to Node 7 than from Node 0 to Node 1. Modern point-to-point architectures moved from a ring topology to a full mesh topology decreasing hop counts. As a result this reduces the importance of SLIT.

Many server vendor whitepapers describe the best practices for VMware ESXi and recommend enabling ACPI SLIT. Do not worry if you forgot to enable this setting, as ESXi does not use the SLIT. Instead, the ESXi kernel determines the inter-node latencies by probing the nodes at boot-time and uses this information for initial placement of wide VMs. A wide VM contains more vCPUs than the core count of a physical CPU. More about wide VMs and virtual NUMA can be found in the next chapter.

CPU System Architecture

Since E5-2600 v1 (Sandy Bridge) the CPU system architecture applied by Intel can be described as a *System-on-Chip* (SoC) architecture, integrating the CPU, GPU, system IO and last level cache into a single package. The QPI and the Uncore are critical components of the memory system and its performance can be impacted by BIOS settings. Available QPI bandwidth depends on the CPU model. Therefore, it is of interest to have a proper understanding of the CPU system architecture to design a high-performance system.

Uncore

As mentioned in chapter 1, the Nehalem microarchitecture introduced a flexible architecture that could be optimized for different segments.

To facilitate scalability, Intel separated the core processing functionality (ALU, FPU, L1 and L2 cache) from the Uncore functionality. A simple way to put it is that the Uncore is a collection of components of a CPU that do not carry out core computational functions but are essential for core performance.

This architectural system change brought the northbridge functionality closer to the processing unit, reducing latency while being able to increase the speed due to the removal of serial bus controllers. The Uncore contains the following elements:

UNCORE ELEMENT	DESCRIPTION	RESPONSIBLE FOR
QPI Agent	Quick Path Interconnect	QPI caching agent, manages R3QPI and QPI Link Interface.
PCU	Power Controller	Core/Uncore power unit and thermal manager, governs P-State of the CPU, C-State of the Core and package. It enables Turbo Mode and can throttle cores when a thermal violation occurs.
Ubox	System Config Controller	Intermediary for interrupt traffic between system and core.
IIO	Integrated IO	Provides the interface to PCIe Devices.
R2PCI	Ring to PCI Interface	Provides interface to the ring for PCIe access.
IMC	Integrated Memory Controller	Provides the interface to RAM and communicates with Uncore through Home Agent.
HA	Home Agent	Responsible for ordering read/writes coming from Ring to IMC. Provides directory cache coherency.
SMI	Scalable Memory Interface	Provides IMC access to DIMMs.

Table 3: Intel Xeon Uncore Elements

Intel provides a schematic overview of a CPU to understand the relationship between the Uncore and the cores. This diagram is recreated to help emphasize certain components.

Please note that the following diagram depicts the *Medium Core Count* (MCC) architecture of the Intel Xeon E5-2600 v4 (Broadwell). This is a single CPU package. The cores are spread out in a 'chop-able' design, allowing Intel to offer three different core counts, low, medium and high. The scalable on-die ring connects the cores with the Uncore components.

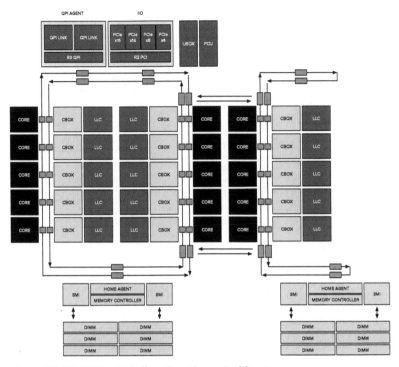

Figure 16: E5-2600 v4 Medium Core Count Architecture

If a CPU core wants to access data it has to communicate with the Uncore. Data can be in the *Last Level Cache* (LLC), thus interfacing with the *Cache Agent* (Cbox). It might require memory from local memory, interfacing with the Home Agent and *Integrated Memory Controller* (IMC). Or it needs to fetch memory from a remote NUMA node. As a consequence, the QPI comes into play. Due to the many components located in the Uncore, it plays a significant part in the overall power consumption of the system. With today's focus on power reduction, the CPU is equipped with an *Uncore Frequency Scaling* (UFS) functionality.

Uncore Power Management

E5-2600 v3 (Haswell) introduces *Per Core Power States* (PCPS) that allows each core to run at its own frequency. UFS allows the Uncore components to scale their frequency up and down independently of the cores. This allows Turbo Boost 2.0 to turbo up and own the two elements independently, allowing cores to scale up the frequency of their LLC and ring on-ramp modules, without having to enforce all Uncore elements to turbo boost up and waste power. Some vendors provide the ability to manage power consumption with the settings Uncore Frequency Override or Uncore Frequency. These settings are geared towards applying performance savings in a more holistic way.

The Uncore provides access to all interfaces, plus it regulates the power states of the cores. Therefore, it has to be functional even when there is a minimal load on the CPU. To reduce overall CPU power consumption, the power control mechanism attempts to reduce the CPU frequency to a minimum by using C-States on separate cores. If a package C-State occurs, the frequency of the Uncore is likely to be lowered.

To avoid this from happening some server vendors provide the BIOS option Uncore Frequency Override. By default, this option is set to Disabled, allowing the system to reduce the Uncore frequency to obtain power consumption savings. By selecting Enabled it prevents frequency scaling of the Uncore, ensuring high performance.

To secure high levels of throughput of the QPI links, select the option Enabled. Keep in mind that this can have a negative (increased) effect on the power consumption of the system.
Some vendors provide the Uncore Frequency options of Dynamic and Maximum. When set to Dynamic, the Uncore frequency matches the frequency of the fastest core. With most server vendors, when selecting the Dynamic option, the optimization of the Uncore frequency is to save power or to optimize the performance. The bias towards power saving and optimize performance is influenced by the setting of power-management policies. When the Uncore frequency option is set to Maximum the frequency remains fixed.

Generally, this modularity should make it more power efficient, however, some IT teams don't want their system to swing up and down but provide a consistent performance. Especially when the workload is active across multiple nodes in a cluster, running the workload consistently is more important that having a specific node to go as fast as it can.

Quick Path Interconnect Link

VM configuration can impact memory allocation. For example, when the memory configuration consumption exceeds the available amount of local memory, ESXi allocates remote memory to this VM.

An imbalance of VM activity and VM resource consumption can trigger the ESXi host to rebalance the VMs across the NUMA nodes. This leads to data migration between the two NUMA nodes.

These two examples occur quite frequently. The QPI architecture impacts the performance of remote memory access, memory migration, and low-level CPU processes (such as cache Snooping and validation traffic). It is imperative when designing and configuring a system that attention must be given to the QuickPath Interconnect configuration.

Xeon CPUs designated for dual CPU setup (E5-26xx) are equipped with two QPI bi-directional links. The QPI links operate at high frequencies measured in giga-transfers per second (GT/s).

Today the majority of E5-2600 v4 (Broadwell) CPUs operate at 9.6 GT/s, while some run at 6.4 GT/s or 8.6 GT/s. Giga-transfer per second refers to the number of operations transferring data that occur in each second in a data-transfer channel. It's an interesting metric, however, it does not specify the bit rate. To calculate the data-transmission rate, the transfer rate must be multiplied by the channel width. The QPI link has the ability to transfer 16 bits of data-payload. The calculation is as follows: GT/s x channel width / bits-to-bytes.

```
9.6 GT per second x 16 bits = 153.6 Gbit per second
153.6 Gbit per second / 8 bits = 19.2 GB per second
```

The purist will argue that this is not a comprehensive calculation, as this neglects the clock rate of the QPI. The complete calculation is:

4.8 GHz
× 2 bits/Hz (Double Data Rate)
× 16(20) (data bits/QPI link width)
× 2 (unidirectional send and receive operating simultaneously)
÷ 8 (bits/byte)
= 38.4 GB/s

Source: https://en.wikipedia.org/wiki/Intel_QuickPath_Interconnect

E5-2600 v3 (Haswell) and E5-2600 v4 (Broadwell) offer three QPI clock rates, 3.2 GHz, 4.0 GHz, and 4.8 GHz.

Intel prefers to provide GT/s values. Therefore, to simplify these calculations, just multiple GT/s by two (16 bits / 8 bits to bytes = 2). Listed as 9.6 GT/s a QPI link can transmit up to 19.2 GB/s from one CPU to another CPU. As it is bidirectional, it can receive the same amount from the other side. In total, the two 9.6 GT/s links provide a theoretical peak data bandwidth of 38.4 GB/s in each direction.

QPI LINK SPEED	UNIDIRECTIONAL PEAK BANDWIDTH	TOTAL PEAK BANDWIDTH
6.4 GT/s	12.8 GB/s	25.6 GB/s
8.0 GT/s	16.0 GB/s	32.0 GB/s
9.6 GT/s	19.2 GB/s	38.4 GB/s

Table 4: Intel Xeon QPI Performance

There is no direct relationship with core-count and QPI link speeds. For example, the E5-2600 v4 (Broadwell) product family features three 8-core count CPUs. Each with a different QPI link speed, but there are also 10 core CPUs with a bandwidth of 8.0 GT/s. To understand the logic, you need to know that Intel categorizes their CPU product family into segments. Six segments exist: Basic, Standard, Advanced, Segment Optimized, Low Power and Workstation.

SEGMENT	LLC SIZE	QPI	CORES	MEMORY
Basic	15-20 MB	6.4 GT/s	6-8	1866 MT/s
Standard	20-25 MB	8.0 GT/s	8-10	2133 MT/s
Advanced	30-35 MB	9.6 GT/s	12-14	2400 MT/s
Segment Optimized	40-55 MB	9.6 GT/s	16-22	2400 MT/s
Frequency Optimized *	> 2.5 MB per core	9.6 GT/s	4-8	2400 MT/s
Low Power	25-35 MB	9.6 GT/s	10-24	2400 MT/s
Workstation	35	9.6 GT/s	12	2400 MT/s

Table 5: Intel Xeon Product Family Segments

* Frequency optimized provides low core count architectures with high frequency operations (up to 3.5 GHz). Additionally, it contains an LLC that exceeds the default 2.5 MB per core configuration.

There is the custom-built segment, which is off the list, but if you have enough money, Intel can look into your problems. The most popular CPUs used in the virtual datacenter are from the Advanced and Segment-Optimized segments. These CPUs provide enough cores and cache to drive a healthy consolidation ratio. Primarily the HCC CPUs from the Segment Optimized category are used. All CPU's from these segments are equipped with a QPI link speed of 9.6 GT/s.

SEGMENT	MODEL NUMBER	CORE COUNT	CLOCK CYCLE	TDP
Advanced	E5-2650 v4	12	2.2 GHz	105W
Advanced	E5-2660 v4	14	2.0 GHz	105W
Advanced	E5-2680 v4	14	2.4 GHz	120W
Advanced	E5-2690 v4	14	2.6 GHz	135W
Optimized	E5-2683 v4	16	2.1 GHz	120W
Optimized	E5-2695 v4	18	2.1 GHz	120W
Optimized	E5-2697 v4	18	2.3 GHz	145W
Optimized	E5-2697A v4	16	2.6 GHz	145W
Optimized	E5-2698 v4	20	2.2 GHz	135W
Optimized	E5-2699 v4	22	2.2 GHz	145W

Table 6: Intel Xeon Advanced and Optimized Segment Details

QPI Link Speed Impact on Performance

When opting for a CPU with lower QPI link speeds, remote memory access will be impacted. The QPI bandwidth test, using the Intel Memory Latency Checker v3.1, revealed an average of ~75% of the theoretical bandwidth when fetching memory from the remote NUMA node.

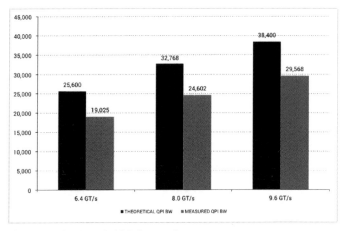

Figure 17: QPI Bandwidth Comparison

The peak bandwidth is more a theoretical maximum number as transfer data comes with protocol overhead. Additionally, tracking resources are needed when using multiple links to track each data request and maintain coherency.

The maximum QPI bandwidth that is available at the time of writing is lower than the minimum supported memory frequency of 1600 MHz. (Intel Xeon E5-2600 v4). The peak bandwidth of quad-channel DDR4 1600 MHz is 51 GB/s, exceeding the 38.4 GB/s combined unidirectional maximum of both QPI links by 32%.

As such, QPI bandwidth can impact remote memory access performance. To obtain the most performance, it is recommended to select a CPU with a QPI configuration of 9.6 GT/s to reduce the bandwidth loss to a minimum. The difference between a 9.6 GT/s and an 8.0 GT/s configuration is a 29% performance drop.

As QPI bandwidth impacts remote memory access, it is the DIMM configuration and memory frequency that impacts local memory access.

> **The reason why we are exploring the nuances of power settings is that high-performance power consumption settings are not always optimal for today's CPU microarchitecture. Turbo Boost allows cores to burst to a higher clock rate if the power budget allows it.**

Intel QPI Link Power Management

Some servers allow you to configure the QPI Link Power Management in the BIOS. When enabled, the buffers in the QPI links are allowed to enter a sleep state when the links are not being used. When there is relatively little traffic, the QPI link shuts down some of its data transmission lanes, this to achieve power consumption reduction. Within a higher state, it only reduces bandwidth, however, when entering a deeper state, memory access will experience a latency penalty.

A QPI link consists of a *transmit circuit* (TX), twenty data lanes, 1 clock lane and a *receive circuit* (RX). Every element can be progressively switched off. When the QPI is under heavy load it will use all twenty lanes, however when experiencing a workload of 40% or less it can decide to modulate to half width. Half width mode, called L0p state, saves power by shutting down at least ten lanes. Typically, when the ten lanes are utilized over 80% of their capacity, the state shifts from L0p back to the full-width L0 state. L0p allows the system to continue to transmit data without any significant latency penalty.

When no data transmission occurs, the system can invoke the L0s state. This state only operates the clock lane and its part of the physical TX and RX circuits. Due to the sleep mode of the majority of circuits (lane drivers) within the transceivers no data can be sent. The last state, L1, allows the system to shut down the complete link, benefitting from the highest level of power savings. A low power state with longer latency and lower power than L0s is activated in conjunction with package C-States below C0.

LOs and L1 states are costly from a performance perspective. Intel's patent US 8935578 B2 indicates that exiting L1 state will cost multiple microseconds and LOs tens of nanoseconds. Idle remote memory access latency measured on 2133 MHz memory is on average 130 nanoseconds. Adding 20 nanoseconds will add roughly 15% latency and that's quite a latency penalty.

STATE	DESCRIPTION	PROPERTIES	LANES
L0	Link Normal Operational State	All lanes and Forward Clock active	20
L0p	Link Power Saving State	A lower power state from L0 that reduces the link from full width to half width	10
L0s	Low Power Link State	Turns off most lane drivers, rapid recovery to the L0 state	1
L1	Deeper Low Power State	Lane drivers and Forward Clock turned off, greater power savings than L0s. Longer time to return to L0 state	0

Table 7: Intel QPI Power Management States

> If the focus is on architecting a consistent high performing platform, we recommend disabling QPI power management in the BIOS. Many vendors have switched their default setting from Enabled to Disabled. Nevertheless, it is wise to verify this setting.

The memory subsystem and the QPI architecture lay the foundation of the NUMA architecture. Last Level Cache is a large part of the memory subsystem. The QPI architecture provides the interface and bandwidth between NUMA nodes. It is the cache coherency mechanisms, that play a great part in providing the ability to span VMs across nodes, but in turn they will impact overall performance and bandwidth consumption.

03

CACHE COHERENCY

When talking about NUMA, it is mostly about the RAM and the core count of the physical CPU. Unfortunately, the importance of cache coherency in this architecture is mostly ignored. Locating memory close to CPUs increases scalability and reduces latency if data locality occurs. However, a great deal of the efficiency of a NUMA system depends on the scalability and efficiency of the cache coherence protocol! When researching the older material of NUMA, today's architecture is primarily labeled as ccNUMA, Cache Coherent NUMA.

> The term 'Cache Coherent' refers to the fact that for all CPUs any variable that is to be used must have a consistent value. Therefore, it must be assured that the caches that provide these variables are also consistent in this respect. Source: hpcresearch.nl

This means that a memory system of a multi-CPU system is coherent. For example, if CPU1 writes to a memory address (X) and later on CPU2 reads X, and no other writes happened to X in between, CPU2's read operation returns the value written by CPU1's write operation.

To ensure the local cache is up to date the Snoopy bus protocol was invented. This protocol allows caches to listen in on the transport of data to any of the CPUs. The listening CPUs replace the old data in their cache if newer data is detected. The interesting thing is that with today's multicore CPU architecture, cache coherency manifests itself within the CPU package as well as between CPU packages. A great deal of memory performance (bandwidth and latency) depends on the Snoop protocol.

Caching Architecture

E5-2600 v1 (Sandy Bridge) introduced new cache architecture. The hierarchy exists of an L1, L2 and a distributed LLC accessed via the on-die scalable ring architecture. Although they are all located on the CPU die, there are differences in latency between them. L1 is the fastest cache and it typically takes the CPU four cycles to load data from the L1 cache, 12 cycles to load data from the L2 cache and between 26 and 31 cycles to load the data from LLC. In comparison, it takes roughly 80 cycles to get the data from local memory while it could take the CPU an incredible 310 cycles to load the data from remote memory (worst-case scenario).

Each core has a dedicated L1 and L2 cache, this is referred to as private cache as no other core can overwrite the cache lines, the LLC is shared between cores. The L1 cache is split into two separate elements, the Instruction cache (32 KB) and the Data cache (L1D) (32 KB). The L2 cache (256 KB) is shared by instructions and data (Unified) and is not considered to be an exclusive cache.

That means that it does not have to contain all the bits that are present in the L1 cache (instructions and data). However, it is likely to have the same data and instructions, as it is bigger (less evictions).

When data is fetched from memory it fills all cache levels on the way to the core (LLC->L2->L1). The reason why it is also in the LLC is because the LLC is designed as an inclusive cache. It must have all the data contained in the L2 or L1 cache.

Data Prefetching

To improve performance, data can be speculatively loaded into the L1 and L2 cache, this is called prefetching.

It's the job of the prefetcher to load data into the cache before the core needs it. Intel has quoted performance improvements up to 30%. The Xeon microarchitecture can make use of both hardware and software prefetching. A well-known software prefetching technology is SSE. SSE stands for *Streaming SIMD Extension*. SIMD stands for *Single Instruction Multiple Data*. SSE provides hints to the CPU which data to prefetch for an instruction. The hardware prefetchers are split between L1 and L2 cache.

The component that actually stores the data in the L1D is called the *Data Cache Unit* (DCU) and is 32 KB in size. The L1D manages all the loads and stores of the data. The DCU prefetcher fetches next cache lines from the memory hierarchy when a particular access pattern is detected. The DCU IP prefetcher attempts to load the next instruction before the core actually requests it. L2 prefetchers also interact with the LLC. When the L2 contains too many outstanding requests, the L2 prefetcher stores the data in the LLC to avoid eviction of useful cache lines.

> **In storage, the unit of transportation is called a block. In cache memory, it is called a cache line.**

The Intel Xeon microarchitecture uses a cache line size of 64 bytes. Two L2 prefetchers exist; spatial prefetcher and streamer prefetcher.

The **spatial prefetcher** attempts to complete every cache line fetched to the L2 cache with another cache line to fill a 128-byte aligned chunk.

The **streamer prefetcher** monitors read requests from the L1D cache and fetches the appropriate data and instructions. Server vendors might use their own designation for L1 and L2 prefetchers:

INTEL	SERVER VENDORS
DCU Prefetcher	DCU Streamer Prefetcher
DCU IP-based Stride Prefetcher	DCU IP Prefetcher
Spatial Prefetcher	Adjacent Cache Line Prefetch[*]
Streamer Prefetcher	Hardware Prefetcher

Table 8: Intel Nomenclature versus Server Vendors Nomenclature

[*] Adjacent Cache Line Prefetch is also referred to as Buddy Fetch (Cisco UCS)

All four prefetchers are extremely important for performance. There are some use cases known where prefetchers consume so much bandwidth and CPU cycles that they reduce performance, but these cases are extremely rare.

Testing prefetcher effectiveness is extremely difficult as synthetic tests are usually focused on measuring best-case scenario bandwidth and latency using sequential access patterns. This is where workload pattern prefetchers shine.

Our recommendation is to have the prefetchers enabled.

Last Level Cache

The L1 and L2 cache are private to the core. It stores data, it reads, writes, or modifies. The LLC is shared amongst the cores. E5-2600 v1 (Sandy Bridge) moved away from a single unified cache entity in the Uncore to a distributed and partitioned cache structure. The total LLC is carved up into 2.5 MB slices and can be fully accessed and utilized by all cores in the system.

It is mentioned in many articles that a cache slice is associated with a core, but the association is just a physical construct. A core cannot control the placement of data in the LLC and has no ability to access anything but the entire LLC. The LLC is accessed through the scalable on-die ring. Latency depends on the number of hops to access the data.

Scalable On-Die Ring

As described previously, the cache is an inclusive cache, signifying that it has to include all of the data that is stored in the lower level caches. The memory addresses are hashed and distributed amongst the slices. This approach leverages the incredible bandwidth of the scalable on-die interconnect while reducing hot spots and contention for the cache addresses. It also helps coherency.

The LLC slices are connected to the scalable on-die ring interconnect. The ring connects the cores and the Uncore. The Uncore contains the *Ring to QPI interconnect* (R3QPI) and the Home Agent servicing the Integrated Memory Controller.

There are two tag arrays, one for data accesses and one for coherency requests and prefetching. The rings run in a clockwise direction as well as a counter-clockwise direction to provide the shortest path between core and cache slice. Intel stated the bandwidth of the ring was ~ 844 GB/s in the Sandy Bridge Architecture. Since E5-2600 v3 (Haswell) the rings are connected by buffered interconnects to allow the rings to operate independently, coinciding with the introduction of *Cluster-on-Die* (COD) cache Snoop mode.

The core scalability results in different die designs. Three core-count configurations exist: *Low Core Count* (LCC), *Medium Core Count* (MCC) and *High Core Count* (HCC). With every new generation Xeon, the classification of the various configurations changes. For example, in E5-2600 v3 (Haswell) eight core CPUs were labeled as LCC, in the E5-2600 v4 (Broadwell) architecture, ten core CPUs are labeled as LCC.

MAX CORE COUNT	DIE DESIGN	CORE COLUMNS	MEMORY CONTROLLERS
10	Low Core Count	2	1
16	Medium Core Count	3	2
22	High Core Count	4	2

Table 9: Core Count Architecture Overview

Cache Snooping

Any core can read data from the LLC slice in the system. Once the data is in the private cache it can be modified. If a cache operation occurs that affects coherence, the owning cache broadcasts this to all other caches. Each cache listens (Snoops) for these messages and reacts accordingly. Cache coherency protocols keep track of these changes and use the invalidation-based-protocol MESI. Within the MESI protocol data in cache can be in four states:

CACHE STATE	DEFINITION	STATE DEFINITION	CACHE LINE EXISTS IN
M	Modified	The cache line is updated relative to memory	Single core
E	Exclusive	The cache line is consistent with memory	Single core
S	Shared	The cache line is shared with other cores. (The cache line is consistent with other cores, but may not be consistent with memory)	Multiple cores
I	Invalid	The cache line is not present in this core L1 or L2	Multiple cores

Table 10: MESI Protocol Overview

Let's use a simple example that shows the sequence of the MESI protocol:

Step 1:
A two-vCPU VM consumes CPU core 1 and 2 runs an SQL server. The VM runs on a four cores CPU in an ESXi host. An SQL query requests memory at address X. The query runs on vCPU1 and core 1 detects that it does not have this data in its L1 and L2 cache. A Snoop request is made to the caching agents.

Both the L1 and L2 cache of core 1 do not contain this data and a request is made to the caching agent. This could be the caching agent of the LLC slice or the Home Agent depending on the Snoop algorithm. The agent will send out a Snoop request to all the cache agents (or the Home Agent) to determine if they have the cache line. At this point, no cache has this data and MESI protocol states that data is in an **Invalid** state for all four cores.

Step 2:
The data is retrieved from memory and stores it into the LLC and the private cache of core 1. The MESI state of this cache line changes and is **Exclusive** for core 1 and invalid for the remaining cores.

Step 3:
Core 1 updates the data, which transitions the state of the cache line from Exclusive to **Modified**.

Step 4:
At this point, another query that runs on core 2 wants X as well. The core checks L1 and L2 and both miss. The request is forwarded to the LLC and it determines X is present. It might not be consistent anymore, therefore a Snoop is sent to core 1 to determine whether the data is modified. It is modified and therefore core 2 retrieves the data. The MESI state of the cache line is changed and it is now in a **Shared** state.

The example provided was based on the traditional MESI protocol, however Intel applies the **MESIF protocol**. With the introduction of **Forwarding (F state)**, it changed the role of the Shared state. With MESI, when data is in a Shared state, each cache owning that cache line can respond to the inquiry.

In a 20-core count system this can create a lot of traffic. As a NUMA system shares its memory address space, it can produce many redundant responses between the CPUs. Often with varying (high) latency!

To solve this problem, one cache line is promoted to the **Forward state**. This cache line is the only one that can respond and forward data. All the other cache lines containing the data are placed in the Shared mode, which now is silent. The F state transitions to the newest version of the data, solving temporal locality problems of the cache, as this cache is the least likely to evict the cache line. The Forwarding state reduces interconnect traffic, as in MESI, all caches in S states respond.

Although we would love to go in-depth on this theory, a detailed explanation of the MESIF protocol is out of the scope of this book. We tried to keep it as simple as possible, losing some interesting details, such as *Cache Valid Bits* (CVB). For more information see the manuscript of J.R. Goodman and H.H.J HUM - MESIF: *A Two-Hop Cache Coherency Protocol for Point-to-Point Interconnects*.

Snoop Modes

A Snoop mode determines which agent will manage Snoop operations issues by the cores. Snoops can be sent by the caching agent (Cbox) of each LLC slice or by the Home Agent. Until now, with every new generation microarchitecture, a new Snoop mode is introduced. These modes are configurable through BIOS settings and have an effect on cache latency and bandwidth consumption, impacting overall performance. Although Intel recommends a default Snoop Mode to the server vendors, not every server BIOS conforms to that recommendation.

Our recommendation is to include QPI Snoop modes in your documentation as a configuration item. If the system is configured with the default option recommended by Intel do not change this without any data-driven reason. Today four Snoop modes are available; one Snoop mode (Cluster-on-Die) is available only if two home nodes are available in the package (MCC and HCC die designs).

Early Snoop

This Snoop mode was introduced by E5-2600 v1 (Sandy Bridge) and is available on all newer generations. Within early Snoop, the caching agent generates the Snoop probe or the Snoop request. Using the scalable on-die ring, it can directly send that Snoop to other cache agents or broadcast it to all the other agents in the system. This model provides a low latency response time, although the amount of broadcasts (especially in HCC die designs) can consume the bandwidth between the NUMA nodes. Typically, this Snoop mode is not recommended when using NUMA optimized workload. Some vendors did not optimize the BIOS defaults and use this Snoop mode even for their newest models. Please check your BIOS!

Home Snoop

This Snoop mode was introduced by E5-2600 v2 (Ivy Bridge) and is available on all newer generations. Instead of each caching agent generating Snoop messages, it is the Home Agent tied to the memory controller that generates the Snoop request. Since the Snoop request has to go to the Home Agent and travel the on-die scalable ring, it has a higher latency than early Snoop. By leveraging a more centralized entity such as the Home Agent, it does reduce the bandwidth consumption. Home Snoop mode is geared towards workloads that are bandwidth sensitive.

Home Snoop with Directory and Opportunistic Snoop Broadcast

This mode uses the Home Agent but it can also speculatively snoop the remote CPU in parallel with the directory read on the Home Agent. The Home Agent contains an in-memory Snoop directory to determine the state of the various cache lines. This reduces Snoop traffic primarily on reads.

The Home Agent snoops in parallel with the directory lookup when it expects bandwidth is available to support the Snoop traffic. When the system gets more heavily loaded, the Snoops are delayed and only sent to the agents. That way the Snoop overhead is kept low in heavily loaded systems and it will use the available bandwidth for data transfer instead. This Snoop mode was introduced by E5-2600 v2 (Ivy Bridge) and was removed in E5-2600 v3 (Haswell). It has been reintroduced by E5-2600 v4 (Broadwell) and is the recommended default Snoop mode by Intel for the E5-2600 v4 (Broadwell) generation. Please check your BIOS settings as not every vendor follows Intel recommendations.

Cluster-on-Die

Although the Home Snoop with *Directory* (DIR) and *Opportunistic Snoop Broadcast* (OSB) has the overall best performance, when running a highly optimized NUMA workload you might want to consider the Cluster-on-Die Snoop mode. This mode provides the best performance for local operations. It provides the lowest LLC hit latency and low local memory latency. Remote memory performance depends on the write activity of the workloads.

Intel published an overview of the Intel Xeon E5 Snoop mode characteristics that provides insight into the relative Snoop mode performance on a NUMA configured system:

PERFORMANCE METRIC	HS WITH DIR+OSB	COD	HOME SNOOP	EARLY SNOOP
LLC Hit Latency	Low	Lowest	Low	Low
Local Memory Latency	Low	Lowest	High	Medium
Remote Memory Latency	Low	Low-High[*]	Low	Lowest

Table 11: NUMA Latency Performance (Lower is Better)

[*]The performance depends on the directory state. If the directory is clean, low latency is expected. If the directory is dirty, high latency can occur.

PERFORMANCE METRIC	HS WITH DIR+OSB	COD	HOME SNOOP	EARLY SNOOP
Local memory Bandwidth	High	High	High	Low
Remote memory Bandwidth	High	Medium	High	Low-Medium

Table 12: NUMA Memory Bandwidth Performance (Higher is Better)

> **If you have your workload correctly sized and you are able to fit workloads within NUMA nodes, Cluster-on-Die can improve performance. If you tend to run a high consolidation ratio and hereby forcing the ESXi CPU scheduler to span small footprint VMs across NUMA nodes, the setting Home Snoop with Directory and OSB might be a better fit.**

Cluster-on-Die Architecture

Cluster-on-Die (COD) is only available on MCC and HCC packages. When enabling COD, it logically divides the CPU into two equal NUMA nodes. It incorporates a part of the scalable ring on-die interconnect that services the Home Agent & Integrated Memory Controller. A MCC and HCC die-design contain two active memory controllers, each servicing two channels. The NUMA nodes are associated with the respective controllers.

It's expected that Intel moves away from the scalable ring on-die interconnect in the upcoming Skylake release. It will be interesting to see how COD is implemented.

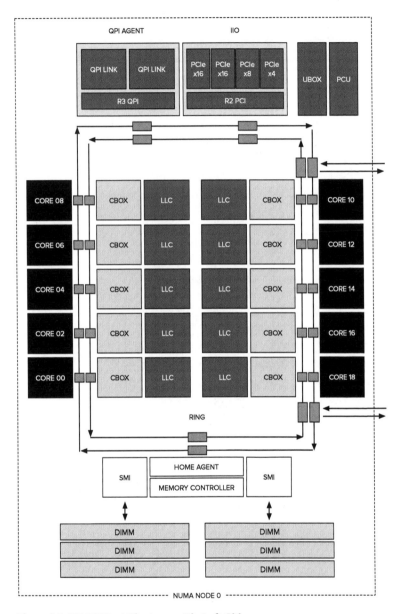

Figure 18: E5-2698 v4 Cluster-on-Die Left Side

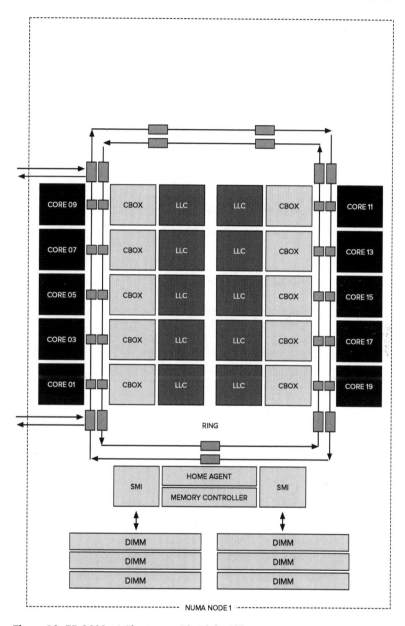

Figure 19: E5-2698 v4 Cluster-on-Die Right Side

Please note that there will be two NUMA nodes in one CPU package! That means there will be four NUMA nodes in a dual socket system.

Marc Lang (@marcandreaslang) demonstrated COD on a 512 GB system. Before COD, the system created two NUMA nodes, each addressing 256 GB per NUMA node.

```
PMEM    /MB: 524194   total: 6555     vmk,204251 other, 313386 free
VMKMEM/MB: 523808 managed:  5852 minfree, 20901 rsvd, 502906 ursvd,  high state
NUMA    /MB: 262048 (171192), 262144 (141810)
PSHARE/MB:    16095 shared,    832 common:    15263 saving
SWAP   /MB:      0   curr,       0 rclmtgt:                  0.00 r/s,    0.00 w/s
ZIP    /MB:      0   zipped,     0   saved
MEMCTL/MB:      0   curr,       0   target,  185230 max
```

Figure 20: Two CPU Packages - Two NUMA Nodes

After enabling COD the system created four NUMA nodes, each addressing 128 GB per NUMA node.

```
9:18:43am up 2 min, 1074 worlds, 0 VMs, 0 vCPUs; MEM overcommit avg: 0.00, 0.00, 0.00
PMEM    /MB: 524194   total: 5093     vmk,179 other, 518921 free
VMKMEM/MB: 523808 managed:  5852 minfree, 14705 rsvd, 509100 ursvd,  high state
NUMA    /MB: 130976 (128830), 131072 (130108), 131072 (130069), 131072 (129529)
PSHARE/MB:     18 shared,     18 common:      0 saving
SWAP   /MB:      0   curr,       0 rclmtgt:                  0.00 r/s,    0.00 w/s
ZIP    /MB:      0   zipped,     0   saved
MEMCTL/MB:      0   curr,       0   target,      0 max
```

Figure 21: Cluster-on-Die Enabled – Four NUMA Nodes in System

COD segments the LLC and the RAM. By segmenting the LLC, it decreases the latency by reducing the number of slices in the NUMA node.

For example, the E5-2699 v4 contains 22 cores. With COD enabled, it creates two affinity domains of 11 LLC slices. Instead of sharing data between all the 22 slices, data will be distributed in 11 LLC slices inside each affinity domain. As a result this configuration decreases the hop count. In addition, the COD in E5-2600 v4 (Broadwell) microarchitecture eliminates cross-buffered interconnect traffic, reducing ring collisions and other overhead that reduces the available bandwidth.

If there is a cache-miss in the LLC within the affinity domain, it will contact the Home Agent responsible for the memory directly. Each Home Agent tracks the memory lines it is responsible for. Therefore, the LLC can contain cache lines of remote memory and traffic will occur across the buffered interconnect if the NUMA scheduler cannot 'affinitize' the process and the memory properly.

ESXi 5.5 update 3 and ESXi 6.0 support COD. Check *VMware KB article 2142499*. As mentioned in chapter 2, ESXi does not use SLIT information to understand topological distance between the physical CPUs. Instead, ESXi determines the inter-domain latencies by probing the CPUs at boot-time and uses this information for initial placement and migration decisions.

Since COD is a boot-time configuration, ESXi has a good view of the latencies of the NUMA domains. Having multiple NUMA nodes presented by a single CPU package is not a new thing. In 2011 AMD released the Magny-Cours architecture, which combined two 6-core Bulldozer CPUs in one package. Unfortunately, a lot of VMware community members reported negative performance results due to the ESXi NUMA round-robin scheduling decisions. The cache architecture of the AMD didn't help.

Snoop Mode Recommendation

If the VMs are right-sized to fit into a single NUMA node, COD could deliver a stellar performance. When operating a large collection of Wide VMs, we recommend selecting the Snoop mode Home Snoop with Directory and Opportunistic Snoop Broadcast (OSB+DIR). COD is all about reducing latency through affinity within a subset of the local Last Level Cache.

04

VMKERNEL NUMA CONSTRUCTS

ESXi server is optimized for the NUMA architecture and as a result it contains a NUMA scheduler and a CPU scheduler. If ESXi runs on a NUMA platform, the VMkernel activates the NUMA scheduler.

The primary role of the NUMA scheduler is to optimize the CPU and memory allocation of VMs. It provides VM initial placement and dynamically load balances VM workloads across the NUMA nodes. The CPU scheduler carries out allocation of physical CPU resources to VMs.

It is crucial to understand that the NUMA scheduler is responsible for the placement of the VM, but it is the CPU scheduler that is ultimately responsible for allocating physical CPU resources and scheduling of vCPUs of the VM. The main reason to emphasize this is to understand how Hyper-Threading fits into CPU and NUMA scheduling.

Before diving into the specifics of NUMA optimizations, let's calibrate the understanding of the various components used at the physical layer, the ESXi kernel layer, and the VM layer.

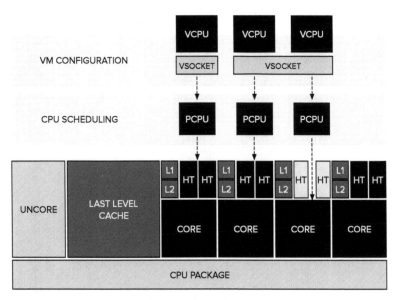

Figure 22: CPU Constructs of Physical, ESXi, and VM Layer

A **host** contains at least one CPU package. In today's datacenter the dual-socket CPU system is by far the most popular configuration. A **CPU package** is the physical CPU piece with the pins. This is inserted in a physical socket. Together with the local memory, they form a NUMA node.

Within the CPU package, a group of **cores** are present. In the example above, the CPU package contains four cores and each core has HT enabled. All cores (and thus HT) share the same cache architecture. The **pCPU** construct exists within the VMkernel layer. A pCPU is an abstraction layer inside the VMkernel and can consume a full core or it can leverage HT. Each HT thread is depicted as a logical processor.

ESXi presents a virtual socket and vCPUs to the VM. A virtual socket can map to a single pCPU or span multiple pCPUs. This depends on the number of vCPUs and the setting *Cores per Socket* (CPS). The vCPU is the logical representation of the pCPU inside the VM. The number of vCPUs and CPS VM settings impact the ability of applications (and operating systems) to optimize its cache usage.

ESXi VMkernel NUMA Constructs

To apply initial placement and load balancing operations, the NUMA scheduler creates two logical constructs, the *NUMA Home Node* (NHN) and the NUMA client.

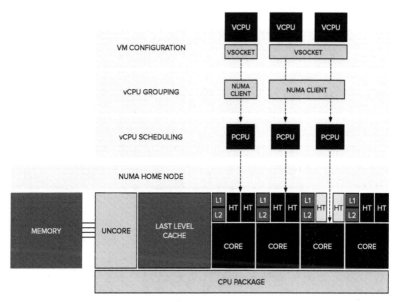

Figure 23: ESXi VMkernel NUMA Constructs

NUMA Home Node

The NUMA home node is a logical representation of a physical CPU package and its local memory. By default, the NUMA home node allows the NUMA client to count the physical cores in the CPU package. This count impacts the default NUMA client size.

This NUMA home node size is important to understand for VM sizing. The NUMA scheduler counts the number of cores within a CPU package. It compares this result to the VM's number of vCPUs and uses this information for initial placement and load balancing decisions. If the number of vCPUs exceeds the physical core count of one CPU package, it is distributed across multiple NUMA nodes.

Distribution can be avoided by reducing the number of vCPUs, or having the NUMA scheduler consider logical processors (HT) by using the advanced setting `numa.vcpu.preferHT=TRUE`. By default, NUMA optimization does not count the logical processors when determining if the VM could fit inside the NUMA home node. For particular workloads that benefit from sharing cache and memory, it might be preferable to have the NUMA scheduler count the available logical processors during the power-on operation. A later paragraph provides more details about the PreferHT setting.

Similar considerations should be applied when sizing memory for the VM. If the virtual memory configuration exceeds the local physical memory attached to a CPU package, then the memory scheduler is forced to allocate memory from another NUMA node. Please note that the NUMA scheduler is focused on allocating local memory as much as possible, it tries to avoid assigning remote memory.

Typically, a CPU package and its local memory are synonymous with a NUMA home node. Exceptions are Intel Cluster-on-Die technology and AMD Opteron (Magny-Cours and newer). When COD is enabled on an Intel Xeon CPU, the CPU package is split up into two NUMA nodes, optimizing the local cache structures.

NUMA Client

A NUMA client is the collection of vCPUs and memory of a VM that fits inside a NUMA home node. The NUMA client is the smallest unit of the NUMA scheduler that is used in initial placement and load balancing operations.

During power-on operations, all vCPUs are counted and compared to the number of physical cores available inside the CPU package. If the vCPU count does not exceed the physical core count of a NUMA node, a single NUMA client is created. A virtual UMA topology is exposed to the VM with a uniform memory address space.

If the number of vCPUs exceeds the number of physical cores inside a single NUMA node, multiple NUMA clients are created for that VM. For example, if a VM is configured with twelve vCPUs and the CPU package contains ten cores, two NUMA clients are created for that VM and the vCPUs are equally distributed across the two NUMA clients.

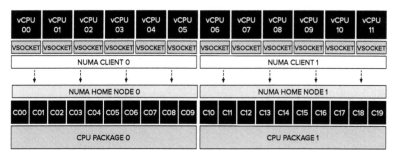

Figure 24: Wide VM on Physical Constructs

Please note that there is no affinity set between a pCPU and a NUMA client. The CPU scheduler can migrate vCPUs between any pCPU provided by the CPU package! This allows the CPU scheduler to balance the workload optimally.

vNUMA Node

If multiple NUMA clients are created for a single VM, then this configuration is considered to be a Wide-VM. The NUMA scheduler provides an extra optimization called *virtual NUMA topology*, commonly referred to as vNUMA. Please note that vNUMA exposes the virtual NUMA topology of the VM, not the entire NUMA topology of the host. In other words, vNUMA shows a tailor-made world to the VM.

In the case of the twelve vCPU VM, vNUMA exposes two NUMA nodes with each six vCPUs to the guest OS. This allows the OS itself to apply NUMA optimizations.

Auto Sizing vNUMA Clients

If multiple vNUMA clients are created, the NUMA scheduler auto-sizes the vNUMA clients. By default, it equally distributes the vCPUs across the least number of NUMA clients. Auto-sizing is done on the first boot of the VM. It optimally sizes the NUMA client for the host it boots on. During the initial boot, the VMkernel adds two advanced settings to the VM:

- `numa.autosize.vcpu.maxPerVirtualNode=X`
- `numa.autosize.cookie = 'XXXXXX'`

The auto-size setting reflects the number of vCPUs inside the NUMA node. This setting will not change, unless the number of vCPUs of the VM changes. This is particularly of interest for clusters that contain heterogeneous host configurations. If your cluster contains hosts with different core counts, you could end up with a NUMA misalignment. In this scenario, the following advanced settings can be used:

- `numa.autosize.once = FALSE`
- `numa.autosize = TRUE`

This forces the NUMA scheduler to reconfigure the NUMA clients on every power-cycle and during each vMotion. Be aware that after its installation and configuration process, some workloads cannot handle this change of microarchitecture well.

> **Be careful using this setting! Only use advanced settings if VMware Global Support Services (GSS) is requesting this.**

Adjusting Virtual NUMA Topology

Sometimes it is necessary to adjust the NUMA client size for application memory bandwidth requirements or for smaller systems. These advanced parameters can help you change the default behavior. As always make a data-driven-decision before you apply advanced parameters in your environment.

numa.vcpu.min

One of the most documented settings is the advanced setting
`numa.vcpu.min`. It's common belief that vNUMA is enabled by default on
VMs with eight vCPUs or more. This is not entirely true. The virtual NUMA
topology is exposed to the VM if two conditions are met:

- The VM contains nine or more vCPUs
- The vCPU count exceeds the core count[*] of the physical NUMA
  node

[*]When using the advanced setting `numa.vcpu.preferHT=TRUE`, logical processors
(HT) are counted instead of cores to determine scheduling options.

numa.vcpu.maxPerMachineNode

Some workloads are bandwidth intensive rather than memory latency
sensitive. In this scenario, you want to use the setting
`numa.vcpu.maxPerMachineNode`. This setting allows you to reduce the
number of vCPUs that is grouped within a NUMA client. It forces the
NUMA scheduler to create multiple NUMA clients for a VM that would
have fit inside a single NUMA home node if the default settings were
used.

Count Threads Not Cores

The advanced parameter `numa.vcpu.preferHT=TRUE` is an interesting one
as it is the source of confusion whether a NUMA system utilizes HT or
not. In essence, it impacts the sizing of the NUMA client and therefore
subsequent scheduling and load balancing behavior.

By default, the NUMA scheduler places the VMs into as few NUMA nodes
as possible. It attempts to distribute the workload across as few cache
structures as it can. During placement, it selects full physical cores for
scheduling opportunity. It wants to live up to the true potential of the
core performance. Therefore, the NUMA client size is limited to the
number of physical cores per CPU package.

Some applications share lots of memory between its threads (cache intensive footprint). They would benefit from having as much local memory as possible and they usually benefit from using a single local cache structure as well. For these workloads, it could make sense to prefer using HTs with local memory, instead of spreading the vCPUs across full cores of multiple NUMA home nodes.

The preferHT setting allows the NUMA scheduler to create a NUMA client that goes beyond the physical core count, by counting the present threads. For example, when running a twelve-vCPU VM on a ten-core system, the vCPUs are distributed equally across two NUMA clients (6-6). When using `numa.vcpu.preferHT=TRUE` the NUMA scheduler counts twenty scheduling possibilities and thus a single NUMA client is created of twelve, which allows the NUMA scheduler to place all the vCPUs into a single CPU package.

Please note that this setting does not force the CPU scheduler to only run vCPUs on logical processors. It can still (and possibly attempts to) schedule a vCPU on a full physical core. The scheduling decisions are up to the CPU scheduler's discretion and often depend on the over-commitment ratio and utilization of the system. The paragraph *Reservations and CPU scheduling* in chapter 6 contains in-depth information about CPU scheduling behavior.

Because logical processors share resources within a physical core, it results in lower CPU progression than if a vCPU runs on a dedicated physical core. Therefore, it is imperative to understand whether your application has a cache intensive footprint or whether it relies more on CPU cycles. When using the `numa.vcpu.preferHT=TRUE` setting, it instructs the CPU scheduler to prioritize on memory access over CPU resources. As always, test thoroughly and make a data-driven decision before moving away from the default!

Maybe we are overstating the obvious, but in this scenario, make absolutely sure that the memory sizing of the VM fits within a NUMA home node. The NUMA scheduler attempts to keep the memory local. If the amount of memory does not fit a single NUMA node, it has to place it in a remote node, reducing the optimization of preferHT.

Please note that numa.vcpu.preferHT=TRUE is a per-VM setting. If necessary this setting can be applied at host level. The *VMware KB article 2003582* contains the instructions to apply the setting at VM and host level. Keep in mind that when you set preferHT on a VM that has already been powered-on once, the originally calculated auto size of the NUMA client is still active. Adjust the auto-size setting in the advanced configuration of the VM or adjust the Cores per Socket for the new values to take effect.

Cores per Socket

The UI setting Cores per Socket (advanced setting: cpuid.coresPerSocket) directly creates a vNUMA node if a value is used that is higher than 1 (and the number of total vCPUs exceeds the numa.vcpu.min count). Using the example of a 16-vCPU VM again, if selecting eight cores per socket, the ESXi kernel exposes two vSockets and groups eight vCPUs per vSocket.

Determining the vNUMA Layout

VMware.log of the VM contains information about the NUMA configuration. Instead of downloading the VMware.log file you can use the command-line tool vmdumper to display the information:

```
vmdumper -l | cut -d \/ -f 2-5 | while read path; do egrep -oi
DICT.*(displayname.*|numa.*|cores.*|vcpu.*|memsize.*|affinity.*)= .
*|numa:.*|numaHost:.*' "/$path/vmware.log"; echo -e; done
```

When using this one-liner after powering-on a ten-vCPU VM on the dual E5-2630 v4 ESXi 6.0 host (ten CPU cores per CPU package) the following NUMA configuration is shown:

```
[root@esxi03:~] vmdumper -l | cut -d \/ -f 2-5 | while read path; do egrep -oi "
DICT.*(displayname.*|numa.*|cores.*|vcpu.*|memsize.*|affinity.*)= .*|numa:.*|num
aHost:.*" "/$path/vmware.log"; echo -e; done
DICT                    memSize = "12288"
DICT                displayName = "DVDStore00"
DICT          sched.cpu.affinity = "all"
DICT                   numvcpus = "10"
DICT numa.autosize.vcpu.maxPerVirtualNode = "10"
DICT        numa.autosize.cookie = "100001"
DICT        cpuid.coresPerSocket = "1"
numa: VCPU 0: VPD 0 (PPD 0)
numa: VCPU 1: VPD 0 (PPD 0)
numa: VCPU 2: VPD 0 (PPD 0)
numa: VCPU 3: VPD 0 (PPD 0)
numa: VCPU 4: VPD 0 (PPD 0)
numa: VCPU 5: VPD 0 (PPD 0)
numa: VCPU 6: VPD 0 (PPD 0)
numa: VCPU 7: VPD 0 (PPD 0)
numa: VCPU 8: VPD 0 (PPD 0)
numa: VCPU 9: VPD 0 (PPD 0)
numaHost: 1 virtual nodes, 10 virtual sockets, 1 physical domains
```

Figure 25: Ten vCPU Single NUMA Client VM

The VM is configured with ten vCPUs (numvcpus). The
cpuid.coresPerSocket = 1 indicates that it is configured with one core
per socket. The last entry summarizes the virtual NUMA topology of the
VM.

All ten virtual sockets are grouped into a single physical domain (PPD),
which means that the vCPUs will be scheduled in a single physical CPU
package that usually is similar to a single NUMA node. To match the
physical placement, a single virtual NUMA node (VPD) is exposed to the
VM. We expand on the VPD and PPD constructs in the paragraph *Virtual
Proximity Domains and Physical Proximity Domains.*

Microsoft Sysinternals tool CoreInfo exposes the CPU architecture in the
VM with great detail. (Linux contains the command numactl). Each
socket is listed and with each logical processor a cache map is
displayed. Keep the cache map in mind when you start to consolidate
multiple vCPUs into sockets.

```
Maximum implemented CPUID leaves: 00000014 (Basic), 80000008 (Extended).

Logical to Physical Processor Map:
*---------           Physical Processor 0
-*--------           Physical Processor 1
--*-------           Physical Processor 2
---*------           Physical Processor 3
----*-----           Physical Processor 4
-----*----           Physical Processor 5
------*---           Physical Processor 6
-------*--           Physical Processor 7
--------*-           Physical Processor 8
---------*           Physical Processor 9

Logical Processor to Socket Map:
*---------           Socket 0
-*--------           Socket 1
--*-------           Socket 2
---*------           Socket 3
----*-----           Socket 4
-----*----           Socket 5
------*---           Socket 6
-------*--           Socket 7
--------*-           Socket 8
---------*           Socket 9

Logical Processor to NUMA Node Map:
**********           NUMA Node 0

No NUMA nodes.

Logical Processor to Cache Map:
*---------           Data Cache          0, Level 1,    32 KB, Assoc   8, LineSize  64
*---------           Instruction Cache   0, Level 1,    32 KB, Assoc   8, LineSize  64
*---------           Unified Cache       0, Level 2,   256 KB, Assoc   8, LineSize  64
*---------           Unified Cache       1, Level 3,    25 MB, Assoc  20, LineSize  64
-*--------           Data Cache          1, Level 1,    32 KB, Assoc   8, LineSize  64
-*--------           Instruction Cache   1, Level 1,    32 KB, Assoc   8, LineSize  64
-*--------           Unified Cache       2, Level 2,   256 KB, Assoc   8, LineSize  64
-*--------           Unified Cache       3, Level 3,    25 MB, Assoc  20, LineSize  64
--*-------           Data Cache          2, Level 1,    32 KB, Assoc   8, LineSize  64
--*-------           Instruction Cache   2, Level 1,    32 KB, Assoc   8, LineSize  64
--*-------           Unified Cache       4, Level 2,   256 KB, Assoc   8, LineSize  64
--*-------           Unified Cache       5, Level 3,    25 MB, Assoc  20, LineSize  64
---*------           Data Cache          3, Level 1,    32 KB, Assoc   8, LineSize  64
---*------           Instruction Cache   3, Level 1,    32 KB, Assoc   8, LineSize  64
---*------           Unified Cache       6, Level 2,   256 KB, Assoc   8, LineSize  64
---*------           Unified Cache       7, Level 3,    25 MB, Assoc  20, LineSize  64
----*-----           Data Cache          4, Level 1,    32 KB, Assoc   8, LineSize  64
----*-----           Instruction Cache   4, Level 1,    32 KB, Assoc   8, LineSize  64
----*-----           Unified Cache       8, Level 2,   256 KB, Assoc   8, LineSize  64
----*-----           Unified Cache       9, Level 3,    25 MB, Assoc  20, LineSize  64
-----*----           Data Cache          5, Level 1,    32 KB, Assoc   8, LineSize  64
-----*----           Instruction Cache   5, Level 1,    32 KB, Assoc   8, LineSize  64
-----*----           Unified Cache      10, Level 2,   256 KB, Assoc   8, LineSize  64
-----*----           Unified Cache      11, Level 3,    25 MB, Assoc  20, LineSize  64
------*---           Data Cache          6, Level 1,    32 KB, Assoc   8, LineSize  64
------*---           Instruction Cache   6, Level 1,    32 KB, Assoc   8, LineSize  64
------*---           Unified Cache      12, Level 2,   256 KB, Assoc   8, LineSize  64
------*---           Unified Cache      13, Level 3,    25 MB, Assoc  20, LineSize  64
-------*--           Data Cache          7, Level 1,    32 KB, Assoc   8, LineSize  64
-------*--           Instruction Cache   7, Level 1,    32 KB, Assoc   8, LineSize  64
-------*--           Unified Cache      14, Level 2,   256 KB, Assoc   8, LineSize  64
-------*--           Unified Cache      15, Level 3,    25 MB, Assoc  20, LineSize  64
--------*-           Data Cache          8, Level 1,    32 KB, Assoc   8, LineSize  64
--------*-           Instruction Cache   8, Level 1,    32 KB, Assoc   8, LineSize  64
--------*-           Unified Cache      16, Level 2,   256 KB, Assoc   8, LineSize  64
--------*-           Unified Cache      17, Level 3,    25 MB, Assoc  20, LineSize  64
---------*           Data Cache          9, Level 1,    32 KB, Assoc   8, LineSize  64
---------*           Instruction Cache   9, Level 1,    32 KB, Assoc   8, LineSize  64
---------*           Unified Cache      18, Level 2,   256 KB, Assoc   8, LineSize  64
---------*           Unified Cache      19, Level 3,    25 MB, Assoc  20, LineSize  64

Logical Processor to Group Map:
**********           Group 0

c:\CoreInfo>_
```

Figure 26: Microsoft CoreInfo Output Ten vCPU Single NUMA Client VM

Virtual NUMA Topology

The vCPU count of the VM is increased to sixteen vCPUs. As a consequence, this configuration exceeds the physical core count. Microsoft Coreinfo provides the following insight:

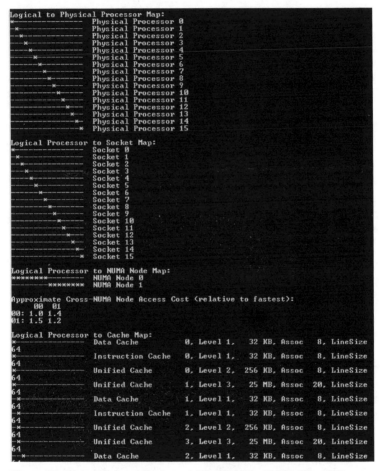

Figure 27: Microsoft CoreInfo Output 16 vCPU Two NUMA Client VM

Microsoft Coreinfo uses an asterisk to represent the mapping of the logical processor to socket map and NUMA node map. In this configuration, the logical processors in socket 0 to socket 7 belong to NUMA node 0.

The CPUs in socket 8 to socket 15 belong to NUMA node 1. The screenshot shown below does not contain the entire logical processor cache map overview. The `vmdumper` command displays the following:

```
[root@esxi03:~] vmdumper -l | cut -d \/ -f 2-5 | while read path; do egrep -oi "
DICT.*(displayname.*|numa.*|cores.*|vcpu.*|memsize.*|affinity.*)= .*|numa:.*|num
aHost:.*" "/$path/vmware.log"; echo -e; done
DICT                    memSize = "12288"
DICT                displayName = "DVDStore00"
DICT         sched.cpu.affinity = "all"
DICT                   numvcpus = "16"
DICT numa.autosize.vcpu.maxPerVirtualNode = "8"
DICT      numa.autosize.cookie = "160001"
DICT      cpuid.coresPerSocket = "1"
numa: Exposing multicore topology with cpuid.coresPerSocket = 8 is suggested for
best performance
numa: VCPU 0: VPD 0 (PPD 0)
numa: VCPU 1: VPD 0 (PPD 0)
numa: VCPU 2: VPD 0 (PPD 0)
numa: VCPU 3: VPD 0 (PPD 0)
numa: VCPU 4: VPD 0 (PPD 0)
numa: VCPU 5: VPD 0 (PPD 0)
numa: VCPU 6: VPD 0 (PPD 0)
numa: VCPU 7: VPD 0 (PPD 0)
numa: VCPU 8: VPD 1 (PPD 1)
numa: VCPU 9: VPD 1 (PPD 1)
numa: VCPU 10: VPD 1 (PPD 1)
numa: VCPU 11: VPD 1 (PPD 1)
numa: VCPU 12: VPD 1 (PPD 1)
numa: VCPU 13: VPD 1 (PPD 1)
numa: VCPU 14: VPD 1 (PPD 1)
numa: VCPU 15: VPD 1 (PPD 1)
numaHost: 2 virtual nodes, 16 virtual sockets, 2 physical domains

[root@esxi03:~]
```

Figure 28: NUMA Constructs Overview 16 vCPU VM

In the previous example, in which the VM was configured with ten vCPUs, the `numa.autosize.vcpu.maxPerVirtualNode=10`. In this scenario, the sixteen vCPU VM has a `numa.autosize.vcpu.maxPerVirtualNode=8`.

The VMkernel symmetrically distributes the sixteen vCPUs across multiple virtual NUMA nodes. It fits the maximum number of vCPUs into the minimum number of virtual NUMA nodes. This results into the distribution of eight vCPUs per virtual node. The VMkernel.log describes this behavior with the following entry: 'Exposing multicore topology with `cpuid.coresPerSocket=8` is suggested for best performance'.

Virtual Proximity Domains and Physical Proximity Domains

Let's look at the NUMA home node and NUMA client in more detail. The VMkernel uses different terminology to identify these constructs. The NUMA client is considered a virtual NUMA topology. It is split up in two elements; the *Virtual Proximity Domains* (VPD) and the *Physical Proximity Domains* (PPD). The VPD is the construct that is exposed to the VM, the PPD is the construct used by NUMA for placement (Initial placement and load-balancing).

Physical Proximity Domain

The PPD auto sizes to the optimal number of vCPUs per physical CPU package based on the core count of the CPU package, unless the setting Cores per Socket within a VM configuration is used.

In ESXi 6.0 the configuration of Cores per Socket dictates the size of the PPD, up to the point where the vCPU count is equal to the number of cores in the physical CPU package. In other words, a PPD can never span multiple physical CPU packages.

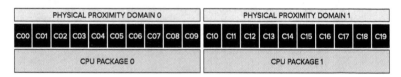

Figure 29: VMkernel NUMA Physical Proximity Domain

The best way to perceive a proximity domain is to compare it to a 'VM to host affinity group', but in this context it is used to map vCPU to CPU cores. The PPD acts like an affinity of a group of vCPUs to all the CPUs of a CPU package.

Please note that the NUMA scheduler is the only system process that uses the proximity group construct. This construct is invisible to the CPU scheduler that is responsible for the vCPU to pCPU scheduling.

The CPU scheduler determines CPU time for a vCPU on an individual basis. The NUMA scheduler uses the PPD to ensure that a particular group of vCPUs is grouped together so they can consume the available resources of a CPU package.

Virtual Proximity Domain

A VPD is the construct that exposes the virtual NUMA topology to the VM. The number of VPDs depends on the number of vCPUs and the physical core count, or the use of the Cores per Socket setting. By default, the VPD aligns with the PPD. If a VM is created with twelve vCPUs on a dual 10-core CPU, two PPDs are created. These PPDs allow the VPDs and its vCPUs to map and consume six physical cores of the CPU package.

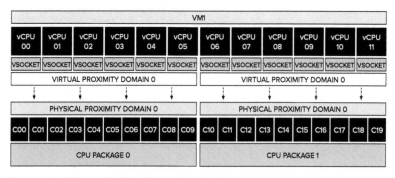

Figure 30: VMkernel NUMA Virtual Proximity Domain

If the default vCPU settings are used, each vCPU is placed in its own CPU socket (`cores per socket = 1`). The VPD to PPD alignment can be overruled if a non-default Cores per Socket setting is used. A VPD spans multiple PPDs if the number of the vCPUs and the Cores per Socket configuration exceeds the physical core count of a CPU package.

For example, a host contains four CPU packages that each contains ten cores. A VM is configured with forty vCPUs and they are divided across two sockets (`cores per socket = 20`). During the power-on operation of the VM, a vNUMA topology is created of two VPDs that each contains twenty vCPUs. These two VPDs span four PPDs.

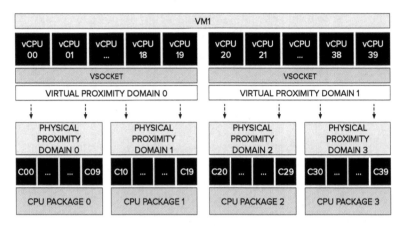

Figure 31: Spanning VPDs Across Multiple PPDs

The Cores per Socket configuration overwrites the default VPD configuration and this can lead to suboptimal configurations if the physical layout is not taken into account correctly.

Specifically, spanning VPDs across PPDs is something that should be avoided at all times. CPU and cache optimizations inside the guest OS and applications can be rendered completely useless by this setting. For example, OS and applications potentially encounter remote memory access latencies while expecting local memory latencies after optimizing thread placements.

It's recommended to configure the VMs Cores per Socket to align with the physical boundaries of the CPU package.

ESXi 6.5 Cores per Socket Behavior

Introduced in ESXi 6.5 NUMA scheduler is the decoupling of Cores per Socket configuration and VPD creation to further optimize virtual NUMA topology.

Up to version ESXi 6.0, if a VM is created with sixteen CPUs and two cores per socket, eight PPDs are created and eight VPDs are exposed to the VM.

```
[root@esxi03:~] vmdumper -l | cut -d \/ -f 2-5 | while read path; do egrep -oi "
DICT.*(displayname.*|numa.*|cores.*|vcpu.*|memsize.*|affinity.*)= .*|numa:.*|num
aHost:.*" "/$path/vmware.log"; echo -e; done
DICT                    memSize = "12288"
DICT                 displayName = "DVDStore00"
DICT          sched.cpu.affinity = "all"
DICT                   numvcpus = "16"
DICT numa.autosize.vcpu.maxPerVirtualNode = "8"
DICT        numa.autosize.cookie = "160001"
DICT        cpuid.coresPerSocket = "2"
numa: Setting.vcpu.maxPerVirtualNode=2 to match cpuid.coresPerSocket
numa: VCPU 0: VPD 0 (PPD 0)
numa: VCPU 1: VPD 0 (PPD 0)
numa: VCPU 2: VPD 1 (PPD 1)
numa: VCPU 3: VPD 1 (PPD 1)
numa: VCPU 4: VPD 2 (PPD 2)
numa: VCPU 5: VPD 2 (PPD 2)
numa: VCPU 6: VPD 3 (PPD 3)
numa: VCPU 7: VPD 3 (PPD 3)
numa: VCPU 8: VPD 4 (PPD 4)
numa: VCPU 9: VPD 4 (PPD 4)
numa: VCPU 10: VPD 5 (PPD 5)
numa: VCPU 11: VPD 5 (PPD 5)
numa: VCPU 12: VPD 6 (PPD 6)
numa: VCPU 13: VPD 6 (PPD 6)
numa: VCPU 14: VPD 7 (PPD 7)
numa: VCPU 15: VPD 7 (PPD 7)
numaHost: 8 virtual nodes, 8 virtual sockets, 8 physical domains

[root@esxi03:~]
```

Figure 32: ESXi 6.0 Cores per Socket Impact on VPD Sizing

The problem with this configuration is that the virtual NUMA topology does not represent the physical NUMA topology correctly.

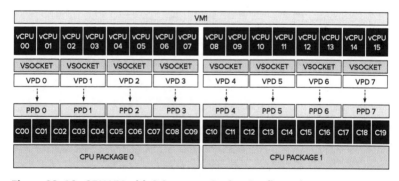

Figure 33: 16 vCPU VM with 8 Cores per Socket Configuration

The guest OS is presented with sixteen CPUs distributed across eight sockets. Each pair of CPUs has its own cache and its own local memory. The OS considers the memory addresses from the other CPU pairs to be remote. When spanning VPDs across multiple PPDs, the OS has to deal with eight small chunks of memory space and optimizes its cache management and memory placement based on its own NUMA scheduling optimizations. The figure below zooms in on two of the eight VPD configurations.

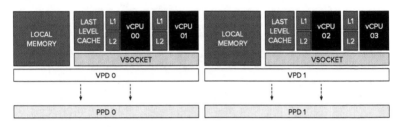

Figure 34: Fragmented VM Cache and Memory Address Space

In reality, the sixteen vCPUs are distributed across two physical nodes, thus eight vCPUs share the same LLC and have access to the physical memory pool. From a cache and memory centric perspective the mapping of a single NUMA node looks more like this:

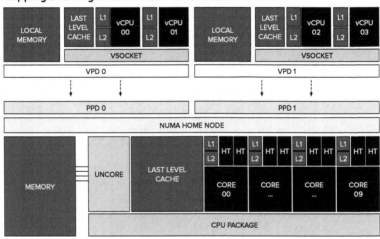

Figure 35: VMkernel NUMA Constructs Scheduled on Physical CPU

Microsoft CoreInfo output of the CPU configuration of the VM:

```
Logical to Physical Processor Map:
*---------------        Physical Processor 0
-*--------------        Physical Processor 1
--*-------------        Physical Processor 2
---*------------        Physical Processor 3
----*-----------        Physical Processor 4
-----*----------        Physical Processor 5
------*---------        Physical Processor 6
-------*--------        Physical Processor 7
--------*-------        Physical Processor 8
---------*------        Physical Processor 9
----------*-----        Physical Processor 10
-----------*----        Physical Processor 11
------------*---        Physical Processor 12
-------------*--        Physical Processor 13
--------------*-        Physical Processor 14
---------------*        Physical Processor 15

Logical Processor to Socket Map:
**--------------        Socket 0
--**------------        Socket 1
----**----------        Socket 2
------**--------        Socket 3
--------**------        Socket 4
----------**----        Socket 5
------------**--        Socket 6
--------------**        Socket 7

Logical Processor to NUMA Node Map:
**--------------        NUMA Node 0
--**------------        NUMA Node 1
----**----------        NUMA Node 2
------**--------        NUMA Node 3
--------**------        NUMA Node 4
----------**----        NUMA Node 5
------------**--        NUMA Node 6
--------------**        NUMA Node 7

Approximate Cross-NUMA Node Access Cost (relative to fastest):
     00   01   02   03   04   05   06   07
00:  1.2  1.1  1.2  1.1  1.7  1.7  1.6  1.7
01:  1.1  1.0  1.0  1.0  1.6  1.6  1.6  1.5
02:  1.3  1.1  1.1  1.1  1.7  1.7  1.7  1.7
03:  1.3  1.3  1.3  1.1  1.7  1.7  1.7  1.7
04:  1.9  1.9  1.9  1.7  1.7  1.7  1.7  1.4
05:  1.7  1.7  1.6  1.6  1.0  1.0  1.1  1.3
06:  1.9  2.0  1.7  1.7  1.1  1.1  1.2  1.3
07:  1.9  1.7  1.7  1.7  1.1  1.1  1.2  1.3
```

Figure 36: Microsoft CoreInfo VM Details

To avoid 'fragmentation' of local memory, the behavior of VPDs and their relation to the Cores per Socket setting has changed. In ESXi 6.5 the size of the VPD is dependent on the number of cores in the CPU package. This results in a virtual NUMA topology that attempts to resemble the physical NUMA topology as much as possible. Using the same example of sixteen vCPUs, two cores per socket, on a dual Intel Xeon E5-2630 v4 (twenty cores in total), the vmdumper one-liner shows the following:

```
[root@esxi03:~] vmdumper -l | cut -d \/ -f 2-5 | while read path; do egrep -oi "
DICT.*(displayname.*|numa.*|cores.*|vcpu.*|memsize.*|affinity.*)= .*|numa:.*|num
aHost:.*" "/$path/vmware.log"; echo -e; done
DICT                 memSize = "12288"
DICT             displayName = "DVDStore00"
DICT       sched.cpu.affinity = "all"
DICT               numvcpus = "16"
DICT numa.autosize.vcpu.maxPerVirtualNode = "8"
DICT       numa.autosize.cookie = "160001"
DICT       cpuid.coresPerSocket = "2"
numaHost: NUMA config: consolidation= 1 preferHT= 0
numaHost: 16 VCPUs 2 VPDs 2 PPDs
numaHost: VCPU 0 VPD 0 PPD 0
numaHost: VCPU 1 VPD 0 PPD 0
numaHost: VCPU 2 VPD 0 PPD 0
numaHost: VCPU 3 VPD 0 PPD 0
numaHost: VCPU 4 VPD 0 PPD 0
numaHost: VCPU 5 VPD 0 PPD 0
numaHost: VCPU 6 VPD 0 PPD 0
numaHost: VCPU 7 VPD 0 PPD 0
numaHost: VCPU 8 VPD 1 PPD 1
numaHost: VCPU 9 VPD 1 PPD 1
numaHost: VCPU 10 VPD 1 PPD 1
numaHost: VCPU 11 VPD 1 PPD 1
numaHost: VCPU 12 VPD 1 PPD 1
numaHost: VCPU 13 VPD 1 PPD 1
numaHost: VCPU 14 VPD 1 PPD 1
numaHost: VCPU 15 VPD 1 PPD 1

[root@esxi03:~]
```

Figure 37: ESXi 6.5 Cores per Socket Impact on VPD Sizing

As a result of having two physical NUMA nodes, only two PPDs and VPDs are created.

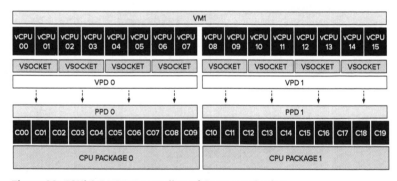

Figure 38: ESXi 6.5 VPD Decoupling of Cores per Socket

A new line appears in ESXi 6.5 when running the vmdumper one-liner. 'NUMA config: consolidation=1' indicates that the vCPUs will be consolidated into the lowest number of proximity domains as possible.

Please note that the setting Cores per Socket has not changed. As a result, multiple sockets are created in a single VPD. Each still creating a fragmented cache address space. In this example, the sixteen vCPUs can be distributed across two NUMA nodes, thus two PPDs and two VPDs are created. Each VPD exposes a single memory address space that correlates with the characteristics of the physical machine.

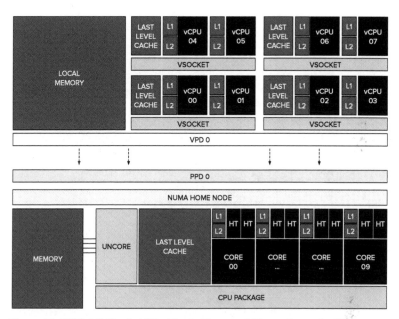

Figure 39: ESXi 6.5 Single VPD, Single Memory Address Space for VM

The Microsoft Windows 2012 guest OS running inside the VM detects two NUMA nodes. The CPU view of the task managers shows the following configuration:

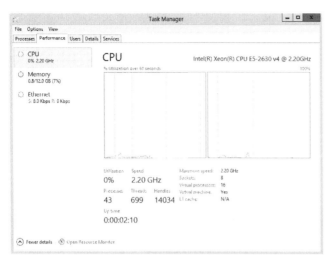

Figure 40: NUMA Node Performance View Windows 2012 Task Manager

The NUMA node view is selected and at the bottom right of the screen it shows that VM contains eight sockets and sixteen virtual CPUs. Microsoft CoreInfo provides the following information:

```
Logical to Physical Processor Map:
*--------------- Physical Processor 0
-*-------------- Physical Processor 1
--*------------- Physical Processor 2
---*------------ Physical Processor 3
----*----------- Physical Processor 4
-----*---------- Physical Processor 5
------*--------- Physical Processor 6
-------*-------- Physical Processor 7
--------*------- Physical Processor 8
---------*------ Physical Processor 9
----------*----- Physical Processor 10
-----------*---- Physical Processor 11
------------*--- Physical Processor 12
-------------*-- Physical Processor 13
--------------*- Physical Processor 14
---------------* Physical Processor 15

Logical Processor to Socket Map:
**-------------- Socket 0
--**------------ Socket 1
----**---------- Socket 2
------**-------- Socket 3
--------**------ Socket 4
----------**---- Socket 5
------------**-- Socket 6
--------------** Socket 7

Logical Processor to NUMA Node Map:
********-------- NUMA Node 0
--------******** NUMA Node 1
```

Figure 41: Microsoft CoreInfo VM NUMA Constructs

With this new optimization, the virtual NUMA topology corresponds more to the actual physical NUMA topology, allowing the OS to correctly optimize its processes for correct local and remote memory access.

Guest OS NUMA Optimization

Modern applications and operating systems manage memory access based on NUMA nodes (memory access latency) and cache structures (sharing of data).

Unfortunately, most applications, even the ones that are highly optimized for SMP, do not balance the workload perfectly across NUMA nodes. Modern operating systems apply a first-touch-allocation policy. When an application requests memory, the virtual address is not mapped to any physical memory. If the application accesses the memory, the OS attempts to allocate it on the local or specified NUMA if possible.

In an ideal world, the thread that creates the memory is the same thread that processes it. Unfortunately, many applications use single threads to create the data. But they use multiple threads to access the data. The threads that access the data are distributed across multiple sockets.

Please take this into account when configuring the VM and especially when configuring the number of cores per socket. The new optimization helps to overcome some inefficiencies created in the OS. However, sometimes it is required to configure the VM with a deviating Cores per Socket setting, for example due to licensing constraints.

If you are required to set Cores per Socket and you want to optimize guest OS memory behavior any further, then configure the cores per socket to align with the physical characteristics of the CPU package. As demonstrated, the new virtual NUMA topology optimizes the memory address space, providing a bigger, more uniform memory slice that aligns better with the physical characteristics of the system.

One element has not been thoroughly addressed is cache address space created by a virtual socket. As presented by Microsoft CoreInfo, each virtual socket advertises its own LLC.

In the scenario of the sixteen vCPU VM on the test system, configuring it with eight cores per socket, it resembles both the memory and the cache address space of the physical CPU package the most.

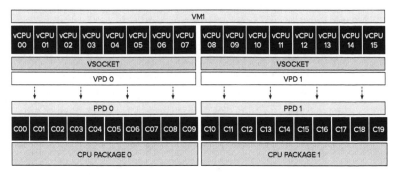

Figure 42: 16 vCPU VM - 8 Cores per Socket Configuration

MS-Coreinfo shows the 16 vCPUs distributed symmetrically across two NUMA nodes. Each socket contains eight CPUs that share LLC, similar to the physical world.

```
Logical Processor to Socket Map:
********--------          Socket 0
--------********          Socket 1

Logical Processor to NUMA Node Map:
********--------          NUMA Node 0
--------********          NUMA Node 1

Approximate Cross-NUMA Node Access Cost (relative to fastest):
      00   01
00: 1.0 1.5
01: 1.5 1.3

Logical Processor to Cache Map:
********--------          Data Cache        0, Level 1,   32 KB, Assoc   8, LineSize
64
********--------          Instruction Cache 0, Level 1,   32 KB, Assoc   8, LineSize
64
********--------          Unified Cache     0, Level 2,  256 KB, Assoc   8, LineSize
64
********--------          Unified Cache     1, Level 3,   25 MB, Assoc  20, LineSize
64
--------********          Data Cache        1, Level 1,   32 KB, Assoc   8, LineSize
64
--------********          Instruction Cache 1, Level 1,   32 KB, Assoc   8, LineSize
64
--------********          Unified Cache     2, Level 2,  256 KB, Assoc   8, LineSize
64
--------********          Unified Cache     3, Level 3,   25 MB, Assoc  20, LineSize
64

Logical Processor to Group Map:
****************          Group 0
```

Figure 43: Single Cache and Memory Address Space

Word of Caution: Migrating VMs from older ESXi versions to an ESXi 6.5 hosts can create PSODs and/or VM Panic if the VMs are configured with a custom Cores per Socket setting. Unfortunately, some vNUMA topology configurations cannot be consolidated properly by the GA release of ESXi 6.5 when vMotioning a VM from an older ESXi version. This is solved by in ESXi 6.5.0a. This patch resorts back to the NUMA scheduler behavior of ESXi 6.0 regarding cores per socket settings. *VMware KB article 2147958* has more information.

NUMA Support for CPU Hot Add

A common question is if CPU Hot Add impacts CPU performance of the VM. It depends on the vCPU configuration of the VM. If CPU Hot Add is enabled, NUMA clients of wide VMs cannot be sized deterministically. As a result, CPU Hot Add is not compatible with vNUMA. If CPU Hot Add is enabled, the virtual NUMA topology is not exposed to the guest OS and could impact application performance.

Remember that NUMA client sizing only happens during power-on operations, while the CPU Hot Add option avoids any power operation. ESXi 6.5 attempts to optimize the configuration, but a NUMA-optimized placement cannot be guaranteed with CPU Hot Add.

Due to this, it is possible that memory is interleaved between the NUMA home nodes for the VM. This often results in performance degradation as memory access has to traverse the interconnect topology. The problem with enabling CPU Hot Add is that this is not directly visible when reviewing the VMs with esxtop. Routinely, most admins check whether NUMA home nodes are reported.

```
4:17:45pm up  6:14, 737 worlds, 1 VMs, 16 vCPUs; MEM overcommit avg: 0.00, 0.00, 0.00
PMEM   /MB: 130961   total: 2357      vmk,8954 other, 119648 free
VMKMEM/MB: 130575 managed:  1920 minfree,  6686 rsvd, 123888 ursvd,  high state
NUMA   /MB: 65423 (59382), 65536 (59882)
PSHARE/MB:      31  shared,      31  common:      0 saving
SWAP   /MB:      0   curr,       0 rclmtgt:               0.00 r/s,   0.00 w/s
ZIP    /MB:      0  zipped,      0   saved
MEMCTL/MB:      0   curr,       0  target,   15974 max

    GID NAME                                         NHN NMIG      NRMEM       NLMEM N%L G!
  35021 SQL02                                        0,1    0       0.00     8600.25 100
```

Figure 44: Esxtop NUMA Statistics - NUMA Home Node

Although esxtop NUMA stats report two NUMA home nodes, it does not mean that NUMA optimizations are applied to the VM. But what happens when the VM is configured with less vCPUs than the core count of the physical CPU package and CPU Hot Add is enabled? Will there be a performance impact? The answer is no! The VPD configured for the VM fits inside a NUMA node, and thus the CPU scheduler and the NUMA scheduler optimize memory operations. It's all about memory locality. Let's make use of some application workload test to determine the behavior of the VMkernel CPU scheduling.

For this test, we installed DVD Store 3.0 and ran some test loads on the MS-SQL server. To determine the baseline, we logged in the ESXi host via an SSH session and executed the command: sched-stats -t numa-pnode. This command shows the CPU and memory configuration of each NUMA node in the system. This screenshot shows that the system is only running the ESXi OS. Hardly any memory is consumed. The metric TotalMem indicates the total amount of physical memory in the NUMA node in KB. FreeMem indicates the amount of free physical memory in the NUMA node in KB.

```
[root@esxi03:~] sched-stats -t numa-pnode
    nodeID      used       idle   entitled    owed  loadAvgPct  nVcpu      freeMem    totalMem
         0        75      19925          0       0           0      0     65330008    66993668
         1        13      19987          0       0           0      0     65853828    67108864
[root@esxi03:~] █
```

Figure 45: Unloaded ESXi Host

An eight vCPU 32 GB VM is created with CPU Hot Add disabled. NUMA
scheduler has selected NUMA node 1 for initial placement and
something consumes ~13759 MB. 67108864 (totalmem) − 53019184
(freemem) =14089680 KB /1024 = 13759,45 MB.

```
[root@esxi03:~] sched-stats -t numa-pnode
     nodeID         used         idle     entitled   owed   loadAvgPct        nVcpu       freeMem      totalMem
          0          151        19849            0      0            0            0      65275796      66993668
          1         7202        12797         7168      0           35            8      53019184      67108864
[root@esxi03:~]
```

Figure 46: 8 vCPU VM on NUMA Node

The following command allows us to verify the VM memory consumption
of the VM.

```
[root@esxi03:~] memstats -r vm-stats -s name:memSize:allocTgt:mapped:consumed:touched -u mb

VIRTUAL MACHINE STATS: Fri Apr 14 05:45:52 2017
------------------------------------------------
   Start Group ID   : 0
   No. of levels    : 12
   Unit             : MB
   Selected columns : name:memSize:allocTgt:consumed:mapped:touched


        name    memSize   allocTgt    consumed     mapped    touched
------------------------------------------------------------------------
   vm.78864      32768      14502       13184      13186      12779
------------------------------------------------------------------------
      Total      32768      14502       13184      13186      12779
------------------------------------------------------------------------
[root@esxi03:~] []
```

Figure 47: VM Memstats

The consumed memory of the VM roughly matches the reduction of
available memory of Node 1. Please note that VM-stats do not include
overhead memory. The VMkernel can consume some additional
overhead in the same NUMA node for other processes. When CPU Hot
Add is enabled (power down VM is necessary to enable this feature),
nothing really changes. The memory for this VM is still allocated from a
single NUMA node.

```
[root@esxi03:~] sched-stats -t numa-pnode
     nodeID       used         idle     entitled   owed   loadAvgPct   nVcpu       freeMem      totalMem
          0         15        19985            0      0            0       0      65277056      66993668
          1         38        19962           27      0            1       8      50843436      67108864
[root@esxi03:~]
```

Figure 48: VM Memory Allocated by Single NUMA Node

To get a better understanding of the CPU scheduling constructs at play here, the vmdumper command provides detailed insight of all the NUMA related settings of the VM:

```
vmdumper -1 | cut -d \/ -f 2-5 | while read path; do egrep -oi
"DICT.*(displayname.*|numa.*|cores.*|vcpu.*|memsize.*|affinity.*)=
.*|numa:.*|numaHost:.*" "/$path/vmware.log"; echo -e; done
```

```
DICT                    numvcpus = "8"
DICT                    memSize = "32768"
DICT                displayName = "SQL00"
DICT numa.autosize.vcpu.maxPerVirtualNode = "8"
DICT        numa.autosize.cookie = "80001"
DICT                vcpu.hotadd = "TRUE"
numaHost: NUMA config: consolidation= 1 preferHT= 0
numaHost: 8 VCPUs 1 VPDs 1 PPDs
numaHost: VCPU 0 VPD 0 PPD 0
numaHost: VCPU 1 VPD 0 PPD 0
numaHost: VCPU 2 VPD 0 PPD 0
numaHost: VCPU 3 VPD 0 PPD 0
numaHost: VCPU 4 VPD 0 PPD 0
numaHost: VCPU 5 VPD 0 PPD 0
numaHost: VCPU 6 VPD 0 PPD 0
numaHost: VCPU 7 VPD 0 PPD 0

[root@esxi03:~]
```

Figure 49: vmdumper Command Displays NUMA Constructs

It shows CPU Hot Add is enabled and the VM is configured with a single VPD that is scheduled on a single PPD. Differently put, the vCPUs of the VM are contained with a single physical NUMA node. It's the responsibility of the NUMA scheduler that physical local memory is consumed. To verify if the VM is consuming local memory, esxtop can be used (memory, f, NUMA stats). You can also use the command sched-stats -t numa-clients to obtain additional insights.

```
[root@esxi03:~] sched-stats -t numa-clients
groupName        groupID    clientID    homeNode    nWorlds    vmmWorlds    localMem    remoteMem    currLocal%    cummLocal%
vm.81204         72144      0           1           8          8            14848284    0            100           100
[root@esxi03:~]
```

Figure 50: 8-vCPU Hot Add NUMA Client

As a result, you can conclude that enabling Hot Add on a NUMA system does not lead to performance degradation as long as the vCPU count does not exceed the core count of the CPU package.

> Hot Add can be enabled on VMs, but it must be clear that vCPUs can be added up to the threshold of the physical core count, to avoid creating a Wide-VM configuration.

What is the impact of disregarding the physical NUMA topology? The key lies within the message that is entered in the VMware.log of the VM after boot:

```
2017-04-1407:33:29;270Z| vmx| I125: NUMA and VPCU hot add are
incompatible. Forcing UMA.
```

The VMkernel is forced into using UMA on a NUMA architecture. As a result, memory is interleaved between the two physical NUMA nodes. In essence, It is load-balancing memory across two nodes, while ignoring the vCPU location. Let's explore this behavior a bit more.
Christmas is coming early for this VM and it gets another 4 vCPUs. Hot Add is disabled again and thus vNUMA is full in play. The vmdumper command reveals the following:

```
DICT                     numvcpus = "12"
DICT                      memSize = "32768"
DICT                  displayName = "SQL00"
DICT numa.autosize.vcpu.maxPerVirtualNode = "6"
DICT        numa.autosize.cookie = "120001"
numaHost: NUMA config: consolidation= 1 preferHT= 0
numaHost: 12 VCPUs 2 VPDs 2 PPDs
numaHost: VCPU 0 VPD 0 PPD 0
numaHost: VCPU 1 VPD 0 PPD 0
numaHost: VCPU 2 VPD 0 PPD 0
numaHost: VCPU 3 VPD 0 PPD 0
numaHost: VCPU 4 VPD 0 PPD 0
numaHost: VCPU 5 VPD 0 PPD 0
numaHost: VCPU 6 VPD 1 PPD 1
numaHost: VCPU 7 VPD 1 PPD 1
numaHost: VCPU 8 VPD 1 PPD 1
numaHost: VCPU 9 VPD 1 PPD 1
numaHost: VCPU 10 VPD 1 PPD 1
numaHost: VCPU 11 VPD 1 PPD 1
```

Figure 51: 12 vCPU NUMA Client Hot Add Disabled

The vCPUs are split up in two virtual nodes (VPD0 & VPD1), each containing six vCPUs. After running the DVD Store query, the following memory allocation occurred:

```
[root@esxi03:~] sched-stats -t numa-pnode
    nodeID        used        idle    entitled    owed    loadAvgPct        nVcpu      freeMem    totalMem
         0          31       19968          17       0             0            6     50596640    66993668
         1          25       19974          17       0             0            6     60624968    67108864
[root@esxi03:~] ▌
```

Figure 52: 12 vCPU vNUMA Hot Add Disabled Memory Allocation

The guest OS (Windows 2012 R2) consumed some memory from node 1. SQL consumed all of its memory from node 0. For people intimate with SQL resource management this might be strange behavior, and it is. To display memory management at the VMkernel layer we had to restrict SQL to only run on a subset of CPUs. We allowed SQL to run on the first four vCPUs. All these were mapped to CPUs located in NUMA node 0.

The NUMA scheduler ensured these CPUs consumed local memory. After powering down and enabling CPU Hot Add, the same test was run again. No NUMA architecture is exposed to the guest OS and therefore a single memory address space is used by Windows. The memory scheduler follows the rules of UMA and interleaves memory between the two physical nodes. And as the output shows, memory is consumed from both NUMA nodes in a balanced manner. The problem is, the executing vCPUs are all located in NUMA node 0. Therefore, they have to fetch a lot of memory from the remote node, creating an inconsistent – less – performing application.

```
[root@esxi03:~] sched-stats -t numa-pnode
    nodeID        used        idle    entitled    owed    loadAvgPct        nVcpu      freeMem    totalMem
         0        3628       16372        3531       0            18            6     50916956    66993668
         1        5168       14831        5071       0            19            6     51352892    67108864
[root@esxi03:~] ▌
```

Figure 53: 12 vCPU vNUMA Hot Add Enabled Memory Allocation

The CPU Hot Add option is a great feature for when you stay within the confines of the CPU package but expect performance degradation, or at least inconsistent performance when going beyond the CPU core count.

NUMA Support for Memory Hot Plug

Memory Hot Plug is supported on a wide-VM. If the Memory Hot Plug option is enabled and memory is added while the VM is operational, the NUMA scheduler allocates the newly added memory across all NUMA nodes. In previous versions, the NUMA scheduler only allocated memory from NUMA node 0.

Advanced Setting numa.consolidate

It can occur that a VM memory configuration exceeds the NUMA node memory configuration. Typically, this happens in multi-socket systems that are used to host monster-VMs. We are seeing an increasing use of VMs with an extreme memory footprint.

In this scenario, the system is equipped with two CPU packages. Each CPU package contains twelve cores. The system has a memory configuration of 128 GB in total. Each NUMA node, if symmetrically configured, should contain 64 GB of memory.

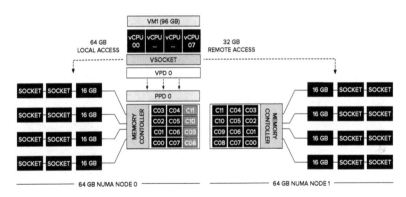

Figure 54: VM with Memory Footprint Exceeding NUMA node

However, if the VM requires 96 GB of memory, only up to 64 GB can be obtained from a single NUMA node. Consequently, 32 GB of memory is retrieved from the remote node. The VM that is powered-on, contains eight vCPUs and is placed inside one NUMA node.

103

Because the VM fits inside one NUMA node, from a vCPU perspective, the NUMA scheduler configures a single PPD for this VM. Running an SQL DB on this machine resulted in the following local and remote memory consumption.

```
[root@esxi03:~] sched-stats -t numa-cnode
  groupName          groupID   clientID   nodeID   time    timePct     memory   memoryPct
  vm.120846           203207          0        0    567        100   65072984          66
  vm.120846           203207          0        1      0          0   32200872          33
[root@esxi03:~] ▋
```

Figure 55: Local and Remote Memory Consumption

The VM consumes nearly 64 GB on its local NUMA node (clientID shows the location of the vCPUs) while it consumes 31 GB of remote memory.

It could be beneficial to the performance of the VM to rely on the NUMA optimizations that exist in the guest OS and application. The VM advanced setting numa.consolidate = FALSE instructs the NUMA scheduler to distribute the vCPUs across as many NUMA nodes as possible. In this scenario, the NUMA scheduler creates two PPDs, allowing a symmetrical configuration of four vCPUs per node.

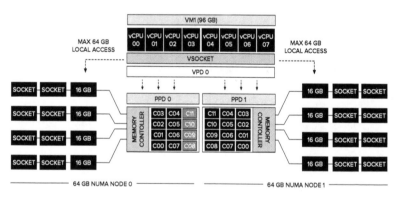

Figure 56: VM Advanced Setting numa.consolidate = false

Please note that the soft affinity node mask applies and that the vCPUs are free to allocate memory from both nodes if required. If the VM is running a single threaded application, you still might end up with a lot of remote memory access, as the physical NUMA node hosting the vCPU is unable to provide the memory demand by itself.

A vNUMA topology will not be exposed if the vCPU count is below nine vCPUs. In the previous used scenario, the VM receives two PPDs but only one VPD. This results in a uniform memory address space inside the VM. The guest OS will detect a single NUMA node.

```
[root@esxi03:~] vmdumper -l | cut -d \/ -f 2-5 | while read path; do egrep -oi "DICT.*(displayname.*|nu
ma:.*|numaHost:.*" "/$path/vmware.log"; echo -e; done
DICT                    numvcpus = "8"
DICT                     memSize = "98304"
DICT                 displayName = "SQL01"
DICT       numa.autosize.cookie = "80001"
DICT        numa.vcpu.preferHT = "FALSE"
DICT numa.autosize.vcpu.maxPerVirtualNode = "8"
DICT            numa.consolidate = "FALSE"
numaHost: NUMA config: consolidation= 0 preferHT= 0
numaHost: 8 VCPUs 1 VPDs 2 PPDs
numaHost: VCPU 0 VPD 0 PPD 0
numaHost: VCPU 1 VPD 0 PPD 0
numaHost: VCPU 2 VPD 0 PPD 0
numaHost: VCPU 3 VPD 0 PPD 0
numaHost: VCPU 4 VPD 0 PPD 1
numaHost: VCPU 5 VPD 0 PPD 1
numaHost: VCPU 6 VPD 0 PPD 1
numaHost: VCPU 7 VPD 0 PPD 1

[root@esxi03:~] sched-stats -t numa-cnode
  groupName         groupID    clientID    nodeID    time    timePct      memory    memoryPct
  vm.122622          211837          0         0      372         96    13080656           96
  vm.122622          211837          0         1       12          3      526336            3
  vm.122622          211837          1         0       12          3      182272            1
  vm.122622          211837          1         1      372         96    15388656           98
[root@esxi03:~]
```

Figure 57: Multiple PPDs with numa.consolidate = false

Size Your VM Correctly

For most workloads, the best performance occurs when memory is accessed locally. The VM vCPU and memory configuration should reflect the workload requirements to extract the performance from the system.

Typically, VMs should be sized to fit inside a single NUMA node. NUMA optimizations are a great help when VM configurations span multiple NUMA nodes. If it can be avoided, aim for a single CPU package VM design. However, if a wide VM configuration cannot be avoided, we recommend researching the CPU consumption of the application. Often HTs provide enough performance to have VMs fit into a single CPU package while benefitting from 100% memory locality. This is achieved by using the preferHT setting. If preferHT is used, we recommend aligning the cores per socket to the physical CPU package layout. This leverages the OS and application LLC optimizations the most.

05

NUMA SCHEDULER

The VMkernel contains a two-level CPU scheduler. It uses a fine-grained CPU scheduler that is responsible for scheduling worlds on physical CPUs using a hierarchical fair-share algorithm that is based on stride scheduling. In conjunction, it uses a longer-term NUMA scheduler that is focused on improving CPU load-balance and memory locality by migrating workloads between NUMA nodes.

Chapter 6 expands on the workings of the fine-grained CPU scheduler. This chapter focuses on the initial placement and load-balancing operations of the NUMA scheduler.

For more information on stride scheduling: Carl Waldspurger published the research paper: *Stride Scheduling: Deterministic Proportional-Share Resource Management*. It's published in 1995, but still an excellent read.

NUMA Scheduling Goals

The goal of NUMA scheduler is to maximize local memory consumption by placing compute and memory on the same node if possible. At the same time the NUMA scheduler balances CPU demand of other active VMs and guarantees fairness. To achieve these goals, NUMA scheduling can be classified into initial placement and workload migration.

Initial placement attempts to maintain balance and improves the resource utilization of the host system by placing the workload on the most optimal (least loaded) NUMA node. Workload migration, commonly referred to as load balancing, can be classified into vCPU migration and memory migration. The NUMA load balancer continually monitors the demand of the VMs and the current resource utilization of the NUMA nodes. By distributing vCPUs and/or memory across nodes, it optimizes memory locality while improving overall resource utilization.

It is key to understand that load-balancing algorithms, focused on satisfying resource entitlement, might not achieve VM placement symmetry. It's a general misconception that a so-called peanut butter spread distribution of VMs across NUMA nodes provides the best performance. Load balancing algorithms apply a cost-benefit and risk calculation. This is used to determine if it makes sense, on both short-term and long-term, to migrate resource consumers or to rebalance scheduling domains. Sometimes the cost of migration and the state of the destination NUMA node (CPU cache and memory environment) outweigh a short-term performance regression.

NUMA Scheduler Initial Placement

When a VM powers on, the NUMA scheduler applies the initial placement algorithm. This new VM (world) has not generated any workload yet. Therefore, the NUMA scheduler cannot derive any information from this world, other than the configuration details itself. Not being able to analyze historical workload patterns poses a significant problem.

One of the toughest challenges in computer science is the prediction of future workload demands. It is extremely difficult when dealing with a highly dynamic environment such as a virtualized datacenter and the one-to-many relationships between VMs. These VMs can run on the same host or run on separate hosts within the vSphere cluster. If they run on the same host then load correlation and load synchronicity are multi layered workload patterns that impact the resource consumption across the NUMA nodes.

However, with the help of some advanced workload algorithms, the NUMA scheduler can determine long-term trends of the overall load patterns on the NUMA nodes. And as a result select the most appropriate NUMA node. The goal of the initial placement algorithm is to provide the best fit for resource availability while attempting to reduce future costs of workload migrations due to host load imbalance or VM resource contention.

Determining Fit

The fundamental step in the initial placement process is to determine whether the VM fits the physical architecture. The first criterion is to have the NUMA scheduler to understand whether the VM vCPUs configuration exceed the core count of a single NUMA node[*]. The bias of initial placement is towards avoiding CPU over commitment. In addition, it determines whether the preferred NUMA node has enough available free memory. To do so, it inspects the two constructs of NUMA home nodes and the NUMA client.

- The **NUMA home node** represents the resource-scheduling domain for CPU and memory resources.
- A **NUMA client** is the collection of the vCPU and memory configuration of a VM.

If a VM is powered-on on a NUMA system, a virtual NUMA topology is created for the VM. Whether this virtual NUMA topology is exposed to the VM or not, depends on if two conditions are met:

- The VM contains nine or more vCPUs.
- The vCPU count exceeds the core count of the physical NUMA node[*].

[*] When using the advanced setting numa.vcpu.preferHT=TRUE, logical processors (HT) are counted instead of cores to determine scheduling options.

As described in chapter 4, a virtual NUMA topology consists of two elements, the *Virtual Proximity Domains* (VPD) and the *Physical Proximity Domains* (PPD). The VPD is the construct that is exposed to the VM. The PPD is the construct used by NUMA for initial placement and load balancing.

```
[root@esxi03:~] vmdumper -l | cut -d \/ -f 2-5 | while read path; do egrep -oi "
DICT.*(displayname.*|numa.*|cores.*|vcpu.*|memsize.*|affinity.*)= ,*|numa:.*|num
aHost:.*" "/$path/vmware.log"; echo -e; done
DICT                  numvcpus = "4"
DICT                   memSize = "32768"
DICT               displayName = "SQL00"
DICT numa.autosize.vcpu.maxPerVirtualNode = "4"
DICT      numa.autosize.cookie = "40001"
numaHost: NUMA config: consolidation= 1 preferHT= 0
numaHost: 4 VCPUs 1 VPDs 1 PPDs
numaHost: VCPU 0 VPD 0 PPD 0
numaHost: VCPU 1 VPD 0 PPD 0
numaHost: VCPU 2 VPD 0 PPD 0
numaHost: VCPU 3 VPD 0 PPD 0

[root@esxi03:~]
```

Figure 58: Virtual NUMA Topology of Four vCPU VM

Initial placement attempts to place the vCPU and memory on the same physical NUMA node. This becomes the home node of the PPD. There are some differences in affinity behavior between CPU placement and memory placement.

Affinity and Node Masks

The vCPUs within a PPD are only scheduled on the home node. If the vCPU count exceeds the core count of the physical CPU package (Wide-VM), then multiple PPDs are created. The PPD acts like an affinity of a group of vCPUs to all the CPUs of a CPU package.

> **A proximity group ensures that a particular group of vCPUs consumes the available resources of a particular CPU package. It is not a construct that is scheduled as an atomic unit. It does not determine whether a specific vCPU gets scheduled on a physical resource.**

Memory is preferentially allocated from the home node. The NUMA scheduler assigns a soft affinity rule to the NUMA home node. It creates a node mask that allows the memory scheduler to allocate memory from that particular physical NUMA node.

In some scenarios, the home node may not have enough memory. In that situation, memory is allocated from a remote node. In essence, local memory is not guaranteed, but the NUMA scheduler maximizes locality.

In the scenario of wide-VMs, the NUMA scheduler applies a node mask to the VM. This node masks lists the NUMA nodes that are used to schedule the VMs PPDs.

For example, in a four NUMA node system the PPDs run on nodes 2 and 3 but not on 0 and 1. If a vCPU that runs on NUMA node 2 and access memory, the memory could be on NUMA node 2 or 3, (2 more likely due to memory locality), but not on 0 and 1 as the node mask does not list these NUMA nodes.

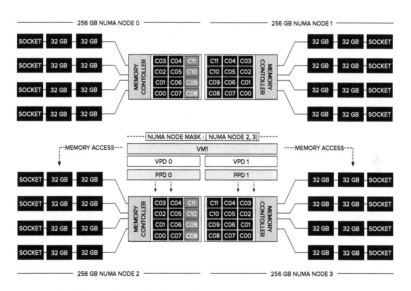

Figure 59: Wide-VM NUMA Node Mask

Keep in mind that the affinity and node mask are constructed during initial placement, but are primarily used for resource allocation and load-balancing decisions. The node mask provides guidance for the memory scheduler to apply a soft affinity rule for memory allocation. If memory contention occurs in both node 2 and 3 and the VM is entitled to more memory, it is possible that the memory scheduler allocates remote memory beyond the affinity mask. Although remote memory is slower than local memory, it still outperforms any form of memory consolidation operations such as ballooning, compressing or swapping.

VM Placement

Once fit is determined it is time to place the PPD(s) on the NUMA nodes. The NUMA scheduler starts off with a round-robin placement scheme. After placing a VM, the scheduler increments the preferred selection of the next NUMA node. In order words, VM1 was placed on NUMA node 2 and 3, for next VM placement, use NUMA node 0. However, maintaining this simple round-robin placement algorithm throughout the uptime of the host is too naive for such a complex system. The number of active VMs is highly dynamic as well as the workload pattern of the VMs themselves. Therefore, the additional metrics resource usage and internode latency are used to determine placement.

Internode Latency

During boot-time ESXi determines the latencies between NUMA nodes (internode latency). Mapping the internode latency is important for large NUMA systems and wide VMs. When placing a wide VM on a large NUMA node system, internode latency helps the NUMA scheduler to determine which two NUMA nodes are close to each other. This helps to place the multiple PPDs near each other and provide low-latency memory access. If memory is 'spilled' over from the NUMA home node to a remote NUMA node (due to memory shortage on the home node) internode latency is used to determine the closest node that has available memory to service these memory requests.

Resource Usage

In addition to internode latencies, the NUMA scheduler determines the entitlement of the VMs running on the NUMA nodes and the normalized load average. To determine the normalized load average of a NUMA system, it uses an *Exponentially Weighted Moving Average* (EWMA) of the NUMA nodes. As described before, prediction of future load balance is quite difficult. The idea behind using statistics such as EWMA is that it flattens out short-term fluctuations and determines long-term trends.

This method helps to address the risk of workload volatility. To some extent it uses historical data as a prologue for the future usage of the home node. Explaining EWMA in-depth is beyond the scope of this book, but to describe it in a simplified way, the EWMA provides a mechanism to determine load averages over time. The strength of EWMA is that it applies a certain weight to the recentness of the data; usage from five seconds ago is more relevant than from an hour ago.

EWMA is used as input to calculate a normalized load average of the NUMA node. The NUMA scheduler compares the normalized load average values of the NUMA nodes to determine which node is the least loaded and thus the preferred NUMA node to select. The command sched-stats -t numa-pnode provides an overview of the normalized load average values of the NUMA nodes (loadAvgPct).

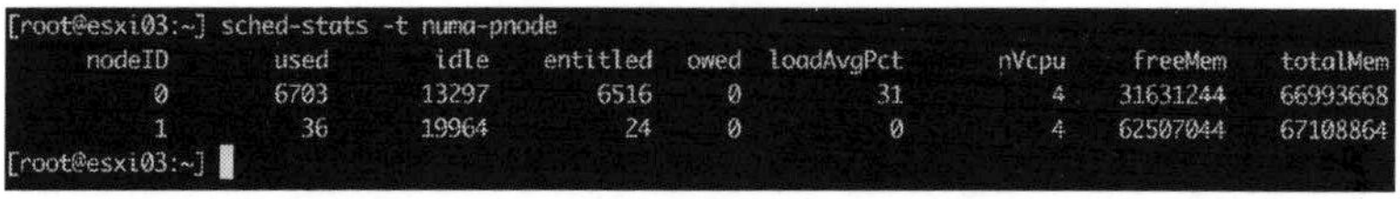

```
[root@esxi03:~] sched-stats -t numa-pnode
    nodeID        used       idle    entitled    owed    loadAvgPct       nVcpu       freeMem      totalMem
         0        6703      13297        6516       0            31           4      31631244      66993668
         1          36      19964          24       0             0           4      62507044      67108864
[root@esxi03:~]
```

Figure 60: Normalized Load Average Value (loadAvgPct)

To provide some background of the command, sched-stats reads the VSI nodes of the ESXi host. If you are a frequent reader of William Lam's excellent blog VirtuallyGhetto.com, you might recognize VSI nodes and the *VMkernel Sys Info Shell* (vsish) interpret tool. That means that the information provided by sched-stats can also be found in the VSI nodes itself.

```
[root@esxi03:~] vsish -e cat /sched/numaStats/numaNodes/0
NUMA node statistics {
   used:7286 msec
   idle:12713 msec
   entitled:6941 msec
   owed:0 msec
   normalized load average:31 pct
   number of vcpus:4
   free memory:32233300 KB
   total memory:66993668 KB
}
[root@esxi03:~] vsish -e cat /sched/numaStats/numaNodes/1
NUMA node statistics {
   used:26 msec
   idle:19974 msec
   entitled:0 msec
   owed:0 msec
   normalized load average:0 pct
   number of vcpus:0
   free memory:65782400 KB
   total memory:67108864 KB
}
[root@esxi03:~] █
```

Figure 61: VSISH NUMA Nodes

We believe in disclosing information and educating the people who work with the systems, rather than obfuscation. But please be careful when using vsish. It allows you to set parameters and as always, you should not make any changes that you are unfamiliar with. Only use this tool to read (cat and get) information or if VMware Support requests so.

Testing Initial Placement

To verify initial placement, a test scenario is created including four VMs. Three VMs running an SQL workload and one VM running a web front-end application on the dual 10-Core Xeon test bed.

NAME	# OF VCPU	MEMORY SIZE
SQL00	4	32 GB
SQL01	4	48 GB
SQL02	4	32 GB
NGN	4	24 GB

Table 13: Test VM Configuration

Initial Placement First VM

SQL00 is running on NUMA node 0 and is generating a workload of roughly 30%. sched-stats -t numa-pnode confirms this:

```
[root@esxi03:~] sched-stats -t numa-pnode
   nodeID      used      idle   entitled  owed  loadAvgPct nVcpu      freeMem     totalMem
        0      6301     13699       6257     0          26     4     54941588     66993668
        1        12     19988          0     0           0     0     65799808     67108864
[root@esxi03:~]
```

Figure 62: SQL00 on NUMA Node 0

Initial Placement Second VM

SQL01 is powered-on and due to the loadAvgPct difference of 26%, the NUMA scheduler selects NUMA node 1 as the home node for SQL01.

```
[root@esxi03:~] sched-stats -t numa-pnode
   nodeID      used      idle   entitled  owed  loadAvgPct nVcpu      freeMem     totalMem
        0      6060     13940       6024     0          30     4     53543624     66993668
        1        37     19963         14     0           2     4     59593224     67108864
[root@esxi03:~]
```

Figure 63: Initial Placement of SQL01 on NUMA Node 1

Unfortunately, sched-stats -t numa-pnode provides a global overview of the physical NUMA nodes. In this scenario two VMs run on the two NUMA nodes, therefore it is easy to determine which VM is running on which node. In a system that runs multiple VMs, the command sched-stats -t numa-clients provides more info in the context of VMs.

```
[root@esxi03:~] sched-stats -t numa-clients
 groupName      groupID  clientID  homeNode nWorlds  vmmWorlds    localMem  remoteMem  currLocal%  cummLocal%
vm.68647         14654        0         0       4            4    12132516         0        100         100
vm.68995         15877        0         1       4            4     6068624         0        100         100
[root@esxi03:~]
```

Figure 64: NUMA-Clients Context

This tool displays the VMX Cartel ID and Group ID. The `groupName` listed in the first column is the VMX Cartel ID. Cartel IDs can be provided by running the command `esxcli vm process list`. Esxtop provides you the group id.

Initial Placement Third VM

Both SQL VMs are running workload. The workload (14%) on NUMA node 1 is less than on NUMA node 0 (31%).

```
[root@esxi03:~] sched-stats -t numa-pnode
      nodeID       used       idle   entitled owed  loadAvgPct nVcpu      freeMem     totalMem
           0       6655      13345       6624    0          31     4     51140004     66993668
           1       5206      14794       5155    0          14     4     55154720     67108864
[root@esxi03:~]
```

Figure 65: LoadAvgPct Difference Between NUMA Nodes

If NUMA scheduler would apply a simple round-robin algorithm, then the next VM would be placed on NUMA node 0. However, due to the normalized load average difference, SQL02 is placed on NUMA node 1.

```
[root@esxi03:~] sched-stats -t numa-pnode
      nodeID       used       idle   entitled owed  loadAvgPct nVcpu      freeMem     totalMem
           0       6571      13449       6522    0          31     4     50606988     66993668
           1       5179      14841       4989    0          22     8     49478008     67108864
[root@esxi03:~]
```

Figure 66: Initial Placement SQL02

The command `sched-stats -t numa-clients` shows that two VMs with each four vCPUs have NUMA node 1 assigned as home node.

```
[root@esxi03:~] sched-stats -t numa-clients
  groupName    homeNode nWorlds   vmmWorlds    localMem   remoteMem  currLocal%  cummLocal%
  vm.68647            0       4           4    14602468           0         100         100
  vm.68995            1       4           4    11778496           0         100         100
  vm.69356            1       4           4     4472636           0         100         100
[root@esxi03:~]
```

Figure 67: VM to NUMA Node Context

Esxtop provides a little bit more context from a VM name perspective.

```
 3:38:05pm up 24 min, 724 worlds, 3 VMs, 12 vCPUs; MEM overcommit avg: 0.00, 0.00, 0.00
PMEM   /MB: 130961   total: 2354      vmk,31027 other, 97579 free
VMKMEM/MB: 130575 managed: 1920 minfree, 7601 rsvd, 122974 ursvd, high state
NUMA   /MB: 65423 (49255), 65536 (47939)
PSHARE/MB:      28  shared,      22  common:      6 saving
SWAP   /MB:      0  curr,       0 rclmtgt:               0.00 r/s,   0.00 w/s
ZIP    /MB:      0  zipped,     0  saved
MEMCTL/MB:      0  curr,       0  target,   74546 max
View VM only
     GID NAME                            NHN NMIG    NRMEM      NLMEM N%L GST_ND0
   15877 SQL01                             1    0     0.00 11704.44 100      0.00
   17180 SQL02                             1    0     0.00  4369.81 100      0.00
   14654 SQL00                             0    0     0.00 14350.22 100 14358.22
```

Figure 68: Esxtop Output

Initial Placement Fourth VM

The placement of the fourth VM is interesting. Two VMs consume resources from NUMA node 1 and one VM is occupying NUMA node 0. From a vCPU perspective, the distribution is 33% to 66%. Four vCPUs are placed on NUMA node 0; eight vCPUs are on NUMA node 1.

As mentioned before, the NUMA scheduler is not in the business of providing peanut butter spreads. It is using historical data to address the risk of workload volatility. The human approach is to address a future look at fluctuation by using what's called implied volatility (expectation of what might happen). I.e. better spread out workload because the VMs might become active all at once. However, this is extremely hard to predict, although historical data is present.

To verify this theory, another VM is introduced on the system. The VM is powered-on and initial placement is placing it on NUMA home 1, similar to the previous VMs, due to the higher normalized load average of NUMA home 0.

```
[root@esxi03:~] sched-stats -t numa-pnode
    nodeID      used      idle  entitled owed loadAvgPct nVcpu    freeMem   totalMem
         0      6633     13366      6446    0         31     4   49077632   66993668
         1      8988     11011      8949    0         25    12   43117712   67108864
[root@esxi03:~]
```

Figure 69: Initial Placement 4th VM

In conclusion, the NUMA initial placement continues to load-balance VMs based on the normalized load average and not on vCPU count. In addition to using the tool esxtop, we recommend to use the command sched-stats -t numa-pnode and sched-stats -t numa-clients to get a more accurate view of the state of the NUMA nodes.

Wide-VM Placement

If a Wide-VM is powered-on, NUMA initial placement is required to distribute the PPDs across the NUMA nodes. If the VM is powered-on on a multi-NUMA node system, initial placement considers internode latency to determine NUMA node proximity. It attempts to place the multiple PPDs of the VM on the NUMA nodes that have the lowest internode latency between each other and have the lowest normalized load average.

SQL00 (four vCPU) is running on NUMA node 0 and is generating a load of roughly 30%. SQL01 and SQL02 are running on NUMA node 1 and generate a combined load of 23%.

```
[root@esxi03:~] sched-stats -t numa-pnode
    nodeID       used       idle    entitled loadAvgPct  nVcpu     freeMem    totalMem
         0       6344      13656        6307         31      4    39985388    66993668
         1       5102      14899        5063         23     12    18379724    67108864
[root@esxi03:~]
```

Figure 70: Average Load on NUMA Nodes 0 and 1

The vCPU configuration of SQL03 is twelve vCPUs and is considered to be a wide VM (10 core physical CPU). Two PPDs are created, containing six vCPUs (maxVcpusPerVPD=6) each.

```
DICT                    numvcpus = "12"
DICT                    memSize = "30720"
DICT           sched.cpu.affinity = "all"
DICT           sched.mem.affinity = "all"
DICT                  displayName = "SQL03"
numaHost: NUMA config: consolidation= 1 preferHT= 0
numa: coresPerSocket= 1 maxVcpusPerVPD= 6
numaHost: 12 VCPUs 2 VPDs 2 PPDs
numaHost: VCPU 0 VPD 0 PPD 0
numaHost: VCPU 1 VPD 0 PPD 0
numaHost: VCPU 2 VPD 0 PPD 0
numaHost: VCPU 3 VPD 0 PPD 0
numaHost: VCPU 4 VPD 0 PPD 0
numaHost: VCPU 5 VPD 0 PPD 0
numaHost: VCPU 6 VPD 1 PPD 1
numaHost: VCPU 7 VPD 1 PPD 1
numaHost: VCPU 8 VPD 1 PPD 1
numaHost: VCPU 9 VPD 1 PPD 1
numaHost: VCPU 10 VPD 1 PPD 1
numaHost: VCPU 11 VPD 1 PPD 1
```

Figure 71: PPD Configuration Wide VM SQL01

Initial placement is forced to separate the PPDs of the VM and therefore this results in the following scenario:

```
[root@esxi03:~] sched-stats -t numa-pnode
    nodeID        used        idle    entitled  owed  loadAvgPct nVcpu       freeMem      totalMem
         0        9085       10896        9015     0          32    10      33570848      66993668
         1        6644       13336        6574     0          24    18      12537396      67108864
[root@esxi03:~] ▊
```

Figure 72: SQL03 PPDs Distributed Across NUMA Nodes

Just to demonstrate the importance of normalized load average on initial placement, a fifth VM (SQL04) is powered on and is configured with two vCPUs. Due to the difference in normalized load, initial placement assigns NUMA node 1 as the home node of SQL04 and increases the vCPU count of NUMA node 1 to 20.

```
[root@esxi03:~] sched-stats -t numa-pnode
    nodeID        used        idle    entitled  owed  loadAvgPct nVcpu       freeMem      totalMem
         0        6733       13268        6702     0          31    10      33053272      66993668
         1        5198       14803        5165     0          23    20      10786064      67108864
[root@esxi03:~] ▊
```

Figure 73: vCPU Distribution Across NUMA Nodes After SQL04 Power-On

119

PPD Internals

The placement of vCPUs on a PPD is pretty much linear; the first six (vCPU 0 to vCPU 5) are placed on pCPUs 0-19 (NUMA node 0). The remaining six vCPUs are placed on pCPUs 20-39 (NUMA node 1). To verify the pCPU count per NUMA node, you can run the command vsish - e ls /hardware/numa/0/pcpus, where 0 is the identification of the NUMA node.

Use esxtop CPU view to identify the pCPUs the VM is currently consuming. Expand the view of the VMs (press e). Use f to toggle the field order and select i to enable the summary stats view.

ID	GID	NAME	NWLD	%LAT_C	%LAT_M	%DMD	EMIN	TIMER/s	AFFINITY_BIT_MASK	CPU	HTSHARING	HTQ
14518	14518	SQL00	15	0.1	0.0	331	8044	64.00	0-39	-	-	-
15645	15645	SQL01	15	0.3	0.0	0	8044	97.00	0-39	-	-	-
16820	16820	SQL02	15	0.1	0.0	0	8044	96.00	0-39	-	-	-
17891	17891	NGN	13	0.3	0.0	0	8584	64.00	0-39	-	-	-
73692	30879	vmx	1	0.0	0.0	0	608	-	0-39	29		
73694	30879	NetWorld-VM-736	1	0.0	0.0	0	1216	-	0-39	9		
73695	30879	NUMASchedRemapE	1	0.0	0.0	0	608	-	0-39	38		
73696	30879	vmast.73693	1	0.0	0.0	0	61	-	0-39	28		
73708	30879	vmx-vthread-16	1	0.0	0.0	0	608	-	0-39	0		
73709	30879	vmx-vthread-17:	1	0.0	0.0	0	608	-	0-39	23		
73710	30879	vmx-mks:SQL03	1	0.0	0.0	0	608	-	0-39	15		
73711	30879	vmx-svga:SQL03	1	0.0	0.0	0	608	-	0-39	0		
73712	30879	vmx-vcpu-0:SQL0	1	0.1	0.0	0	7297	-	0-39	1		
73715	30879	vmx-vcpu-1:SQL0	1	0.0	0.0	0	7297	-	0-39	1		
73716	30879	vmx-vcpu-2:SQL0	1	0.0	0.0	0	7297	-	0-39	17		
73717	30879	vmx-vcpu-3:SQL0	1	0.1	0.0	0	7297	-	0-39	7		
73718	30879	vmx-vcpu-4:SQL0	1	0.0	0.0	0	7297	-	0-39	11		
73719	30879	vmx-vcpu-5:SQL0	1	0.0	0.0	0	7297	-	0-39	3		
73720	30879	vmx-vcpu-6:SQL0	1	0.0	0.0	0	7297	-	0-39	25		
73721	30879	vmx-vcpu-7:SQL0	1	0.1	0.0	0	7297	-	0-39	37		
73722	30879	vmx-vcpu-8:SQL0	1	0.1	0.0	0	7297	-	0-39	21		
73723	30879	vmx-vcpu-9:SQL0	1	0.1	0.0	0	7297	-	0-39	30		
73724	30879	vmx-vcpu-10:SQL	1	0.2	0.0	0	7297	-	0-39	36		
73725	30879	vmx-vcpu-11:SQL	1	0.1	0.0	0	7297	-	0-39	33		
73713	30879	LSI-73693:0	1	0.0	0.0	0	608	-	0-39	25		
73714	30879	PVSCSI-73693:1	1	0.0	0.0	0	608	-	0-39	14		
32102	32102	SQL04	11	0.4	0.0	0	2646	88.00	0-39	-	-	-

Figure 74: Esxtop CPU Summary Stats View

It is possible to swap PPDs between NUMA nodes, but that is the responsibility of the NUMA load balancer. Please note that it is possible to have multiple PPDs of the same VM on a NUMA node. This is the result of the Cores per Socket configuration (that does not align with the physical layout of the NUMA node) and the advanced setting of Numa.FollowCoresPerSocket, which is set to 1.

What happens if the setting `numa.vcpu.preferHT=TRUE` is applied to SQL03? All vCPUs are consolidated into a single PPD because the pCPU count of the NUMA nodes exceeds the vCPU count of the VM. Please remember to adjust the `numa.autosize.vcpu.maxPerVirtualNode` setting in the VM if it is already been powered-on once. This setting overrides the `numa.vcpu.preferHT=TRUE` setting.

```
[root@esxi03:~] sched-stats -t numa-pnode
     nodeID      used      idle   entitled loadAvgPct nVcpu      freeMem   totalMem
          0        66     19933         44          2     4     37724456   66993668
          1       134     19865         99          0    14     15698148   67108864
[root@esxi03:~] sched-stats -t numa-pnode
     nodeID      used      idle   entitled loadAvgPct nVcpu      freeMem   totalMem
          0      2446     17554         17          2    16     37688896   66993668
          1       247     19753         86          0    14     15669488   67108864
[root@esxi03:~] 
```

Figure 75: PreferHT Wide VM Placement

As expected, the VM is placed in its entirety on NUMA node 0. However, another interesting thing occurs. The other VMs do not generate any workload. Therefore, the normalized average load percentage is close to zero. Although NUMA node 0 has a non-zero load average percentage, initial placement assigned NUMA node 0 as home node of SQL03.

Initial Placement Load Threshold

This behavior is due to the load difference between the NUMA nodes. If the load difference between NUMA nodes is fewer than 5%, the default round-robin initial placement scheme is applied and since the last placement was SQL04 on NUMA node 1, SQL03 is going to be placed on NUMA node 0.

Initial Placement Focus

In essence, NUMA scheduler initial placement applies a round-robin algorithm with focus on normalized load averages and internode latency. As a result, the VMs, or more specifically, the vCPUs distribution does not have to be uniform across NUMA nodes.

NUMA Scheduler Load Balancing

Due to the complexity and the increasing scale of modern workloads, it is challenging to achieve a perfect fit when placing VMs.

Workloads have lifecycles, usually aligned with the state of the project it supports. During the initial phase of the project, a lot of testing occurs, which introduces a lot of load. During the early stages of production, the application needs to acquire new users and use cases. Workload and utilization will ramp-up through time, until it is nearing the end of its lifecycle and being replaced by a newer application. Whether the application fits inside the infrastructure, is mostly dependent on an accurate assessment of potential workload, done by the IT-team.

Unfortunately, it is difficult to assess the interaction of the workload with the rest of the environment and the underlying machine architecture of the virtual infrastructure. Studying the interaction between workloads and microarchitecture is interesting but difficult to do. Virtual infrastructures are a collection of hosts, networks and storage infrastructures and they all have an important role in providing the best possible performance to the VMs. Zooming in, we find ourselves studying the interaction of micro architectural components. We look at elements such as NUMA nodes and we want to determine how on-chip caches and internode latencies impact workloads. How does it operate in isolation and how does it interoperate with local and external workloads?

If workloads, albeit running in different VMs, run on the same host, then load correlation and load synchronicity impact the resource consumption across the NUMA nodes.

Load Correlation defines the relationship between workloads running on different machines. This can be triggered by an event that initiates multiple processes, for example, a search query on the front-end webservers. This results in utilization of both the front-end and back-end applications.

Load Synchronicity is often caused by load correlation but can also exist due to collective user activity. It is common to see spikes in workload at specific hours, think about log-on activity in the morning. For every action, there is an equal and opposite reaction. Quite often, load correlation and load synchronicity will introduce periods of collective non or low utilization (break-time, shift changes), which reduce the displayed CPU utilization.

Both load correlation and load synchronicity are workload patterns that cannot be predicted by initial placement and as a result are the concern of the NUMA load balancer.

NUMA Scheduler Objectives

The objectives of the NUMA scheduler are to avoid CPU contention on its scheduling domains (the NUMA nodes) while maintaining memory locality for the VMs. To achieve both objects is a difficult task, especially when dealing with fluctuating workloads. To give a classic example, if NUMA node imbalance is determined, the NUMA scheduler migrates a VM to the NUMA node where CPU contention is lower. While this behavior is perfect to address the long-term CPU imbalance, It is difficult to solve the short-term CPU imbalance, as memory has to follow to maintain memory locality. The scheduler has to distribute the VMs in a manner where the workload characteristics demands can be satisfied while dealing with fairness, without burdening the microarchitecture.

Over more than ten years of the existence of the ESXi NUMA scheduler (ESX2 introduced the NUMA scheduler) it helped the VMware CPU engineers to understand how workloads behave and to fine-tune the schedulers. The latest generation of the NUMA scheduler takes many elements of the microarchitecture into account when determining the optimal load balance. As a result, the NUMA scheduler sometimes distributes VMs in a manner that occasionally may defy common knowledge.

An integral part of performance in today's microarchitecture is the shared Last Level Cache. It has become the central connection between the cores on the CPU package. VMs spanning multiple NUMA nodes are common today, thus cache coherency operations between NUMA nodes have greater impact. This leads to scheduling behavior that takes the aspects of cache sharing and communication into account.

At times, multiple VMs are scheduled on the same NUMA node, just to benefit from having the same data in the cache. Although this might increase CPU ready time due to CPU contention, it could outperform the same set of VMs if they are distributed across NUMA nodes.

NUMA scheduling decisions are difficult to explain with just a quick glance at some performance metrics in esxtop. The following paragraphs provide a more in-depth view at the behavior of the NUMA scheduler.

Determining CPU Imbalance

To deal with the fluctuation of load the NUMA scheduler evaluates the state of the NUMA nodes every two seconds. This timeframe is called the NUMA balancing epoch. The NUMA scheduler examines the load of the NUMA nodes and determines whether it should rebalance. To do so, the NUMA scheduler keeps track of fairness. It calculates a metric called owed and in essence, this is the difference between the VM entitlement of CPU resources and the actual usage of the CPU resources. A higher owed metric means that the VM is entitled to more CPU time.

In addition, the NUMA scheduler tracks the owed metric at the NUMA node level. To determine the imbalance, it compares the sum of VM owed of both NUMA nodes to each other. By default, at least a 10% load imbalance needs to exist between nodes in order for the NUMA scheduler to consider a load balancing operation.

And last, but certainly not least, the NUMA scheduler keeps track of the overall CPU load within the NUMA node. If the CPU load is over 90%, the NUMA scheduler initiates a load balance operation.

If a load balance operation is necessary, the NUMA scheduler may make one load balance decision during this particular load-balance epoch. These decisions can be categorized in short-term migrations, long-term migrations or locality migrations.

Short-Term Migration

The first migration operation that the NUMA scheduler will attempt is a one-way move.

One-Way Move

The NUMA scheduler analyzes the owed metric of the NUMA nodes and determines which VM migration can reduce the load-imbalance. It will migrate a PPD with all its vCPUs from its NUMA home node to the other, less contended, NUMA node.

vCPUs migrate and immediately VM memory will follow. What once was remote memory is now local memory and memory residing in the previous NUMA home node is transferred over time. Memory cannot be migrated instantly. Dynamically throttled memory migration is done to avoid saturating the CPU-interconnect. More about page migration can be found in a later paragraph.

Unfortunately, this simple algorithm can become victim of thrashing. Thrashing is the act of moving the same VM between nodes in consecutive epochs. In other words, trashing is the act of the NUMA scheduler playing ping-pong with a VM between NUMA nodes. To avoid thrashing, the NUMA scheduler applies a long-term fairness threshold.

Swap

If multiple epochs cannot create a one-way move that resolved the load imbalance sufficiently, the NUMA scheduler can resort to swapping two NUMA clients (PPDs). The swap combination that reduces the load imbalance the most will be selected and executed.

Long-Term Fairness Migration

One of the challenges the NUMA scheduler faces, is the choice between performance and NUMA node load balance. In some situations, it can occur that the number of VMs and their entitlement pose a problem for the NUMA scheduler to reach a balanced state without trashing the bandwidth between the NUMA nodes. In essence, there is no perfect placement to provide performance and fairness.

One of the most popular examples to explain this challenge is the situation of three VMs and two NUMA nodes. All three VMs run similar workload that exceeds the physical capabilities of the physical CPU. VM1 and VM2 are located on NUMA node 0, VM3 is located on NUMA node 1. VM1 and VM2 are not receiving the resources they are entitled to and therefore NUMA node 0 has a higher owed metric than NUMA node 1. Migrating one VM to another node would reduce the owed metric of NUMA node 0, but this will recreate the problem at NUMA node 1. This usually leads to another migration, ergo it is thrashing the interconnect bandwidth.

However, the NUMA scheduler can hold out on avoiding trashing for so long, it cannot ignore the fairness principle forever. Therefore, the option Long Term Fairness Interval exists. What it does is that the scheduler keeps track of the short-term fairness for five epochs. If the long-term owed is high, the VM will be migrated to another NUMA node.

```
[root@esxi03:~] vsish -e get /config/Numa/intOpts/LTermFairnessInterval
Vmkernel Config Option {
   Default value:5
   Min value:0
   Max value:1000
   Current value:5
   hidden config option:0
   Description:duration of long term fairness interval in terms of NUMA rebalanc
e period, 0 indicates that long term fairness is disabled
}
[root@esxi03:~]
```

Figure 76: Long Term Fairness Interval

If you set the `Long Term Fairness Interval` to 0, thrashing will be avoided every epoch and you can end up with VMs that may not receive their entitlement for a long time. On the flipside, there is a tradeoff between long-term fairness and memory locality. Migration leads to remote memory access. When ping-ponging VMs across nodes, interconnect bandwidth is consumed due to continuous remote memory access. By disabling long-term fairness, memory locality should be more stable. We recommend monitoring NUMA migrations by using the command `sched-stats -t numa-migration`.

```
[root@esxi03:~] sched-stats -t numa-migration
groupName            groupID    clientID  balanceMig loadMig localityMig longTermMig  monitorMig pageMigRate
vm.68620             14574      0         70       0     0          0          0        1294
vm.68833             15717      0         64       0     2          0          0          80
vm.69023             16788      0         58       0     4          0          0        1093
[root@esxi03:~]
```

Figure 77: Sched-stats -t numa-migration Output

If particular VMs experience a higher number of long-term migrations, it might be a good idea either to manually move them to another ESXi host in the vSphere cluster or review their resource allocation units (reservation, shares & limit). Changing the `LTermFairnessInterval` setting to 0 should be your last resort.

Locality Migrations

When CPU load balancing is not necessary, the NUMA scheduler looks to see if it can improve locality by applying locality migrations.

Memory Locality Migration

Sometimes memory page migration for a particular VM does not make sense if a large amount of remote memory is assigned to the VM. In these situations, the NUMA scheduler can apply a locality migration. By default, the NUMA scheduler only applies a node swap if the improvement of memory locality is more than 20%. After the swap completes, memory load balancing occurs to move the remaining data to the new NUMA home node.

Communication Locality Migration (Action-Affinity)

The communication locality migration is an interesting one and we believe this is the one type of migration that has some people pull their hairs out as it can be difficult to determine the cause of this situation.

Communication locality migration is better known as *action-affinity*. Action-affinity is designed to optimize sharing of the CPU cache. The VMs, which are subject to this locality migration, share data and share the same IO context or communicate heavily with each other. The problem is that this action-affinity may cause an imbalance on NUMA nodes by assigning multiple active VMs to the same NUMA node.

To provide a simple example that demonstrates action-affinity perfectly, two VMs run on a dual CPU system. Initial placement applies the default round-robin scheme and each VM is placed on a separate NUMA node.

```
[root@esxi03:~] sched-stats -t numa-pnode
    nodeID      used       idle   entitled  owed  loadAvgPct  nVcpu    freeMem    totalMem
         0        34      19966         17     0           0      4   61210204    66993668
         1       160      19840        868     0           2      4   62271088    67108864
[root@esxi03:~]
```

Figure 78: Round-Robin Placement

Sched-stats -t numa-clients output verifies that each VM is placed on a different NUMA node.

```
[root@esxi03:~] sched-stats -t numa-clients
  groupName          homeNode  nWorlds   vmmWorlds   localMem   remoteMem  currLocal%  cummLocal%
  vm.68599                  0        4           4    3948452           0         100         100
  vm.68823                  1        4           4    3537764           0         100         100
[root@esxi03:~]
```

Figure 79: Sched-stats -t numa-clients Output

Both systems communicate with each other (front-end and back-end) and the NUMA scheduler detects this communication and migrates the VM from NUMA node 1 to NUMA node 0.

```
[root@esxi03:~] sched-stats -t numa-pnode
     nodeID        used         idle    entitled owed  loadAvgPct nVcpu      freeMem     totalMem
          0        12985        7015       12921    0          36     8     53789900     66993668
          1            8       19991           0    0           0     0     59651588     67108864
[root@esxi03:~] ▊
```

Figure 80: VM Imbalance due to Action-Affinity

Sched-stats -t numa-clients output verifies that the current home node of VM.68823 is now NUMA node 0.

```
[root@esxi03:~] sched-stats -t numa-clients
   groupName        homeNode nWorlds   vmmWorlds    localMem    remoteMem  currLocal%  cummLocal%
   vm.68599                0       4           4     9404364            0         100         100
   vm.68823                0       4           4     3209256      5628804          36          53
[root@esxi03:~] ▊
```

Figure 81: HomeNode Output

At this point, the only two VMs running on the ESXi host are now placed on a single NUMA node. You would think that spreading the workload across the NUMA nodes should improve performance due to the availability of more resources. However, some VMs communicate heavily with each other and could benefit from a warmed-up cache. Having the data already at the cache layer avoids the costly latency of retrieving data from memory structures. However, other VMs could benefit from having more CPU cache resources available to them, to avoid LLC contention.

The challenge is to verify exactly whether the workload is benefitting from the action-affinity or not. Monitoring ready time is not enough, because sometimes accruing a little bit of ready time is still better than incurring cache coherency invalidations across LLCs or cache-misses. The best way, and this paradigm should be applied to all performance testing, is to test and measure real-time performance. If you run an SQL database, measure its throughput when action-affinity is occurring and when it is not. Or measure the time in which the query is completed. Eventually that is what counts, the user-experience, not just some trivial number showing up in a command-line monitoring tool.

To verify if your system is experiencing locality migrations, two commands can be helpful: sched-stats -t numa-global and sched-stats -t numa-migration.

The command `sched-stats -t numa-global` outputs the migration count of the entire system since boot-time.

```
[root@esxi03:~] sched-stats -t numa-global
NUMA Global Stats
------------------------------------
balanceMigration: 0
loadMigration: 0
localityMigration: 3
longTermFairnessMigration: 0
monitorMigration: 0
localMemory: 14297084
remoteMemory: 5036924
[root@esxi03:~]
```

Figure 82: Numa-global Stats Output Number of Locality Migrations

The command `sched-stats -t numa-migration` provides a more granular view, accounting the types of migrations per VM.

```
[root@esxi03:~] sched-stats -t numa-migration
  groupName       balanceMig loadMig localityMig longTermMig  monitorMig pageMigRate
  vm.68599              0         0         0           0           0          0
  vm.68823              0         0         3           0           0       4958
[root@esxi03:~]
```

Figure 83: NUMA Migrations Per VM View

If action-affinity is creating an imbalance so severely that CPU ready time is accrued, it can be switched off. Setting the ESXi host advanced setting `WeightActionAffinity` to 0 does this.

| Numa.LocalityWeightActionAffinity | 130 | Benefit of improving action affinity by 1. |

Figure 84: Host Advanced Setting

Memory Load Balancing

Although the NUMA scheduler maximizes locality, it often occurs that remote memory is allocated to satisfy memory requests from the VM. Once remote memory is allocated, the NUMA scheduler attempts to migrate remote memory to the local NUMA node whenever this is possible.

If local memory frees up, the NUMA scheduler migrates the remote memory. To be more precise, it selects a page on the original home node and it copies over the data to the new home node. It then remaps the virtual memory address to the new physical memory address without any impact on the guest OS. Memory operations are now applied on local memory pages and as a result this remapping eliminates further remote access of that data.

In the interest of overhead reduction, page migration is done in a cost-effective manner. The NUMA scheduler applies an algorithm that includes node latency difference and the degree of local versus remote memory pages.

The memory page migration rate depends on the degree of remote memory pages and the desired state of memory in relation to its distribution. There are many different configurations of remote memory when it comes to the desired state of memory. For example, the vCPUs of the VM run on both nodes, but memory is located on a single node, then memory balance will be executed.

The migration rate depends on the locality rate and is dynamic throughout the process. If most pages are located on the remote memory node, a higher migration rate is applied. The rate reduces if the majority of pages are local.

To demonstrate this behavior, a scenario was created where the VM was requiring more memory than the local NUMA node could provide. The NUMA scheduler allocated 188 MB of remote memory to the VM.

The command `sched-stats -t numa-global` displays the overall NUMA statistics of the system. In this scenario, only one VM is running on the system. Therefore, the system statistics are equal to the per-VM statistics.

```
[root@esxi03:~] sched-stats -t numa-global
NUMA Global Stats
-----------------------
balanceMigration: 382
loadMigration: 0
localityMigration: 0
longTermFairnessMigration: 0
monitorMigration: 0
localMemory: 74741976
remoteMemory: 4247320
[root@esxi03:~]
```

Figure 85: ESXi Host Global Statistics

The command `sched-stats -t numa-migration` provides a per-VM overview of NUMA migration. Every few seconds we ran the command to determine the current memory page migration rate and it is evident that the migration rate slowly reduces over time.

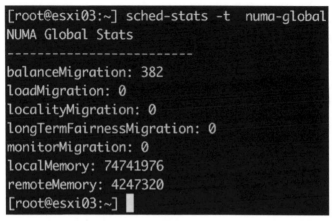

```
[root@esxi03:~] sched-stats -t numa-migration
groupName        groupID    clientID  balanceMig loadMig localityMig longTermMig  monitorMig pageMigRate
vm.68744         14958      0         0       0    2           0          0          117
[root@esxi03:~] sched-stats -t numa-migration
groupName        groupID    clientID  balanceMig loadMig localityMig longTermMig  monitorMig pageMigRate
vm.68744         14958      0         0       0    2           0          0          110
[root@esxi03:~] sched-stats -t numa-migration
groupName        groupID    clientID  balanceMig loadMig localityMig longTermMig  monitorMig pageMigRate
vm.68744         14958      0         0       0    2           0          0          110
[root@esxi03:~] sched-stats -t numa-migration
groupName        groupID    clientID  balanceMig loadMig localityMig longTermMig  monitorMig pageMigRate
vm.68744         14958      0         0       0    2           0          0          109
[root@esxi03:~] sched-stats -t numa-migration
groupName        groupID    clientID  balanceMig loadMig localityMig longTermMig  monitorMig pageMigRate
vm.68744         14958      0         0       0    2           0          0          108
[root@esxi03:~] sched-stats -t numa-migration
groupName        groupID    clientID  balanceMig loadMig localityMig longTermMig  monitorMig pageMigRate
vm.68744         14958      0         0       0    2           0          0          106
[root@esxi03:~] sched-stats -t numa-migration
groupName        groupID    clientID  balanceMig loadMig localityMig longTermMig  monitorMig pageMigRate
vm.68744         14958      0         0       0    2           0          0          101
[root@esxi03:~] sched-stats -t numa-migration
groupName        groupID    clientID  balanceMig loadMig localityMig longTermMig  monitorMig pageMigRate
vm.68744         14958      0         0       0    2           0          0          79
```

Figure 86: Insight on Page Migration Rate

The global stats (`sched-stats -t numa-global`) confirm that the amount of remote memory is reduced. After a minute, the global stats and the `numa-migration` stats are queried again and at that point 90 MB of total 32 GB of memory is remote and the NUMA scheduler is transferring the remote memory with a page migration rate of 22 pages per second.

```
[root@esxi03:~] sched-stats -t numa-migration
 groupName          groupID    clientID  balanceMig loadMig localityMig longTermMig  monitorMig pageMigRate
 vm.68744           14958         0          0        0        0            2           0          0          75
[root@esxi03:~] sched-stats -t numa-global
NUMA Global Stats
---------------------------
balanceMigration: 0
loadMigration: 0
localityMigration: 2
longTermFairnessMigration: 0
monitorMigration: 0
localMemory: 16330228
remoteMemory: 147704
[root@esxi03:~] sched-stats -t numa-global
NUMA Global Stats
---------------------------
balanceMigration: 0
loadMigration: 0
localityMigration: 2
longTermFairnessMigration: 0
monitorMigration: 0
localMemory: 32914932
remoteMemory: 90360
[root@esxi03:~] sched-stats -t numa-migration
 groupName          groupID    clientID  balanceMig loadMig localityMig longTermMig  monitorMig pageMigRate
 vm.68744           14958         0          0        0        0            2           0          0          22
[root@esxi03:~]
```

Figure 87: Page Migration Slowed Down

Dynamic page migration rate is designed to avoid overhead. Usually, older pages are less relevant and sometimes it is more efficient to have them expire on the old home node than to copy them and have inactive memory consume memory space.

In addition the NUMA scheduler wants to maintain a healthy amount of bandwidth available between NUMA nodes and avoids creating a denial-of-service to the rest of the VMs if it needs to migrate memory. The NUMA scheduler initiates memory migration with a rate of roughly 8000 pages per second if a substantial number of remote pages exists.

```
[root@esxi03:~] sched-stats -t numa-migration
 groupName      balanceMig loadMig localityMig longTermMig  monitorMig pageMigRate
 vm.68620           36        0        0            0           0          433
 vm.68833           34        0        2            0           0          8000
 vm.69023           26        0        4            0           0          1133
[root@esxi03:~]
```

Figure 88: Default Migration Rate

The page size is 4 KB (of contiguous memory). If it is migrated with a rate of 8000 pages per second, the rate is 32 MB per second. In extreme cases, the page migration rate can burst up to 250,000 pages per second. In that scenario, the memory migration process eats up 980 MB per second.

Currently, the lowest QPI speed of the recent CPU family boasts a unidirectional bandwidth of 12.8 GB per second. Although this is theoretical bandwidth, a single page migration process should not create interconnect bandwidth contention.

In one scenario, we witnessed 25 GB of memory being migrated in approximately 10 minutes. From a CPU perspective, this generated a load of 3%. When a page migration occurs, the command `ps` shows a world called `NUMASchedRemapEpochIntitialize`.

The default page migration rate is designed to generates a modest impact on the overall system. It becomes interesting when VM trashing occurs over a longer period of time. As said before, it is better to manually migrate VMs to another hosts in the vSphere cluster or to adjust resource entitlement with the appropriate resource.

06

CPU SCHEDULER

The primary goal of the ESXi CPU scheduler is to maximize physical CPU utilization while ensuring fairness of resource consumption. If the CPU scheduler detects an idle physical CPU, and ready worlds are available, then it will move that world to that idle physical CPU. This generally improves utilization, which will lead to higher application performance.

> **What is a world? Just consider it as a process or thread. It is just a different terminology inside the VMkernel. A vCPU can be a world, but also a kernel thread that is responsible for handling disk I/O.**

However, the act of migration has some negative performance impact attached to it. In particular, the cache state of the VM. The CPU scheduler has to determine whether it makes sense to migrate to an available physical CPU with a cold cache or to wait a few CPU quanta and preserve the cache state.

As it turns out, preserving cache state generally provides a better application performance than opting for the first available physical CPU resource. It is for the reason that fetching data from other caches or main memory is slower than a CPU quantum.

> **The CPU scheduler uses a default time slice (quantum) of 50 milliseconds. A quantum is the amount of time a vCPU is allowed to run on a physical CPU before another vCPU of the same priority gets scheduled. When a vCPU is consuming the physical CPU, it is not available for other vCPUs and can introduce queuing.**

> **Please note that most workloads won't use a full CPU quantum, it can block (waiting on IO) before using up its quantum. This reduces the effective time slice the vCPU is occupying the physical CPU. The advanced setting** `cpu.quantum` **allows you to change the default setting, however it is not advised to change this setting.**

The CPU scheduler wakes up if a vCPU needs to be scheduled on a physical CPU. In addition, it is getting scheduled every 2 to 30 milliseconds to verify the physical CPU load and VM demand and it determines whether vCPU migrations would improve utilization.

The CPU scheduler determines which worlds are entitled to CPU time. The CPU scheduler time-slices the available CPU resources amongst the entitled worlds. The state a world is in depends on whether or not the world is consuming CPU time. Many CPU states exist. The most interesting states a world can be in are idle, ready, running and waiting.

CPU States

When a world is created, it can either be transitioned to the run state or to the ready state. It depends on whether a CPU resource is available or not. If a CPU is available, the world directly enters the run state. If all physical CPU resources are busy, then the world waits its turn to run and is assigned a ready state.

A world transitions into a run state when the CPU executes the world's instructions. If the instructions are carried out successfully, the world is de-scheduled and enters a wait state until it has instructions to run again.

During run time, the instructions may require input or access to an external resource (external to the CPU), i.e. data in memory or data from disk. During the completion of an external event, the world is placed in a wait state. The world informs the CPU scheduler that it can be de-scheduled as it is waiting for the results of the external event. There are events where a world is woken up due to unrelated events, but that is beyond the scope of the book.

If the external event is completed, the world is scheduled to run again. If the previous pCPU is available, the world is transitioned to the run state again and the instructions are executed. If the pCPU is not available, the state of the world will be changed to ready.

In scenarios where there are enough free CPU resources available for other worlds to run (i.e. the ESXi host is in an under-committed state), the CPU scheduler does not de-schedule the world that runs an idle busy wait loop from the context of this world. This allows the CPU scheduler to immediately continue to run the world when it receives the data. This helps the CPU scheduler to provide the best response time, as it doesn't have to wait for the world to be scheduled again.

How does the CPU scheduler know which worlds to run and which worlds are in a ready state? It does so by determining priority and applying fairness. To understand relative priority and fairness, accounting needs to get a coherent view of the state of the resource consumers and resource producers.

CPU Scheduler Accounting

The fundamental element of the CPU scheduler is the accounting algorithm. Accounting provides the CPU scheduler a holistic view of all the workloads that are present on the ESXi host. Keep in mind that the CPU scheduler manages the VMkernel worlds as well as all VM worlds. A VM consists of multiple worlds: besides the vCPU world, VM *Mouse Keyboard and Screen* (MKS) subsystem worlds, CD-ROM and the VMX file.

Although the vCPU world generates the greater part of the CPU load, sometimes a physical CPU is required to run the other worlds. Worlds like VMX, CDROM and MKS are considered to be auxiliary worlds.

The accounting algorithms are used to determine the exact amount of CPU time that is charged to the world. The fairness algorithm uses this data to determine the MHzPerShare. The accounting algorithm is also responsible for estimating the EWMA of the pCPU and load the worlds used for CPU load balancing itself. Accounting manages calculating the historical CPU usage used by reporting. After selecting an eligible pCPU, the CPU scheduler keeps track of whether the vCPU receiving its demand.

The demand is the amount of time the vCPU can consume. However, due to sharing the microarchitecture of the pCPU (Hyper-Threading) and the utilization of a host, the CPU scheduler keeps track of stolen time. This stolen time is subtracted from the demand to provide an estimation of the CPU time used by the vCPU and the time it could have used if there were no 'stolen' cycles.

Stolen Time

Stolen time occurs due to various reasons. Common reasons for stolen time are over-commitment of the pCPUs, microarchitecture behavior or overlap time cycles due to latency of completion of an external event.

Microarchitecture Behavior

Stolen time can occur due to the behavior of Hyper-Threading and power-management. When both logical processors of a core are busy, the worlds make less progress. Detailed information about Hyper-Threading and the HT-Busy state can be found in the *Hyper-Threading* paragraph. The physical CPU can run in a different power mode due to *Dynamic Voltage Frequency Scaling* (DVFS). A pCPU gets charged less when operating at a lower frequency than its default operating frequency (nominal frequency).

Interestingly, when reviewing esxtop to troubleshoot a problem, the metric %USED takes stolen time due to HT and power management into account. In essence, the metric %USED reflects the 'quality' of the physical resource. Please keep in mind that Turbo Boost activity is also reflected in the %USED metric. In Turbo Boost, the active pCPU can leverage excessive CPU power of other idling cores. More information about Turbo Boost Technology can be found in chapter 7: *Host Power Management*.

Overlap Time

If a vCPU world is executing instructions on a pCPU, the instructions may require data from an external source. In this scenario, the execution does not make any progress as the system is servicing this IO request. In esxtop %OVRLP reflects the time the execution is halted due to servicing an interrupt and is therefore subtracted from the %RUN time.

Esxtop metrics formula: %USED = %RUN + %SYS - %OVRLP

If a service handles an I/O request, then accounting charges this time to the issuing VM. This is because the VMkernel sustains CPU costs to schedule the world that needs to handle the I/O request of the VM.

In esxtop, the metric %SYS reflects the time being charged to the VM. For example, network processing is done by VMkernel threads and then charged back as system time to the VM. In ESXi 5.0 it was accounted to vCPU 0, but in 6.0 it was changed to the VMkernel scheduling time and it was accounted to the VMX world of the VM. ESXi 6.5 solves this accounting artifact by introducing new worlds, such as NetWorld-VM-xxx. This is doing the network processing for the VM and is therefore associated with the VM. The esxtop expanded view shows the following:

```
 9:28:07pm up 1 day  6:55, 728 worlds, 1 VMs, 2 vCPUs; CPU load a
PCPU USED(%): 0.0 0.0 0.5 0.0 0.0 0.2 0.0 0.0 0.0 0.0 0.0 0.0 0.0
PCPU UTIL(%): 0.2 0.0 1.0 0.1 0.0 0.2 0.0 0.0 0.0 0.0 0.0 0.0 0.0
CORE UTIL(%): 0.3     1.0     0.3     0.0     1.1     1.0     0.0
```

ID	GID	NAME	%USED	%RUN	%SYS	%WAIT
92010	139143	vmx	0.03	0.05	0.00	100.00
92012	139143	NetWorld-VM-920	0.00	0.00	0.00	100.00
92013	139143	NUMASchedRemapE	0.00	0.00	0.00	100.00
92014	139143	vmast.92011	0.04	0.09	0.00	100.00
92016	139143	vmx-vthread-6	0.00	0.00	0.00	100.00
92017	139143	vmx-mks:VM00	0.00	0.00	0.00	100.00
92018	139143	vmx-svga:VM00	0.00	0.00	0.00	100.00
92019	139143	vmx-vcpu-0:VM00	0.52	0.85	0.00	99.45
92021	139143	vmx-vcpu-1:VM00	0.33	0.50	0.00	99.80
92020	139143	LSI-92011:0	0.00	0.00	0.00	100.00
92023	139143	vmx-vthread-7:V	0.00	0.00	0.00	100.00

Figure 89: CPU Accounting Networld-VM-920

When the VM is generating a lot of network traffic, it will not be accounted as %RUN time to the NetWorld-VM-xxx world. This helps to better identify the 'costs' of running this VM on your ESXi host.

Ready Time

Ready time represents the percentage of time that the VM is in a ready to run state but that it is waiting for the availability of a pCPU. Ready time is considered stolen time. Interestingly enough, when defining a CPU limit, you as the admin are stealing pCPU time from the vCPU. As such, the ready time incurred by a limit is also being accounted to ready time. To check whether a limit is set and is increasing ready time, verify the metric %MLMTD in esxtop.

Esxtop metrics formula: %WAIT + %RDY + %CSTP + %RUN = 100%

Please note that a lot of content is available about ready time. A common covered rule of thumb is that ready time higher than 20% is bad and you need to do something. The only way to determine whether the reported ready time is bad, is to view the expanded mode of the VM and then look at a per-world stat. By default, esxtop shows the group state, where the ready time is shown as an accumulation of the VM worlds.

There is really no quick and fast rule about ready time. To determine whether ready time has impact on your application, is to do real life benchmarks. This allows you to understand whether your application can handle ready time or that it absolutely cannot tolerate ready time.

Be aware that the CPU scheduler is designed to optimize for performance, but in doing so, a conscious decision has been made to accept some latency to improve overall throughput and responsiveness. Sometimes it makes sense to incur ready time for two milliseconds to leverage data that is present in the local cache. Migrating to a less busy CPU can provide you that faster enter time of actually running, but then it will move to a blocking state as the data needs to be retrieved from memory or remote cache.

Monitoring ready time over a longer period of time is a good indication that you are running increased consolidation ratios or that the workload has increased. Typically, you do not want to use a tool such as esxtop for trend analysis. Better tools for this are vCenter, VMware vRealize or third-party tooling such as SolarWinds or CloudPhysics.

If vCenter is used to view and monitor ready time, please realize that the shown metric is a summation value unlike the percentage value shown in esxtop. *VMware KB article 2002181* contains the accurate calculation methods to help you get a uniform metric. To give an example, if vCenter reports an average ready time of 70 for the VM and you are looking at the real-time view with a 20 second update interval, you need to apply the following calculation:

*(CPU summation value / (<chart default update interval in seconds> * 1000)) * 100 = CPU ready %*

```
(70 / (20s * 1000)) * 100 = 0.35% CPU ready
```

Please note that this value is the ready time in percentage for the entire VM. If this VM contains four vCPUs, then 0.35 / 4 = 0.087% is a rough average of the ready time value per vCPU.

The reason why we are calling it a rough average is that ready times are experienced per vCPU and there are many applications that are single threaded or they execute some operations as a single thread operation.

A great example is the SQL Maintenance operation of Index reorganize. As the SQL DB remains online, SQL issues this process as a single threaded operation, so other CPUs can process incoming queries and keep the database available. The vCPU responsible for providing the performance for the Index reorganize process may incur ready time. Therefore, we strongly recommend expanding the details in esxtop to determine whether the workload is uniformly distributed across vCPUs.

Monitor Ready Time VMKernel Processes

An indicator that the VMkernel may suffer from the workload it is required to service, is its own ready time. If the ready time for the VMkernel services is increasing, VMs will suffer.

Idle

If a guest OS has nothing to do anymore, it will spin up a process called idle loop. In esxtop %idle reflects the percentage of time spent in the idle loop and applies to vCPU worlds only. It can impact vCPUs, because it has to schedule vCPU time to allow progress of the time service within the guest OS.

Wait

Wait reflects the percentage of time the vCPU spent in wait state. Please note that the wait time in esxtop contains the idle time as well. Therefore, it can be high. It is recommended to focus on the VMWAIT metric when troubleshooting as this provides a more accurate view if the vCPU is waiting on external input such as I/O completion.

Esxtop metrics: %WAIT + %RDY + %CSTP + %RUN = 100%

VMWAIT

The total percentage of time the world spent in a blocked state waiting for events.

RUN

The metric %RUN reports the percentage of total scheduled time to run. %run is based on the wall clock time, meaning how many percent of the time the vCPU consumed the physical CPU resources. As a result, a high %RUN value shows that the vCPU is using a lot of CPU resources. It does not necessarily mean that the VM is constraint for CPU resources.

Performance Isolation and Fairness

Satisfying fairness is the act of scheduling worlds based on the dynamic entitlement. The CPU scheduler has to observe the global progression of scheduling the worlds while complying with the priority of all active VMs. Activity in combination with shares, reservations, and limits determine the overall priority of the VM.

Whenever a world wants to run, the CPU scheduler kicks in and attempts to schedule the world on an available physical CPU. If a physical CPU becomes idle, the CPU scheduler reviews the ready worlds and selects the world that has the highest priority and schedules it. Priority is dynamically calculated, based on the ratio of consumed CPU time over its fair share.

Dynamic Entitlement defines a target that represents the ideal amount of resources eligible for use. Both DRS and the host resource schedulers compute this target and it is up to the VM to use the available resources or not.

Entitlement is comprised of static and dynamic elements. User-specified resource settings are static elements, while dynamic elements are based on estimated demand and system contention levels.

A VM has a separate dynamic entitlement target for both the CPU and the memory resources. If a VM consumes more resources than its fair-share, then it is considered to be a lower priority VM. If a VM consumes less than its fair share, then it is considered a higher priority VM. Actual consumption changes dynamically. Therefore, actual priority also changes dynamically.

Fair Share

How is fair share calculated? It is mainly determined by resource configuration. The resource allocation settings shares, reservations, and limits can be set at CPU level. Interestingly enough, limits and shares have similar behavior on CPU as on memory, CPU reservations act differently. Let's review the resource allocation settings:

Shares

The number of shares indicates the proportional value of the VM on the same hierarchical level. If active utilization is equal between two VMs, the VM with twice as much shares is entitled to consume twice as many CPU cycles as the other VM.

Reservation

A reservation is a guarantee of the specified amount of physical resources, regardless of the total number of shares in its environment.

Limit

A limit is a mechanism to restrict physical resource usage of the VM. A limit ensures that the VM will never receive more CPU cycles than specified, even if extra cycles are available on the host.

Transient Ownership of CPU Reservations

It is important to understand that when a VM does not use its CPU cycles, these CPU cycles are redistributed to other active VMs. This behavior even occurs when the VM is configured with CPU reservations.

By redistributing the available CPU cycles and not allowing the VM to unnecessary hold on to its entitled CPU resources, the VMkernel attempts to achieve better fairness among the VMs and optimally use all available host resources. To achieve this goal, the CPU scheduler calculates the MHzPerShare metric. This metric identifies which VMs are 'ahead' of their entitlement and which VMs are 'behind' and do not fully utilize their entitlement.

MHzPerShare is calculated by dividing the MHzUsed by the number of shares (MHzPerShare = MHzUsed / Shares). MHzUsed is the current utilization of the VM measured in Megahertz. Shares indicates the configured number of shares of the VM.

The VMkernel calculates the MHzPerShare number of each active VM and the VM with the **lowest** MHzPerShare value receives the highest priority of scheduling. If the VM with the lowest MHzPerShare value does not consume the allocated cycles, the cycles become available to the VM with the next lowest MHzPerShare value.

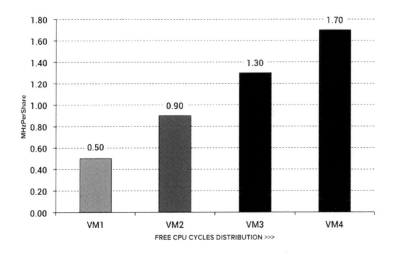

Figure 90: Free CPU Cycles Distribution Based on MHzPerShare

P1 \\ CPU RESOURCES

For example, the VM1 is only using 500 MHz and has 1000 shares. This results in an MHzPerShare value of 0.5. VM2 has 1000 shares and is using 900 MHz at the moment but it wants to use more. Because VM2 has the lowest MHzPerShare value of all the other VMs, it has the highest priority to receive the CPU cycles. If VM2's demands are satisfied, the remaining CPU cycles are available to VM3 and so forth.

Reservations play an important part in this calculation. Reservations precede shares and guarantee the amount of physical resources, irrespective of the total number of outstanding active shares. This means that the CPU cycles specified in the reservation are always available to the VM, even if another VM has a lower MHzPerShare value. When calculating the MHzPerShare value, reservations and shares interact with each other as follows:

In this scenario, an ESXi host contains two CPUs running at 3 GHz. The ESXi host runs three VMs: VM1, VM2 and VM3. VM1 runs a memory intensive application and consumes 500 MHz. VM1 is configured with 1000 CPU shares and 1000 MHz of CPU reservation. VM2 and VM3 both run a CPU intensive application and are competing for resources. VM2 is configured with a reservation of 2500 MHz and has 1000 shares. VM3 is configured with two vCPUs. It has a normal share setting (no reservation). As a result, 2000 shares are assigned to it.

VM	# OF CPUs	SHARES	RESERVATION
VM1	1	1000	1000 MHz
VM2	1	1000	2500 MHz
VM3	2	2000	0

Table 14: VM Shares and Reservations Overview

If VM1 runs at 500 MHz, the MHzPerShare value equals 0.5 (MHzPerShare = 500/1000). Although it has 1000 MHz CPU reservation, the 500 MHz fulfills its demand. The CPU scheduler distributes the remaining cycles to the other active VMs. VM2 uses its reservation and consumes 2500 MHz. VM2's MHzPerShare value equals 2.5 (2500/1000). At the same time, VM3 awakes from an idle state and wants to consume 2000 MHz. Its MHzPerShare at this point is 0 and hereby has the highest claim.

VM	CONSUMED MHz	SHARES	MHzPerShare
VM1	500	1000	0.5
VM2	2500	1000	2.5
VM3	0	2000	0

Table 15: VM MHzPerShare Overview

Fairness allows VM3 to claim up to 2.5 MHzPerShare, thus it is potentially entitled to 2000 x 2.5 = 5000 MHz. VM3 consumes 2000 MHz and at that instance its MHzPerShare value is 1. At this point 1000 MHz of unclaimed resources are still available on the system. Now VM1 has the highest claim (lowest MHzPerShare), but does not require it. VM3 has the second highest claim, but its requirement is also satisfied. That allows VM2 to consume the remaining resources of the physical CPU it runs on.

> **Please keep in mind that a vCPU can only use one core at a time. That means that the vCPU can never exceed the speed of the physical CPU. The operations pushed down from the vCPU to the physical CPU needs to fit inside the physical CPU. As a consequence, a reservation can never exceed the number of the vCPUs * MHz rating of the physical CPU.**

In this scenario, VM2 runs on the second CPU and VM1 and VM3 share the first CPU. Although the CPU scheduler allows VM2 to consume up to 1000 MHz, it is already using 2500 MHz of the consumed 3000 MHz. Therefore, during this cycle, VM2 receives the remaining free 500 MHz.

CPU Limit

When the administrator sets a limit, it will restrict the CPU usage of that particular VM. It cannot exceed this limit, even if the MHzPerShare is the lowest and unused resources are available on the system. A limit should not be set without reason.

World Placement

Once the CPU scheduler selects a world to schedule, the CPU scheduler applies a load-balancing algorithm to determine the best suitable physical resource. Besides providing fairness to the active VMs, the CPU scheduler is optimized to maximize the CPU utilization of the ESXi host. The goal is to provide as much CPU resources to the VM worlds as possible to get the best system throughput. As a result, the CPU scheduler takes scheduling overhead into account when making a decision where to place the world.

Applying world placement decisions on the fact of CPU core utilization alone would possibly not provide the optimal performance (progression) of the worlds. As mentioned before, the policy of the CPU scheduler is to preserve the on-chip cache state and to minimize migration cost. The CPU scheduler uses a load balancing algorithm during world placement that is designed to avoid Hyper-Threading contention, but it also attempts to avoid last level cache contention.

Intel Hyper-Threading technology exposes two logical processors, both utilizing and consuming the physical resources of a single core.

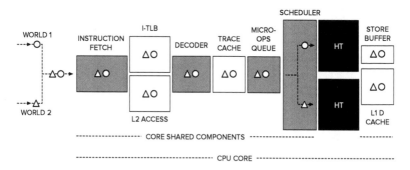

Figure 91: Multiple Worlds Processed by HT

If multiple worlds are scheduled on these logical processors, each logical processor cannot consume 100% of physical resources. It needs to share the L1 and L2 cache. They need to share the access to the scalable on-die ring for LLC operations and local and remote memory operations.

Sharing these parts of the microarchitecture impacts the overall performance of the HT. Therefore, if the CPU scheduler detects multiple available worlds and enough idle physical cores available, these worlds will be scheduled on separate physical cores.

This behavior impacts the scheduling decision for multiple vCPU VMs as well. To achieve uniform progress of sibling vCPUs of the VM, the CPU scheduler avoids scheduling these sibling vCPUs on both logical processors of the same core. More info about vCPU progress can be found in the *co-scheduling* paragraph.

Keep in mind that we are still discussing CPU placement inside a single CPU package that shares the same last level cache. The CPU scheduler prefers to place the worlds that frequently communicate with each other on the same CPU package to benefit from sharing the same data. Leveraging data already present in the cache can dramatically improve performance and offload microarchitecture and in some cases even the rest of the virtual infrastructure (network and storage).

Sharing cached data is important in NUMA systems. Worlds can be scheduled on different NUMA nodes and they experience an increase of latency due to possible remote last level cache data retrieval, or worse remote memory.

Load Balancing

The CPU load balancer is a classic example of a VMkernel service that just works. It's our recommendation that it shouldn't be tinkered with and should be left alone. The focus of the load balancing process is to improve CPU utilization and responsiveness by maintaining a proper distribution of worlds across the available pCPUs.

The load balancer can initiate a world migration if a pCPU becomes idle due to fairness imbalance, or when a new world wants to run. To determine whether a migration makes sense, the CPU scheduler calculates a goodness factor.

The goodness factor takes into account the pCPU load, the use of Hyper-Threading and the cache state of the vCPU. Even if idle pCPUs appear, it may not always make sense to move existing worlds due to various criteria.

Take the example of two pCPUs. One is available immediately, while another is utilized at the moment. Therefore, multiple time scales are used to determine pCPU to find the correct pCPU. If Hyper-Threading is enabled, the CPU scheduler takes the logical processor load into account. Besides the individual pCPU utilization, the sibling pCPU load is taken into account as well. An idle pCPU with a lower utilized sibling pCPU (logical processor) is more suitable than an idle pCPU that has a higher utilized sibling pCPU that will contest for incoming load for core resources.

In NUMA systems, the NUMA scheduler determines the placement of the vCPU on the CPU package, but it is the responsibility of the CPU scheduler to place the vCPU on a pCPU within the CPU package. The NUMA scheduler keeps track of local memory usage and tries to avoid migrating to improve CPU workload while having to migrate large amounts of memory between nodes.

The CPU scheduler does not need to worry about migrating data, but keeps the cache state of a vCPU. If the vCPU has a large footprint in the cache, it makes more sense to endure a little bit more CPU ready time. The costs to replenish the cache with data that needs to be retrieved from memory will be higher. It may introduce more block (wait) states for the vCPU, resulting in performance degradation instead of improvement. The command `sched-stats -t vcpu-migration-stats | grep vcpu` provides insight in the CPU migrations happening on the system.

pcpu_idle	fairness	wakeup_corun	ht_balance	affinity	vcpu_affinity	vcpu_cosched
111	0	98	1	2	8	4
46	0	11	1	3	0	14
45	0	6	2	2	0	33
82	0	7	2	3	0	40

Figure 92: Selection of Stats Provided by vcpu-migration-stats Command

Intel Hyper-Threading

Although the performance improvement of enabling HT is not an additional 100%, it does provide more scheduling options to the CPU scheduler. Because the CPU scheduler is aware if a VM is running on a full core or using a logical processor, it accounts the time used differently.

> To quote the vSphere 5.1 CPU scheduler technical paper: 'To reflect the asymmetry, the CPU scheduler charges CPU time partially if a world is scheduled on a partial core. However, if the world has been scheduled on a partial core for a long time, it might have to be scheduled on a whole core to be compensated for the lost time'.

Since ESXi 2.1, Hyper-Threading support is enabled by default in the VMkernel and every following version has introduced improvements to maximize performance.

What is Hyper-Threading?

Let's take a step back and review what Intel Hyper-Threading is and what it isn't. HT allows a single core to run two independent threads (worlds in our case) simultaneously. To do so, hardware threads, commonly called logical processors, are present on the core. What is interesting, is that both logical cores share the on-chip cache and the functional units of the core (*Floating Point Unit (FPU) and Arithmetic/Logical Units (ALU)*). These are flexibly shared between the logical processors depending on the aggregated activity of both logical processors.

That means if one logical processor is idle, the active one can consume all the functions and cache of the core. If a logical processor is active but it uses a small amount of cache, the other active logical processor can consume more cache. In essence, the size of the logical processor is dynamic.

As a result of sharing parts of the microarchitecture of the core, these two logical processors cannot provide the same performance as two individual cores. However, when both logical processors are utilized, this leads to aggregated throughput increase. In some scenarios, this can lead to throughput reduction of each separate world running on these logical processors. In those cases, the CPU scheduler adjusts its accounting.

Hyper-Threading Accounting

One important thing to understand is the accounting of CPU time. The CPU scheduler accounts for used CPU time measured in full core seconds and not in logical processor seconds.

If a logical processor on a busy core services a world, i.e. the other logical processor is also executing instructions of a world, then the world is getting a 'discount' in used CPU time from the CPU scheduler.

If a world is scheduled on a logical processor and the other logical processor is idle, then the CPU scheduler charges a full 100% of the CPU time. If both logical processors are executing instructions at the same time, then the CPU time is discounted by 37.5% to each world. This discount is used to recalculate the entitlement. As a result, it allows the world to be scheduled again and receive its full entitlement. This discount is a part of a concept called 'stolen time' that is covered in the *vCPU Demand* paragraph. If both logical processors are executing instructions, this state is called HT Busy.

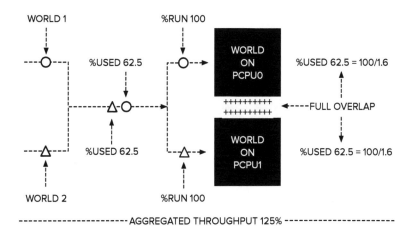

Figure 93: HT Busy Accounting

The VMkernel usually schedules vCPU worlds of different VMs on logical processors. In the previous scenario, the vCPU consumed the full logical processor and thus experienced a 100% run time. However, the CPU scheduler recognizes the reduced efficiency and therefore discounts the real used CPU time by applying the formula %RUN / 1.6 = %USED.

The interesting thing is that the CPU scheduler labels the logical processor as a pCPU. This is because the logical processor has the ability to function as a full core.

It is possible that two separate vCPUs consume the logical processors of a core without an overlap in time. Remember that most vCPUs do not fully utilize their quantum. If no overlap occurs, the vCPU is able to use the full core and therefore is charged for a full 100% of the CPU time.

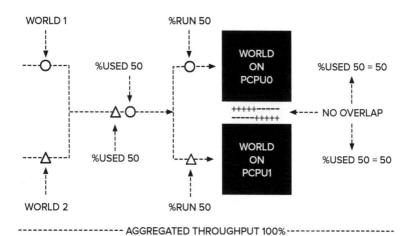

Figure 94: No Overlap Use of Logical Processors

Because the logical processor has the full core to its disposal, %RUN equals %USED. But what if there is a partial overlap in logical processor usage? In that case, the time of overlap is only discounted.

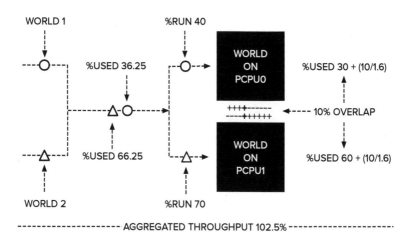

Figure 95: 10% HT Busy Overlap

Enable or Disable Hyper-Threading

There has always been a discussion whether to enable or disable Hyper-Threading. Either the old recommendation of disabling ESX 2.x stuck, or the lack of practical performance testing led to the decision of disabling HT. One statement that is often heard is the fact that the VM could not determine whether it was running on a logical processor or not.

Interestingly enough, from a guest OS perspective, the CPU exposed to the guest OS by the VM is the equivalent to a single non-Hyper-Threaded core. This has no consequence as the *Virtual Machine Monitor* (VMM) just communicates the CPU instructions (Run, Idle, Halt, etc.) from the guest OS to the CPU scheduler in the VMkernel. The CPU scheduler takes CPU accounting and world placement into account when determining priority and fairness.

VM Setting HT Sharing

Please note that up to vSphere 5.0, the advanced CPU setting *HT-Sharing* at VM level could determine whether a VM could share cores with other VMs or not. vSphere 5.0 HT *Sharing Internal* stopped working, in ESXi 5.1 *HT sharing Any* was available. In ESXi 5.5 it was removed from the CPU scheduler. However, the UI did not reflect that change. ESXi 6.5 removed all the UI remnants.

Disable HT to Avoid Sizing Mistakes

Another reason to disable HT is to avoid VM sizing mistakes. We would recommend determining and defining a standard consolidation ratio based on full cores and allowing the CPU scheduler to use HTs to schedule all the existing worlds. Remember a VM consists of vCPUs and many auxiliary worlds. In addition, the VMkernel needs to schedule its own processes as well. Typically, they are all great candidates to shortly run on a logical processor. Disabling HT usually creates the situation that you want to avoid in the first place.

Catering to Diva Virtual Machines

If you have a VM that wants only the best and nothing but the best (a real diva), then we recommend to look into using the *latency sensitivity* setting with a full core reservation. The CPU scheduler will ensure that no other world is scheduled on the sibling logical processor when a vCPU with exclusive reservation is scheduled on a CPU core. More details can be found in a later paragraph.

Please note that from this point forward pCPU is used from the point of view from the CPU scheduler, i.e. the highest abstraction of a physical CPU core resource. This can be a logical processor that has the full core to its disposal or a logical processor that has to share the core resources with the busy sibling logical processor.

Co-Scheduling

The typical guest OS assumes all detected CPUS are constantly present and run at the same pace. However, the CPU scheduler schedules and de-schedules worlds (vCPUs) separately according to fairness and priority. As a result, not all vCPUs may be running. This can impact the uniform progress the guest OS expects. The independent scheduling behavior can cause skew, which is the difference in progress between the vCPUs of the same VM. The problem with a skew that is too large is that it breaks the assumption of the guest OS and could possibly cause a crash of the guest OS. Therefore, it is necessary to control the skew by co-scheduling the vCPUs as much as possible.

For better understanding of co-scheduling, it is good to know what it is not, and that is gang scheduling. Gang scheduling is the act of scheduling a group of worlds until it is able to schedule all worlds at the same time. Unfortunately, a lot of users perceive ESXi to gang schedule vCPUs of a VM. A lot of outdated wisdom is still spread on the Internet about co-scheduling. This quote was found on a popular VMware forum at the end of 2015:

> *"One thing people don't realize is that for a VM to do anything, it has to have ALL of the cores provisioned to it before it can process an operation - even if that operation is a simple (1 + 1 = 2)."*

The problem is that this is an accurate description of the behavior of the strict co-scheduling algorithm of a system that we do not use any longer. It describes the behavior of the CPU scheduler present in ESXi 2.x, which was released in 2004.

ESXi 3.x introduced the relaxed co-scheduling. In earlier versions of ESXi, the CPU scheduler used to co-stop all vCPUs once the skew was too large. Since ESXi 4.0, skew is being tracked per individual vCPU. This allows for a much greater granular co-stop behavior.

Granular Co-Stop

Once the skew per vCPU accumulated enough, it stops only the leading vCPU if its skew is large enough. The skew between CPUs is tracked by each vCPU relative to the slowest. The interesting part is the 'restart' of co-stopped vCPUs. In early versions, all lagging vCPUs were scheduled together again. Opportunistically, all the vCPUs of the VM were queued. Now that only the leading vCPU is de-scheduled, this vCPU is placed in the ready queue once the skew between the vCPU and the slowest vCPU is acceptable again.

If a co-stopped VM is required to run, the CPU scheduler will detect the vCPU worlds it can schedule. The CPU scheduler does not consider worlds that are in a wait state. If the number of available pCPUs is smaller than the number of available vCPUs, the CPU scheduler multiplexes the vCPUs across the pCPUs. The CPU scheduler Intermittently schedules the vCPUs that have not run for a while. For example, if six vCPUs are ready to run, but only four pCPUs are available, the CPU scheduler selects four vCPUs. It schedules them on the four pCPUs and cycles through the CPUs, so progression remains uniform.

Co-Run & Hyper-Threading

To avoid skew as much as possible, the CPU scheduler avoids placing the vCPUs on the logical processors of the same core. It is difficult to have sibling vCPUs progress uniformly when they are forced to use logical processors of the same core. Scheduling the same logical CPU possibly leads to more skew. However, both vCPUs can still be scheduled on logical processors of different cores in the same CPU package. Having Hyper-Threading enabled, provides the CPU scheduler the extra flexibility when mapping vCPUs to pCPUs to co-run.

When a co-stopped vCPU needs to run to satisfy its demand, and the CPU scheduler detects that no full core is available, it will de-schedule a lower priority world. This ensures that no other workload is scheduled on the sibling logical processor. This way, the world that is behind owns a full core.

Tracking Co-Scheduling Problems

Co-scheduling problems normally occur if the vCPU to pCPU consolidation ratio is high while running a great number of active VMs.

Co-stop becomes problematic if your application inside the VM is running parallelized operations across all the vCPUs. A great example is Microsoft SQL, which can execute high impact queries across the number of CPUs that are specified in the Max Degree of Parallelism setting. To know more about tuning SQL, we recommend visiting David Klee's site davidklee.net.

Both vCenter and esxtop show statistics to track co-stop. The co-stop counter can be found in the advanced chart options (Select VM > Monitor > Performance > advanced > CPU > Co-stop.)

Within esxtop the co-scheduling attempts can be tracked by viewing the %CSTP value. This value represents the percentage of time that the VM is ready to execute but that it is waiting for the availability of multiple CPUs as the VM is configured to use multiple vCPUs.

If a VM is configured with VM snapshots, esxtop shows a high value of %CSTP. Consolidation of snapshots can help reduce or eliminate %CSTP.

Oversized VMs and Co-Stop

Oversized VMs can introduce a lot of co-stops. In most cases, adding more CPUs to a VM does not automatically guarantee an increase of throughput of the application. Some workloads just do not take advantage of all the available CPUs, especially single-threaded applications.

A single-threaded application can only be scheduled on one CPU at a time and will not benefit from the multiple CPUs available. The problem lies within the way the guest OS or the application leverages those CPU resources. If the guest OS is smart, it keeps on executing a particular thread on the same CPU. This improves caching and it has the least impact on the CPU scheduler. Due to tracking the skew per vCPU, it allows the CPU scheduler to understand whether other vCPUs are idle. As a result, the CPU scheduler grants the idle vCPUs the same progress as the fastest sibling vCPU and therefore does not co-stop the VM.

It gets messy when the guest OS or application round-robins its threads across the available CPUs. This leads to overhead such as interrupts or context switches and cache misses. In addition, each vCPU makes progress. Most likely it happens in a non-uniform matter, resulting in co-stopping the vCPUs. This leads to performance impact to that particular VM and in worse cases other VMs as well, due to the scheduling overhead such as vCPU migrations.

Although relaxed co-scheduling reduces the requirement of the VMkernel to simultaneously schedule all vCPUs of the VM, it is still necessary to maintain progress of each vCPU of the VM to keep them acceptably synchronized. To check whether the VM is oversized and/or does not handle multi-threading well and is using one vCPU only, you can check the %WAIT metric and %CSTP. %WAIT indicates the waiting and idling time.

Scheduling Affinity

ESXi allows you to define a CPU affinity for each VM. CPU affinity restricts the assignment of vCPUs to a subset of pCPUs. The question most users have is if it offers performance advantages for the VM. Yes, we believe it can, but only in an extreme limited number of specific cases. Read: for 99.8% of the time it will get you in trouble! Maybe even 99.9%. But some people just like to live dangerously. Keep in mind that additional changes to the virtual infrastructure are usually required to obtain a performance increase over the default scheduling techniques. Setting CPU affinity by itself will not result in any performance gain, but usually a performance decrease.

By using CPU affinity, you restrict the CPU scheduler to schedule the vCPUs of that particular VM only on the selected pCPUs. A CPU affinity does not remove the selected pCPUs from the scheduling options from other VMs. In other words, it **does not** exclusively reserve those physical CPU resources to that particular VM. It allows you to introduce VM-to-processor placement constraints for the CPU scheduler. Typically, it will not help in most cases we witnessed in the field.

When Will CPU Affinity Help?

Under a controlled environment, some specific workloads benefit from using CPU affinity. When the VM workload is cache bound, it profits from aggregated caches. If the workload has high intra-thread communications and is running on separate CPU sockets, setting CPU affinity might have the opposite effect. It may negatively impact the performance of the application.

CPU affinity is also used to assign a pCPU to a vCPU, but this requires a lot of changes and it increases management. Be aware that it never dedicates the physical CPU to the VM as the VMkernel schedules all its processes across all available pCPUs, regardless of any custom setting a VM has. The scheduling overhead for the CPUs stays the same whether CPU affinity is set on the VM or not. You just reduce the vCPU's choice.

To determine if your application fits this description is a challenge and maintaining such configurations usually results in a nightmare. Generally, CPU affinity is only used for licensing restrictions, performance simulations and load testing. It is better left unused for every other case. Setting CPU affinity results in less choice for the CPU scheduler to schedule the VM, but there is more to it.

Controlled Environment

CPU affinity does not equal isolation of a physical CPU. In other words, when a VM is pinned to a physical CPU it does not control or own that CPU. The CPU scheduler still considers that physical CPU a valid CPU to schedule other VMs on. If isolation of a CPU is the end goal, then all other residing VMs on the host (and VMs that are created in the future) must be configured with CPU affinity as well. The specific CPU(s) assigned to the VM must be excluded from all other VMs. Setting CPU affinity results in manual CPU micro management and can be a nightmare to maintain.

Some try to maintain cache footprint by pinning a particular VM to a pCPU. Although L1 and L2 are private, they are relatively small. Thus, by the time the VM is scheduled again, the other worlds that are using the vCPU have already filled the L1 and L2 cache with their data. Last Level Cache is a completely different story as it is shared amongst all the cores in the CPU package. No affinity has impact on any form of cache retention, good or bad!

Resource Entitlements

On the grounds that CPU affinity will not automatically isolate the CPU for that specific VM, shares and reservations should be set to guarantee a specific performance level.

The scheduler attempts to maintain fairness for all VMs. It is possible that other VMs are scheduled on the set of CPUs specified in the affinity set of the VM.

Adjust the VM shares and reservations accordingly. This ensures priority over other active VMs. Please note that CPU reservations are friendly. Although the vCPU is guaranteed a specific portion of physical resources, an external thread or other VM might use the vCPU. This thread will not instantly be de-scheduled.

In the case where multiple VMs are affinity bound to the same CPU, it is possible that the CPU scheduler cannot meet the specified reservation. Be aware that admission control ignores affinity. Multiple VMs can have a full reservation equal to a full core but still need to compete with other affinity bound VMs.

Host Admission Control

Admission control is mostly associated with vSphere High Availability. However, admission control is active at the host level as well. It is actually responsible for the decision whether a VM is powered-on or not.

A reservation can be defined as a hard *Service Level Agreement* (SLA). Under all circumstances, the resources that are protected by a reservation must be made available to that VM. Even if every other VM is in need of resources, the CPU scheduler cannot reclaim these resources as it is restricted by this Hard SLA. To meet the SLA, the host admission control verifies if it has enough free unreserved resources available during the power-on operation of the VM. If it doesn't have the necessary unreserved resources available, the host cannot meet the hard SLA. And as a result the host rejects the power-on operation of the VM.

Affinity Configuration

What recommendations can be provided to make affinity configuration as successful as possible?

Cache Level

If a VM is spanned across two CPU packages, it effectively results in having two Last Level Caches available to the VM.

Today's CPU architecture offer dedicated L1 and L2 cache per core and a shared LLC for all cores inside the CPU package. Because access to Last Level Cache is faster than (normal) memory, it might make sense to span the VM across two processor packages to increase the amount of available LLC.

However, the inter-socket communication speed reduces -or removes- the positive effect of having low-latency cache available. If the workload can fit inside one cache (small cache footprint) and it uses intensive intra-thread communication, then placement in a single CPU package is preferred over spanning it across multiple packages.

Hyper-Threading

If a VM runs on a Hyper-Threading enabled system, it is best to set the CPU affinity to the logical CPUs that do not belong to the same core. The HT threads on a core are translated by the VMkernel as logical CPUs. They are consecutively numbered. For example, core 1 contains pCPU0 and pCPU1, core 2 contains pCPU2 and pCPU3, etc. If CPU affinity is set to logical CPUs belonging to the same core, both vCPUs of the VM need to compete with each other for physical CPU resources. By scheduling a VM on logical CPUs of different cores, the vCPUs do not have to compete. This benefits the vCPUs' throughput because the VMkernel allows the vCPU to use the entire cores' resources. This occurs if only one logical CPU per core is active.

NUMA

If CPU affinity is set on a VM running in a NUMA architecture, the VM is treated as a NON-NUMA client and gets excluded from NUMA scheduling. Therefore, the NUMA scheduler will not set a memory affinity for the VM to its current NUMA node and the VMkernel can allocate memory from every available NUMA node in the system.

Consequently, the VM may end up running on a different NUMA node than where its memory is residing. This results in unnecessary memory latency and possible higher %Ready time, as the instruction must wait until the memory is fetched from a remote node.

Scheduling Affinity Alternative

To control licensing constraints, CPU affinity could be a great tool. In almost every other case CPU affinity is better left unused.

Scheduling worlds is very complex. Scheduling threads belonging to multiple VMs with different priorities, activity, progress and still considering optimal use of the underlying CPU and memory architecture, is extremely complex. The CPU scheduler is aware of all these components and together with the cluster scheduler vSphere DRS, it can see to it that the VMs receive their resource entitlement.

If the VM must have access to specific and isolated physical resources, other mechanisms such as the Latency Sensitivity setting, made available in vSphere 5.5, are better suitable. Latency Sensitivity introduced a new form of scheduling affinity: exclusive affinity in combination with the Latency Sensitivity setting.

Latency Sensitivity Setting

The premise of the Latency Sensitivity setting is that the VM needs to be immune to all kinds of operation delays. When jitter and latency are impacting the performance of the application in a noticeable way, Latency Sensitivity settings can be helpful.

The Latency Sensitivity setting focuses on three key areas to reduce latency and scheduling overhead:

- CPU Scheduling
- Memory
- Network

Adjustments to network and memory behavior will be covered in their respective parts of the book.

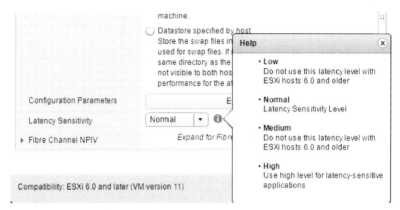

Figure 96: VM Setting Latency Sensitivity Options

To have no scheduling delays at vCPU level, a high enough CPU reservation has to be set to evoke exclusive affinity at the physical CPU level.

However, keep in mind that you can set Latency Sensitivity to high without a CPU reservation. If this configuration is used, the VM is powered-on, but the CPU scheduler cannot guarantee exclusive use of the physical CPU. When selecting the option High, the UI displays the following warning:

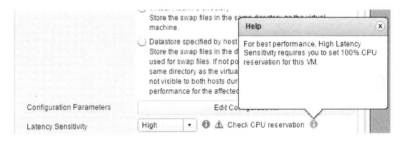

Figure 97: Check CPU Reservation Warning

Please keep in mind that both settings, Latency Sensitivity and CPU reservation, are hot configurable. However, the CPU scheduler can only apply exclusive affinity during power-on operations. Therefore, it is recommended to apply these settings when the VM is powered off.

If DRS detects a VM with Latency Sensitivity enabled, it creates a VM-Host affinity rule for this VM. The VM-Host affinity rule is created to prevent migration to avoid any performance impact due to vMotion. This rule is a preferential rule (should-rule) and allows DRS to move the VM during maintenance mode and if the host is 100% utilized. It is important to know that the automatic created rule is not visible from the UI. This to avoid human error while administrating the environment.

CPU Full Core Reservation

Setting a reservation can be quite a challenge, especially if you want to achieve a full core reservation. The UI allows you to specify the amount of MHz that is equal to the total amount of MHz that is available in the system.

This is quite an interesting situation, as the VMkernel cannot allocate any more cycles directly to the guest OS in the VM than the amount of MHz that is equal to the number of vCPUs * the normal CPU operation rate of the physical CPU core.

For example, the test system is equipped with two Intel Xeon E5-2630 CPUs. Each CPU contains ten cores running at 2.20 GHz.

```
[root@esxi03:~] vsish -e get /hardware/cpu/cpuModelName
Intel(R) Xeon(R) CPU E5-2630 v4 @ 2.20GHz
[root@esxi03:~]
```

Figure 98: CPU Model Name

If the VM is configured with two vCPUs, the maximum amount of MHz the VMkernel can provide to the guest OS is 2 x 2200 MHz = 4400 MHz. Unfortunately, the UI is not clear on this limitation. In this scenario, the reservation is set to 8000 MHz. The reconfiguration of the VM completes successfully. However, whenever the VM is powered-on, an error is thrown.

```
haTask-2-vim.VirtualMachine.powerOn-122325797
Power On this virtual machine
DVDStore00
Failed - Module 'MonitorLoop' power on failed
```

- Module 'MonitorLoop' power on failed.
- Group host/user: Invalid CPU allocation requested for virtual machine vmm0:DVDStore00. (min: 8000 mhz, max: -1, minLimit: -1, shares: -3)
- Could not power on virtual machine. CPU min outside valid range.
- Failed to power on VM.
- Failed to start the virtual machine

Figure 99: Power-on VM Error

'Min' is the internal definition of a reservation. Max -1 is the internal definition for unlimited. The error message 'CPU min outside valid range' indicates that the reservation is set above the capabilities of the physical CPUs.

Typically, users apply a reservation that is close to the normal CPU operation rate. However, this does not enable exclusive affinity. To avoid these errors and apply a full-core reservation successfully, we recommend to review the summary of the ESXi host, or use the command `vsish -e get /hardware/cpu/cpuModelName` to retrieve the CPU MHz spec of your host.

> **Please keep in mind that exclusive affinity can impact consolidation ratios due to providing exclusive physical CPU access.**

07

HOST POWER MANAGEMENT

Host power management might be one of the biggest enigmas in virtual infrastructure environments. Its use case appears to be unappealing at first sight, yet it can help to unlock the full potential of modern CPUs. Static power plans with monikers such as *High* or *Maximum Performance,* trick you into believing you obtain the maximum level of performance. In reality, it is more geared towards providing a consistent degree of performance, while dramatically reducing the effectiveness of the Turbo Boost functionality.

Turbo Boost allows cores to operate above their base operating frequency via dynamic control mechanisms. This is a useful feature for a system that deals with fluctuating workloads. Let's take a closer look at the seemingly uninteresting world of power management and discover which model suits your workload best.

Power Management Control

Power management is controlled at two levels: at the BIOS level of the host and at the vSphere level. While it is rare to find workload that is impacted by the ESXi defaults. It is quite common to come across an ESXi host that is configured with a suboptimal power management setting in the BIOS. For economic reasons, most servers are shipped with a Balanced or Dynamic power management policy enabled in the BIOS. These default BIOS settings have caused, and are still producing, massive amounts of troubleshooting tickets at vendors around the globe.

Never ask a global support services employee about BIOS controlled P-States / frequency scaling being the shipped default unless you are willing to listen to them rant for an hour. Ok, this might be a little bit exaggerated. But the point is, many customers have lost countless hours of compute power due to longer query times or longer completion times. Which is caused by the inability of the hardware power management to take workload patterns into account.

Most IT organizations or IT professionals that have been burned by this experience, and skew away from using BIOS Dynamic power management policies. As a result they set everything to maximum performance in the server hardware BIOS. Selecting this option isn't necessarily a wrong decision, but more elegant solutions are available that provide more flexibility. The different power management policies in both the BIOS and vSphere are covered in detail in a later paragraph.

Current CPU microarchitectures can leverage power-saving technology in such a way that it can shift the available thermal budget from idle cores to boost the performance of existing workloads. Therefore, the focus of this chapter is different than most collateral on host power management. Instead of using vSphere *Host Power Management* (HPM) for creating energy-efficient servers, we are exploring the possibilities of Turbo Boost technology to attain peak performance of today's CPU microarchitecture. The peak performance of Turbo Boost technology depends on energy-saving states. Let's start by exploring these constructs first.

CPU Power Management Technology

One of the core techniques in computer architecture to conserve power is the use of *Dynamic Voltage and Frequency Scaling* (DVFS). By reducing the frequency of the CPU, less power is consumed. Please note that this will also reduce throughput at the same rate. I.e. you will not save power over the same amount of work. When voltage is reduced, it only cuts the power consumption. However, switching at a certain frequency requires enough 'pressure' (voltage) so frequency has to be reduced as well.

Now every cycle at a lower voltage is more efficient though, hence you save power over the same amount of work (it will just take longer). This technology in Intel CPU is known as *Enhanced Intel SpeedStep* (EIST). Intel CPUs up to the E5-2600 v2 (Ivy Bridge) regulated voltage at CPU package level and pushed this to the individual CPU cores. This level of coarseness combined with the granularity of the CPU scheduling at core level might not make it a winning combination. Think about what happens if a lot of VMs are idling, while one VM with a small number of vCPUs is pushing a lot of workloads. If only the BIOS power management would manage the CPU, the overall load utilization of the CPU package would warrant for a lower frequency and voltage of the CPU cores, resulting in degradation of performance.

Tremendous advancements have been made in CPU design. E5-2600 v3 (Haswell) introduced *Fully Integrated Voltage Regulators* (FIVR), which allows a more granular DVFS power budget per core that helps to fine-tune the CPU power consumption by allowing core independent power saving states. This aligns perfectly with the virtualization workload, where individual VMs each use a fraction of the total available cores. As we all know, workloads are not 100% active all of the time (which is the original premise of virtualization). In addition, not all workloads demand 100% CPU performance when active. What we often see is that virtualization is that core utilization difference might be higher (i.e. that some cores are at e.g. 70% while others are at 20%). Bare metal seems more balanced (e.g. all cores at 40%). Combine this hardware feature with the intelligence of the VMkernel and you do have a more successful combination.

Two constructs are mainly used to reduce power consumption of a CPU core, sometimes even a complete CPU package. These constructs are called P-States and C-States. In short, a P-State is an execution power saving state. The CPU is active and processing workload. A C-State is an operating (idle) power saving state. A C-State allows the CPU package to shut down a particular core and parts of the CPU package to save energy while balancing response times. C-States can apply to individual cores but also to the entire CPU package.

P-States

A P-State is an *Advanced Configuration and Power Interface* (ACPI) defined processor performance state and leveraged by EIST. In essence, each P-State has a predefined voltage and frequency point.

Every CPU model has a fixed number of performance states. The number of P-States is processor specific. Commonly, modern CPU families provide up to ten to twelve states. Power states are labeled as P0, P1, P2, etc. In the test system, the E5-2930 v4 reports the following P-States to ESXi:

P-STATE	FREQUENCY	TDP
P0	2201 MHz	85 W
P1	2200 MHz	85 W
P2	2100 MHz	79 W
P3	2000 MHz	74 W
P4	1900 MHz	70 W
P5	1800 MHz	65 W
P6	1700 MHz	61 W
P7	1600 MHz	57 W
P8	1500 MHz	53 W
P9	1400 MHz	48 W
P10	1300 MHz	45 W
P11	1200 MHz	40 W

Table 16: Overview P-States Intel Xeon E5-2630 V4

Without Turbo Boost enabled, you'd see one less P-State. By default, the system assigns P0 to Turbo Boost and increases the P-State base frequency with one MHz. The VSI nodes list the power reduction specifications. The power consumption is an estimation of when all cores in the CPU package are all running at that particular P-State. With the introduction of FIVR, cores are allowed to run in different P-States individually. Therefore, these power reduction numbers might not be accurate.

P-States Selection

The power management policy uses P-States to indicate to the CPU how much performance it would like to receive on a particular core (E5-2600 v3 and newer). Even though a pCPU can run at 2.2 GHz, power saving modes might reduce the frequency and allow the CPU to run from 2 GHz to 1.2 GHz. If the OS determines that a core can run at a lower performance state due to its workload demand, it votes for the desired P-State. It is the CPU package that ultimately decides which P-State is selected for a core. FIVR helps the CPU package to provide the recommended state.

With CPU packages without FIVR, a different behavior occurs. The cores within a CPU package all share the same voltage and frequency (P-State). The exceptions to this rule are the cores that are idling. Their frequency is zero. Although the power management policy requests different P-States for each core, a compromise of frequency and voltage is necessary. Because they share the same voltage plane, there can only be one P-State effective. For example, if workload A utilizes pCPU0 for 50% and workload B utilizes pCPU1 for 20%, the CPU package selects a P-State that matches the 50% workload. In essence, it will always vote for the maximum value. This behavior, and especially the improved behavior due to FIVR, helps to free up thermal budget for Turbo Boost.

If vSphere Power Management is enabled, the VMkernel starts voting for P-States when the utilization of a pCPU drops below the threshold of 60%. The default algorithm in ESXi balances between performance versus power management trade-off. The balanced power management policy only votes for a particular P-State if the workload will go just as fast or close to it.

ESXi HOST POWER MANAGEMENT POLICY	P-STATE THRESHOLD
High Performance	P-State Disabled
Balanced	60%
Low Power	90%

Table 17: vSphere HPM P-State Thresholds

Once the lowest common voted P-State per core changes, it starts the transition to the new desired effective P-State, as it has to ensure the active core still operates correctly. As a result, it does not transition between states in one big move, but gracefully in subtle increments.

ACPI Domain Coordination

Some systems allow you to select the ACPI Domain Coordination. These are usually found in older systems where processors imposed restrictions on which P-State the cores could be placed in. Cores were grouped in domains to which the P-State was applied to collectively. With the introduction of FIVR, all cores can run independently but sometimes the BIOS still contains these settings.

There are three classes of ACPI Domain Coordination: SW_ALL, SW_ANY and HW_ANY. When set to an SW state, the system allows the software to initiate the P-State transition. This is either on any CPU within the domain (SW_ANY) or it transitions all the cores in the domain (SW_ALL). When selecting HW_ANY, you allow the hardware to coordinate P-State transitions. ESXi expects systems to have ACPI Domain Coordination set to HW_ANY.

C-States

While P-States are execution power saving states (the CPU is still active and processing), the C-States are operating (idle) power saving states. C-States allow the CPU package to shut down cores and parts of the CPU microarchitecture to save energy while balancing response times. C-States can apply to individual cores but also to the entire package.
The C0 state is the active power state in which the core is executing instructions. In this state, P-States are possible. If all the instructions are completed, the OS idles. In this state, the OS sends a HLT (Halt) instruction to the CPU.

Idle time is not as uncommon as people think. In reality, when CPU utilization is less than 100%, part of the time the core is executing instructions and the rest of the time it is idle. If the OS sends the HLT instruction, the core stops and waits until an interrupt occurs to service the device that has sent the signal. The time between receiving a HLT instruction and an interrupt is where the power consumption is reduced.

Interestingly enough the HLT instruction was already present in the 8086, but it wasn't until the 486DX4 that Intel leveraged the HLT state as a mean to save power. The 486DX4 introduced the C1 state. In C1, the core is in a HLT state and power gates most of the core logic. C3 and C6 are deeper C-states in which they turn off parts, caches are flushed into higher order caches and consume less power and produce less heat.

Pentium 4 introduced SSE3 that included the Monitor/MWAIT instructions. These instructions help improve multi-threaded applications. When multiple threads share data, synchronization has to occur between threads to ensure correct operation. One common scenario is that one thread is waiting on another thread to reach the point of synchronization.

Monitor/MWAIT was introduced to help the OS to optimize intra-process thread synchronization. It avoids relatively expensive *Inter-Processor Interrupt* (IPI). This is an interrupt that allows one core to interrupt another core if its action is required. This could be for example the flushing of *Translation Lookaside Buffers* (TLB). The TLB construct is handled extensively in the *Memory section* of this book. An IPI is also used to get an idle core out of its HLT state when there is a job to do. The Monitor/MWAIT state does not need an IPI. The core monitors the specified memory address, which e.g. indicates that the thread is ready to run. When the write to the address is registered, the core will automatically leave HLT state and gets to work. The VMkernel uses MWAIT. However, the VMM does not virtualize MWAIT states for VMs.

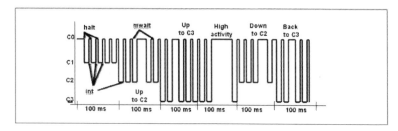

Figure 100: Halt and MWAIT Induced C-States (source: Intel)

Due to the interaction with system cache, C0 and C1 are considered Snoopable C-States, whereas C3 and C6 are referred to as non-Snoopable C-States as they move and flush specific cache levels.

The challenge with deep C-States is that they introduce wakeup latencies. C-States provide the biggest power savings, thus providing the best opportunity for higher Turbo Boost frequencies. If you disable deep C-States, you will lose an estimated 30 to 40% Turbo Boost increase. This is important to understand for obtaining the maximum performance of the CPU packages.

> **It is recommended to determine whether your workload will be impacted from deep C-States.**

The ACPI standard dictates that the restart latency must be small enough to not have the OS consider the latency aspect of the state when deciding to schedule instructions on the pCPU. There are multiple C states, and various definitions of the C-State exist. ACPI uses consecutively numbered C-States, while Intel is using C0, C1, C3 and C6. In this book, we use the Intel C-State nomenclature.

Core C1 State

This is the low-power idle state. The core is put into a C1 state if a HLT instruction is received. In the case of the ESXi server, the ESXi scheduler schedules the idle thread to run on a pCPU, which executes the HLT instruction on the pCPU.

The core stops the central internal CPU clock signal, making it consume less power. The C1 state allows the APCI and bus interface unit to stay active and run at full speed. This ensures that the core receives interrupts and it returns to a normal operating state. Besides device interrupts, the core can (temporarily) exit C1 state and go back to C0 state to address cache coherence Snoops. The data in the cache structures is still available, which allows the core to process the Snoop request and then swiftly return to the C1 state. This sequence is called the *Stop Clock Snoop State*.

Be aware that issuing a HLT instruction requires ring 0 access. It can only be run by privileged system software such as the VMkernel. A VMs idle threads can issue HLT but it will be intercepted by the VMM and the VMkernel deschedules the vCPU. ESXi does not present any deep C-State capabilities to VMs. From its perspective the 'hardware' doesn't support them.

Core C1E State

The C1E state is an altered version of the C1 state, often referred to as Enhanced Halt. In addition to stopping the central internal clock, it reduces CPU voltage to reduce leakage. The voltage and frequency are reduced to the lowest point possible. In essence, C1E equals C1 + the lowest frequency P-State.

The C1E state is completely transparent to the OS. The OS issues a regular C1, and the CPU microcode will engage and move to a C1E state. Although it is transparent to the OS, ESXi records whether C1E is enabled or not in the boot log / VMkernel. If a core in a C1E state receives a cache Snoop, it transitions to a Snoop state. This allows the core to exit the C1E state to respond to cache Snoop transactions, but uses a lower voltage instead of returning to the nominal voltage.

According to Intel, the difference in latency between entering C1 versus C1E is supposed to be undetectable. Independent research shows that the wake-up latency is detectable.

Therefore, it is recommended for low-latency workloads to disable it. However, if you are not running low-latency workloads and still crave high performance, C1E assists Turbo Boost in reaching its full potential. Our recommendation is, before turning off C1E, ensure that the label of low-latency workload is accurate. Don't label your workload as low-latency if the VM just needs better performance than the other active workloads.

> **C1E is the only relevant setting in the BIOS that is not configurable from the ESXi level. You need to configure this setting in the server BIOS.**

Core C3 State

The C3 state is the first C-State where components are shut down. As a result, the internal clocks are stopped. On most systems the APCI and the bus controller are also stopped. The C3 is considered to be a non-Snoopable state, as it does not need to respond to cache coherence traffic active in the CPU package. The data residing in L1 and L2 cache are flushed into the Last Level Cache.

Core C6 State

The C6 state is the deep C-State where all cached data is stored in static RAM. Its architectural state is also saved to the static ram. This allows the CPU package to reduce the voltage of the core to 0 V. Waking up from this state requires the core to load the architectural state from static RAM, which results in substantial wake-up latency.

Package C-State

As described earlier, C-State can be applied to cores as well as the complete CPU package. In general, the CPU package exposes two Package C-States: Package C3 and Package C6. Whereas the core C-State is applied to the individual core and its components, the Package C-State applies to the complete CPU package.

Besides reducing power to cores, Uncore components such as the scalable ring are being powered down as well. Typically, Package C-States are uncommon in ESXi hosts as the VMkernel distributes its worlds across all available cores. To drop a complete CPU package into a C6 state, all cores are required to be in the core C6-State.

Independent Uncore Frequency Scaling

As described in chapter 2 - *System Architecture*, the Uncore is a collection of components of a CPU that does not carry out core computational functions but is essential for core operations. In the E5-2600 v3 (Haswell) microarchitecture, the Uncore runs in a separate clock domain than the cores. This allows the Uncore to have a dynamic behavior. Some server vendors, such as Dell, allow you to adjust the Uncore frequency as well. For example, the Dell BIOS contains the feature Uncore Frequency with the options Dynamic and Maximum.

If the option Maximum is selected, the Uncore frequency runs at the rated frequency. The Uncore within the microarchitecture (Haswell) runs at 3.0 GHz. It runs at 2.7 GHz in the E5-2600 v4 (Broadwell) microarchitecture. If the option Dynamic is selected, the Uncore attempts to operate at a similar frequency as the fastest (throttled) core.

C-State Selection

An accurate prediction of sleep length is required to select the optimal C-State. Each C-State has a minimum idle period to be cost-effective. This is the target residency. The wake-up latency is an estimation of time necessary to return to the C0 state. The trade-off is made between power savings and wake-up latency. Deeper C-States save more power, and at least C3 is necessary for additional Turbo Boost performance, but requires longer exit time to restore the state.

Predicting a shorter period leads to selecting a shallow C-State, while a deeper C-State would be more profitable, energy-wise.

Conversely, predicting a longer sleep time might result in selecting the C6 state, adding unnecessary state restart latency to the interrupt process time. Intel does not provide residency and restart latency statistics of newer microarchitectures. The most recent statistics provided by Intel are from the E5-2600 v1 (Sandy Bridge) microarchitecture.

C-STATE	RESIDENCY	WAKE-UP LATENCY
C0	ACTIVE	ACTIVE
C1	1 μs	1 μs
C3	106 μs	80 μs
C6	345 μs	104 μs

Table 18: E5-2600 v1 C-State Residency and Wake-Up Latency

According to the academic paper *Experimental Evaluation of Speed Scaling Systems* E5-2600 v4 (Broadwell) has the following residency thresholds and restart latencies:

C-STATE	RESIDENCY	WAKE-UP LATENCY
C0	ACTIVE	ACTIVE
C1	1 μs	2 μs
C1E	20 μs	10 μs
C3	100 μs	40 μs
C6	400 μs	133 μs

Table 19: E5-2600 v4 C-State Residency and Wake-Up Latency

The restart latency states the time it takes for the core to return to the operating state. The C3 or C6-State flush their cache, you can expect additional latency due to cache misses.

Intel Turbo Boost Technology

Intel Nehalem microarchitecture introduced Intel Turbo Boost Technology. Turbo Boost can be seen as dynamic (supported) overclocking. The CPU package is allowed to operate at a particular temperature to guarantee consistent performance. If the CPU package exceeds the Turbo Boost thermal threshold, it reduces the voltage and frequency of individual cores or other components.

Most CPU packages are not 100% utilized all of the time. Some VMs are processing data while other VMs are idling. Some instructions retrieve their data from the cache while waiting on retrieval from disk. This dynamic behaviour and the increased core count provide an excellent basis for a more dynamic distribution of frequency and voltage amongst the cores within a CPU package (E5-2600 v3 and newer).

The ability of Turbo Boost is highly dependent on the level of energy savings of inactive cores. When cores are idle, they do not consume as much power as active cores. In combination with the OS, the CPU packages place individual cores in lower P-States or C-States. The reduction of power consumption results in thermal headroom allowing Turbo Boost to increase the voltage of active cores. It dynamically distributes frequency where it is needed the most.

Please note that the High Performance power management policies restrict the CPU package from using P- and C-States. If either BIOS or vSphere power management policies are set to High Performance, Turbo Boost cannot provide the performance boost described in the next paragraphs.

Turbo Boost Basics

A CPU package has a specified nominal frequency. For example, the E5-2630 v4 has ten cores, each running at a nominal frequency of 2.20 GHz. The *Thermal Design Power* (TDP) value provides some insights in the power consumption of the CPU. Please note that the TDP value indicates how much heat the cooling system needs to dissipate to avoid the CPU exceeding its thermal envelope (maximum temperature). As the TDP indicates an amount of energy per time unit, the unit Watt is used. It does not indicate how much power the CPU actually uses. Although Intel does not provide these specifications, it is quoted by many sources that the peak power is approximately 1.5 times the TDP rating. The TDP value of the E5-2630 v4 is 85 Watts.

The CPU has a limit on the current consumption, the power consumption and the temperature of the processor. Depending on the activity of the cores, and the instructions they process, Turbo Boost decides whether to provide more frequency and voltage to particular active cores.

E5-2600 v1 (Sandy Bridge) introduced Turbo Boost 2.0. It focuses on the overall thermal temperature of the CPU package to decide whether to increase or decrease the power. The CPU package sustains Turbo Boost as long as it is operating within its thermal limit. The level of effectiveness of the cooling system impacts the duration of the Turbo Boost. The more heat extracted from the core, the more time it can run at the increased frequencies. Takes this into account when configuring fan speed in the BIOS.

Turbo Bins

Turbo Boost dynamically increases until the upper limit is reached. Frequency increase occurs in predefined deltas, referred to as *Turbo Bins*. In all current CPUs, this is done at increments of the *Front Side Bus Clock* (BCLCK) speed of 100 MHz (Nehalem is the only one that uses a 133 MHz delta).

Turbo Boost is indicated as x/x/x for a CPU with three cores. The first number shows the number of possible turbo bins when no cores in the package are not in a deep C-State.

Each following number assumes one additional core is in deep C-State and notes the turbo bins for the remaining cores. The turbo mode notation for the 2630 v4 is 2/2/2/3/4/5/6/7/9/9. The numbers 2 indicates that all ten cores are active. Turbo Boost can increase the frequency of all cores to 2.4 GHz. That is (2x 100) 200 MHz above the rated frequency of 2.20 GHz.

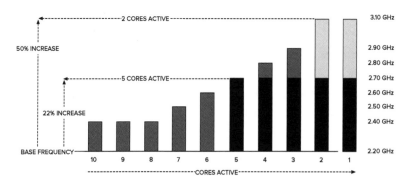

Figure 101: Turbo Bins Intel Xeon E5-2930 V4

If five cores are active, these five cores can operate at 2.70 GHz (2200 + (5 x 100). That is a 22% performance increase. If only two cores are active, both cores can operate at 3.10 GHz. The two cores get an extra 50% of their rated frequency. When reviewing the popular CPU packages, notice the difference in Turbo Boost frequency range.

MODEL (V4)	CORE COUNT	CLOCK CYCLE	MAX. TURBO	FREQUENCY INCREASE	TDP
E5-2650	12	2.2 GHz	2.9 GHz	31%	105W
E5-2660	14	2.0 GHz	3.2 GHz	60%	105W
E5-2680	14	2.4 GHz	3.3 GHz	38%	120W
E5-2690	14	2.6 GHz	3.5 GHz	34%	135W
E5-2683	16	2.1 GHz	3.0 GHz	42%	120W
E5-2695	18	2.1 GHz	3.3 GHz	57%	120W
E5-2697	18	2.3 GHz	3.6 GHz	56%	145W
E5-2697A	16	2.6 GHz	3.6 GHz	38%	145W
E5-2698	20	2.2 GHz	3.6 GHz	63%	135W
E5-2699	22	2.2 GHz	3.6 GHz	63%	145W
E5-2699A	22	2.4 GHz	3.6 GHz	50%	145W

Table 20: Turbo Boost Specifics

We recommend taking the Turbo Boost frequency into account when researching new server hardware.

Measure Turbo Mode Effect

The Power Usage screen in esxtop show the C-States and P-States of the cores. Both C- and P-States are numbered consecutively from 0. P0 is the full speed + turbo bins. Please note that P0 doesn't show the many Turbo Bins that are available due to overall TDP and number of deep idling sibling cores.

P1 is the base speed; Pn indicates the remaining P-States. C0 state is the active state, C1 can be C1 or C1E, depending if C1E is enabled in the BIOS. The deeper C-States don't match the Intel C-State numbering (it doesn't even match the ACPI c-state numbering).

As mentioned before, Intel C-States are numbered as C0, C1, C3 and C6. Esxtop presents the numbers C0, C1, C2, and C3. If the BIOS only exposes one deep state, this may be shown as C0, C1, and C2. You can verify the deep C-States in VSI as /power/pcpu/*/cstate/2. In ESXi 6.5 the Power Usage screen of esxtop provides insight about the use of Turbo Boost.

The APERF/MPERF ratio indicates whether Turbo Boost is active. MPERF stands for *Maximum Performance Frequency Clock Count*, where APERF stands for *Actual Performance Frequency Clock Count*. Both MPERF and APERF are *Model-Specific Registers* (MSR) that are part of the CPU and are used to track and coordinate P-States. These MSRs are per logical process and monitor the performance while not idle. The counter ignores the C1 (HLT) state, as this results in a 0 MHz frequency. So simply put, the APERF/MPERF ratio is providing insights about how fast the processor is running while it is in C0-state.

The APERF/MPERF ratio is a frequency ratio. It does not show an exact MHz value of the CPU operating speed. Instead, it indicates the performance of the CPU during the measured interval. If the %A/MPERF column shows a value less than 100, the CPU is operating at a lower frequency than its nominal frequency. Please check the setting in the BIOS. If this number is significantly lower than 100 while experiencing high load, the P-State option might be configured incorrectly.

If the column shows a value of 100, it is running at its rated (base) frequency, and if the column shows a value above 100, then the core is leveraging Turbo Boost. The APERF/MPERF ratio shown in esxtop is in real-time.

CPU	%USED	%UTIL	%C0	%C1	%C2	%P0	%P1	%P2	%P3	%P4	%P5	%P6	%P7	%P8	%P9	%P10	%P11	%A/MPERF
0	0.0	0.1	0	2	98	100	0	0	0	0	0	0	0	0	0	0	0	125.6
1	130.8	100.0	100	0	0	100	0	0	0	0	0	0	0	0	0	0	0	128.6
2	0.0	0.0	0	9	91	100	0	0	0	0	0	0	0	0	0	0	0	129.2
3	127.1	100.0	100	0	0	100	0	0	0	0	0	0	0	0	0	0	0	128.6
4	59.6	100.0	100	0	0	100	0	0	0	0	0	0	0	0	0	0	0	128.6
5	65.7	100.0	100	0	0	100	0	0	0	0	0	0	0	0	0	0	0	128.6
6	0.0	0.0	0	9	91	21	0	0	0	0	0	0	0	0	0	0	79	116.3

Figure 102: APERF/MPERF Counter in Esxtop

In the screenshot above, the Power Usage screen of esxtop is expanded with the %A/MPERF column and it provides quite some interesting information.

```
Esxtop > P (Power Usage) > F (Field Order) > F %APERF/MPERF =
percentage of APERF to MPERF ratio.
```

For example, a four vCPU VM is running an application that consumes each CPU for 40 to 70%.

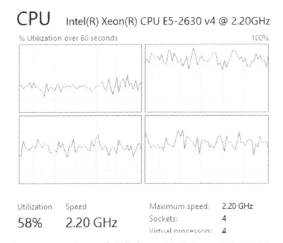

Figure 103: Microsoft Windows 2012 Guest OS CPU Consumption

The %UTIL column in esxtop shows the percentage of time that the pCPU was active. To be precise, it is the time the idle thread was not running on the pCPU, this is based on the TSC *(Time Stamp Counter)*.

Nehalem introduced a newer TSC that is called an invariant TSC. It will run at a constant rate in all P- and C-States. The OS can use the TSC for wall clock and high precision timer services. TSC reads are extremely efficient and do not incur the overhead associated with interrupt or tick driven timekeeping.

As described in an earlier chapter, the metric %USED reflects the quality of the physical resource. To be precise, it uses the *Non-Halted Core Cycles* (NHCC) counter. As a result, Turbo Boost activity is also reflected in the %USED metric. In this scenario (displayed by the figure above), CPU1 is utilized for 57.5% by the vCPU of the VM, but the quality of the CPU time is above normal operation, i.e. 70.9%. A lower value in %USED compared to the %UTIL value means that either the HT and/or frequency scaling is active. The %A/MPERF ratio/value helps you to identify whether the CPU is operating in Turbo Boost and thus the VM is running on a faster CPU.

The %A/MPERF indicates that the Turbo effect is 126.2%, which comes close to the 23% difference between the %USED and %UTIL value.

Energy Efficient Turbo

Hardware vendor power management focuses on energy efficiencies. Turbo Boost technology tends to hurt energy efficiency, especially when it selects a frequency that provides a little performance increase. *Energy Efficient Turbo* (EET) only allows for a particular Turbo Boost frequency when the energy used is proportional to the performance obtained. It takes memory performance (memory stalls) into account and long-term activity of cores. EET is managed by the hardware and measures stall data at a rate that may be insufficient to make a proper assessment of the dynamic workload behavior of the various VMs consuming the CPU cores.

We recommend not using Energy Efficient Turbo if you plan to leverage the full capabilities of the CPU package.

Use vSphere Host Power Management

We recommend using vSphere Power Management and not use any vendor specific BIOS power management profiles. It is necessary to enable all power management features such as C-States, P-States and Turbo Boost Technology in the BIOS, regardless of which host power management policy you select in vSphere. The reason is that we want vSphere to manage these features.

The benefit of having vSphere control the power management abilities of the CPU package, is that these settings can be programmatically modified without the need of a host reboot. It allows for creating a power management baseline that can be adjusted on the fly. This is especially valuable when dealing with large clusters. We know of one vSphere environment that changes the vSphere Power Management during a power outage. While running on the UPS, the ESXi servers are switched to a low power policy to reduce power consumption and lengthen the window to safely power down the VMs. Levering PowerCLI, they programmatically change the nature of power consumption of the cluster.

As a policy is applied instantly and requires no reboot, it also allows for easier troubleshooting of power management related issues.

Please note that some BIOS versions enable PCI Power Management if the power management setting is not configured with the High Performance setting. This can lead to inconsistent behavior of PCIe cards (Flash devices, 10 GbE cards) and sometimes even frozen conditions. Ensure PCI Power Management is disabled after selecting a custom power management setting in the BIOS or talk to the vendor if they don't include it as a separate option.

Deterministic Frequency

If you are designing an environment that runs low-latency applications, or workloads that cannot endure any inconsistent responsiveness, we recommend using the High Performance policy. This also applies when using vSAN.

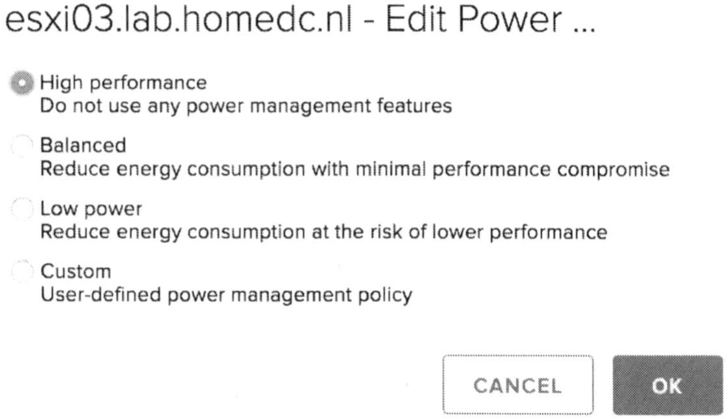

esxi03.lab.homedc.nl - Edit Power ...

⦿ High performance
Do not use any power management features

○ Balanced
Reduce energy consumption with minimal performance compromise

○ Low power
Reduce energy consumption at the risk of lower performance

○ Custom
User-defined power management policy

CANCEL   OK

Figure 104: vSphere Power Management Policy

If **absolute** consistency is necessary, we recommended disabling Turbo Boost Technology as well. Again, we recommend enabling this feature in the BIOS, but programmatically adjusting this in vSphere. Select the Custom user-defined power management policy in vSphere and select the Advanced System settings and set the value to 99 of the Power.MaxFreqPCT setting.

> **Please note that the custom policy defaults to Balanced. If you need to disable TB, but also want to set MinFreqPct to 99, UseCStates to False.**

Balanced Power Management Policy

By default, the power policy in ESXi 6.5 is set to Balanced. Please note, that although this policy has a similar name to BIOS power management policies, it should not be compared with the BIOS policy.

The Balanced policy is optimized to provide the performance the workload requires while leveraging the P- and C-States efficiently. It is important to know that the BIOS version is aimed mostly towards saving power, while the vSphere version is aimed to provide performance first, energy saving second.

The compelling part is that this policy turns your ESXi host in a flexible powerhouse, dynamically distributing frequency where it is needed the most. By leveraging the power and idle states, it can free up valuable TDP headroom. It can provide CPU cores, that run at a higher frequency than their nominal frequency, to active workloads. The drawback is that it does not necessarily provide a consistent performance pattern if the overall workload fluctuates heavily.

To spin this positively, sometimes you experience good performance and sometimes you experience stellar performance. As beauty is in the eye of the beholder, this behavior can be interpreted incorrect. Good performance is sometimes seen as sub-par if stellar performance is considered the baseline. Having a consistent performance baseline would make more sense if you cannot interpret the performance baseline in the correct context.

To be clear, this is not a definitive performance test, as the EULA is strict about publishing performance test results! Therefore, we urge you to run your own tests. Maybe they provide a better improvement, maybe they provide less benefit. To give you a better idea what's possible, we performed a test of a four vCPU VM running DVD Store 3.0 on the dual Intel Xeon 2930 v4 system. The following table contains five random test results. We performed each test on the host with vSphere High Performance power management policy enabled and then continued to run the same test with Balanced policy enabled. We ran each pair of tests more than 50 times to have a better sample size. The numbers presented are the number of orders completed in a 5-minute test time period.

HIGH PERFORMANCE	BALANCED	INCREASE OF ORDERS
26043	28361	2318
25853	28529	2676
26190	28222	2032
25923	28125	2202
25820	28085	2265

Table 21: DVD Store 3.0 Test Results Difference of HPM Policies

On average, using the Balanced power management policy resulted in 2298 more orders completed in each 5-minute test run. During the test, the Power Usage screen of esxtop showed the %A/MPERF stats and the percentage of votes the CPU package from the VMkernel received for a particular state for a particular core.

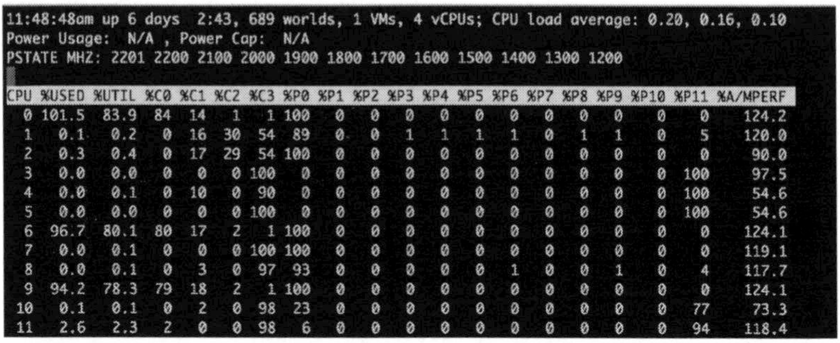

```
11:48:48am up 6 days  2:43, 689 worlds, 1 VMs, 4 vCPUs; CPU load average: 0.20, 0.16, 0.10
Power Usage:  N/A , Power Cap:  N/A
PSTATE MHZ: 2201 2200 2100 2000 1900 1800 1700 1600 1500 1400 1300 1200

CPU %USED %UTIL %C0 %C1 %C2 %C3 %P0 %P1 %P2 %P3 %P4 %P5 %P6 %P7 %P8 %P9 %P10 %P11 %A/MPERF
  0 101.5  83.9  84  14   1   1 100   0   0   0   0   0   0   0   0   0    0    0   124.2
  1   0.1   0.2   0  16  30  54  89   0   0   1   1   1   1   0   1   1    0    5   120.0
  2   0.3   0.4   0  17  29  54 100   0   0   0   0   0   0   0   0   0    0    0    90.0
  3   0.0   0.0   0   0   0 100   0   0   0   0   0   0   0   0   0   0    0  100    97.5
  4   0.0   0.1   0  10   0  90   0   0   0   0   0   0   0   0   0   0    0  100    54.6
  5   0.0   0.0   0   0   0 100   0   0   0   0   0   0   0   0   0   0    0  100    54.6
  6  96.7  80.1  80  17   2   1 100   0   0   0   0   0   0   0   0   0    0    0   124.1
  7   0.0   0.1   0   0   0 100 100   0   0   0   0   0   0   0   0   0    0    0   119.1
  8   0.0   0.1   0   3   0  97  93   0   0   0   0   1   0   1   0   1    0    4   117.7
  9  94.2  78.3  79  18   2   1 100   0   0   0   0   0   0   0   0   0    0    0   124.1
 10   0.1   0.1   0   2   0  98  23   0   0   0   0   0   0   0   0   0    0   77    73.3
 11   2.6   2.3   2   0   0  98   6   0   0   0   0   0   0   0   0   0    0   94   118.4
```

Figure 105: Esxtop Power Usage Screen During a Test Run

Interestingly enough, the VMkernel can request a certain P-State but the CPU package does not have to apply this state to the core. If esxtop displays a value, it means that the vote happened at least once during the sample period. Not necessarily for the whole esxtop sample time. To illustrate this point, a slide from Intel presented shows how fast an E5-2600 v3 (Haswell) CPU can exit and enter states.

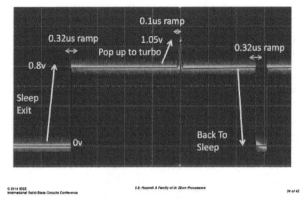

Figure 106: Intel Example of Turbo Mode Ramp-Up Duration

Intel states the CPU needs 0.32 microseconds to exit sleep state and 0.1 microseconds to ramp up to turbo frequencies. Using the 0.1-microsecond example, you could have 10,000,000 changes in frequency during the shortest sample period of esxtop (2 seconds). The following screenshot shows the ESXi host free from running any workload while configured with the default power policy (Balanced). Due to the absence of load, most pCPUs are in a deeper C-State and the most economic P-State (P11).

CPU	%USED	%UTIL	%C0	%C1	%C2	%P0	%P1	%P2	%P3	%P4	%P5	%P6	%P7	%P8	%P9	%P10	%P11
0	0.0	0.1	0	1	99	1	0	0	0	0	0	0	0	0	0	0	99
1	0.0	0.0	0	0	100	35	0	0	0	0	0	0	0	0	0	0	65
2	0.0	0.1	0	9	91	49	0	0	0	0	0	0	0	0	0	0	51
3	0.0	0.0	0	3	97	37	0	0	0	0	0	0	0	0	0	0	63
4	0.0	0.0	0	0	100	0	0	0	0	0	0	0	0	0	0	0	100
5	0.0	0.0	0	0	100	8	0	0	0	0	0	0	0	0	0	0	92
6	0.0	0.0	0	4	96	44	0	0	0	0	0	0	0	0	0	0	56
7	0.0	0.0	0	0	100	0	0	0	0	0	0	0	0	0	0	0	100

Figure 107: C-State and P-State Utilization (Balanced HPM Policy)

Let's switch over to the High Performance policy. Immediately all pCPUs exit C2 state and all pCPUs vote for 100% P0-state. P0 is the state in which the pCPU runs at least at the nominal frequency, maybe leveraging Turbo Boost Technology as well.

CPU	%USED	%UTIL	%C0	%C1	%C2	%P0	%P1	%P2	%P3	%P4	%P5	%P6	%P7	%P8	%P9	%P10	%P11
0	0.0	0.2	0	100	0	100	0	0	0	0	0	0	0	0	0	0	0
1	0.5	0.7	1	99	0	100	0	0	0	0	0	0	0	0	0	0	0
2	0.2	0.5	1	99	0	100	0	0	0	0	0	0	0	0	0	0	0
3	0.0	0.2	0	100	0	100	0	0	0	0	0	0	0	0	0	0	0
4	0.2	0.4	0	100	0	100	0	0	0	0	0	0	0	0	0	0	0
5	0.0	0.2	0	100	0	100	0	0	0	0	0	0	0	0	0	0	0
6	0.0	0.2	0	100	0	100	0	0	0	0	0	0	0	0	0	0	0
7	0.1	0.3	0	100	0	100	0	0	0	0	0	0	0	0	0	0	0
8	0.3	0.5	1	99	0	100	0	0	0	0	0	0	0	0	0	0	0
9	0.1	0.3	0	100	0	100	0	0	0	0	0	0	0	0	0	0	0
10	6.5	6.2	6	94	0	100	0	0	0	0	0	0	0	0	0	0	0

Figure 108: C-State and P-State Utilization (High-Performance HPM Policy)

Although all pCPUs vote for 100% P0-State, some pCPUs are in C1-state. The C1-state indicates that the CPU is in a HLT state. In a HLT state, the CPU is not executing any instructions. This does not lead to additional latency as it can return to the C0-State (executing) incredibly fast. The VSI Shell provides incredibly detailed insights: run the command vsish -e cat /power/pcpu/<pcpunumber>pstate/<p-statenumber>.

For example: vsish -e cat /power/pcpu/2/pstate/10 provides the stats of the P-State 10 of pCPU2. One of the interesting stats is the total resident time. This command lists the number of microseconds the VMkernel voted for having the pCPU in the P10 State. It shows the stats since the boot of the ESXi host.

```
[root@esxi03:~] vsish -e cat /power/pcpu/2/pstate/2
P-state {
    Frequency: 2100 MHz
    Power: 79 W
    Bus Latency: 10 usec
    CPU Latency: 10 usec
    Dependent PCPUs:none
    Coordination Type:: 254 -> HW_ALL
    Total Resident Time: 0 usec
    Available: 1
}
[root@esxi03:~] vsish -e cat /power/pcpu/2/pstate/10
P-state {
    Frequency: 1300 MHz
    Power: 45 W
    Bus Latency: 10 usec
    CPU Latency: 10 usec
    Dependent PCPUs:none
    Coordination Type:: 254 -> HW_ALL
    Total Resident Time: 0 usec
    Available: 1
}
[root@esxi03:~]
```

Figure 109: VMkernel P-State pCPU2 Overview

Rethink Your Power Management Strategy

Power management must be the topic that every blog covers once during its lifetime. Mostly the recommendation is set to the power management policy to High Performance in the BIOS as it provides the best performance and consistent response times. The debate whether to choose vSphere HPM over the BIOS, and set it to High Performance in vSphere, is usually met with a set-and-forget attitude. It doesn't matter where it is configured, it will be set once, and we will not reconsider this. And actually, this is quite understandable.

However, we firmly believe that a lot of workloads in the enterprise space do not belong to the latency-sensitive category. Not that many workloads warrant the non-compromising BIOS High Performance power management profile.

vSphere allows you to change power management profiles on-the-fly, without a reboot! Therefore, you can start by using the High Performance policy and test the impact of the Balanced policy by changing the setting when an appropriate time slot appears.

Please note that power management settings are designed to cope with real life scenarios, i.e. multiple VMs running fluctuating workloads. Testing the impact of various power management policies on an idle system with one VM blasting a static workload is a scenario that does not provide you real insight. As always, try to use workload that you run on a daily basis in your datacenter.

P2

MEMORY RESOURCES

PROLOGUE

After more than a decade of unfulfilled promises, radical new memory technologies and system-level architectures are finally reaching production. Within just the past few months, Intel started shipping 3D XPoint memory, and HP unveiled a working 160-TB prototype of The Machine. Such advances are creating exciting opportunities for researchers, architects, and developers to innovate and rethink conventional hardware and software designs.

While it is too early to predict exactly how things will unfold, several trends seem clear. Compared to DRAM, emerging memory technologies tend to be denser and less expensive, enabling much larger configurations. Like DRAM, they are byte addressable with low latency. Like flash, they are non-volatile, with asymmetric costs for reads and writes, and some limitations on durability.

These properties are disruptive to earlier designs optimized around different tradeoffs. Memory-centric processing that assumes 'big data' will always remain resident becomes feasible. Disaggregated architectures become attractive, such as memory blades providing flexible pools of memory for multiple hosts via high-speed interconnects. Storage stacks can use persistent load/store operations instead of traditional block reads/writes, but must carefully flush data from volatile on-die caches using recently-introduced CPU instructions for consistency. Software overheads that were previous hidden by slower media are no longer acceptable.

Despite dreams of simplified systems where a single memory type replaces both DRAM and persistent storage, it seems more likely that sophisticated management of a complex memory hierarchy will become increasingly important. Hypervisors and the OS can exploit locality transparently via adaptive caching and tiering.

Virtualization can also abstract away many differences, as with existing demand-paged virtual memory and virtualized NUMA topologies. But system software should still provide explicit controls and performance monitoring to help high-performance applications optimize their own behavior.

Before long, your vSphere cluster may contain huge DRS memory resource pools that you can carve up flexibly for both VM memory and persistent storage. Disaggregated memory could make vMotion effectively instantaneous, with no need for bulk data transfer. Users may be more concerned about physical attacks on VM memory, no longer exotic when memory is non-volatile.

In any case, I am confident that engineers, architects, and admins will have their hands full modeling and optimizing challenging memory system tradeoffs to ensure everything works smoothly.

Carl Waldspurger

Carl Waldspurger has a long record of innovation in systems software and resource management. As a consultant and technical advisor, he works closely with engineering and research teams on a range of topics including resource management, storage caching, security, and hardware support for processor-level QoS.

While at VMware, Carl led the design and implementation of processor scheduling and memory management for the ESX hypervisor, and was the architect for VMware's Distributed Resource Scheduler (DRS). Prior to VMware, he was a researcher at the DEC Systems Research Center. Carl holds a Ph.D. in computer science from MIT. He is active in the research community, has published numerous academic papers, and is an inventor with more than a hundred issued patents.

08

MEMORY ARCHITECTURE

Processor speeds and core counts are important factors when designing a new server platform. However, the memory subsystem can have equal or a greater impact on application performance than the processor speed.

ESXi 6.5 supports up to 12TB per server. With the possibility of creating high-density memory configurations, care must be taken when designing the ESXi host. The availability of DIMM slots does not automatically mean expandability without introducing performance consequences. Especially when you want to increase the existing memory capacity.

The CPU type and generation impacts the memory configuration. When deciding on a new server platform you get presented with a wide variety of options. A great example is the DIMM layout of today's most popular server hardware. The server boards of the Cisco UCS B200 M4, Dell PowerEdge 730 Gen 13, and HP Proliant DL380 Gen 9 servers all come equipped with dual processors and 24 memory slots (12 per CPU).

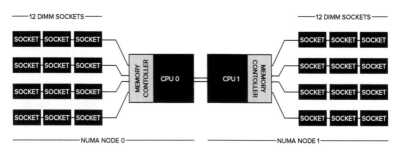

Figure 110: Memory Architecture Modern Server Systems

The Intel Xeon E5-2600 microarchitecture uses multiple onboard memory controllers to provide multi-channel memory architecture. Multi-channel configurations, DIMM ranking, DIMM types, memory frequency and DIMM placement are critical considerations when designing your new server platform. If these factors are not accounted for, future scalability may be impeded and/or the memory subsystem will likely not perform as expected.

Dual In-Line Memory Module

Today's CPU microarchitectures contain Integrated Memory Controllers. The memory controller connects through a channel to the DIMMs. DIMM stands for *Dual In-line Memory Module* and it contains memory modules that provide 64 bits of data. If *Error Checking and Correction* (ECC) memory is used the data-width is 72-bits per memory module, 64-bits for data + 8 bits of ECC data.

Dual In-line refers to pins on both side of the module. A DDR3 DIMM is a 240-pin dual in-line memory module. A DDR4 DIMM contains 288 pins. This design results in having 144 pins at the front side and 144 pins at the backside.

Some servers use *Small Outline DIMMs* (SO-DIMM). A DDR3 SO-DIMM has 204 pins. The DDR4 equivalent sports 260 pins. Aside from the pin difference, the module packaging of DDR4 deviates from the DDR3 packaging. The key notch is placed at a different location on the *Printed Circuit Board* (PCB). In addition, the pin arrangement is different. Towards the middle of the PCB, there is a change gradient, making some pins longer. From pin 35, the length per pin increases (Detail B). This design results in less resistance when installing the DIMM module. This avoids damaging the product.

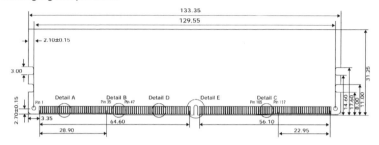

Figure 111: DDR4 Module Packaging

Standard DDR3 DIMMs operate at 1.5 volts. Low-voltage DDR3 DIMMs operate at 1.35 volts. DDR4 modules require 1.2 volts. Low voltage DDR4 is not yet announced but it is estimated to operate at 1.05 volts.

Memory Organization

There are many different configurations of a DIMM, yet they still provide the same capacity. For example, a 32 GB ECC DIMM is available with the following specifications:

- 32 GB - 2Rx4 DDR4 RDIMM PC4-19200 2400 MHz
- 32 GB - 2Rx4 DDR4 LRDIMM PC4-19200 2400 MHz
- 32 GB - 4Rx4 DDR4 LRDIMM PC4-17000 2133 MHz

The specs contain details about: the memory organization (2Rx4), the buffer availability (LRDIMM) and the speed (PC4-19200). All instrumental for designing a high performing platform while providing the memory capacity required. Let's start with taking a closer look at the memory organization.

Dynamic Random-Access Memory

A DIMM contains memory chips, to be more precise, *Dynamic Random-Access Memory* (DRAM) *Integrated Circuits* (IC). DRAM chips are arranged in ranks. Each rank is connected to the memory controller by address busses that carry clock, control and address signals. A 64-bit data bus transfers the data to and from the DRAM chips.

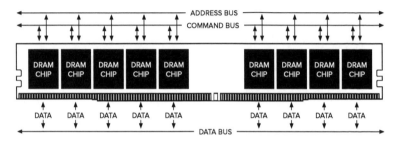

Figure 112: DRAM Chips on DIMM

A DIMM is organized in a rank arrangement of DRAM chips that are grouped together to provide 64 bits of data (not including the 8 bits of ECC data). All DRAM chips in a rank are controlled simultaneously by the same address, command, and chip select signals. As a result, they all respond to the same memory address, although each with a different segment of data corresponding to that memory address. Three configurations are possible.

- 1R - Single Rank
- 2R - Dual Ranks
- 4R - Quad Ranks

A memory channel can support a maximum number of ranks. Rank configuration impacts performance! Each DRAM chip provides a number of bits. Modern DRAM chips provide 4 bits (x4) or 8 bits (x8). For example, a single rank DIMM can contain eight DRAM chips, providing each 8 bits of data or it can contain sixteen DRAM chips providing each 4 bits of data.

If the DIMM is equipped with ECC, additional DRAM chips are used to store the ECC bits. This results in one extra DRAM chip in an 8-bit DRAM configuration, or two extra DRAM chips in a 4-bit DRAM configuration.

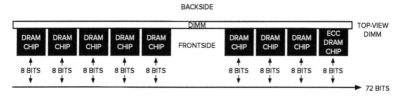

Figure 113: Single Rank DIMM Using 8-Bits DRAM Chips

If 4-bit DRAM chips are used, the DRAM chips organization could look as follows:

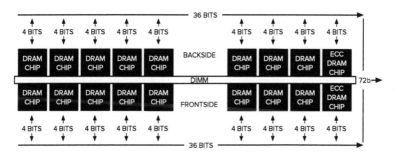

Figure 114: Single Rank DIMM Using 4-Bits DRAM Chips

A DRAM chip is responsible for storing data. Instead of creating one massive memory array inside a DRAM chip, a DRAM chips consists of multiple banks each containing memory. Distributing the memory array across multiple banks increases performance and reduces power consumption.

A bank is sub-divided into tens of subarrays called tiles. Each tile contains a set of cells that share circuitry that act as address decoders for the rows and columns of a cell. A bank is a 2D memory array of cells and is organized into rows and columns. A DRAM row is often referred to as a DRAM page.

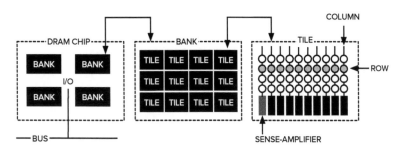

Figure 115: DRAM Organization

A memory address is partitioned by the memory controller and maps to different pieces of the DRAM:

- Column Address (C)
- Row Address (R)
- Bank Address (B)
- Bank Group Address (BG) (DDR4)

The memory controller selects the bank that contains the memory block. The memory controller retrieves the row and stores this in the sense amplifiers, commonly referred to as the row buffer. This row contains data blocks of multiple columns. Once stored in the buffer, the memory controller pinpoints the exact column where the data is stored and retrieves the data from the particular sense-amplifier.

Memory Geometry Notation

The configuration of the DIMM module is described with a memory geometry notation. A popular 16 GB DDR4 ECC DIMM module is available in the following configuration: 16 GB 2R x4. This data point informs us that this DIMM is dual-ranked (2R) and has a memory-width of 4 bits (x4) per DRAM chip. This is a common notation amongst server vendors.

When selecting a dual ranked 16GB ECC DIMM with a memory width of 4-bits a quick calculation shows us that a total of 36-DRAM chips are present on the DIMM.

To satisfy the 64-bit memory bus, each rank requires 16-DRAM chips (memory width/memory bus width). Two more DRAM chips are necessary to store the ECC bits. As a result, each DRAM chip stores up to 2048 bits.

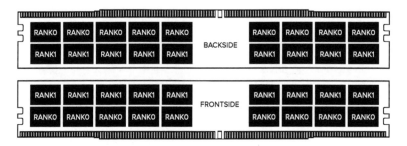

Figure 116: Dual-Ranked DIMM Containing 36 DRAM Chips

Chip Density

DDR3 DRAM chips are available with a memory width of x4 and x8. DDR4 is available with DRAM chip memory widths of x4, x8 and x16. Generally DIMMs with higher density chips, for example x8, are cheaper to produce than x4. This is because of the simple reason that fewer components cost less to produce.

There should be no performance difference between density configurations. Crucial Memory goes as far to compare it to the lug pattern on a wheel *"The wheels are going to work the same – the difference is in how they're made"*.

DDR3 has eight banks per DRAM chip. DDR4 increases the bank count to 16. This is interesting to know because the benefit of more banks is the avoidance of bank conflicts. DRAM requires that a DRAM page or bank is open before it is accessed. Once a DRAM page is read from a bank, it takes a minimum period of time before another page of the same bank can be opened. This is called the *Row-Cycle Time* (tRC).

A page miss can happen if the access to a different page is required before the tRC has completed. This introduces latency that is equal to the remaining portion of the tRC. This sequence is called a bank conflict.

The number of banks that are available impact the frequency at which bank conflicts occur. DDR organizes banks differently than DDR3. DDR4 is designed to support high-speed multi-core processors. It is expected to have the cores separately cycle through different banks. Therefore DDR4 contains bank groups. Instead of having eight independent banks per DRAM chip, DDR4 contains four bank groups with four banks in each group. DDR4 has significantly smaller row sizes than DDR3, 512 bits versus 2048 bits in DDR3 and as a result the DRAM chip can cycle through banks at a higher rate than DDR3 DRAM chips. This improvement helps DDR4 to achieve better overall latency even with a higher *Column Address Strobe* (CAS) latency.

Rank Support

As general-purpose server motherboards have a finite number of DIMM slots, quad-ranked DIMMs are the most effective way to achieve the highest memory capacity. Unfortunately, you are unable to fill up every DIMM slot in the system with quad rank DIMMs due to the chip-select limitation.

The Intel Xeon E5-2600 microarchitecture has a maximum number of logical ranks per each memory channel. As a result, this impacts DIMM configuration and possibly memory capacity. For example, if all three DIMMs are populated with quad-ranked DIMMs, a total of 12 ranks are active on the channel. This configuration exceeds the logical rank limit of the memory controller and as a result, it will not recognize the last DIMM.

The memory controller uses the address, command and data bus to communicate to all the available ranks on the DIMMs that are connected to the channel. To engage with all the ranks, a control operation (control line) is required to select one rank out of several connected ranks on the same channel. This control line is called a *Chip-Select* (CS). When data is required from that rank or is available for that rank, the chip select pin on the DIMM is kept in an active state for that particular rank.

The select pins of all the other ranks on the channel are kept in the inactive state ignoring all signals on the channel. Intel Xeon E5-2600 memory controllers support a maximum of eight logical ranks per channel.Please keep in mind that ranks can be accessed independently, they cannot be accessed simultaneously as the data lines are still shared between the ranks on a channel.

Registered and Unregistered DIMM

There are two primary types of DIMMs, registered and unregistered. *Unregistered DIMM* (UDIMM) are targeted towards the consumer market for systems that do not need to support large amounts of memory. An UDIMM allows the memory controller to address each memory chip individually and in parallel, this is often referred to as unbuffered access.

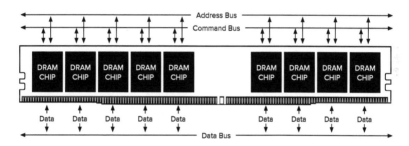

Figure 117: Unregistered DIMM

Each memory chip places a certain amount of capacitance on the memory channel and this weakens the signal. As a result, a limited number of memory chips (18 to be exact) can be used, while maintaining stable and consistent performance.

ESXi hosts running virtualized enterprise applications require a high concentration of memory. However, with these high concentrations, the connection between the memory controller and the DRAM chips can become overloaded, causing errors and delays in the flow of data. CPU speeds increase and therefore memory speeds have to increase too. Consequently, higher speeds of the memory bus leads to data flooding the channel faster, which results in the occurrence of more errors.

To increase scale and robustness, a register is placed between the DRAM chips and the memory controller. This register, sometimes referred to as a buffer, isolates the control lines between the memory controller and each DRAM chip. This reduces the electrical load, allowing the memory controller to address more DRAM chips, while maintaining stability. In total 72 DRAMs per DIMM are allowed. *Registered DIMMs* are referred to as RDIMMs.

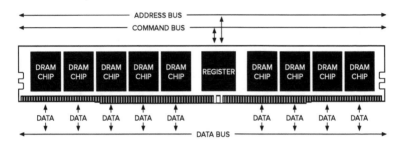

Figure 118: Registered DIMM

There is a slight performance difference between unregistered and registered DIMMs. The register buffers each read and write operation for one cycle between the bus and the DRAM chip. As a result, an operation on a registered DIMM is running one clock cycle behind the same operation done on an unregistered DIMM. This difference disappears if multiple DIMMs are installed per channel. As the electrical load increases on the channel, the memory controller adjusts the timing for address and control lines. Consequently, every command follows the 2N timing, resulting in an extra clock cycle for every command. In general, ESXi hosts are equipped with multiple DIMMs. In this configuration RDIMMs perform better due to their lower latency and higher bandwidth capabilities.

Load-Reduced DIMM

DDR3 memory introduced *Load Reduced DIMMs* (LRDIMMs). LRDIMMs operate under the same principle as a RDIMM as it buffers both the control and data lines from the DRAM chips. However, the register is replaced with *an Isolation Memory Buffer* (iMB).

Similar to RDIMMs the memory controller detects the iMB and not the individual DRAM chips. The introduction of a register allows the increase of DRAM chips from 18 to 72 per DIMM module. This provided the much-needed capacity required for modern day compute usage. The register only buffers the command and address bus. However, the data bus remains unbuffered and connects directly to the multiple ranks of DRAM, thus exposing a separate load per rank.

DDR3 LRDIMM solved this by having the memory buffer isolate the ranks from the host. As a result, this reduces the electrical load. The buffer abstracts the DRAM chips and especially the rank count, increasing performance and capacity. The abstraction of rank count is done via rank multiplication. This technique allows multiple physical ranks to appear as a single logical rank of larger size.

Rank multiplication requires LRDIMM aware memory controllers. Fortunately, with the introduction of LRDIMMs, memory controllers have been enhanced to improve the utilization of the LRDIMMs memory capacity.

Generally, memory controllers of systems prior to 2012 were 'rank unaware' when operating in rank multiplication mode. Due to the onboard register on the DIMM it was unaware whether the rank was on the same DIMM and it had to account for time to switch between DRAMs on the same bus. This resulted in lower back-to-back read transactions performance, sometimes up to a 25% performance penalty. Many tests have been done between RDIMMs and LRDIMMs operating at the same speed. In systems, with rank unaware memory controllers, you can experience a performance loss of 30% when comparing LRDIMMs and RDIMMs.

Systems after 2012 are referred to generation 2 DDR3 platforms and contain controllers that are aware of the physical ranks behind the data buffer. Allowing the memory controller to adjust the timings and providing better back-to-back reads and writes. With the introduction of a new memory controller of E5-2600 v2 (Ivy Bridge), the bandwidth drop was reduced and latency was slightly improved. Providing the same capacity, LRDIMMs operate at a higher transfer-rate.

The screenshot on the next page is published in the IDT DDR4 LRDIMM white paper and shows the bandwidth drops of LRDIMM and RDIMMs in the three Intel Xeon architectures. On the far right the E5-2600 v1 (Sandy Bridge) is shown, the middle graph shows the Intel E5-2600 v2 (Ivy Bridge) and the left is the E5-2600 v3 (Haswell). Source: IDT DDR4 LRDIMM whitepaper.

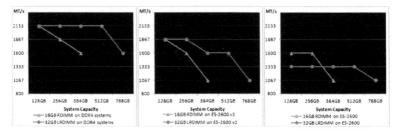

Figure 119: LRDIMM versus RDIMM Speed Improvement

The reason why latency is higher in LRDIMM architecture is due to the use of the memory buffer. The fastest way is always a direct line. With unbuffered DIMMs the memory controller communicates directly with the DRAM chip. With registered DIMMs the memory controller sends control and management messages to the register but still fetches data straight from the DRAM chip. DDR3 LRDIMMs use a memory buffer for all communication, including data. That means that the distance of data travel, often referred to as trace lengths is much longer.

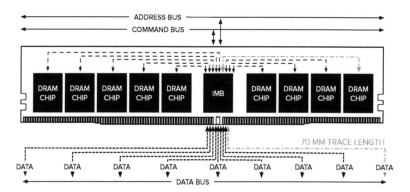

Figure 120: DDR3 LRDIMM - 70 mm Trace Length

DDR4 LRDIMM uses the same principle, but has a different architecture. Bidirectional *Data Buffers* (DB) close to the DRAM chips replace the iMB to reduce the I/O trace lengths.

A *Registered Clock Driver* (RCD) buffers and re-drives commands and addresses to the DRAMs. Both on the front and on the back of the PCB DRAM data loads are placed and share the same data bus. All four *Data Loads* (DL) are connected to a single bidirectional data buffer to produce a 4:1 electrical load reduction.

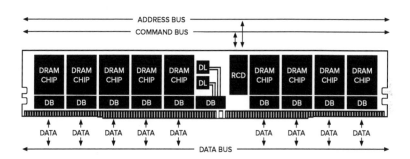

Figure 121: DDR4 LRDIMM

With DDR3 LRDIMMs, a trace length is up to 77 millimeters, DDR4 LRDIMM trace lengths are claimed to be between two and eight millimeters. DDR4 LRDIMMs trace lengths are comparable to DDR4 RDIMM trace lengths.

With DDR3 the added component latency of the memory buffer is approximately 2.5 ns when compared to an RDIMM, the component delay of DDR4 LRDIMM is approximately 1.2 ns. The reduction of trace lengths decreases the impact on signal integrity, which in turn allows DDR4 DIMMs to operate at a higher bandwidth when using a 3 *DIMMs Per Channel* (DPC) configuration. Anandtech.com compared the memory bandwidth of RDIMMs against LRDIMM in various DPC configurations

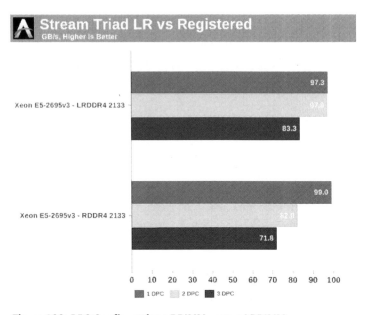

Figure 122: DPC Configurations RDIMM versus LRDIMM

In the article *Intel Xeon E5 Version 3: Up to 18 Haswell EP Cores* on Anandtech.com Johan De Gelas (@ServerAce) noted the following:

> **Registered DIMMs are slightly faster at 1 DPC, but LRDIMMs are clearly faster when you insert more than one DIMM per channel. We measured a 16% to 18% difference in performance. It's interesting to note that LRDIMMs are supposed to run at 1600 at 3DPC according to Intel's documentation, but our bandwidth measurement points to 1866.**

By using a buffer for each DRAM chip the latency overhead is thus significantly lower on DDR4 LRDIMMs. Compared to RDIMMs at the same speed with one DPC the latency overhead will be small, but as soon as more DIMMs per channel are used, the LRDIMMs actually offer a lower latency as they run at higher bus speeds.

Forward look: 3DS/TSV RDIMMs

Introduced in 2014, 3DS/TSV is aimed at high-density memory configurations. 3DS stands for three-dimensional stacking. The architecture uses a master-slave die design. Only the master die communicates with the memory controller.

The 3DS design moves away from the buffer-per-DRAM chip used in DDR4 LRDIMM. Each buffer consumes between four to seven watts and introduces a slight increase in latency. The maximum number of loading limits high-speed operations.

TSV stands for *Through Silicon Via* and allows the use of a vertical interconnect between the DRAM chips to stack one upon another. DRAM chips on traditional RDIMMs and LRDIMMs use wires for connection to the PCB. This new technology uses through-silicon vias. Simplified, they drilled a high number of (fine) holes in the DRAM chips and filled each hole with electrodes. This construction allows electrical connection through the DRAM chips vertically.

The increase of connection points compared to the few wires used in conventional DRAM allows for a better signal integrity. Each wire-bond is approximately ten times larger than one TSC bond, this allows for higher stacking capability and thus higher DRAM densities.

The bonds are much more energy efficient and due to the stacking method, it allows turning off DRAM chips that are not engaged. Powering down unnecessary hardware I/O circuitry provides a significant power consumption reduction.

Unfortunately, we could not verify it ourselves, but the memory vendor claims the power savings can reach up to 56% when the DRAM is idle (on standby) and ~30% when the DRAM is operating. The availability is limited at the time of writing the book, but it can be expected to see 3DS RDIMMs appear in server vendor catalogs soon.

Memory Protection

You can build the fastest server platform on earth, but the moment an error occurs all your efforts go to waste. There are multiple levels of memory protection. Protection usually decreases performance due to copying bits or increasing security checks. Selecting a memory protection technology depends on your *Reliability, Availability and Serviceability* (RAS) requirements. Therefore, these technologies are described briefly without providing any recommendation.

Memory leaks and memory corruption are two major forms of malfunctions that impact RAS. Poor build quality chips, faulty circuitry or heavy voltage fluctuations cause a lot of the previously mentioned problems. Interestingly enough, background radiation and cosmic radiation can also cause errors. Memory errors can be classified into two categories: hard errors and soft errors. A hard error is cause by a physical defect, and as a result the memory has to be replaced to avoid repeatable data corruption. A soft error is where the value of the data is wrong, but no physical defect has occurred.

An interesting read is the research paper *DRAM Errors in the Wild: A Large-Scale Field Study* by Bianca Schroeder of the University of Toronto and Eduardo Pinheiro, and Wolf-Dietrich Weber of Google. The paper studied the incidence and characteristics of DRAM errors in a large fleet of servers. Although most organizations do not operate an ESXi host fleet of similar size of Google's server fleet, memory density per ESXi server grew tremendously over the last few years. As such, most conclusions made by Google in 2008 can be of guidance for today's ESXi host fleet.

Memory Refresh Rate

Data is stored in a DRAM chip as a charge. A DRAM chips slowly leaks. Thus the data location loses charge over time. To make things worse, every time a data location is read it loses charge.

To maintain a healthy level of charge DRAM 'refresh reads' the data and writes the data back to that location. This process occurs within the DRAM chip itself. The data bus does not see the data. The only operation seen in the system is the memory controller instructing the DRAM to refresh.

The DDR standard defines the retention time. This is the time window in which a cell needs to be refreshed within a 64 ms interval. Most server vendors set the memory refresh rate to one. This memory refresh setting indicated how fast the memory refresh occurs with a refresh window. When increasing the memory refresh setting to two, you double the refresh rates within the retention time interval. This can impact high bandwidth workloads.

The double refresh rate mitigates the *Row Hammer error* (a security exploit). In short, Row Hammer is a vulnerability in which the same row of memory is repeatedly accessed (open, read, close). More details about Row Hammer can be found in the research paper titled *Flipping Bits in Memory Without Accessing Them: An Experimental Study of DRAM Disturbance Errors*. By reducing the refresh time from 64 ms to 32 ms, the potential window for executing Row Hammer is reduced.

DDR4 memory supports *Targeted Row Refresh* (TRR), which makes the DRAM chips more able to withstand the large number of malicious operations, however a recent test has shown DDR4 chips are not immune to Row Hammer completely. If you are concerned about this particular security exploit, enable double memory refresh. As always, it is recommended to test the behavior and verify the impact of settings on your application landscape.

A factor to take into account is the temperature of the memory. The temperature range for operation is from -40°C to +85°C. Temperature of the memory beyond +85°C is referred to as the extended temperature range. If this occurs the retention time is reduced to 32ms to account for higher leakage rates. Please take this dynamic setting into account when deciding to configure the fan speed of your server. DDR4 features *Temperature Controlled Refresh* (TCR) that dynamically changes the refresh rate based on the temperature.

Memory Patrol Scrubbing

Patrol Scrub is a variant of memory scrubbing, which cyclically reads each memory location to detect soft-errors. Once detected, the soft-errors are corrected with an error correcting code.

Typically, the memory is searched at a predetermined interval to prevent errors from accumulating. The system initializes Patrol Scrub during idle times, however in highly utilized systems this might not be possible. Some system vendors recommend turning off Patrol Scrubbing when running latency-sensitive workloads to avoid a negative performance impact. But they admit it is difficult to establish proof that Patrol Scrub has an effect on performance. Some systems allow configuring the Patrol Scrub Interval. A lower number equals a shorter time interval between scrubs and consume more memory bandwidth.

Cisco enables Patrol scrubbing by default and does not specifically go into detail whether to enable or disable the feature. In other enhanced memory configuration documentation, Patrol Scrub plays a notable role in its strategy to prevent data decay. Dell enables Patrol Scrub in the various Performance System Profile settings. When selecting the Dense Configuration optimized that is especially designed for high-density memory configurations the Extended scrub is selected. With the standard Patrol Scrub the entire memory configuration is scrubbed every 24 hours. The extended Patrol Scrub aims to search the entire memory array once every hour. HP recommends disabling this setting when tuning for low-latency applications.

When Patrol Scrub is disabled, the system checks for memory ECC errors when a memory address is read or written.

Error Checking and Correction Memory

ECC memory is essential in enterprise architectures. With the increased capacity and the speed at which memory operates, memory reliability is of the utmost concern.

DIMM Modules equipped with ECC contain an extra DRAM chip for each group of eight DRAM chips that store data. Contrary to Patrol Scrub this process is done outside the DRAM chip. The memory controller uses the extra DRAM chip to record parity or use it for error correcting code. When data is read and it is corrupted but correctable, the memory controller writes the corrected data back to the data location.

The reason why DIMMs with 4-bit DRAM chips cannot be mixed with DIMMs with 8-bit DRAM chips is that the structure influences the method from which ECC detects whether an error can or cannot be corrected.

The error correcting code provides *Single Bit Error Correction and Double Bit Error Detection* (SEC-DED). When a single bit goes bad, ECC can correct this by using the parity to reconstruct the data. When multiple bits are generating errors, ECC memory detects this but is not capable to correct this.

The trade-off for protection of data loss is cost, and also performance reduction. ECC can reduce memory performance by around 1 to 2% on some systems, depending on application and implementation. The performance loss is due to the additional time needed for ECC memory controllers to perform error checking. Please note that ECC memory cannot be used in a system containing non-ECC memory.

Advanced ECC

ECC provides single bit error correction and double bit error detection but some organizations would like to have a higher level of reliability. Advanced ECC detects and corrects single-bit memory errors, and corrects 4-bit memory errors within a DRAM chip (x4) and can detect errors of two DRAM chips as well. This capability is known as a *Single Device Data Correction* (SDDC). To provide this level of recoverability, two memory channels run in lockstep mode. In lockstep mode, the 64 bits are distributed between two memory channels. The SEC-DED capabilities of both DIMMs are combined to offer redundancy. If one DRAM chip fails, the data is reconstructed. Cisco does not explicitly state whether it uses advanced ECC\SDDC in it maximum-performance memory RAS config profile. The Dell memory performance profile Optimizer does not leverage Advanced ECC mode, but uses an independent channel configuration. HP enables Advanced ECC by default.

Sparing Mode

Various sparing techniques can be applied to provide memory redundancy. This approach impacts the overall memory capacity, as a portion of memory capacity must be reserved so that it can be used when other DIMM fails.

Rank sparing: One rank is held in reserve. If a rank fails, the data of the failing rank is transferred to the spare rank. Basic math tells us that if rank sparing is enabled on 4R DIMMs it consumes 25% of the total capacity, if rank sparring is enabled on 8R DIMMs 12.5% of total capacity is reserved.

DIMM sparing: One DIMM is held in reserve. If a DIMM fails, the data of that failing DIMM is transferred to the spare DIMM.

Sparing is a pro-active feature, it can only transfer data before It is too late. If memory errors are becoming too frequent the system decides to migrate the data. The server vendor sets these thresholds.

09

MEMORY SUBSYSTEM BANDWIDTH

It is important to understand that server memory is not a monolithic resource. It is possible to experience different performance-levels between identical DIMMs in a server. DIMM types and placement impact performance. Additionally, designing for capacity may result in choosing between capacity and performance.

Described in chapter 09, each rank introduces electrical load on the channel and with the introduction of each load it impacts the ability to maintain signal integrity (the ability to distinguish the actual data value 1 or 0). To safe guard data integrity, the memory speed drops when the maximum number of DIMMs is used in a channel. In certain configurations, DIMMs will run slower than their listed maximum speeds.

Before drilling deeper into performance reduction when using multiple DIMMs per channel, let's zoom into the relation between bandwidth and frequency.

DIMM Bandwidth

Often memory vendors use different terminology. Sometimes MHz is used to indicate bandwidth, other times transfer rate per seconds (MT/s). The metric that seems to resonate the most is the bandwidth per second in megabytes. E5-2600 v3 (Haswell) and newer require DDR4 DIMMs. Although the JEDEC standard list data rates up to 3200 MT/s, Cisco, Dell, HP and Fujitsu offer DDR4-2400 DIMMs in the popular server ranges at the time of writing this book.

DDR4 TYPE	MEMORY CLOCK	I/O BUS CLOCK	DATA RATE	MODULE	PEAK TRANSFER RATE
1866	233 MHz	933 MHz	1866 MT/s	PC4-14900	14933 MB/s
2133	266 MHz	1066 MHz	2133 MT/s	PC4-17000	17066 MB/s
2400	300 MHz	1200 MHz	2400 MT/s	PC4-19200	19200 MB/s
2666	333 MHz	1333 MHz	2666 MT/s	PC4-21300	21300 MB/s
3200	400 MHz	1600 MHz	3200 MT/s	PC4-25600	25600 MB/s

Table 22: DDR4 Standard Rates

Despite the fact that DDR4-2400 is often rated as 2400 MHz, it does not actually operate at 2400 MHz, but at 1200 MHz generating two operations per cycle. Before DDR, *Synchronous DRAM* (SDRAM) was the standard of computer memory (1970-2000). SDRAM issued an operation on the rising edge of a clock, thus the number operations equaled the frequency of the memory (Hertz).

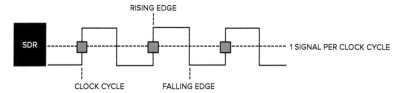

Figure 123: SDRAM Single Data Rate

Double Data Rate

DDR stands for *Double Data Rate* which means data is transferred on both the rising and falling edges of the clock signal. As a result, transfer rate is roughly twice the speed of the I/O bus clock. Therefore, Hertz/frequency and operation-rate are not synonyms anymore. Hertz equals frequency, while megatransfers per second simply indicates what memory does. But to be honest, in everyday life this is nitpicking.

If the I/O bus clock runs at 1200 MHz per second, the effective rate is 2400 mega transfers per second (MT/s). I.e. 1200 million **rising** edges per second and 1200 million **falling** edges per second of a clock signal running at 1200 MHz.

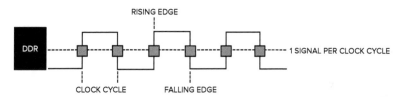

Figure 124: Double Data Rate

Interestingly enough, only data signals follow the DDR pattern. Address and control signal follow the SDRAM pattern, once per clock cycle on the rising edge of the clock cycle.

The transfer rate refers to the number of operations transferring data that occur in each second in the data-transfer channel. Transfer rates are generally indicated by MT/s or gigatransfers per second (GT/s). 1 MT/s is 10^6 or one million transfers per second. Similarly, 1 GT/s means 10^9, or one billion transfers per second.

Therefore, It is more interesting to calculate the theoretical bandwidth. The transfer rate itself does not specify the bit rate at which data is being transferred. To calculate the data transmission rate, one must multiply the transfer rate by the information channel width. The formula for a data transfer rate is:

```
Channel width (bits/transfer) × transfers/second = bits
transferred/second
```

This means that a 64-bit wide DDR4-2400 DIMM can achieve a maximum transfer rate of 19,200 MB/s. To arrive at 19,200 MB/s multiply the memory clock rate (300) by the bus clock multiplier (4) x data rate (2) = 2400 x number of bits transferred (64) = 153,600 bits / 8 (bits to bytes) = 19200 MB/s.

Two elements impact the effective memory bandwidth of a server, number of memory controllers in a CPU package and the number of DIMMs per channel.

Effective Memory Bandwidth

The CPU microarchitecture determines the maximum memory frequency. E5-2600 v4 (Broadwell) low core count microarchitecture supports up to 2133 MHz, medium and high core count configurations support up to 2400 MHz.

The difference between a ten core E5-2630 v4 and a twelve core E5-2650 v4 is not only two extra cores. It provides an additional 13% memory bandwidth. With the shared memory architecture, each core in the system will benefit from this.

The main reason why there is a difference in maximum frequency is due to the memory controller configuration of the CPU package. In low core count CPU packages, only one memory controller exists that is responsible for managing the four different channels. In medium and high core count CPU packages two memory controllers are present managing two channels each.

Memory Channel

E5-2600 v3 (Haswell) introduced quad-channel memory architecture. These multiple independent channels increase data transfer rates due to concurrent access of multiple DIMMs. When operating in in quad-channel mode, latency is reduced due to interleaving. The memory controller distributes the data amongst the DIMMs in an alternating pattern. This allows the memory controller to access each DIMM for smaller bits of data instead of accessing a single DIMM for the entire chunk of data. This way more bandwidth is available for accessing the same amount of data across channels instead of traversing a single channel when it stores all data in one DIMM.

> **Please note that interleaving memory across channels is not the same as the Node Interleaving setting of the BIOS. When enabling Node Interleaving the system breaks down the entire memory range of both CPUs into a single memory address space. It maps 4 KB addressable regions in a round robin fashion from each node. More info can be found in chapter 2. Channel interleaving is done within a NUMA node itself.**

> **Skylake microarchitecture is expected to move from a 4-channel 3 DPC configuration to a 6-channel 2 DPC configuration. Avoiding the 3 DPC penalty while increasing memory bandwidth by adding two channels.**

Memory Region

Memory channel interleaving has the largest impact on performance, particularly on throughput. To leverage memory channel interleaving optimally, the CPU creates regions.

The memory controller groups memory across the channels as much as possible. When creating a one DPC configuration, the CPU creates one region (Region 0) and interleaves the memory access.

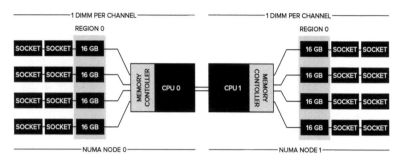

Figure 125: Memory Channel Interleaving Region 0

Quad-channel mode is activated when four identical DIMMs are put in quad-channel slots. When three matched DIMMs are used in Quad-channel CPU architectures, triple-channel is activated, when two identical DIMMs are used, the system will operate in dual-channel mode. This sequence occurs for each region! Our recommended is to design for balanced memory channel interleaving, maintain an equal distribution of DIMMs per region.

DIMM Per Channel Configuration

If the memory controller supports up to three DIMMs per channel, it results in a maximum of twelve DIMM slots per CPU package, however some vendors choose to provide eight DIMM slots per CPU package.

If one DIMM is used per channel, this configuration is commonly referred to as one DIMM Per Channel (1 DPC). Two DIMMs per channel (2 DPC) and if three DIMMs are used per channel, this configuration is referred to as 3 DPC.

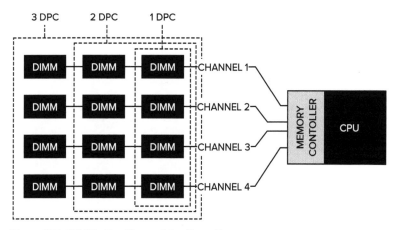

Figure 126: DIMMs Per Channel Configuration

Adding memory capacity can be done through higher density DIMMs (32 GB instead of 16 GB) or by using all available DIMM slots. Due to the maximum of eight physical ranks, the use of high density DIMMs are generally limited to two DIMMs per channel. Three 4R DIMMs would introduce twelve physical ranks on the channel, which exceeds the eight ranks per memory rank limit of currents systems. If 2R DIMMs are used, three DIMM slots can be used. However, when adding more DIMMs per channel, throughput per DIMM decreases.

DIMM Population Guidelines

Although the register of a RDIMM mitigates the control, address and clock signal problems, the multiple data loads of each DIMM on the data bus generates a lot of signals. At high frequencies, the number of DRAM chips can affect the quality of the signals. Maintaining signal integrity is important for correctness and as a result the data bus dictates DIMM population guidelines and their respective operation frequencies.

DIMM population guidelines create a challenge whether the capacity can be solved by using higher capacity DIMMs or taking the throughput hit as more capacity is only obtainable by populating all DIMM sockets.

Populating the channels with two DIMMs (2 DPC) does not drastically impact throughput. The system allows to DIMMs to run at native speed. However, it becomes interesting when choosing between 2 DPC and 3 DPC configurations.

RDIMM DPC Effective Transfer Rate

Popular server vendors offer DDR4 memory configuration with three possible values 1866, 2133 and 2400 MT/s for the transfer rate of the memory. If a two DIMMs per channel configuration is used, the memory maintains its rated transfer rate. If three DIMMs are used, the transfer rate of all DIMMs in that channel is downscaled to a lower rate. For example, installing 16 GB 2R 2400 MHz DIMMs in a 3 DPC configuration results in an effective transfer rate of 1866 MT/s.

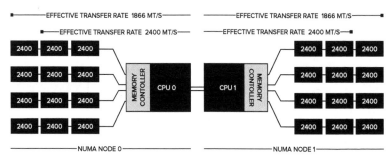

Figure 127: Effective Operation Rate of 3 DPC Configuration

The theoretical bandwidth drops from 19,200 MB/s to 14,933 MB/s. This is a 22% bandwidth reduction. Interestingly enough the effective frequency of a 3 DPC configuration remains the same for all three common DIMM transfer rates. Table 23 contains the results of Cisco, Dell, and HP documentation.

VENDOR	MT/s	RANK	GB	1DPC (MT/s)	2DPC (MT/s)	3DPC (MT/s)	PERFORMANCE REDUCTION
Cisco	2400	2R	32	2400	2400	1866	22%
Cisco	2400	1R	16	2400	2400	2133	11%
Dell	2400	1R\2R	All	2400	2400	1866	22%
HP	2400	1R	All	2400	2133	1866	11%/22%
HP	2400	2R	16	2400	2400	1866	22%
Cisco	2133	1R\2R	All	2133	2133	1866	12%
Dell	2133	1R\2R	All	2133	2133	1866	12%
HP	2133	1R\2R	All	2133	2133	1600	25%
Cisco	1866	1R\2R	All	1866	1866	1600	14%

Table 23: RDIMM DPC Performance

Source Cisco: UCS-b-series-blade-servers/b200m4-specsheet.pdf (Page 17)
Source Dell: www.dell.com/learn/us/en/2684/campaigns/memory-speeds-and-population
Source HP: c04375623.pdf (HPE Proliant DL360 Generation 9 (Gen9) (Page 57)
Source HP: HP DDR4 SmartMemory

At the time of writing the book Dell & HP do not offer 1866 MT/s DIMMs anymore. If maximum capacity (3 DPC) is needed without resorting to LRDIMMs, the most economical method is to equip the ESXi with 2133 MT/s DIMM as this result in the same effective transfer rate similar to 2400 MT/s.

LRDIMM DPC Effective Transfer Rate

To achieve more memory density, higher capacity DIMMs are required. As you increase capacity of memory modules, you are forced to increase the rank count of memory. For example, single rank has a maximum capacity of 16 GB while dual rank RDIMMs have a maximum capacity of 32GB per DIMM. LRDIMMs range from 32 GB to 128 GB (For historical reasons, at the time of writing this book, a 128 GB LRDIMM has a list price of 12,339 US Dollar).

Enterprise Memory

HPE 128GB (1x128GB) Octal Rank x4 DDR4-2400 CAS-20-18-18 Load Reduced Memory Kit

809208-B21

€ 11.616.00 * incl. BTW

Figure 128: Let's Have a Laugh In Five Years

Comparing 32 GB LRDIMMs and 32 GB Quad Rank RDIMMs it becomes apparent that LRDIMMs allow for higher capacity while retaining the bandwidth. For example, a Gen 12 Dell R730 contains two Intel Xeon E5 2600 CPU, allowing up to 3 TB of RAM. The system contains 24 DIMM sockets and allows up to 128 GB DDR4 DIMMs up to 2400 Mhz.

VENDOR	MT/s	RANK	GB	1DPC (MT/s)	2DPC (MT/s)	3DPC (MT/s)	PERFORMANCE REDUCTION
Cisco	2400	4R	All	2400	2400	2133	11%
Dell	2400	4R	All	2400	2400	2133	11%
HP	2400	All	All	2400	2400	2400	0%
Cisco	2133	4R	All	2133	2133	1866	11%
Dell	2133	1R\2R	All	2133	2133	1866	11%
HP	2133	2R\4R	All	2133	2133	1866	11%
Cisco	1866	4R	All	1866	1866	1866	0%

Table 24: LRDIMM Memory Transfer Rate of DPC Configuration

At the time of writing the book Dell & HP do not offer 1866 MHz DIMMs anymore. LRDIMMs frequency drops less when operating in a 3 DPC configuration. Most configurations drop 11% instead of the 22% experienced with RDIMM configurations. HPE Memory documentation states there is no frequency loss in 3 DPC. It is unclear how this is achieved. It's recommended to request additional information from the vendor during the purchase process.

DDR4 Bandwidth and CAS Timings

As described in the section *Dynamic Random-Access Memory* in chapter 8 the memory area of a memory bank inside a DRAM chip is made up of rows and columns. To access the data, the chip needs to be selected, then the row is selected, and after activating the row the column can be accessed. At this time, the actual read command is issued. From that particular moment to the moment the data is ready at the pin of the module, that is the CAS latency. It's not the same as load-to-use as that is the round-trip time measured from a CPU perspective.

CAS Latencies (CL) increase with each new generation of memory, but as mentioned before latency is a factor of clock speed as well as the CAS latency. Generally, a lower CL will be better, however, they are only better when using the same base clock. If you have faster memory, higher CL could end up better. When DDR3 was released it offered two speeds, 1066MHz CL7 and 1333 MHz CL8. Today servers are equipped with DDR3 1600 MHz CL9 memory and those servers are ready to be upgraded. DDR4 was released with 2133 MHz CL13. Today, major server vendors offer 2400 MHz @ CL17. To work out the unloaded latency is:

```
(CL/Frequency) * 2000.
```

This means that 1600 MHz CL9 provides an unloaded latency of 11.25ns, while 2400 MHz CL17 provides an unloaded latency of 14.16ns. Resulting in a performance drop of 25.9%. However, there is an interesting correlation with DDR4 bandwidth and CAS latency. Memory vendors offer DDR4 2800 @ CL 16. Using the same calculation 2800 MHz CL16 provides an unloaded latency of (16/2800) * 2000 = 11.42ns. Almost the same latency at DDR3 1600 MHz CL9! 2800 MHz CL14 provides an unloaded latency of 10ns, resulting in similarly loaded latencies while providing more than 75% more bandwidth.

Memory Module Installation Guidelines

DIMM types impact future expandability of the server. Due to the maximum number of ranks support per channel, care must be taken when initially designing the server spec of the server. In general performance is optimized when each channel is populated and identical. If a heterogeneous configuration is used, please apply the following population schemes:

- Do not mix different types of DIMMs. Mixing RDIMMs, LRDIMMs and TSV-RDIMMs is not supported.

- When mixing memory modules with different capacities, populate the sockets with memory modules with highest capacity first.

- DIMMs of different ranks can be used in the same channel, however, always populate the higher number rank DIMM first. For example, in a 2 DPC configuration, the first DIMM would be the 2R-DIMM, the second DIMM in the channel would be the 1R-DIMM.

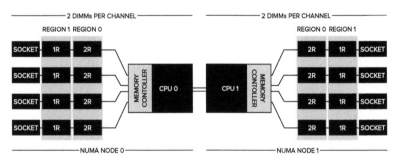

Figure 129: Rank Placement Order

10

MEMORY TOPOLOGY DESIGN

Creating a NUMA architecture that provides enough capacity per CPU is a challenge considering the impact memory configuration has on bandwidth and latency. If a cache miss occurs, the memory controller responsible for that memory line retrieves the data from RAM. Fetching data from local memory could take 80 cycles, while in extreme cases it could take the CPU a stellar 310 cycles to load the data from remote memory. This chapter combines previous content to achieve consistently high performance.

Memory Speed

To obtain the best-rated memory speed is a rather straightforward exercise. Just select the highest number and you are good to go. DIMMs with a rated 2400 MT/s should outperform DIMMs with an operational rate of 2133 MT/s.

DDR4 TYPE	MEMORY CLOCK	I/O BUS CLOCK	DATA RATE	MODULE	PEAK TRANSFER RATE
1866	233 MHz	933 MHz	1866 MT/s	PC4-14900	14933 MB/s
2133	266 MHz	1066 MHz	2133 MT/s	PC4-17000	17066 MB/s
2400	300 MHz	1200 MHz	2400 MT/s	PC4-19200	19200 MB/s

Table 25: Theoretical Operational Rate of DDR4 DIMMs

However, the theoretical operational rate of a DIMM is an indication of the operations per second in the most optimal situation. The operational speed of memory depends on several factors:

- Rated memory speed of the CPU
- Rated memory speed of the DIMM
- Number of DIMMs per channel
    - Number of ranks per DIMM
    - DIMM type

The combination of number of ranks per DIMM and the DIMM type dictate the performance degradation and the supported DIMM population per CPU package. As we are designing a multi-CPU host architecture, the interconnect speed is a point of interest. The selection of a DIMM is therefore not as straightforward of an exercise as it looks. The required memory capacity impacts the overall memory operation rate. It might be more economical selecting a lower rated operational rate DIMM to get the best possible performance while satisfying the memory capacity requirement.

CPU Selection

It's recommended to select a CPU with a medium or high core count as both microarchitectures contain 2 memory controllers in a CPU package.

SEGMENT	LLC CACHE SIZE	QPI SPEED	CORE COUNT	MEMORY SPEED
Basic	15-20 MB	6.4 GT/s	6-8	1866 MHz
Standard	20-25 MB	8.0 GT/s	8-10	2133 MHz
Advanced	30-35 MB	9.6 GT/s	12-14	2400 MHz
Segment Optimized	40-55 MB	9.6 GT/s	16-22	2400 MHz
Frequency Optimized *	> 2.5 MB per core	9.6 GT/s	4-8	2400 MHz
Low Power	25-35 MB	9.6 GT/s	10-24	2400 MHz

Table 26: CPU Segment Overview

Medium and high core count microarchitectures are grouped in the Advanced Segment and the Segment Optimized SKUs of Intel. In addition to the 2 memory controllers, the CPU package supports up to 2400 MHz and the QPI operates at 9.6 GT/s.

SEGMENT	MODEL NUMBER	CORE COUNT	CLOCK CYCLE	MAX TURBO	TDP
Advanced	E5-2650 v4	12	2.2 GHz	2.9 GHz	105W
Advanced	E5-2660 v4	14	2.0 GHz	3.2 GHz	105W
Advanced	E5-2680 v4	14	2.4 GHz	3.3 GHz	120W
Advanced	E5-2690 v4	14	2.6 GHz	3.5 GHz	135W
Optimized	E5-2683 v4	16	2.1 GHz	3.0 GHz	120W
Optimized	E5-2695 v4	18	2.1 GHz	3.3 GHz	120W
Optimized	E5-2697 v4	18	2.3 GHz	3.6 GHz	145W
Optimized	E5-2697A v4	16	2.6 GHz	3.6 GHz	145W
Optimized	E5-2698 v4	20	2.2 GHz	3.6 GHz	135W
Optimized	E5-2699 v4	22	2.2 GHz	3.6 GHz	145W
Optimized	E5-2699A v4	22	2.4 GHz	3.6 GHz	145W

Table 27: Advanced & Segment Optimized Overview

We recommend selecting a CPU from the advanced and segmenting optimized SKU. Leveraging multiple memory controllers that support the highest memory speed and QPI bandwidth.

Memory Channel

The memory controller connects via a channel to the DIMMs. E5-2600 v4 (Broadwell) supports up to four channels per CPU package. When operating in quad-channel mode, latency is reduced due to interleaving. The memory controller distributes the data amongst the DIMM in an alternating pattern, allowing the memory controller to access each DIMM for smaller bits of data instead of accessing a single DIMM for the entire chunk of data. This provides the memory controller more bandwidth for accessing the same amount of data across channels instead of traversing a single channel storing all data into a single DIMM.

We recommend populating all 4 channels to achieve Quad channel memory interleaving.

Memory Capacity

When designing a system that provides memory capacity while maintaining performance requires combining memory ranking and DIMM type knowledge.

Common enterprise server platforms contain up to 12 DIMM sockets per CPU package. This results in a maximum of three DIMMs per memory channel. In general, this number of available DIMM sockets drives the decision to obtain the lowest capacity DIMM (cheaper) and fill every DIMM socket to attain the required memory capacity.

However, a channel supports a limited amount of ranks due to maximal capacitance. As a result, memory ranking impacts the total memory capacity of each channel and operational performance. The memory capacity requirement primarily drives the choice of DIMM type.

DIMM Type

DIMM type and maximum number of ranks are intertwined. A channel can control eight memory ranks. Each rank can provide a limited capacity. RDIMMs expose the ranks on a channel. The max capacity of a RDIMM is 32 GB per DIMM as of this writing. By leveraging rank multiplication LRDIMMs do not face this problem and can increase the capacity per DIMM. Therefore, if the memory capacity requirement per ESXi host exceeds 786 GB (32 GB x 24 DIMM sockets) LRDIMMs are required. If both RDIMMs and LRDIMMs are able to provide the capacity the choice is dictated by cost and overall performance level if a 3 DPC configuration is required.

RDIMMs are cheaper than LRDIMMs and have slightly better performance than LRDIMMs when comparing them in an isolated scenario. However, due to the buffered structure LRDIMMs offer more memory capacity per DIMM while minimizing the performance degradation in a high capacity memory design (3 DPC).

Ranks Per DIMM

Common server vendors offer RDIMMs in single rank (1R) or dual rank (2R) configurations. The largest capacity 2R DIMM is 32 GB. This result in a 96 GB per channel multiplied by four equals 384 GB per CPU package (NUMA node). If It is not required to provide 768 GB per ESXi host, the next DIMM size is 16 GB. Some vendors offer these DIMMs in 1R and 2R configurations. This raises the question which one to select.

A rank is responsible for a single 64-bit cache line. That's in general the size of an operation. Thus, having multiple ranks on a single DIMM allows for more bandwidth. Remember, ranks can be accessed independently but not simultaneously. They can't be active sending and receiving data simultaneously due to sharing of the data bus, but one rank can receive write data, while the other rank is performing read-related operations. To quote the *Intel 64 and IA-32 Architectures Optimization Reference Manual*:

> **"In addition, using more ranks for the same amount of memory, results in somewhat better memory bandwidth, since more DRAM pages can be open simultaneously".**

The decision tree shows the consequences from a capacity perspective. Although quad-rank 32 GB RDIMMs exist, they reduce the overall capacity per channel. Please note that this diagram illustrates the capacity per channel, multiple by four to obtain the total capacity by NUMA node.

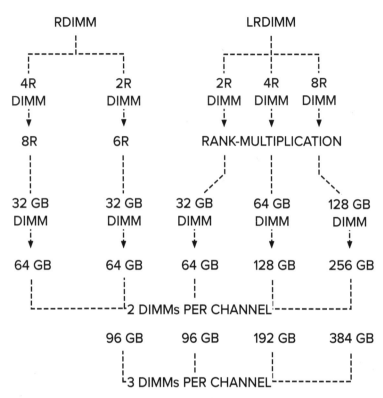

Figure 130: Memory Capacity per Channel

DIMMs Per Channel

Even if the numbers of ranks are within the maximum number of ranks, performance is degraded when populating all three DIMMs per channel.

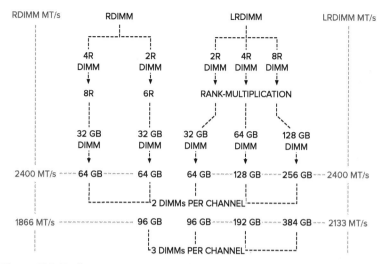

Figure 131: Performance DIMMs per Channel Configuration

On average the megatransfers per second (MT/s) of 2400 MT/s RDIMMs drop 22% if operated in a 3 DPC configuration. Cisco and Dell 2133 MT/s RDIMMs drop 12%, HP drops to 1600 MT/s (25%).

VENDOR	1 DPC (MT/s)	2 DPC (MT/s)	3 DPC (MT/s)	REDUCTION
Cisco	2400	2400	1866	22%
Dell	2400	2400	1866	22%
HP	2400	2400	1866	22%
Cisco	2133	2133	1866	12%
Dell	2133	2133	1866	12%
HP	2133	2133	1600	25%

Table 28: 2400 MT/s RDIMM DPC Performance

VENDOR	1 DPC (MT/s)	2 DPC (MT/s)	3 DPC (MT/s)	REDUCTION
Cisco	2400	2400	2133	11%
Dell	2400	2400	2133	11%
HP	2400	2400	2400	0%
Cisco	2133	2133	1866	11%
Dell	2133	2133	1866	11%
HP	2133	2133	1866	11%

Table 29: 2400 MT/s LRDIMM DPC Performance

This means if the capacity requirements require the use of 32 GB the best choice is to use LRDIMMs from a performance perspective. Instead of having a performance decrease 22% like RDIMMs, they only provide a reduction of 12%. Reducing the theoretical peak transfer rate from 19,200 MB/s to 17,066 MB/s.

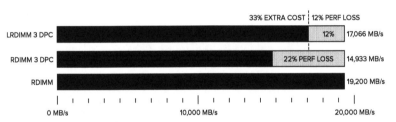

Figure 132: 3 DPC Performance Loss and Related Cost

However, when comparing cost, the list price of LRDIMM is on average 33% higher than RDIMM. The performance requirements should provide guidance whether the extra 10% performance over RDIMMs validates the price increase of 33%.

The examples use a 32 GB DIMM, which provides a maximum of 96 GB per Channel. This results in 384 GB per NUMA node. In total 768 GB of memory in an ESXi host. Most ESXi hosts at the time of writing of this book do not have a memory capacity that exceeds 512 GB. If using 16 GB DIMMs, the capacity per channel is restricted to 48 GB, resulting in a memory capacity per NUMA node of 192 GB.

When creating a system containing 384 GB, using 16 GB and populate every DIMM slot results in a memory frequency of 1866 MHz, while using (and let's not forget, paying for) 2400 MHz RDIMMs. Interestingly enough we found many different memory configurations that successfully provided the memory capacity, but were unable to provide consistent performance.

Unbalanced NUMA Configuration

The cardinal rule is to configure both NUMA nodes identically. The capacity and DIMM population should be identical of each NUMA node. We've seen some unbalanced memory configurations. We want to highlight the impact of these configurations.

In this example, the system is configured with 128 GB of memory. Both NUMA nodes are configured identically and contain 64 GB. Each NUMA node benefits from the quad-channel mode and has its region 1 filled. Note that each NUMA node controls its own regions.

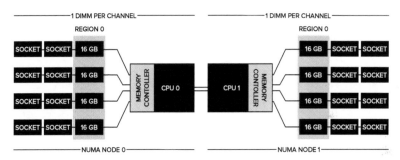

Figure 133: Identical NUMA Node Configuration

Unbalanced NUMA Node Configuration

In this example, additional memory capacity is installed in the system, specifically 64 GB in NUMA node 0. NUMA node 0 contains 128 GB. NUMA node 1 contains 64 GB.

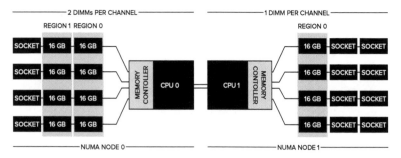

Figure 134: Unbalanced 192 GB Memory Configuration

CPU 0 will create two regions and will interleave the memory across the four channels and benefit from this extra capacity. However, this level of optimization of local bandwidth would not help the VMs that are scheduled to run on NUMA node 1. Because there is less memory available, it could require fetching memory remotely. Remote memory access experiences the extra latency of multi-hops.

Unbalanced Channel Configuration

Adhering to the 'treat your NUMA nodes equally' mantra, the DIMMs are distributed equally across the NUMA nodes. In this scenario both nodes contain 96 GB of RAM. The CPUs create two regions, region 0 (64 GB) interleaves across four channels, region 1 (32 GB) interleaves across two channels.

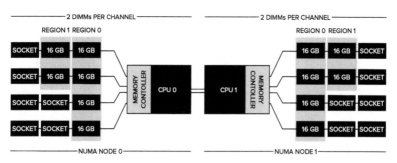

Figure 135: Unbalanced Channel Configuration

Native DIMM speed remains the same (MT/s). However, some performance loss occurs due to control management overhead. With local and remote memory access in mind, this configuration does not provide consistent memory performance.

Data access is done across four channels for region 0 and two channels for region 1. Data access across the QPI to the other memory controller might fetch the data across two or four channels. Low core count CPU configurations contain a single memory controller whereas medium and high core count CPU configurations contain two memory controllers. This memory layout creates an imbalance in load on memory controllers with medium and high core count CPU configurations as well.

When adding more DIMMs to the channel, the memory controller consumes more bandwidth for control commands. By adding more DIMMs, more management overhead is created which reduces the available bandwidth for read and write data. The question arises; do you solve the capacity requirement by using higher capacity DIMMs or take the throughput hit by moving to a 3 DPC configuration?

Mixed DIMM Capacity Configuration

Mixed configurations are supported however some requirements and limitations exist when using mixed configurations:

- RDIMMs and LRDIMMs must not be mixed
- RDIMMs of type x4 and x8 must not be mixed
- The configuration is incrementing from bank 1 to 3 with decreasing DIMM sizes. The larger modules should be installed first.

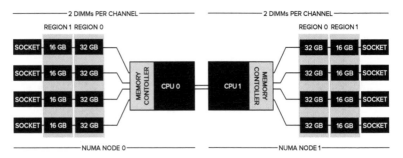

Figure 136: Mixed DIMM Capacity Configuration

To get the best performance, select the memory module with the highest rank configuration. This allows for the largest capacity configuration, while maintaining throughput performance. Looking at the memory prices at the time of writing the book, DDR4 32 GB memory modules are the sweet spot.

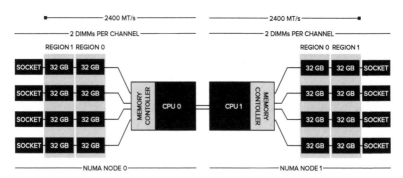

Figure 137: Homogeneous 2 DPC NUMA Node Configuration

11

VMKERNEL MEMORY MANAGEMENT

The VMkernel manages the physical memory of an ESXi host. A small part of the system's memory is used to run the VMkernel and its processes. The remaining memory is available to the VMs. To run VMs the VMkernel abstracts the physical memory to dynamically allocate memory to the active VMs. The VMkernel manages physical memory without the knowledge of the guest OS. In turn, the guest OS manages its own memory space without informing the VMkernel.

To be aware of this mutual disconnect allows you to further understand the impact of each memory reclamation technique. In turn this helps you with designing a proper consolidation ratio for your environment. Memory reclamation techniques are covered in the next chapter.

This chapter explores memory from an application point of view and how it interacts with guest OS software, the hypervisor and the hardware layer. This chapter's goal is to provide insight into why certain VMkernel settings contribute more to host memory capacity instead of application memory performance, for example disabling of large pages.

Memory should provide capacity and performance to the applications running inside the VMs. We all have the same requirements for ideal memory, as it should provide:

- Zero access latency time
- Zero cost of memory operations
- Infinite capacity
- Infinite bandwidth

There are methods to achieve close to zero access time and methods to access memory in parallel to achieve high levels of bandwidth by using caching. Part 1 of the book covered the physical structure of caching and how to provide a consistent latency from a physical structure as well. It's interesting to explore how the VMkernel interacts with the hardware, but before we arrive at that point it is helpful to understand how virtual memory and virtualized memory interact with each other.

Large Pages

Modern CPU Micro architectures are equipped with virtualization-optimized techniques to improve memory address translation performance for virtualized workloads. Natively these optimizations leverage large memory pages and ESX 3.5 started to use large pages for VM memory mapping by default. A consequence of using large pages is that memory pages are not shared when the ESXi host experiences no memory pressure. Some organizations prefer to increase their consolidation ratio by disabling large pages and subsequently rely on *Transparent Page Sharing* (TPS) to share memory.

However, disabling large pages in modern CPU architectures comes with a great penalty. We feel that this impact is somewhat trivialized by some. The most common remark is that it is only a 20% to 30% CPU increase and because they are not overcommitted on CPU resources they can take that hit. Well unfortunately the penalty is actually more a memory latency impact than a utilization problem. Every cycle = time, thus more utilization for a process equals increase in time. Think about the full stack, when an CPU instruction requires data, its fetched from cache, if It is not there, It is fetched from memory, if It is not there, It is fetched from disk. By injecting memory latency on purpose, one might ask why optimize the rest of the stack.

Proper design does not scrutinize a single step in a process while trivializing others. To help understand how detrimental disabling large pages can be for modern systems, we are going to explore hardware constructs such as the TLB, virtual memory and virtualized memory.

Virtual Memory and Virtualized Memory

Two concepts commonly used when discussing memory management in a virtual infrastructure is virtual memory and virtualized memory, but they are not the exactly same. In total three levels of memory mapping are used in virtualized environments. In the guest OS two levels exist, virtual memory and physical memory. Both concepts can be a bit misleading to most of us now, but consider the fact that these concepts were invented long before x86 virtualization was in play.

Virtual memory was introduced to abstract physical memory. As a result, operating systems provide a dedicated memory address space to each application. It allows applications with large memory demands to run on computers with smaller memory capacity. The developer does not have to worry about to aligning certain memory instructions to the physical limitations of a host. Another benefit about the abstraction is the security and stability concept. Applications cannot overwrite each other's memory pages as they are presented with an isolated memory address space. However, these virtual memory address spaces must be mapped to the actual physical memory pages.

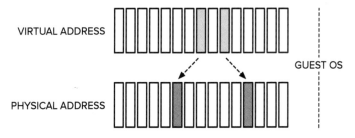

Figure 138: Virtual to Physical Memory Mapping

It's the responsibility of the OS to transparently map the virtual memory addresses to physical memory addresses. Keep in mind that we are talking about an OS running inside a VM. The mapping virtual address to physical address occurs in the guest OS running inside the VM. That's why that a virtual memory address inside the guest OS is referred to as *Guest Virtual Address* (gVA). A physical memory address inside the guest OS is a Guest Physical Address (gPA). The physical memory detected by the guest OS inside a VM is virtualized host physical memory (hPA), often referred to as machine memory.

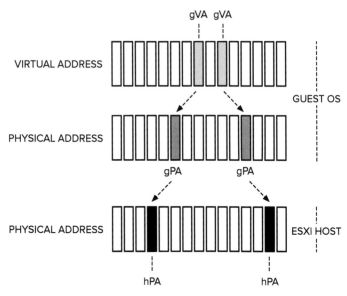

Figure 139: Guest to ESXi Host Memory Mapping

Memory Mapping

The OS is responsible for mapping virtual addresses to physical addresses. It maintains these mappings in a page table for each address space. The virtual address is generated by an instruction inside a process. The memory page table maps the virtual address to physical addresses in memory.

Modern operating systems use a large 64-bit virtual address space. To support this large range of addresses a single page table is not optimal. Smaller page tables are much faster, thus modern operating systems and CPU microarchitectures use a four-level hierarchical page table. Please note that in modern host systems memory page tables are managed by hardware and software together. It's the method of cooperation between hardware and software that impacts the memory performance.

Page Table Walk

If an application want to retrieve data from memory the virtual address needs to be translated to a physical address. The process that retrieves the physical address is referred to as a *page table walk*.

A control register inside the CPU contains the address of the page table, this control register is called CR3, and the helps the process to locate the page directory. It then proceeds to walk through the four levels. Each level contains a small portion of the address. The process differs slightly if the page table entry points to a large page (2 MB), then it does not have to go through all four tables in the case of a small page (4 KB).

To go into detail about the roles of each table within this process is out-of-scope. If you are interested we recommend the academic paper *Performance Implications of Extended Page Tables on Virtualized x86 Processors* by Tim Merrifield and Reza Taheri.

It can happen that the memory is swapped out to disk, then the page table entry points to disk instead of a physical memory address. If that data is needed, the system transparently retrieves the data from disk, and places it into physical memory and adjusts the mapping in the page table. This process is called demand paging.

With this in mind, we can argue that physical memory is the cache for pages on the disk. However, this cache is considered slow when comparing it to CPU cache. The page table is stored in memory.

That means that to translate a virtual memory address to physical memory address, additional memory operations are required. This is costly from a memory latency and bandwidth perspective (think at scale here, the system is generating incredible amounts of memory operations). The industry attempts to reduce this cost by introducing another cache. The TLB reduces time in the critical path of application performance.

The TLB is a hardware structure and caches frequently access mappings. Each CPU core in a CPU package contains multiple TLBs. A TLB is considered to be a part of the *Memory Management Unit* (MMU). The MMU is not a physical component on the CPU but is a collection of software functions and hardware components. The overall responsibility for the MMU is to translate addresses.

Memory Management Unit

If the OS runs inside a VM, the OS maintains the page tables similar to running the OS in a native system. However, the VMkernel restricts the vCPU of a VM to have direct access to the MMU on the CPU as this would result in loss of control of the host memory address space.

Because the vCPU cannot directly run at a higher privilege on the physical CPU, particular data structures are duplicated. This MMU can be either virtualized by the VMM or can be executed in hardware by the use of hardware virtualization technology.

Software-Assisted Memory Virtualization

In software-based memory management unit virtualization the VMM maintains the mappings from guest physical memory to host physical memory addresses in its internal data structures. In addition, the VMM maintains shadow page tables in which it stores the gVA to hPA mappings. Although the MMU is virtualized, the VMM stores the most recently used virtual (vPA) to host physical address mappings (hPA) in the TLB.

The VMM synchronizes the shadow page tables to the guest page tables. When the guest OS requests a vGA to vPA, the VMM services this access request and walks its shadow page table and returns the actual hPA location to the VM. This results in tracking this effort on various levels within the CPU and software. Overall the translation done by the VMM is quite efficient, however each time the guest OS adjust its gVA to gPA mapping the VMM needs to adjust its shadow pages as well. This synchronization of mappings can turn into a major performance penalty when the VM runs a memory intensive application.

Second Level Address Translation

To accelerate this important process, both Intel and AMD developed a *Second Level Address Translation* (SLAT) technology that provides hardware assist. Intel released *Extended Page Tables* (EPT) with the Westmere microarchitecture. EPT is a part of Intel *Virtualization Technology* (VT). AMD released *Rapid Virtualization Indexing* (RVI) with the third generation of Opteron (Barcelona). ESXi supports SLAT, also known as nested pages, since version 3.5. The whitepaper *Performance Evaluation of Intel EPT Hardware Assist* reports performance gains up to 48%. SLAT is often referred to as hardware-assisted memory virtualization. VT must be enabled in the server BIOS!

Hardware-Assisted Memory Virtualization

The VMkernel determines whether or not to use hardware support for MMU virtualization based on various factors such as the guest OS type and the physical hardware. For example, hardware MMU is used by default if a VM contains a 64-bit guest OS and runs on an EPT-enabled CPU architecture.

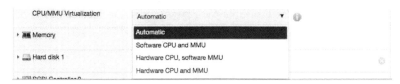

Figure 140: CPU/MMU Virtualization Option

The hardware is able to dynamically manage guest MMU operations and translate gVA to hPA directly. The advantage of having the hardware manage all memory operations of the VMs on the host is it reduces the need for the VMM to sync their shadow pages each time the guest OS adjust its virtual to physical (gPA) mapping. This improves performance tremendously for multi-vCPU VMs and hosts that run a large number of VMs.

This hardware assistance has one drawback. It suffers performance penalties on TLB miss. To avoid or reduce TLB misses as much as possible, large pages are used to back small pages and large pages from the guest OS. Before zooming in on large pages and the effect it is having on resource management operations, let's have a closer look at the TLB.

Translation Lookaside Buffer

In its basic forms a memory mapping translation has to occur before the cache can be accessed to determine whether the data is in cache instead of memory.

The process without involving a TLB in a native system is as follows: the virtual page number is sent to the MMU, the MMU provides the *Page Table Entry Address* (PTEA). Based on that PTEA the memory is accessed and gets the *Page Table Entry* (PTE). With the PTE the translation occurs in the MMU to get the Physical Address and then accesses the cache. This process accesses physical memory twice before hitting the cache.

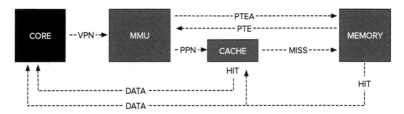

Figure 141: Address Translation Before Data Retrieval

If the data is not in the cache, memory is accessed. When the page is not in memory this is called a page fault, the data is retrieved from disk. As the cache is inclusive, all data is written to the cache when retrieved from memory or disk.

Please note that a page table can be stored in the cache if it is recently used. But depending on the active working set of all the VMs it could or could not be in the cache. Therefore, we chose to depict the worst-case scenario!

As the page table is in memory an extra step is required to access the memory. To avoid this cost a cache is created that keeps track of recently used address mappings to avoid having to do a page table lookup. This cache is the TLB.

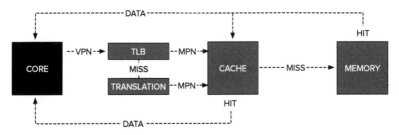

Figure 142: TLB Lookup in Data Retrieval Process

If a virtual address is requested the TLB is accessed and the search result is an address that can be used to access the machine memory. This sequence is called a TLB hit.

Since Sandy-Bridge, each CPU core includes two levels of TLBs. Instead of one big TLB, two different sized TLBs are used to keep TLB misses to a minimum while still providing excellent performance. It's stated that the TLB architecture provides about 3 translations per clock cycle.

To make it even faster a separate TLB is used for instructions and another for data. The unified level 2 TLB on modern CPU architectures has room for 1536 entries, this number is regardless of the memory page size, it can be an entry for a 4 KB page as well as a 2 MB page.

LEVEL	PAGE SIZE	ENTRIES
Instruction	4 KB	128
Instruction	2 MB/4 MB	8 per Thread
First Level Data	4 KB	64
First Level Data	2 MB/4 MB	32
First Level Data	1 GB	4
Second Level Data	Shared by 4 KB and 2 MB Pages	1536
Second Level Data	1 GB Pages	16

Table 30: TLB Parameters of Broadwell Microarchitecture

Virtually Indexed Physically Tagged Cache

The interesting thing is that TLB translation latency is considered not fast enough for the critical path. Therefore, the L1 cache is redesigned in modern CPU microarchitectures to be a *Virtual Indexed Physically Tagged* (VIPT) cache. This allows the system to access both the cache and the TLB in parallel.

The cache is indexed using virtual addresses. The virtual page number is used to query the TLB. In parallel with the TLB access, the virtual address is interpreted as a cache address. Once you get the physical address from the TLB you compare it to the tag used in the cache with the physical frame number provided by the TLB. If the tag matches the physical frame-number it is a hit and the data is retrieved from cache. This is much faster than waiting for the TLB to translate the virtual memory address and then access the cache and cycle through the cache to determine if the data is present in the cache.

TLB MISS

If the requested address is not present in the TLB, it could be a TLB miss or a page fault. By walking the page table, it can be determined whether the miss is merely a TLB miss or a page fault.

A TLB miss when dealing with virtualized workloads can be quite costly. In native systems (OS on bare metal) a page walk can take up referencing four tables. With nested page tables, it can take up as many as twenty-four memory references to get the physical memory frame. For comparison, the industry moved to a VIPT cache because it cannot wait for a TLB access that sits next to L1 cache in the CPU core itself.

The reason why it can take up that many memory references is that walking the guest page table structure incurs multiple page-table walks of the EPT structure. A guest page table walk is combined with a nested page table walk for each level. A combination of page sizes can exist within the system. If large pages (2 MB) are used, the page table walk has to deal with one less level in each direction.

GUEST	HOST	# MEMORY REFERENCES
Small	Small	24
Large	Small	20
Small	Large	19
Large	Large	15

Table 31: Memory References of Guest Host Page Combinations

Due to the size of the TLB, TLB misses occur more frequently than page faults. TLB misses can occur due to compulsory misses (i.e. data is being entered into the system for the first time), or due to capacity misses. Compulsory misses are just a fact of life! You cannot do anything about them. Capacity misses happen if the stream of entries exceeds the capacity of the TLB. This is exactly the reason why large pages are used. By covering a larger memory range, it typically leads to a higher rate of TLB hits. As a result, avoiding the costly overhead of a page walk.

Impact of Disabling Large Pages

Think about the level of inconsistencies that are introduced when opting to disable large pages in a system. Some addresses might be in the TLB. Some parts of a page table might be in the cache. And sometimes a page walk consists of memory access and cache access intertwined with the some cache misses. As a result, you are treating yourself to inconsistent memory performance. By using large pages, you are reducing pressure on the TLB. This increases performance and above should provide more consistent performance. Disabling large pages is not only consuming more CPU cycles, it is introducing inconsistent memory latencies. Maybe your applications might not be impacted that much by this inconsistent memory behavior. But if you are trying to optimize performance at any level (CPU, storage or network) for a single application running in your environment, the last recommendation we would do is disable large pages. Cache performance and memory performance are fundamental for any subsequent layer in your system. If you ignore this you might wonder if other optimizations are as fruitful as you hope them to be.

> **If you want to keep performance consistent and avoid memory access latency as much as possible, do not disable large pages on the ESXi host!**

One of the reasons why large pages are disabled is the perceived saving of TPS. Large pages are not shared if the system is not experiencing memory pressure. Please read chapter 12, *Transparent Page Sharing* to understand the current state of memory sharing before disabling Large Pages. If you still wish to disable large pages, you can adjust the following advanced setting: `LPage.LPageAlwaysTryForNPT=0`

Host Overhead Memory

CPU and memory resources are necessary to run the hypervisor. With every new release the engineering team seeks out to reduce the resource overhead of the VMkernel to improve the VM consolidation ratio per host. Let's explore how ESX manages memory for itself and the VMs.

The biggest improvement was with the introduction of ESXi 5.0, which provided a resource consumption reduction of 40%. The change of MinFree (chapter 12) improves consolidation ratios of hosts with large memory configurations tremendously. For example, the memory reserved for the host by MinFree was reduced from 15.3 to 3.1 GB.

The VMkernel implements hierarchical portioning of CPU and memory resources using resource groups. These are similar to Resource Pools. These resource groups are organized in the form of a tree and top-level resource group (HOST) has four child resource groups. These are all not visible to the user.

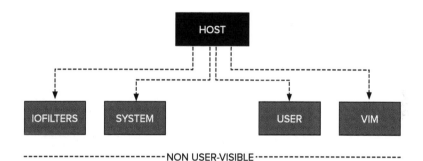

Figure 143: Non-Visible Host Resource Groups

The VMkernel leverages the following resource allocation settings to manage the CPU and memory.

SETTING	DESCRIPTION
mem.shares	Indicates the relative priority between the resource group and its siblings.
mem.limit	Indicates the maximum memory that can be consumed by all memory consumers inside the resource group.
mem.resv	Indicates the amount of memory that is guaranteed to be available to the memory consumers inside the resource group.
mem.resvLimit	The VMkernel is able to increase reservations for RG's automatically, the mem.resvLimit indicates the maximum mem.resv value of a RG

Table 32: Resource Groups Resource Allocation Settings

Reservations on these resource groups differ in behavior from user-created resource pools. Reserved memory is not claimed up front for the resource consumers, but will increase reserved memory when needed. If needed it can reclaim memory from other resource consumers that are not protected by memory reservations. The UI lists the maximum system resource reservations in the configure menu of the host.

DRS mirrors the cluster resource pool tree to each host and maps the appropriate resource settings to each resource pool node if the host is a part of a DRS cluster. The /host/user hierarchy is expanded with the resource pool structure.

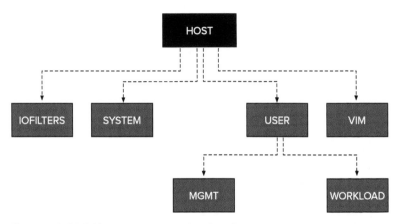

Figure 144: DRS Cluster RP Tree at Host Level

The host local scheduler computes the entitlement and distributes the resources between resource pools and VMs if needed.

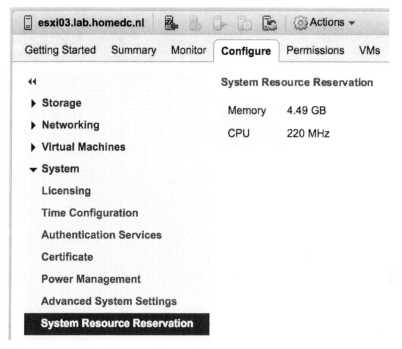

Figure 145: System Resource Reservation

However, the VMkernel might not have allocated all of its reserved memory. You can verify this by using performance monitor (advanced > Memory > VMkernel consumed. Or by using the command-line tool memstats with the following options:

```
memstats -r comp-stats -s
total:kernelCode:dataAndHeap:buddyOvhd:vmkClientConsumed -u mb
```

```
COMPREHENSIVE STATS: Sun Apr  9 12:25:23 2017
---------------------------------------------------
 Unit            : MB
 Selected columns : total:kernelCode:dataAndHeap:buddyOvhd:vmkClientConsumed


---------------------------------------------------------------------
    total kernelCode dataAndHeap  buddyOvhd vmkClientConsumed
---------------------------------------------------------------------
   130961        20          14        32             2289
---------------------------------------------------------------------
[root@esxi03:~] ▊
```

Figure 146: Memstats VMkernel Memory Consumption

The host admission control takes into the memory reservations of these resource groups into account when performing power-on operations of VMs or when new resource groups are created or altered. Alteration of reservations of non-user visible groups can happen when new services are installed and introduce kernel modules for example.

VMs are placed in the user resource group. The VMkernel uses the other three resource groups for various functions. The Idle resource group is empty. The system resource group contains child resource pools for processes, low-level kernel services and drivers. The VIM resource group contains child resource groups for each host management process such as DCUI, hostd, VPXA, etc.).

Some of the services are configured with a static memory reservation regardless of the host configuration. Other services are configured with a memory reservation that scales with the memory configuration of the host. Some services get more memory assigned due to the number of active VMs. Because of this behavior, it is difficult to accurately predict an overhead consumption for each host.

Figure 147 shows the breakdown of each VMkernel process and its related overhead. Each block represents a VMkernel component and the size of the block indicates the relative memory consumption of this component compared to the other components.

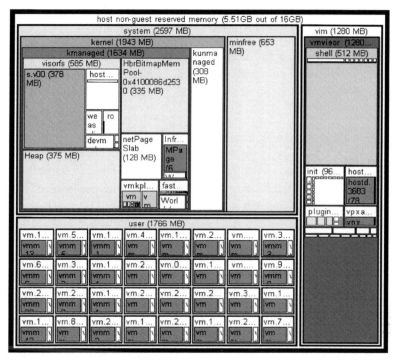

Figure 147: Breakdown of VMkernel Overhead Running 32 single vCPU VMs

Prior to ESXi 6.0, the advanced system resource allocation option in the configure menu showed the resource group structure. This was a relic from the good old service console days. Some third-party vendors recommended setting a specific CPU and memory reservation for the service console so their backup and monitor software operated smoothly. Since we do not have a service console anymore and the VMkernel is able to manage the reservations automatically (and much faster and fine-grained than most humans) it does not make sense to change the resource groups and their resource allocation settings.

The fact of life is that you need resources to run a datacenter OS. In some cases (lab environments primarily) the VMkernel might consume more than half the total amount of resources. But let's be realistic, this software is optimized in such a way that it provides performance while not hoarding loads of resources, but you cannot expect to run this platform on 100 MB of RAM.

Memory reclamation on the resource groups follows a similar pattern as memory reclamation of VMs. Ballooning, compression and even hypervisor level swapping occurs to free up memory when the VMkernel determines memory pressure. Chapter 12 covers memory states and memory reclamation techniques in detail.

VM Overhead Memory

ELLC VM running on an ESX host consumes some memory overhead additional to the current usage of its configured memory. This extra space is needed by the VMkernel to create and maintain internal data structures such as the VM frame buffer and to some extent a memory translation-mapping table (mapping guest physical memory to host physical memory).

When using software MMU virtualization the dynamic overhead totally depends on the workload and can change while the VM is running. The shadow page tables play an important role in sizing the dynamic overhead as it can shrink and grow according to the guest OS workload. When the VMM wants to add more shadow page tables, it will request an increase in the amount of overhead memory. The following configuration items impact the total memory overhead reservation:

- Number of CPUs
- Amount of RAM
- Video Card Settings: (often used for VDI VMs)
    - Number of displays
    - Amount of video memory
    - 3D Support

The vSphere client (or UI) does not show the static overhead anymore. In previous versions, the UI showed the worst-case scenario of VM overhead when the VM was powered off. ESXi 6.5 just shows the actual overhead memory consumption. 0 MB when powered down, the actual up-to-date consumption when powered-on.

Figure 148: VM Memory Overhead Consumed

VM memory overhead consists of two parts, static overhead and dynamic overhead:

Static Overhead

Static overhead is the minimum overhead that is required for the VM startup. Both the host as well as DRS uses this metric for admission control and vMotion calculations. The destination host must be able to back the VM reservation and the static overhead otherwise the vMotion will fail.

Dynamic Overhead

Once the VM has started up, the VMM can request additional memory space. This is why you see the VM memory overhead change over time. The VMM will request the space, but the VMkernel is not required to supply it. If the VMM does not obtain the extra memory space, the VM will continue to function but this can lead to performance degradation. The VMkernel treats VM overhead reservation the same as VM-level memory reservation and it will not reclaim this memory once it used.

Overhead Memory Used by Admission Control

As mentioned before, the host and DRS admission control will not allow the VM to be powered up if reservations cannot be guaranteed, this means that the effective memory reservation for a VM is the configured memory reservation (VM-level reservation) plus the overhead reservation.

Although each VM memory overhead is small relative to the host memory configuration, however it can become a significant amount of memory when running high consolidation ratios.

VM Level Resource Allocation Settings

The configured memory size of a VM is the virtual address space of the VM. The VM allocates and consumes memory from the free memory pool of the user resource group of the host. Typically, the amount of memory consumed is equal to the amount of demand of the guest OS and its applications. However, when the demand of all the active VMs exceeds the amount of available memory of the USER resource group, the VMkernel recalculates distribution of these resources on the dynamic entitlement of each VM.

Entitlement

The *VMware vSphere 5.1 Clustering Deep Dive* states the following about entitlement:

> **The entitlement of a VM defines a target that represents the ideal amount of resources eligible for use. The host-local scheduler computes this target and it is up to the VM or resource pool to use the available resources or not. Entitlement is comprised of static elements and dynamic elements. The static elements are based on user-provided resource specifications, while dynamic elements are based on estimated demand and the level of contention in a system. A VM has a separate entitlement target for both CPU and memory.**

In essence, the tasks of the memory scheduler are rather straightforward and that is to compute the memory entitlement for each VM. If the memory entitlement is lower than the currently consumed memory, its task is to reclaim memory.
The memory entitlement of a VM is based on the memory resource allocation settings (Shares, Reservation, Limit) and its memory demand. The memory demand is determined by the active memory.

As the VMkernel is unable to accurate determine the working set size of the applications inside the VM, therefore it relies on a statistical sampling technique. And that technique is active memory, which has proven to be pretty accurate. To investigate memory activity properly, let's review memory allocation terminology.

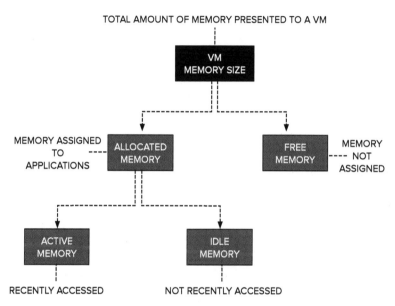

Figure 149: Memory Terminology

A simplistic representation of the various memory allocation concepts is as follows:

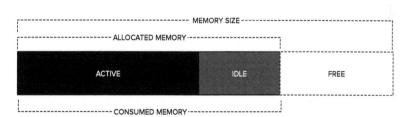

Figure 150: Memory Allocation Concepts

Please note that active, idle, and free memory are often distributed in a random manner. This diagram does not depict real world scenarios, but functions as a simplistic indicator of the various memory allocation concepts. Unfortunately, due to the information gap, It is not always clear to the VMkernel that some of the allocated memory is idle within the VM. This behavior is described in detail in chapter 12.

But once that idle memory was a part of the demand of the VM. Demand describes the amount of memory that a VM actively wants to use. The VMkernel determines the entitlement of the VM by calculating the entitlements of all the VMs based on their activity and their relative priority, which is derived from the resource allocation settings.

To provide the best performance for your VM, you must ensure that the entitlement exceeds the demand of the VM. The trick is to keep both values close to each other to obtain the best consolidation ratio without wasting precious host resources.

If the consumed memory (how much memory is allocated to the VM) exceeds the entitled memory (how much memory is the VM allowed to have) and the host experiences memory pressure, the VMkernel reclaims the memory up to the entitlement mark.

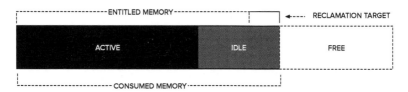

Figure 151: Reclamation Target

Therefore, the reclamation is based on VM entitlement and memory consumed. The applied reclamation techniques depend on the memory state of the VMkernel. The relative priority of the VM is calculated using the following parameters:

SETTING	DESCRIPTION
Configured Memory Size	Specifies the maximum entitlement
Reservation	Indicates the minimum entitlement value
Limit	Indicates the maximum entitlement value
Shares	Specifies the relative priority of the VM compared to other VMs.
Idle Memory Tax	Impacts entitlement based on share value by taxing idle memory. If the VM contains idle memory, entitlement is reduced.

Table 33: Resource Entitlement Parameters

The maximum entitlement value of a VM is determined by comparing the value of the configured memory size and limit. If a limit is set, lower than the VM configured memory size. The limit specifies the maximum entitlement.

Reservation

Internally referred to as MIN, reservations determine the minimum entitlement of a VM once it has allocated the memory. Its primary goal is to protect the physical memory allocation against memory reclamation. And thus, is an excellent mechanism to guarantee consistent memory performance for this VM.

Impact of Memory Management on the VM

Memory reservations guarantee that physical memory pages are backed by machine memory pages all the time, regardless of memory pressure. You might choose to set the memory reservation equal to the configured memory, this guarantees the best performance for the VM all of the time. But using this policy impacts the virtual infrastructure.

Admission Control

Configuring memory reservation has impact on admission control. There are three levels of admission control:

- Host Level
- High Availability
- Distributed Resource Scheduler

Host Level: When a VM is powered on, admission control verifies the amount of available unreserved CPU and memory resources. If the memory scheduler cannot guarantee the memory reservation and the memory overhead of the VM, the VM is not powered on.

HA and DRS: Admission control also exists at HA and DRS level. The HA admission control policy 'Host failures tolerate' uses the configured memory reservation as a part of the calculation of the cluster slot size. The number of slots available equals the number of VMs that can run inside the cluster. Thus, the combination of large reservations and the host failures tolerate policy can lead to a reduced consolidation-ratio of the vSphere cluster. The HA Deep Dive at yellow-bricks.com provides in-depth information about HA admission controls and its policies.

Allocation of Memory

Please note that setting a reservation does not automatically mean that the VM has allocated the memory, this depends on the memory consumption of the guest OS running inside the VM. For example, Linux operating systems only allocate memory when needed. If a 10 GB Linux VM with a 10 GB memory reservation runs an application that consumes 6 GB (including guest OS usage), the reservation of physical host memory is 6 GB. This 6 GB will be protected against memory reclamation. Windows touches all memory during the boot process and therefore allocates all the memory.

The memory scheduler allows other VMs to allocate memory that is unused. Thus, in the case of the Linux machine, the remaining 4 GB will be available for all other VMs to allocate. However, once the Linux machine requires the memory and no unallocated memory is available, the memory scheduler will reclaim memory from VMs that are not protected by a reservation. It allocates this memory to the Linux VM. Once a VM has accessed memory that is protected by a memory reservation it will remain available for that VM only. The memory scheduler will not reclaim this memory during memory pressure.

This memory is allocated to the VM and to that VM only. Even if the VM becomes idle and other VMs are in dire need of this memory, the memory scheduler has to search and provide memory from somewhere else.

There is an advanced option that fully allocates all the memory during power-on operation and as a result will have its memory protected by the reservation. The setting is called pre-allocation and can be enabled by setting the advanced setting option: `sched.mem.prealloc = True`. This setting is primarily used for memory latency sensitive workloads that cannot risk waiting for the memory scheduler to reclaim memory from other VMs. Reservations on resource pool behave differently, the performance study: *DRS Cluster Management with Reservation and Shares* published by VMware April 06, 2017 covers this subject in great detail.

Shares

Shares determine the relative priority of VMs and resource pools at the same hierarchical level and determine how resources (total system resources - total reservations) are divided.

Relative Priorities

Shares are pool-relative, which means that the numbers of shares are compared between the child-objects of the same parent. This can be directly beneath the host resource group of the host or in a mirrored DRS cluster resource pool structure.

By default, for each MB configured the VM receives ten shares. Please note that the absolute values do not matter. Instead of providing ten shares per MB, you can assign 1 share per MB or 1000 shares per MB, the relative priority is determined by comparing your shares to the shares of other siblings. For example, two VMs running on the host; VM01 has 16000 shares and VM02 has 4000 shares. VM1 has 4 times more shares than VM02 and therefore the ratio is 4:1.

The entitlement between the MIN (Reservation) and the Max (Limit) is determined by the share value. The memory scheduler computes the dynamic entitlement LLC 15 seconds and updates the memory allocations. If the host a part of a DRS cluster, this metric is pushed to DRS. If memory contention occurs on the host, the memory scheduler reclaims memory resources. The target is the memory allocated based on the share value. Chapter 12 covers memory states and memory reclamation techniques in detail.

Limit

The limit determines the maximum amount of physical resources the memory scheduler can allocate to the VM. Even if enough free resources are available inside the host, the memory controller enforces the limit.

Limits are not visible to the guest OS and can therefore impact behavior of the guest OS and the active applications. A guest OS sizes and tunes its caching algorithms based on the available memory it is presented. In the case of a VM it is the configured memory. If a limit is set that is smaller than the configured memory size it may use memory that is not backed by physical memory. The memory scheduler is required to balloon\compress or swap out other parts of the memory address space available to the VM. This behavior does not only negatively impact the performance of the VM, it increases the host load as well as the memory scheduler needs to actively run memory reclamation techniques to satisfy the limit requirement.

By default, the limit is set to unlimited and this is done to allocate memory for user-worlds assisting the VM outside the memory address space of the guest OS. Some administrators have the habit of adjusting the default setting and aligning the limit with the configured memory size of the VM. This impacts the VM performance as the memory scheduler is forced to reclaim memory from the VM for its memory overhead. Please note that the limit is not dynamically adjusted when the memory size of the VM is increased, increasing the risk of having more memory not being backed by host physical memory.

Memory Idle Tax

Shares can be tool to dynamically create relative priority in a system. Only the shares of powered-on VMs are compared to each other, as a result resources' flow to the VMs that are consuming resources actively. The challenge with comparing share values between powered-on VM is that it does not take idle memory into account. This can lead to memory hoarding by unproductive VMs, while active VMs with a lower number of shares suffer under severe memory pressure. Idle memory tax resolves this problem by charging the VM more for an idle memory page than an active memory page. To be precise the Idle Memory Tax is set to 75% and this result in an idle page costing four times more than an active page. You can adjust the advanced setting Mem.IdleTax, but we have no idea why you should change it.

12

MEMORY RECLAMATION TECHNIQUES

The Information Gap

The guest OS is not aware that it is running inside a VM and manages the memory as it is permanently and exclusively access to it. The guest OS remaps virtual to physical memory if and when needed. Microsoft Windows is a good example of this behavior. Microsoft Windows does not delete the contents of a memory page if this memory address is reused by the same application. If the content is not necessary anymore, the memory manager includes this page in its free page list. Windows allows its applications to overwrite the old data with the new data, however the VMkernel is not informed of this behavior, thus the VMkernel just continues the stale date. Please note that Windows only zero's out the page if the memory page is made available for other applications.

Similar to the importance of the data, the VMkernel does not know how important this data is to the guest OS or to its applications. Is it a driver, data used a kernel process or cached data? The VMkernel just knows which machine page belongs to which VM. This 'shroud' obscuring the context of the memory page is the reason why kernel swapping can be so disastrous for VM performance. It could grab a stale memory page. It could be as well the most used memory page in the system.

MinFree

The threshold defined by the MinFree calculation determines the amount of memory that the VMkernel should keep free to prevent performance and correctness issues. Once this threshold is surpassed, the VMkernel applies various memory reclamation techniques depending on the severity of the memory pressure.

The VMkernel uses this amount of memory free to handle dynamic allocation requests efficiently. The VMkernel of ESXi versions up to 5.0 kept 6% of the memory free. Due to the increase of system memory of new systems the 6% was kind of wasteful.

ESXi 5.0 replaced the static MinFree percentage with a dynamically modifying MinFree and the free memory state thresholds that triggers specific memory reclamation techniques. Linking the memory state thresholds to the MinFree state allows auto-scaling of the free memory state thresholds when MinFree is modified.

Calculating MinFree

A sliding scale is applied to the available memory that the VMkernel manages. This amount of memory is less than the total amount of memory installed in the system due to overhead of hardware and ESXi itself. As shown, the overhead is on average 512 MB.

MEMORY SIZE IN GB	VMKERNEL MANAGED IN MB	MEMORY IN GB
256	261712	255.58
384	392772	383.57
512	523808	511.53
768	785922	767.50
1024	1048070	1023.50
2048	2096720	2047.58
3072	3145203	3071.49

Table 34: VMkernel Managed Memory

This accuracy is important as it impacts the (end) range of calculating the MinFree. Please note that the VMkernel managed memory range of your systems might be slightly different due to the hardware used or the patch level of ESXi. If you want to calculate the MinFree threshold yourself, use the VMkernel memory range is to review the memory screen in esxtop. Or execute the following command:

```
[root@esxi00:~] memstats -r comp-stats -s total:minFree:free:managedByMemSched -u mb

COMPREHENSIVE STATS: Tue Mar  7 04:53:24 2017
---------------------------------------------------
 Unit            : MB
 Selected columns : total:managedByMemSched:minFree:free


---------------------------------------------------
   total managedByMemSched     minFree       free
---------------------------------------------------
   65501            65175        1266      11858
---------------------------------------------------
[root@esxi00:~]
```

Figure 152: Memstats Displaying MinFree

The sliding scale is partitioned in four parts: a 256 GB host configuration is used for this example.

PERCENTAGE	MEMORY RANGE	EFFECTIVE RANGE	RESULT
6%	0-4 GB	4096 MB	245.76
4%	4-12 GB	8192 MB	327.68
2%	12-28 GB	16,384 MB	327.68
SUBTOTAL		28,762 MB	901.12
1%	Remaining Memory	233,040 MB	2330.40
Total MinFree			3231.52

Table 35: MinFree Calculation of 256 GB Host

The table is split up in two parts. The first part is the range calculation of the first 28 GB of memory of a host. It is reasonable to assume that servers that run ESXi 6.5 contain more than 32 GB of memory. Therefore, the first three steps are equal for all ESXi 6.5 hosts.

The interesting step in this calculation is the 1% of remaining memory. This is truly the sliding scale part of the equation as it differs for various memory configurations (256 GB, 512 GB, 1024 GB, etc.).

It is dynamically adjusted if the memory configuration of the host is expanded. Using the 256 GB memory configuration as an example. The 1% is calculated across the range of 233,040 MB (261,712 MB -/- 28,762 MB). This is the result of 261,712 MB of VMkernel managed memory minus the 28,762 MB (4096 MB + 8192 MB + 16,384 MB) used for the preceding percentage calculations. MinFree does not do anything by itself. The result of the MinFree calculation is used to derive the memory state of the ESXi host.

Memory State

In ESXi 6.5 five memory states exists; High, Clear, Soft, Hard and Low. These states trigger the VMkernel to start or stop using various memory reclamation techniques. The memory state of the ESXi can be verified by reviewing the esxtop memory screen. Or you can use the following vsish command: `vsish -e cat /sched/globalStats/memory/memStats | grep memory-state`

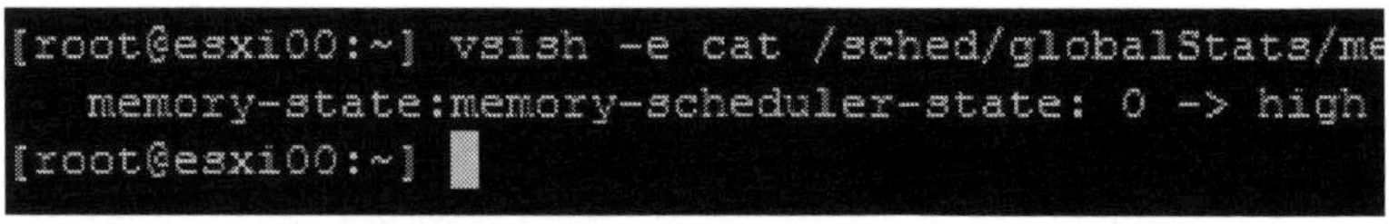

```
[root@esxi00:~] vsish -e cat /sched/globalStats/me
    memory-state:memory-scheduler-state: 0 -> high
[root@esxi00:~] █
```

Figure 153: Memory State Query Using VSISH

Memory State Transition Points

The VMkernel applies one or more memory reclamation techniques when memory pressure occurs. A more aggressive method of memory reclamation is applied with the increase of memory pressure. This may impact VM performance. As a result, memory reclamation is relaxed when memory pressure decreases. To avoid oscillation between two states, different memory state transition points are active with reference to the memory pressure condition. More specifically, the VMkernel uses two transition points for a memory state, one if memory pressure increases and one when memory pressure decreases.

MEMORY STATE	MEMORY PRESSURE INCREASE	MEMORY PRESSURE DECREASE
HIGH	301% of MinFree	401% of MinFree
CLEAR	300% of MinFree	400% of MinFree
SOFT	64% of MinFree	100% of MinFree
HARD	32% of MinFree	48% of MinFree
LOW	16% of MinFree	24% of MinFree

Table 36: Memory State Transition Points

As shown, the memory state transition points are derived from the MinFree threshold. It is important to understand that these thresholds are the transition points for that particular level. When memory pressure is increasing, the host enters the listed memory state. Let's use an ESXi host with 256 GB memory as an example.

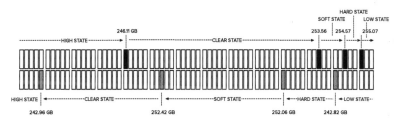

Figure 154: Memory Transition Points Host with 256 GB Memory

In total the VMkernel manages 261,712 MB. The calculated MinFree equals 3231 MB. The ESXi host is in a high memory state until memory consumption surpasses the Clear Threshold. Once memory consumption is more than 252,019 MB (246.11 GB) the system transitions to a Clear memory state. The threshold of Soft state is set to 64% of MinFree (3231 MB * 0.64 = 2068 MB) As a result the system transitions to the Soft state if more than 261,712 MB -/- 2068 MB = 259,644 MB is consumed. If memory consumption increases beyond 260,679 MB (254.57 GB) the system is in a Hard state. The last state the system can transition to is the Low state and this happens when the overall memory consumption exceeds 261,192 MB. A little over 400 MB remains for the system to maintain correctness of operations.

The VMkernel attempts to avoid this situation by applying various methods of memory reclamation. Each memory state applies particular memory reclamation techniques, customize to the level of aggressiveness required to save the system for running out of memory. Unfortunately, aggressive reclamation impacts VM and system performance. To avoid oscillation between two states, the system is required to reclaim more to return to a higher state.

For example, the system transitions to the clear state when more than 252,019 MB is consumed, yet to return to the high state (the state above the clear state), less than 248,791 MB can be consumed. (300% of MinFree, versus 400% of MinFree). That means that the system will apply a form of memory reclamation technique long beyond the initial (and well known) memory state thresholds. Please be aware of this behavior if operating ESXi systems with memory consumption nearing 96%.

The command `memstats -r comp-stats -s total:minFree:free:numHigh:numClear:numSoft:numHard:numLow:memState -u mb` provides great insight in the current state and the number of times the host was in a particular state.

```
COMPREHENSIVE STATS: Tue Mar  7 04:39:19 2017
------------------------------------------------
Unit              : MB
Selected columns  : total:minFree:free:numHigh:numClear:numSoft:numHard:numLow:memState

----------------------------------------------------------------------------------------------
  total    minFree      free    numHigh   numClear    numSoft    numHard    numLow memState
----------------------------------------------------------------------------------------------
  65501      1266      11858        23         22          0          0          0    High
----------------------------------------------------------------------------------------------
[root@esxi00:~]
```

Figure 155: Memstats Comp-Stats Overview

By default, the command shows much more information, but by using the −s option, specific columns are displayed. This example shows that the host contains 64 GB and has a MinFree of 1266 MB. Since it last boot, the system has been in High state 23 times but also 22 times in Clear state. It's a great tool to get a better understanding whether a host has been under severe memory pressure.

Please note that the advanced configuration setting Mem.MemMinFreePct is still available, yet as the system dynamically manages the MinFree it is set to 0.

Memory Reclamation Techniques per State

Several memory reclamation techniques exist to reclaim memory from VMs. The memory reclamation techniques are transparent page sharing, memory ballooning, memory compression, and memory swapping. Each memory state applies one or more memory reclamation technique.

MEMORY STATE	SHARE	BALLOON	COMPRESS	SWAP	BLOCK
HIGH	X				
CLEAR	X				
SOFT	X	X			
HARD	X		X	X	
LOW	X		X	X	X

Table 37: Memory Reclamation Techniques Active per Memory State

The Clear, Soft, and Hard states focus on providing the best performance possible, while each step introduces a more drastic reclamation technique to prevent memory starvation. The Low state is required for correctness. It protects the VMkernel from crashing resulting from memory starvation.

Transparent Page Sharing

TPS is a passive and opportunistic memory reclamation technique. TPS is a process in the VMkernel that runs in the background. It searches for the opportunity to collapse different memory pages (with identical content) into one memory page. The TPS process exists out of two separate processes. There is a process of identifying identical pages and a process of sharing (collapsing) identical pages. TPS cannot collapse pages immediately when starting a VM.

The identification process scans the memory pages of the powered-on VMs and identifies page copies by their contents. Not eLLC page is compared to all other pages in the system, but a more efficient hashing is used to identify pages with identical contents. These hash value summarizes the page content and function as a hint. These hints are stored into a hash table and contain entries of the other hashed pages and the pages that are already collapsed and shared. The command `memstats -r pshareHint-stats -u mb` provides insight of the current hint stats of the ESXi server.

```
[root@esxi00:~] memstats -r pshareHint-stats -u mb

PSHARE HINT STATS: Tue Mar  7 04:58:40 2017
---------------------------------------------------
  Unit             : MB
  Selected columns : (all)


---------------------------------------------------
     type           totAdd        totRemove         active
---------------------------------------------------
   regular          551597          551396            201
   lpage           7163773         7125078          38694
---------------------------------------------------
   Total           7715370         7676475          38895
---------------------------------------------------
[root@esxi00:~] █
```

Figure 156: PSHARE Hint Statistics

If the hash of a new page matches a hash that is present in the hash table then the sharing process is activated to do a full comparison of the page content to verify if the page is truly identical. If the match exists, the *Copy-On-Write* (COW) technique is used to collapse the page into a single page and share this page. The redundant memory page is reclaimed and can be allocated to another memory instruction.

By default, TPS operates at a cycle of 60 minutes (Mem.ShareScanTime) to scan a VM for page sharing opportunities. TPS will scan 4MB/s per 1 GHz CPU. (Mem.ShareScanGHz).

This means that a slow(er) CPU equals slow(er) TPS process. (But is it a secret that a slow CPU will offer less performance that a fast CPU?). The advanced setting Mem.ShareRateMax sets the maximum number of per-VM scanned pages to 1024 pages per second. The defaults can be altered, but it is advised to keep to the default.

The seasoned administrator and architect noticed that sharing amongst VMs is left out of the previous description and that is because the default focus area of TPS has changed over time. Throughout the years, new CPU instruction extensions were introduced, we moved from 32-bit to 64-bit operating systems. CPU architectures moved from UMA to NUMA and due to the success of the platform, it became subject to security vulnerability scrutiny.

Hardware MMU Impact on TPS

When introduced, 32-bit workloads using memory pages of 4 KB were common. TPS is designed to work with 4K pages and scans and collapses as fast as it can. With the introduction of AMD *Rapid Virtualization Indexing* (RVI) and Intel *Extended Page Tables (EPT)* hardware support for virtualization was introduced. By using hardware MMU, *Nested Page Tables* (NPT) replaced the shadow page tables used to virtualizing x86 processors. Large pages (2MB) reduce the additional overhead of using NPT. Unfortunately, TPS does not collapse large pages by default, thus a tradeoff is introduced between better memory savings versus better performance.

Hardware MMU, NPT and the inability of to collapse large pages by TPS were introduced under the radar and caught many IT organizations off-guard. For many, memory savings were more important than obtaining higher performance increase and thus this improvement was perceived as negligible compared to the additional overhead it created. This happened in the timeframe 2008/2009 and still up to this day you will hear or read 'expert' advice of disabling large pages. The scar runs deep.

Consolidation ratios are extremely important, however disabling large pages in 2017 will not bring back the consolidation-ratios back of 2008 and this is due to NUMA systems and security-focussed changes.

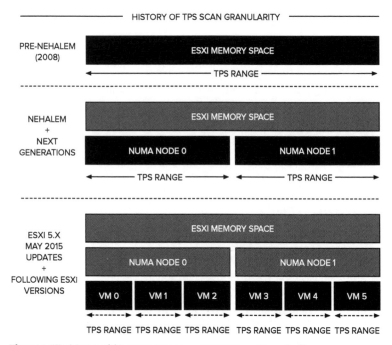

Figure 157: CPU Architecture Impact on TPS Scan Granularity

NUMA Architecture Impact on TPS

NUMA allows the best memory performance by allocating memory pages as close to a CPU as possible. Sharing of identical pages between NUMA nodes impact performance. It can increase memory access latency for a VM on Node 0 accessing a shared page of another VM that runs on Node 1. To avoid unnecessary memory access latency and reduce the overall bandwidth consumption of the QPI, ESXi delimits the sharing domain to a NUMA node. Sharing is still active within the NUMA nodes and it depends on the salting level whether Intra-VM or Inter-VM page sharing occurs within the NUMA node.

The advanced setting: `VMkernel.Boot.sharePerNode` allows you to alter the default setting. As most default settings in ESXi, only change this setting if you are sure that it benefits your environment.

TPS Salting

The paper *Wait a minute! A fast, Cross-VM attack on AES* presents an attack between VMs using TPS. In short it shows a method to attack a VM and recovers an AES encryption key from a VM using cache timing and TPS within the same ESXi host. It is an interesting read and a elaborate method of getting information while the attacker already has access to the system. Nevertheless, we are not here to judge the validity of security hacks. Thus, in the spirit of maintaining a stable and robust platform VMware decided to remove this threat by introducing the salting technique to TPS.

> **VMware reworked the TPS code and the salting technology was included in version: ESXi 5.5 Update 2d (Q1, 2015), ESXi 5.1 Update 3 (12/4, 2014) and ESXi 5.0 Update 3d (Q1, 2015).**

In essence, the default behavior of TPS focuses on intra-VM memory sharing. It only scans and collapses small pages that contain identical content. Or it will collapse large pages into small pages and consolidate identical content if the ESXi host operates in a Clear memory state. It will also avoid consolidating small pages into large pages of the VM during the Clear State operations of the host. Please note that this can impact EUC workloads, with many nearly identical VMs and vFork bases systems that rely on inter-VM TPS.

Salting Explained

In encryption salting is the act of adding random data to make a common password uncommon. This makes it unlikely that this password shows up in any common password list. This slows down the attack.

VMware adopted this concept to group VMs. If the VMs contain the same random number they are perceived to be trustworthy. If the random number doesn't match, no memory page sharing occurs between these VMs. By default the vc.uuid of the VM is used as random number. And because the vc.uuid is unique randomly generated string for a VM in a vCenter, it will never be able to share pages with other VM.

Adjusting Default Behaviour

To Salt pages, two settings must be activated, one at the host (VMkernel) level and one at the VM level. By default, the VMkernel setting is Mem.ShareForceSalting is set to 2. If it is set to 0, TPS shares memory between VMs in the traditional way. Please note this will only be within the same NUMA node while being in a Clear memory state while using large pages. If large pages is disabled on the ESXi system, small pages are consolidated at each memory state of the ESXi host.

MEM.SHAREFORCESALTING	SHARING
0	Inter-VM
1	Between VMs with identical Salt value
2	Intra-VM

Table 38: Host TPS Salting Advanced Setting

If Mem.ShareForceSalting is set to 1 VMs can share their identical memory pages if their salting value is identical. By default the vc.uuid is used, thus Mem.ShareForceSalting=1 requires the per-VM setting sched.mem.pshare.salt. The per-VM setting overrules Mem.ShareForceSalting=2 and shares identical memory pages between VMs running on the same NUMA node.

To enable Inter-VM sharing within a group of VMs, power-off the VMs and add the sched.mem.pshare.salt advanced setting along with a unique string but identical on all VMs within this trusted 'sharing-domain'.

Intra-VM TPS and Zero-pages Sharing

The TPS sharing range has been reduced by many different changes. Keep in mind that an ESXi host free of memory contention, i.e. the host is continually operating in High State, sharing of memory between VMs and within the VM is not active. Is it safe to say that TPS is not used at all? Fortunately, ESXi recognizes zero-pages and collapses them as soon as possible.

Memory pages that contain all 0x00 content are zero pages. During the boot process of Microsoft Windows the OS checks how much memory it has by zeroing out pages it detects. As a result, the VMkernel allocates the entire configured memory of the VM filled with zeroes. Instead of allowing these pages to consume physical memory, the VMkernel collapses them regardless of their size (large or small).

The VMkernel pools the zero pages per NUMA node and can be review within esxtop under shared pages (SHRD), and the shared saved statistic (SHDSVD). These statistics are not shown by default. Switch to the memory screen (M) and press f to select field options. Enable COWH (Copy-on-Write) by pressing N. Sharing zero-pages does not happen immediately as TPS requires time to scan, share and reclaim memory.

```
5:44:07pm up 8 days 18:45, 628 worlds, 6 VMs, 28 vCPUs; MEM overcommit avg: 0.38, 0.39, 0.49
PMEM  /MB: 65501   total: 1826       vmk,52675 other, 10999 free
VMKMEM/MB: 65175 managed:  1266 minfree,  5657 rsvd,  59517 ursvd,  high state
PSHARE/MB:  11220  shared,        91  common:   11129 saving
SWAP  /MB:      0   curr,         0 rclmtgt:             0.00 r/s,   0.00 w/s
ZIP   /MB:      0 zipped,         0   saved
MEMCTL/MB:      0   curr,         0  target,   57153 max

NAME               MEMSZ      GRANT      CNSM      SZTGT      TCHD   TCHD_W      ZERO      SHRD  SHRDSVD      COWH
SQL00           24708.37 24590.48 23657.04 23763.68    343.51     7.04    917.48    921.44   918.96 22357.91
NGN             24663.13  4338.75  1268.00  1458.19     54.65     6.97   3035.86   3058.28  3056.46   791.46
DCX0            16501.05 16400.10 10004.26 10100.43    411.48     6.79   6378.32   6379.24  6379.05  2151.90
VCSA            16495.05 16399.25 15786.89 15889.97   1219.97    334.46    582.60    644.98   597.11 11402.98
DPDK-PKTGEN02    4174.89   961.12   860.91   994.05     78.28     47.86     84.00     93.89    85.09   822.49
DPDK-PKTGEN01    4156.46   642.89   535.06   625.07     67.81     47.68     85.11     95.21    92.94   509.73
```

Figure 158: Copy-On-Write Statistics in Esxtop

Windows boot-process is the common example used to illustrate the usefulness of sharing zero-pages, but interestingly enough the vCenter Server Appliance benefits as well as it generates a substantial number of zero-pages. In this example, the ESXi server runs 6.5 and runs with a default-salting configuration.

The memory state is high thus no memory pressure exists. Even with only Intra-VM TPS enabled, zero-page sharing provides a saving of 11129 MB (PSHARE/MB saving) and is only using 91 MB (PSHARE/MB shared) to provide this saving. The command memstats -r pshare-stats provides an overall impression of the number of zero pages and the amount of shared memory.

```
[root@esxi00:~] memstats -r pshare-stats

PSHARE STATS: Mon Mar  6 19:12:24 2017
------------------------------------------
    Unit                : KB
    Peak chain length : 58
    Peak chain index  : 364519
    Peak ref. count   : 56474
    Selected columns  : (all)

----------------------------------------------------------------------------
        cow         cow1        zero       used  reclaimed     totAdd  totRemove
----------------------------------------------------------------------------
   11460676        48428    11349124      63972   11396704   11653380   11541836
----------------------------------------------------------------------------
[root@esxi00:~] ▌
```

Figure 159: Pshare Hint Statistics

Interestingly the windows OS keeps several memory-page lists to allocate memory pages to demanding applications. The zero-page list contains zeroed out pages to safely allocate memory to a process demanding memory. If an application returns a memory page to the OS, Windows scrubs the freed memory before allocating it to another process. This is an ongoing process and the scan process of TPS picks up the new zeroed-out pages and marks them for sharing. As a result, you will see a fluctuation of zero pages and sharing within the system.

Clear State Uses TPS for Memory Reclamation

If the ESXi host is operating in a High state, large pages are scanned and hints are installed for the small pages within the large page region. If the system transitions to a Clear state large pages will be broken into small pages and collapsed into shareable pages within the NUMA boundary.

When the system is in the clear state it also does not allocate large page regions for small pages, allowing the TPS process to identify and collapse identical pages more quickly than default behaviour. When the system returns to the High state, the small pages are promoted to large pages again. The purpose of the clear state and the interaction with TPS is that it attempts to avoid entering the Low state while making the best use of large pages and small pages. If the VM is protected by a memory reservation, large pages belonging to this particular VM are not collapsed and shared.

Memory Ballooning

The ballooning memory reclamation technique is solely used at the Soft State. This technique operates together with the guest OS. Unfortunately, there is some latency involved with ballooning due to the fact it has to work together with the guest OS to provide the most savings while keeping performance impact to a minimum.

To fully understand the beauty of the balloon driver, It is crucial to understand that the VMkernel is not aware of the guest OS internal memory management mechanisms. Guest OS's commonly use an allocated memory list and a free memory list. When a guest OS makes a request for a page the VMkernel backs that memory page with a physical memory page. When the guest OS stops using the page, it will internally remove the page from the allocated memory list and place the address on the free memory list. Because no physical data is removed the VMkernel keeps storing this data in physical memory.

The official name for the balloon driver is *VMware Memory Control Driver* (vmmemctl) and is distributed as a guest model in the VMware Tools for Microsoft Windows, Linux, FreeBSD, and Solaris guests. If the VMware Tools software is not installed, the VMkernel is unable to initiate the balloon driver in the guest OS and therefore reclaims memory forcefully by using compression and swapping instead. By default, the balloon driver can claim up to 65% of the VM memory configuration.

Altering the value of the setting *Mem.CtlMaxPercent* can change this behavior. As always, be sure to know what you are doing before altering a default value.

When the balloon driver is utilized, the balloon driver inside the VM requests the guest OS to allocated a certain number of pages. Typically, the guest OS provides pages from the free list. Once this list is depleted, it will allocate pages from the cache list. Both lists do not eat up any active pages belonging to the OS or application. In turn the balloon driver informs the VMkernel which physical pages to free up for other VMs. The pages are pinned by the driver so that the guest OS cannot reuse them. It is interesting to note that the guest OS uses its own memory reclamation techniques to reclaim the memory from its applications. One important construct in this process is the guest OS swap file. It's important to have enough guest OS swap space available for the Balloon driver to perform optimally. This requirement should be taken into account when designing the guest OS baseline. A lot of IT organizations are downsizing the guest OS template without truly considering this impact of this design.

At the VMkernel layer a single zeroed page is use and all pinned pages are mapped to this physical page. The balloon driver operates asynchronously and has varying latency as it depends on the guest internal memory pressure. When the ESXi host is no longer under memory pressure, the VMkernel instructs the balloon driver to release the allocated pages back to the guest OS.

Of all memory reclamation techniques, the balloon driver introduces the least amount of performance impact. However, it does require time to reclaim the memory. The VMkernel initiates ballooning when memory consumption is already beyond 96%. Assuming monitoring tools are used, it should be something out of the ordinary that is going on which eats up memory faster than the balloon driver can reclaim.

Many recommendations state that for better performance you should turn off the balloon driver. This in fact, could not be further from the truth.

The balloon driver is activated when memory pressure occurs. It does not cause memory pressure itself, it is a reclamation technique trying to save the system while being as gentle as it can. Disabling this balloon driver doesn't take away – or solve – your memory pressure. This problem is caused by aggressive over commitment of system resources. Disabling the balloon driver pushes the problem down the stack. And that's where swapping rears its ugly head. I'd rather opt for sedation and cure the problem with a well-executed operation than go full battlefield triage while ending up blindly amputating limbs left right and center.

The Balloon Driver as a Performance Indicator?

The balloon driver is not indicator of a performance problem! The balloon driver is used by the VMkernel to reclaim physical memory pages by asking various VMs to get rid of their junk data. It asks the guest OS to provide some RAM which it will not use anymore. The guest OS does not start by handing over memory pages that contain valid data, but provides memory pages in the free list that contain useless data.

As described, the balloon driver is only used in the Soft state and the VMkernel stops engaging the balloon driver when transferring to the Hard state. Connect this with the latency involved in reclaiming and you will notice that the balloon driver is taking up less than 25% of the guest OS memory. If more than 30% of the guest OS memory space is occupied by the balloon driver than it is time to investigate. Typically, a low percentage of balloon activity is usually not a problem.

To get more insights into the balloon target of a VM and the number of ballooned pages the command `memstats -r vm-stats -s name:memSize:max:ballooned:balloonTgt` provides the following stats:

```
[root@esxi00:~] memstats -r vm-stats -s name::memSize:max:ballooned:balloonTgt

VIRTUAL MACHINE STATS: Mon Mar  6 23:26:44 2017
------------------------------------------------
  Start Group ID  : 0
  No. of levels   : 12
  Unit            : KB
  Selected columns : name:memSize:max:balloonTgt:ballooned

------------------------------------------------------------------
       name    memSize      max balloonTgt  ballooned
------------------------------------------------------------------
   vm.68174   16777216       -1          0          0
   vm.68333   16777216       -1          0          0
   vm.88677   25165824       -1          0          0
   vm.93889   25165824       -1          0          0
------------------------------------------------------------------
      Total   83886080                   0          0
------------------------------------------------------------------
[root@esxi00:~] ▊
```

Figure 160: VM-stats Showing Balloon Target and Ballooned Pages

Unfortunately, there is no method to monitor ballooning activity via API-calls. One popular workaround is to place the guest OS swap file on its own virtual disk and monitor the disk IO.

Java and the Balloon Driver

VMware KB article 1008480 recommends setting the memory reservation equal to the configured memory size of the VM if Java is running inside the VM. The *Java VM* (JVM) memory is an active heap space in which objects are constantly created and garbage collected. The JVM expects full access to its memory space to operate adequately. As a result, no pages that reside in the JVM heap should be paged out.

Does that mean you should disable the balloon driver? No! Absence of the balloon driver will trigger compression or swapping during memory over commitment, which result in forcibly reclaiming memory. If the host is expected to be over-committed, then it is recommended to set a reservation. No reclamation is done at physical layer if a reservation is set and thus no reclamation technique is initiated for this VM. This recommendation is only valid if memory over commitment is expected. If the hosts in the cluster are under commitment, no reservation is necessary as it affects vSphere High Availability Slot Sizes.

Memory Compression

vSphere 4.1 introduced memory compression. Memory compression occurs if the host enters the hard state. The VMkernel always attempts to compress memory before swapping, as it faster to retrieve the page from a compressed state than to read it from flash or spinning disk. Research indicated that 70 to 99% of the VM memory pages are highly compressible.

Memory compression occurs on 4 KB pages. The VMkernel strives to share the page first before it attempts to compress the page. If the page is compressible to 2 KB or less, the VMkernel stores it in the per-VM compression cache. Otherwise, the VMkernel swaps out the page.

If the compression cache is full, one compressed page is replaced to make room for a new memory page. The old page will be swapped out. Interestingly enough, ESXi never swaps out compressed files directory, to avoid the additional overhead during a swap-in operation of the page. Pages are first uncompressed before swapping out to disk. If the host experiences prolonged resource contention, memory compression will become the first stop before ultimately ending up as a swapped page.

If the guest OS wants to access the data, the VMkernel first checks the compression cache before it checks the swap file. If the VMkernel finds the page, it decompresses the page and restores it in the VM guest memory. Compression and decompressing use CPU cycles, but it is still more efficient than incurring disk I/O. It avoids swapping to disk, isolating the operations within the host system while improving the page-fault latency. Decompression often takes sub-ms compared to a swap operation, which can take up too many milliseconds. In general, the decompression is in faster by one or two orders of magnitude then swapping.

Per-VM Compression Cache

It is important to know for host design that the compression cache consumes the VMs memory space. The VMkernel does not allocate host physical memory to store the compressed pages, in essence, the compression cache of a VM consumes its own memory space.

The compression cache is fully transparent to the guest OS and if the host is not experiencing memory pressure the size of the cache is zero. The size of the compression cache is fully dynamic. When the host enters the hard state, and the VMkernel selects pages from the VM to swap out, the compression cache starts to grow. By default, the compression cache size is restricted to 10% of the VM memory and is controlled by the advanced setting Mem.MemZipMaxPct. Please note that this setting is a host-level setting. This setting impacts all VMs that run on that host.

Managing Compression Cache

For example, the memory compression cache can take up to 3.2 GB of physical host memory for a 32 GB VM. A quick calculation shows that this space allows the VM to store up to 6.4 GB of memory.

Adjusting the default size of the memory compression cache can have a contradictive effect. By decreasing the cache size more swapping can occur, increasing the page fault latency of the VM. Increasing the cache size can lead to reduced availability of host physical memory during normal operations. Regardless of the memory state of the ESXi host compressed pages remain compressed until the guest OS requires the data. As a result, the compressed data lingers and continues to occupy valuable physical host memory. Physical memory that could otherwise be used to host the active working set of the VM. Esxtop and memstat commands reveal a lot of useful information about the compression cache. The Zip (Q) field expands esxtop with information about the compression cache size and the active zip operations. Memstat provides additional details such as the compression time and overall stats on how much data was compressed and uncompressed. Time is listed in ms!

```
[root@esxi03:~] memstats -r zip-stats -s name:totalCache:zipped:unzipped:zipRejected:avgZipTime:avgUnziptime -u MB

VIRTUAL MACHINE COMPRESSION STATS: Wed Apr 19 15:44:16 2017
----------------------------------------------------------
  Start Group ID   : 0
  No. of levels    : 12
  Unit             : MB
  Selected columns : name:totalCache:zipped:unZipped:zipRejected:avgZipTime:avgUnzipTime

--------------------------------------------------------------------------------------
          name totalCache     zipped  unZipped zipRejected avgZipTime avgUnzipTime
--------------------------------------------------------------------------------------
     vm.159977        508       2652       466        1119         73           35
--------------------------------------------------------------------------------------
         Total        508       2652       466        1119         73           35
--------------------------------------------------------------------------------------
[root@esxi03:~] █
```

Figure 161: Memstats Zip-Stats

VSISH provides more details about the compression and decompression time. Use the mem client id shown in the memstats output to retrieve the details from the VSI shell.

```
[root@esxi03:~] vsish -e cat /sched/memClients/159977/memzipInfo
mem client memzip stats {
    cache size:510816 KB
    used cache size:510226 KB
    maximum cache size:3355440 KB
    number of free half pages:249
    number of free quarter pages:92
    total memory compressed:2716516 KB
    total memory decompressed:501632 KB
    total memory faulted:475384 KB
    total memory rejected:1146464 KB
    total memory selected as a swap candidate:0 KB
    rejection rate:28
    average page size:1289
    average compression time:73 usec
    minimum compression time:10 usec
    maximum compression time:245 usec
    average decompression time:33 usec
    minimum decompression time:5 usec
    maximum decompression time:102 usec
    average hit rate:0
    average adjusted hit rate:0
}
[root@esxi03:~] █
```

Figure 162: VSISH MemzipInfo Output

Memory compression reduces the performance impact of memory reclamation tremendously, team this with host cache swapping to flash devices and the memory reclamation penalty is severely reduced.

Memory Swapping

When the ESXi host enters the hard state, it resorts to swapping. Swapping is the most aggressive form of memory reclamation and is there to avoid the system of running out of memory. During the hard state, the VMkernel selects the memory page without any interaction with the guest OS. You can argue that it goes in blind, just random select pages to reclaim. Now there is some sense of intelligence or at least finesse as the VMkernel determines if that memory page is shareable or compressible. If not it will swap out this page into one of its swap files. Also, the VMkernel turns to itself to see whether some processes could perform good enough with less memory and reclaims memory from user worlds and processes used for virtualizing VMs (VMX).

ESXi 6.5 has three different kinds of swap files. The system swap file is the designated space to reclaim memory from its user worlds. The VMX swap files are used to reclaim memory from the processes directly tied to running a VM. The third swap file is the VM swap file, which allows reclaiming memory from the VMs memory space.

System Swap

A system swap space is available to the VMkernel to swap out memory pages from its user-worlds. The primary goal of the system swap file is to reclaim memory without compromising user fidelity. A host must be able to respond sufficiently fast all the time. Within the VMkernel distinguish is being made between visible user worlds and invisible user world. This distinction is from a user-experience perspective. User worlds such as the hostd impact user experience if too much memory is reclaimed from this user world, that is why it is preferred to reclaim memory from user-invisible worlds.

By default, the system swap is enabled with the options 'Use host cache if available' and 'Can use datastore specified by host for swap files'. Typically, these options are not enabled by most, and therefore most systems do not leverage the possibility of system swap by default.

The system swap consumes up to 1 GB of disk space. If the system swap is configured to use a host swap directory, a `sysSwap*.swp` file appears in this directory.

Name		Size		Modified		Type
.sdd.sf				04/09/2017, 9:11:26 AM		Folder
sysSwap-ds-58626395-8a10-dfd0-99f2-0cc47a6f23aa.swp		1,048,576 KB		04/18/2017, 1:17:32 PM		File

Figure 163: System Swap File in Swap Directory

VMX Swap Files

To reduce the VM overhead in times of memory pressure, vSphere 5.0 introduced a VMX swap file. Admittedly the name VMX swap file can be a bit confusing, as it synonyms for most with the VMX file. However, VMX stands for VM eXecutable and is therefore not tied to the VMX file directly.

The VMX swap file allows reducing the amount of memory reserved for the VMX process while the host is experiencing memory pressure. It allows the system to reduce the overhead memory reservation dynamically for each active VM.

> **Interestingly enough, this is the only reservation connected to a VM that can be reclaimed by the VMkernel during memory pressure. The overhead memory is dynamic and the VMkernel adjust its reservation automatically during normal operations. As a result, it can also reduce the reservation and swap the memory to a swap space in time of need.**

The VMX swap file is considered to be a private swap file. It is exclusively linked to a VM. When a VM is powered on, two swap files appear in the VM directory. One for the VMX process and one swap file for the guest memory address space. If a host local swap directory is enabled, the swap files are stored in this directory.

Name	Size
⬜ .sdd.sf	
⬜ SQL02-66026eb7.vswp	25,165,824 KB
⬜ sysSwap-hls-58626395-8a10-dfd0-99f2-0cc47a6f23aa.swp	1,048,576 KB
⬜ vmx-SQL02-1711435447-1.vswp	112,640 KB

Figure 164: VMX Swap Files in Host Swap File Location

By default, the VMX initial file size is 110 MB and can be adjusted adding the VM advanced setting `sched.swap.vmxInitialFileSize` and specifying a file size. Typically, the system knows best. To disable VMX swapping, add the advanced setting: `sched.swap.vmxSwapEnabled` value: `False`. If no swap space is defined, the memory pages of the VMX are pinned and the VMkernel cannot consolidate memory used by the VMX processes.

VM Swap File

A VM swap file is available for the VM memory that is not protected by a memory reservation. The size of the swap file is calculated as follows: `Configured memory - memory reservation = size swap file size.` Configured memory is the amount of 'physical' memory seen by guest OS. For example, the configured memory of VM is 16 GB – memory reservation of 12 GB = 4 GB swap file size.

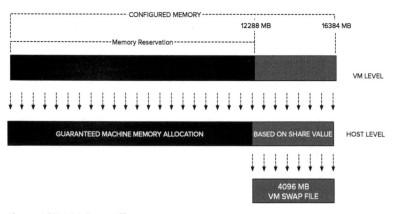

Figure 165: VM Swap File

The VMkernel uses the memory reservation setting to calculate the VM swap file because reserved memory will be backed by machine memory all the time. The difference between the configured memory and memory reservation is eligible for memory reclamation.

By default, the VM working directory stores the VM swap file. An alternative datastore can be used to store the VM swap file. It can be a local device or a shared datastore. The swap file is a file in a Thick Provision Lazy Zeroed format. When the VM powers on, the VMkernel creates the file and allocates the appropriate disk space. The swap file is zeroed out on demand. This behavior allows the VMkernel to create the swap file swiftly.

vSAN 6.2 provides the option called Sparse VM Swap Objects that allows you to create thin-provisioned swap files. Instead of 100% reserving the memory of a vSAN datastore for the VM swap file object now storage capacity is consumed when the host is swapping. The administrator is required to ensure enough vSAN capacity is available if this scenario occurs otherwise the VM will fail. For more information about this feature, please visit CormacHogan.com or Yellow-Bricks.com and use the appropriate search term.

Alternative Swap File Locations

Storing the VM swap file in an alternative location is often done for one of the two reasons, speed or saving expensive shared storage space by reducing shares storage footprint.

If a memory reservation is not protecting the VM configured memory, the full memory configuration size is consumed as disk space. If you are running thousands VMs with an average memory size of 32 GB, realize that just only the swap files consume 32 terabytes of shared storage. Depending on the probability of memory pressure, it might be a hefty tax.

An interesting strategy to save disk space is to configure a (partial) memory reservation on each VM to reduce the footprint of swap files on the shared storage solution. This strategy is appealing for organizations that focus on never to overcommit ESXi host memory. In essence, it boils down to a comparison of cost per gigabyte of memory versus the cost of gigabyte per shared (NAND Flash) storage. Storing the VM swap file on an alternative swap file location might have an impact on some services.

Impact 1 - Increase vMotion Time
During normal operations, the destination ESXi host has no ability to connect to the local swap datastore of any other host. You would not want to do this, as latency will go through the roof. Swapping + round trip network fetching would probably feel like you're running your application on an i386 again. If a VM migrates with vMotion, the destination host creates a new VM swap file in its local swap file directory. The time to create the file and extracting the memory pages from the source swap file increase the vMotion time.

Impact 2 – Storage Management of Swap File Directory Across Cluster
Keep in mind that the destination swap file directory must contain enough space to create the Thick Provision Lazy Zeroed VM swap file. If the local swap directory does not have enough space, the ESXi host tries to store the VM swap file in the working directory of the VM. You need to ensure enough free space is available in the working directory otherwise the VM not allowed to be powered up.
Assuming you chose for a local swap directory, you want to ensure that this functionality is available for VMs in your cluster. This result in additional management overhead ensuring enough storage capacity is available on every local swap file directory in case a vMotion occurs.

The vMotion network is used for moving the memory pages from the source host to the destination host. Memory pages are extracted from the VM swap file in the local swap directory and are copied into the stream of the in-memory pages from the source host to the destination host. The destination host is not aware which pages originate from swap file and which pages come from in-memory, they are just memory pages that need to be stored and made available to the new VM.

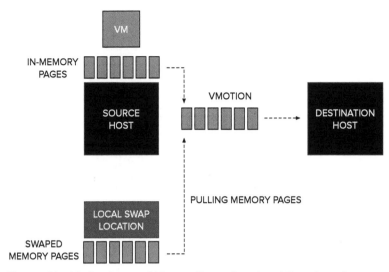

Figure 166: vMotion Swapped Memory Pages from Local Swap Location

Alternative Swap file location

If a host is a member of a vSphere cluster, the swap file location is managed by a collection of settings. The first step is to change the cluster-level setting of the swap file location. In the general setting section of the cluster configuration, select swap file location and click on edit. This screen provides the option 'Datastore specified by host'.

Figure 167: Selecting an Alternative Datastore Location

On each host in the cluster, go to the Configure tab, select the Swap File Location option and click on edit.

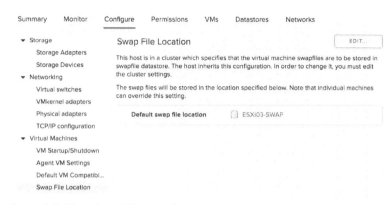

Figure 168: Host Swap File Location

From this point forward the VMkernel stores both the VMX and the VM swap file of each VM it services in this location. Swap files of active VMs remain on the previously configured location until the VM power cycles. This option allows selecting any device formatted with VMFS. Using a local flash device for this option leads to reduced swap-in and swap-out times. vSphere 6.5 provides additional swapping features that leverages flash technology optimally.

Host Swap Cache

vSphere 5.0 introduced the option Swap to Host Cache, and it became quickly know as Swap to SSD as it would only leverage flash devices. vSphere 5.5 introduced the Virtual Flash Host Swap Cache Configuration, which operates similarly to Host Cache Configuration. vFlash allows to facilitate the host swap cache configuration from its framework. The only operational difference between these two features is the disk format it uses. Host Cache Configuration uses VMFS datastores, while vFlash uses Virtual Flash File System datastores.

VMware produced no official performance report of a performance difference between two file systems. Therefore, we cannot provide clear directives on which feature to use. As both functions operate similar on the backend, this section covers both.

Why Swapping to Flash Devices?

Pages are swapped in synchronously, which makes it a part of the performance critical path. The latency of this IO is essential to VM performance as a swap in operation blocks the progress a VM. A VM cannot continue until the swap-in process is completed. Leveraging the performance, a flash device offers helps to reduce the swap-in latency tremendously. Interestingly enough, pages are swapped out asynchronously as this reduces the swap out time. The swap-out rate determines the reclaim memory performance.

Shared Swap Files

The Host Swap Cache Configuration creates a repository of swap files that are available to all active VMs running on the host. During the configuration of the feature, the necessary space is allocated for the host cache. The VMkernel creates multiple swap files of 1 GB in the space allotted to the swap cache. For example, selecting 20 GB of swap space results in 20 swap files of each 1 GB.

The following screenshot shows the Host Cache Configuration and the Virtual Flash Host Swap Cache Configuration. Both features are configured to consume 20 GB and each creates 20 separate swap files of 1 GB in size. (The screenshot cropped for legibility).

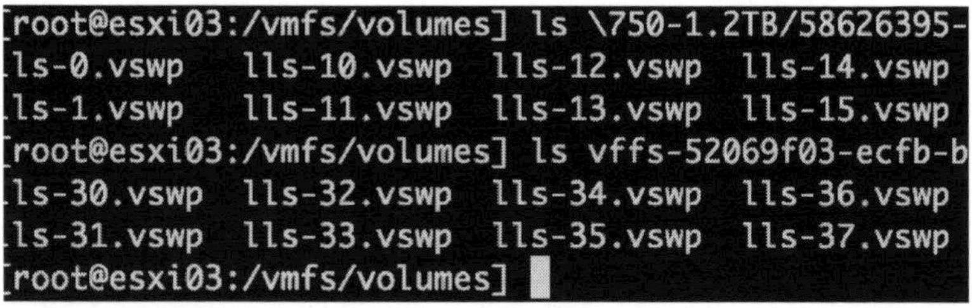

```
[root@esxi03:/vmfs/volumes] ls \750-1.2TB/58626395-
ls-0.vswp    lls-10.vswp  lls-12.vswp  lls-14.vswp
ls-1.vswp    lls-11.vswp  lls-13.vswp  lls-15.vswp
[root@esxi03:/vmfs/volumes] ls vffs-52069f03-ecfb-b
ls-30.vswp   lls-32.vswp  lls-34.vswp  lls-36.vswp
ls-31.vswp   lls-33.vswp  lls-35.vswp  lls-37.vswp
[root@esxi03:/vmfs/volumes] █
```

Figure 169: Multiple Swap Files in Host Swap Cache

The active VMs share these swap files. The system does not create a particular swap file for each active VMs. I.e. you can have one active VM and have 20 swap files stored in the swap space, or you can have 80 active VMs, there would still be 20 swap files. The VMkernel shares the swap files amongst the VMs during memory contention. There is no direct method of controlling per-VM priority consumption of swap space. It is the VM memory entitlement that determines which VM is subjected to memory reclamation.

Implementing the host swap cache configuration does not remove the need for per-VM swap files. A regular VM swap file is created for every powered-on VM following the standard calculation. However, the host swap cache follows a write-back scheme, resulting in swapped out data being in solely one place. If space is running low on the flash device, older pages are written to the per-VM swap file. An interesting design option is to use host swap cache with flash devices and store the VM and VMX swap files on low-cost spindles. If the host swap cache is sized accordingly, swapping to per-VM swap file should be non-existent.

The duration of a vMotion process is prolonged as vMotion reads in the page from the flash device and transfer the data to the destination host. The flash device performance should help with decreasing the overhead experienced with swap files stored on spinning disks.

Unswap

As described above, swap-in operations are detrimental to VM performance. The VMkernel selects memory pages to swap out randomly for each VM. Due to the information gap, the VMkernel does not have any knowledge how important this memory page was to that VM. The page could belong to the working set of an application, or it could be a page that is in one of the free/standby list of the OS.

Consequently, It is hard for the VMkernel to determine the value of swapping in. A VM request for this memory address confirms its validity. It is uncertain whether a premature swap-in helps to avoid the latency of a disk access if a page fault occurs. And due to this, the VMkernel rather prefers a performance hit for a particular VM, than to waste precious physical memory resources by filling it up with potential useless data. In this case, the needs of the many outweigh the needs of the few.

However, if the memory pressure was the cause of an uncommon event, for example, a few host outages at the same time, it might be interesting to swap the memory pages back into the physical memory to avoid any delay of application operations. For this reason, the command UNSWAP is available for a manual swap in action for VMs.

Please note that the option unswap only works with per-VM swap files. If your host is configured with a host swap cache, the VMkernel is unable to unswap the memory pages and will report the following entry in the vmkernel.log file.

```
Swap: VM 163011: 4805: Regular swap file is empty
Swap: VM 163011: 4805: Finish swapping in reg file. (faulted 0
pages, pshared 0 pages). Success
```

The vmstats command shows us that this VM has swapped out more than 8 GB. You may have noticed that there is no ballooned memory. Typically, the balloon driver attempts to reclaim memory up to 65%, but for this exercise, we disabled the balloon driver.

```
[root@esxi03:~] memstats -r vm-stats -u mb -s name:worldGrp:memSize:max:consumed:swapped:Ballooned

VIRTUAL MACHINE STATS: Thu Apr 27 15:48:48 2017
-------------------------------------------------------
  Start Group ID   : 0
  No. of levels    : 12
  Unit             : MB
  Selected columns : name:worldGrp:memSize:max:consumed:ballooned:swapped


---------------------------------------------------------------------------------------------------
        name    worldGrp    memSize      max    consumed  ballooned     swapped
---------------------------------------------------------------------------------------------------
    vm.165805      165805      32768    10240       10249          0        8804
---------------------------------------------------------------------------------------------------
       Total                  32768                10249          0        8804
---------------------------------------------------------------------------------------------------
[root@esxi03:~] ▊
```

Figure 170: Memstat Swapped and Ballooned

The VM-stats command shows the VMX Cartel ID of the VM. However, the UNSWAP command requires the world id of the VM. One of the quickest methods to determine the world-id is by issuing the command `esxcli vm process list`.

```
[root@esxi03:~] esxcli vm process list
SQL00
    World ID: 165806
    Process ID: 0
    VMX Cartel ID: 165805
    UUID: 42 03 33 60 2b 56 3e 71-7d b4 95 07 1c ec ab 95
    Display Name: SQL00
    Config File: /vmfs/volumes/58ef6760-2ad9a448-20d9-0cc47a6f23aa/SQL00/SQL00.vmx
[root@esxi03:~] ▊
```

Figure 171: Esxcli Command to Determine World ID

This command shows both the World ID as well as the VMX Cartel ID allowing you to match both IDs quite easily. You can start the unswap process by using the localcli command. In our example, we want to unswap the 8804 MB that is currently located in the swap file.

The command to unswap is as follows: `localcli --plugin-dir=/usr/lib/vmware/esxcli/int vm process unswap --world-id 165806 -s 8804 -u mb`

The command immediately returns to the prompt. However it does not imply that the command is completed, the process can take a while, depending on the amount of memory to swap-in. To follow process, you can tail the vmkernel.log: `tail -F /var/log/vmkernel.log | grep Swap`

```
[root@esxi03:~] tail -F /var/log/vmkernel.log | grep Swap
2017-04-27T15:50:02.757Z cpu4:167110)Swap: vm 165806: 4864: Starting prefault for the reg file
```

Figure 172: Tail VMkernel.log

Or you can log in to the vSphere Web Client and adjust the monitor performance chart. We've configured chart to show the consumed memory and the swapped memory. The screenshot clearly shows when the unswap command was issued.

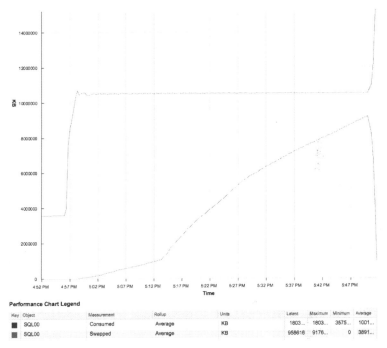

Performance Chart Legend

Key	Object	Measurement	Rollup	Units	Latest	Maximum	Minimum	Average
■	SQL00	Consumed	Average	KB	1803...	1803...	3575...	1001...
■	SQL00	Swapped	Average	KB	958616	9176...	0	3891...

Figure 173: VM Performance Chart WebClient

After swapping in 8804 MB the VMkernel logs the entry:

```
Swap: VM 165806: 4864: Starting prefault for the reg file
Swap: VM 165806: 4864: Finish swapping in reg file. (faulted
2253824 pages, pshared 66616 pages). Success.
```

We verify if the swap file is empty by running the memstats command again. Unfortunately, when we decided to swap in the 8+ GB the VM was still swapping out memory, hence the non-zero report of the performance chart. Typically, you issue a swap-in command when the host is free of memory pressure. The command does not require a precise swap-in target. You can also provide a larger target number to avoid the scenario depicted above.

Block Execution

Block execution is the final state, the state in which the VMkernel tries its utmost best not to run out of memory. Most of you will never see a block execution happen as it appears most VMware engineers focused on memory management report not being able to get the VMkernel in this state as swapping reliefs the memory pressure fast enough to avoid this dreaded state.

However, if the VMs allocate memory at a faster rate than the current swap-out rate, then the VMkernel enters the Low state. The VMkernel blocks new memory allocations from VMs as long as it is in Low state until the memory reclamation techniques have reclaimed enough memory to revert to the Hard state. If a memory page is selected it will be checked to see whether it can be shared, compressed before swapping out.

The command `memstats -r comp-stats -s total:minFree:free:numHigh:numClear:numSoft:numHard:numLow:memState -u mb` provides great insight in the current state and the number of times the host was in a particular state since boot.

```
COMPREHENSIVE STATS: Tue Mar  7 04:39:19 2017
------------------------------------------------
  Unit            : MB
  Selected columns : total:minFree:free:numHigh:numClear:numSoft:numHard:numLow:memState
------------------------------------------------------------------------------------------
    total    minFree      free    numHigh    numClear    numSoft    numHard    numLow memState
    65501       1266     11858         23          22          0          0         0     High
------------------------------------------------------------------------------------------
[root@esxi00:~]
```

Figure 174: Memory State Overview

P3

STORAGE RESOURCES

PROLOGUE

The advent of powerful commodity server platforms led to the ability to run all functions of an IT environment in software. Compute virtualization has been used extensively for more than a decade for cost and operational benefits. More recently, *Software Defined Networking* (SDN) and *Software Defined Storage* (SDS) are also becoming mainstream. For storage, the ubiquity and (eventually) cost effectiveness of *Solid-State Drives* (SSDs) sealed the future of storage. It is all software on commodity hardware. That applies to enterprise products and certainly hyper-scale storage in public clouds.

Going forward, the storage industry is approaching another inflection point, perhaps more significant than what we witnessed with SDS. This is driven by two major trends. First is the emergence of a new generation of persistent memory technologies. Initially available in the internals of NVMe devices, we should expect to see soon products in a DIMM form factor. The properties of these devices will be disruptive to the architectures of existing storage systems. For the first time in the history of Computing, storage will be faster than the network. Imagine storage accessible in sub-microsecond latencies on the memory channel of a CPU. The implications will be profound. Over the next 3-5 years, we shall see a race in the industry for who's going to offer the best storage platform for the new types of storage hardware.

Interestingly, the second trend is all about the commoditization of storage platforms. IT organizations are moving towards hybrid infrastructures, which consist of a combination of private and public clouds. In such dynamic and heterogeneous environments, the industry's focus will shift to data management across storage silos and physical boundaries. The value will be on data services that are not confined within a specific storage platform.

Examples include snapshots for getting immutable copies of data out of one storage silo and seamlessly ship them to another location or cloud, for protection (backup, DR) or for transformation for further processing (e.g., warehousing). When data can move seamlessly across a hybrid IT environment, one needs tools for data monitoring, control and governance. In my opinion, it is inevitable that the storage industry will be moving in that direction – evolve from selling data persistence products to offering global data management services. Exciting times ahead for all of us!

Christos Karamanolis

Christos is a Fellow, Principal Engineer and the CTO of the Storage and Availability Business Unit at VMware. He has 25 years of research and development experience in distributed systems, fault tolerance, storage, and storage management. He has co-authored more than 20 research papers in peer-reviewed journals and conferences and holds over 20 granted patents with several pending.

13

HOST-LOCAL STORAGE ARCHITECTURE

Consistent performance is provided by data locality. CPU and data want to be together. And in a perfect world, the CPU would have vast amounts of data storage space directly connected to its registers. Unfortunately, we don't live in a perfect world. We need to battle economics and deal with physics.

Reducing distance between resources is a primary objective within every layer of the computer architecture. You can't beat physics, thus by removing distance you decrease time spent traveling. Distance generally introduces additional components to process the signal. Each component adds latency. In a worst-case scenario, this latency is inconsistent, providing a variable user experience. Of course, this statement is made with economics in mind. There are ways to create an infrastructure with a lot of external components (non-host-local) that performs extremely well, but we are talking Bond villain like budgets here.

The previous sections of the book focused on optimizing the data path between memory and cache and the data placement between cache and CPU register. Optimizations that shave off time in the nanosecond (ns) range. We are talking about a unit of time equal to one billionth of a second. A scale so small it is unfathomable for us humans, so let's move it closer and use a more comprehendible scale of seconds, minutes, hours, days and years.

If the CPU retrieves data from the L1 cache, it typically takes 0.5 ns, but for the sake of simplicity this becomes one ns, and we substitute one ns for one second. We discovered that in a NUMA system a local memory reference takes about 70 ns and a remote memory reference up to 130 ns. By using the one-second scale, a remote memory reference takes two minutes and ten seconds. If we need to fetch data from a traditional storage array using spindles, It is common to experience eight milliseconds of latency. That is eight million nanoseconds! On our one-second measurement scale that equals to 133333.34 minutes - or - 2222.22 hours - or - 92.59 days. Interesting to see, many people want to optimize local and remote memory operations in NUMA systems, but trivialize storage latency.

To reduce that number drastically, we can take advantage of the advancements the industry has made in recent years. Hardware and software technologies such as *Non-Volatile Memory express* (NVMe), (3D-) NAND flash, and 3D XPoint (*pronounced 3D cross point*) provide the fundamentals to obtain consistent storage performance. These solutions are faster in orders of magnitude than traditional centralized storage solutions. As a comparison, the device latency of a gen-1 Intel 3D XPoint device is below 10 microseconds. Intel states that in worst-case scenario, any read or write operation will be completed in less than 150 microseconds. That is still 150,000 times more than an L1 cache reference, but 41.7 hours sounds much better than 92.59 days. It also shows that software is now the primary factor of latency! A later paragraph will cover the overhead of software in depth.

Bringing the storage device closer to the application is a big step in cutting down latency and reducing the number of components in between. When selecting a host-local storage device you can choose between different interfaces and protocols. Although the physical distance is reduced, the logical distance can differ between host controller interfaces. Complex protocol stacks are suboptimal for performance. Therefore, the NVMe protocol is designed to use the least number of software layers to reduce latency and decrease the number of CPU cycles spent on processing I/O.

Designing a system that provides high-performance consistently does not stop at selecting a fast device, both the software and hardware characteristics need to be taken into account. This chapter focuses on host-local storage architecture focusing on the details of device interfaces, device drivers and finally the various storage devices available today.

The storage section primarily focuses on modern host-local storage solutions, but does not ignore particular VMkernel scheduling constructs that exist to connect to centralized storage solutions.

Transport Interconnect

Which technology is the best fit for your architecture, operations, and workload? Each acceleration technology has its benefits and its trade-offs. NAND-Flash encounters architectural bottlenecks that mechanical spindles do not face. In turn, 3D XPoint eliminates bottlenecks that NAND-Flash encounters. And we are sure that its successor will solve limitations of 3D XPoint technology while introducing new ones as well. It is a never-ending race to zero.

Today's *Non-Volatile Memory* (NVM) components (NAND-Flash and 3D XPoint) are hitting a performance wall when using traditional interfaces. These interfaces and protocols were created in a pre-solid state world and cannot provide the bandwidth or speed that non-volatile memory components require. To solve the performance limitations, new standards such as NVMe and device interfaces such as M.2 are designed from the ground up to exploit the performance levels of modern host-local storage devices. Today's choice of interfaces include *Serial Advanced Technology Attachment* (SATA), *Serial Attached SCSI* (SAS) and *Peripheral Component Interconnect Express* (PCIe). We intentionally left out M.2 from this list. Often confused as an interface definition, but in actuality it is a form-factor standard. M.2 devices, formerly known as *Next-Generation Form Factor* (NGFF), are available with an SATA bus connector or a PCI-E connector.

> **The reason why it is called M.2 is that it stands to replace both mSATA and mini PCI Express.**

Another architecture + form factor we omitted from the list is *Memory Channel Storage* (MCS). MCS leverages the DIMM socket and interfaces with the memory controller on the CPU. It attempts to leverage the parallel channels of the memory bus, however current implementations of MCS implement a DDR3-to-SATA bridge controller. Multiple devices are necessary to obtain parallelism.

The popular interfaces to connect your non-volatile memory resource are SATA 3.0, PCIe 3.0 and SAS-3. As most PCIe devices utilize a PCIe x4 Gen 3 host interface, we listed the theoretical transfer rate and bandwidth separately. This allows you to properly compare SAS devices with a PCIe 3.0 x4 device.

INTERFACE	RAW BIT STREAM	TRANSFER RATE	BANDWIDTH
SATA 3.0	6 GT/s	6.0 Gb/s	600 MB/s
PCIe 3.0	8 GT/s	8.0 Gb/s	985 MB/s
SAS-3	12 GT/s	12.0 Gb/s	1200 MB/s
PCIe 3.0 (x4)		31.5 Gb/s	3930 MB/s

Table 39: Theoretical Bandwidth of Popular Interfaces

Please keep in mind that the theoretical bandwidth is not entirely available for data transfer as some bits are used for encoding. The Host Networking chapter contains detailed information about the encoding, but in essence, SAS-3 endures a 20% overhead for encoding, while PCIe 3.0 only sustains an overhead of 1.54%

SATA

Modern servers contain SATA-3 controllers that provide a theoretical transfer rate of 6 Gbits per second. SATA Revision 3.2 was released in 2013 and introduced SATA Express. The SATA Express is an interface that supports both SATA and PCI Express devices.

The host connector is backward compatible with the SATA connector, allowing connection of two SATA devices. Instead of continuing iteration of SATA native speed, it was clear that it would take too long to catch up to the current solid-state performance levels. By adopting PCIe, bandwidth, and scalability levels are immediate up to par. Or so it seemed. Early SATA Express connects the device with two PCIe 2.0 lanes, providing a theoretical bandwidth of 1 GB/s. A small leap from 600 MB/s to 1 GB/s. Newer SATAe devices and server chipsets support PCIe 3.0, doubling the theoretical bandwidth from 1GB/s to 2GB/s.

U.2 (SFF-8639)

Although it is a big step forward from 600 MB/s to 2 GB/s, many considered the two PCIe lanes a limitation. PCIe add-in cards often leverage 4 PCIe lanes. The SFF-8639 connector was introduced to compete with the bandwidth of PCIe add-in cards. The name SFF-8639 won't make it to the list of words we love because, well, it doesn't roll off the tongue that well. In June 2015, the SSD Form Factor Working group decided it was better to replace the name with U.2 (U dot 2). This name aligns more with the new and hip M.2 connector instead of old and dusty SATA moniker. The U.2 connector is available with PCIe 2.0 support and PCIe 3.0 support. All U.2 devices of major vendors do not support AHCI but are NVMe devices. As a result, a 2.5-inch NVM device with a U.2 interface could be as fast as a PCIe add-in-card, with more friendly serviceability functionality such as hot plug.

Interestingly enough, U.2 is leveraging NVMe and PCIe technology. Yet due to the connector being mechanically identical to the SATA Express device plug it is considered an SATA technology.

> **Please ensure that the firmware of the ESXi host is able to boot the NVMe storage device.**

SAS

SAS controllers are available from multiple vendors, there is no universal SAS controller equivalent to the SATA AHCI controller. This results in a variety of software drivers for the on-chip or external HBA. The major factor of SAS development was to manage higher performance flash devices and spinning media such as 15K RPM HDDs.

SATA uses a half-duplex mode of communication. It can either read or write data to the device. SAS leverages multiple full-duplex data channels, allowing it to read and write simultaneously, providing faster throughput of data. Today's SAS standard is providing a theoretical bandwidth of 12 Gbit/s. This is simply not enough for modern flash devices. Luckily, a new SAS specification is on the horizon. SAS-4 specification states 24 Gbit/s, but the SCSI Trade Association reports that the maximum bandwidth of the first-generation devices will have 19.2 Gbps.

SAS-3 exceeds the bandwidth of a single lane of a PCI-e device, however PCIe uses multiple lanes for scalability. For example, a PCIe 3.0 x4 device can deliver nearly 4 GB/s of theoretical bandwidth. Therefore, the industry focused on moving the non-volatile memory onto the PCIe interface. The PCIe interface offers more bandwidth while reducing the connectivity complexity.

Newer standards of existing interfaces are on the horizon, SAS-4 and PCIe 4.0 specifications are expected to be released somewhere in the year 2017. The Host Networking chapter contains detailed information about the theoretical bandwidth of various PCIe specifications.

PCIe Architecture

Chapter 2 introduces Uncore and its components. The Integrated I/O component within the Uncore is responsible for providing the interface to PCIe devices. The E5-2600 v1 (Sandy Bridge) integrated PCIe 3.0 on the processor die. The platform controller hub that is contained within the chipset that is external to the CPU, takes care of PCIe 2.0 connections. The PCIe architecture is a point-to-point topology that connects every device with separate links. A PCIe link supports full-duplex communication between the two PCIe devices. The most common configuration leverages a connection between the host endpoint (the PCIe root complex) and a PCIe device itself.

A link is composed of one or more lanes. Generally, NVMe devices use four lanes, a well-known exception is the Samsung PM1725 that uses eight lanes.

Each lane contains two pairs of wires. One pair of wires is to receive data, the other pair of wires is to send data. PCIe supports up to 32 lanes per link, PCIe links are available in lane configurations: 1, 2, 4, 8, 12, 16 and 32. Each PCIe 3.0 lane has a transfer rate of eight gigatransfers per second.

Storage controllers benefit the most from increased numbers of lanes. The E5-2600 v4 (Broadwell) supports up to 40 lanes. The allocation of lanes depends on the server model, i.e. how many PCIe expansion slots it contains. The most common configuration for NVMe devices is a PCIe 3.0 x4 connection (four lanes per link). The amount of bandwidth is adequate for today's read and write performance of the drives. If such a device would be an x16 device, it unnecessary reduces the available lanes (and thus bandwidth) for other devices. Most often servers are expanded with high-speed NICs, which are also in need of large amounts of bandwidth.

During power-on operations the *Integrated I/O component* identifies what devices are connected and creates a mapping. It automatically adjusts lanes to the lower common denominator. For example, when placing an x8 card in an x4 slot, the card uses four lanes to communicate. The opposite is true as well, an x4 card in an x8 slot utilizes four lanes.

A PCIe 3.0 slot connects to the Integrated IO components on the CPU package. The PCIe root complex of that NUMA node has control over that PCIe device. When another NUMA node is generating data, it has to push that data across the QPI to the PCIe root complex of the owning NUMA node. That means that the data path to an NVMe device is non-uniform. As a result, it is critical to select the CPU with the highest QPI bandwidth.

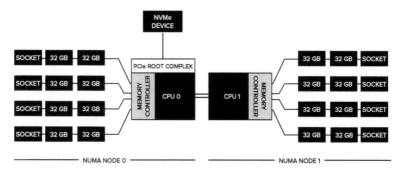

Figure 175: NUMA Node Controlling PCIe NVMe Device

Unfortunately, not many vendors publish their PCIe mapping online. Luckily, we found the spec sheet of the Cisco UCS C460 M4 High-Performance Server (Rev E.5 - May 6, 2017) that lists the following:

SLOT NUMBER	CPU CONTROLLED	LANES	CONNECTOR
1	1	x8	x8
2	1	x16	x16
3	2	x4	x16
4	2	x8	x16
5	2	x8	x16
6	4	x8	x8
7	3	x16	x16
8	4	x8	x16
9	3	x16	x16
10	4	x8	x16

Table 40: PCIe Expansion Slot Numbering Cisco UCS C460

Maybe a picture explains the complex layout of connections, bandwidth and PCIe interfaces better. As you will notice, just the length of the interface does not imply it will operate at the expected speed. Work with your server vendor to determine which PCIe interface is suitable for your PCIe based storage device. Please note that the PCI lanes are non-uniformly distributed.

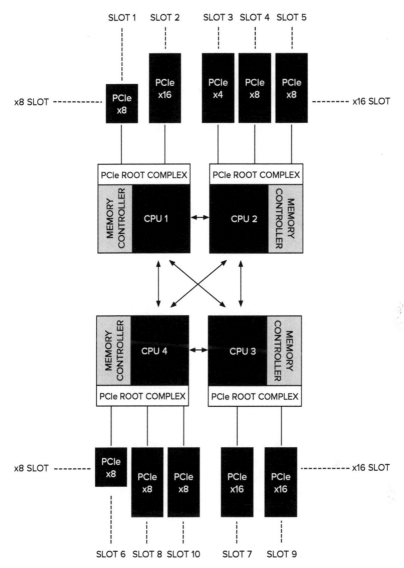

Figure 176: Cisco UCS C460 PCIe Expansion Slot Layout

Before selecting, installing and configuring a device, validate that the device is on the official VMware Compatibility Guide. If designing for vSAN, please ensure the device is listed on the VMware Compatibility Guide for vSAN (vmwa.re/vsanhcl). Just like vSphere, vSAN has strict requirements considering components.

It is therefore important to verify a certified driver is available for the device to ensure correct vSphere and vSAN operations.

Transport Protocols

Increasing performance and consistency relies upon two key factors: simplicity and proximity. Typically, each additional layer in software and/or hardware introduces delay due to increased process time. Protocols such as SATA, SCSI and SAS were designed to support spinning media, while NVMe is built with non-volatile memory and future memory technologies in mind. This difference has a profoundly positive impact on the latency of the I/O.

AHCI

SATA is using the *Advanced Host Controller Interface* (AHCI) as a command protocol. AHCI is fundamentally similar to *Integrated Drive Electronics* (IDE) but augmented with support for operations defined in the SATA specifications such as hot swapping and power management. AHCI was developed to connect the host bus adapter to rotating media. Bus overhead of one or more microseconds per command were deemed as negligible as the duration time of a read operation would take milliseconds. However, with today's media, this overhead is substantial.

The host bus adapter of SATA is incorporated in the system chipset, often referred to as the Southbridge. The *Host Bus Adapter* (HBA) inside the Southbridge also implements various RAID management features. The Intel Xeon E5-2600 v3 (Haswell) moved the Southbridge (and Northbridge) onto the Platform Controller Hub chipset. This move improved performance.

One of the challenges is that the system chipset is either an Intel or AMD implementation, depending on the CPU chipset. Modern storage platforms such as vSAN require the disk controller to run in a particular mode, for example pass-through mode, HBA mode or JBOD mode. In some cases, the system board does not expose those modes and thus become either unsupported or unusable with newer storage platforms.

Keep in mind that the driver for the system chipset is commonly not developed with the modern storage platform use case in mind. Typically, it is optimized for the original use case, slow spinning media. SATA is not optimized at the hardware or the software level for non-volatile media. SATA should be considered as a low-cost interface where cost, not performance, is the major decision factor.

Serial Attached SCSI

SAS offers a faster physical interface and a notably better protocol than SATA. SAS uses the SCSI command set to transfer data to the storage device. The native command set makes SAS a more efficient choice than SATA for flash devices. For example, where SATA uses a hardware-assisted I/O queue called *Native Command Queue* (NCQ), SAS uses *Tagged Command Queue* (TCQ).

NCQ versus TCQ

NCQ orders the commands in the most optimal way for the head of a traditional HDD to travel the shortest path. Interestingly enough this feature also works for flash devices. When used with a flash device it leverages the pipeline-rescheduling algorithm to distribute the I/O across the device. Flash cannot execute read and write I/Os on the same group of chips simultaneously, by ordering these commands NCQ achieves I/O parallelism. Unfortunately, the SATA NCQ is restricted to 32 requests or actually 31 due to a bug in the specification.

In TCQ a tag is applied to several commands. A device processes the command in a certain way, based on its tag. The 'Ordered' tag requires the device to process the commands in the same way as they arrived.

The tag 'Head of Queue' prioritizes the command and forces the drive to execute that command directly after the current command. The 'Simple' tag allows the device to control the sequence of the command. Simple is the same method of NCQ operations. It allows the device to order the commands, as it knows its own layout best.

The system can continue to issue commands while the flash device is in a busy state. The storage controller on the flash device can continue to fetch new commands, maximizing the bandwidth.

Simply put, NCQ and TCQ are out-of-order execution mechanisms. Originally designed for spinning media, it turns out that it is even more critical in flash devices than expected. It helps to deal with the complex housekeeping tasks of NAND devices. Write amplification and wear-leveling operations (which we cover in a later paragraph in detail) result in delayed commands. SAS uses a deeper command queue than SATA. A deeper queue depth combined with TCQ helps to leverage the parallelism capabilities of a flash device much better than the SATA protocol. Although SAS is scalable, up to thousands of devices compared to PCIe devices, the reality is that a few PCIe NVMe devices can saturate today's CPU microarchitectures.

NVMe

NVMe is designed from the ground up for non-volatile memory technology such as NAND and 3D XPoint over PCIe. The NVMe Consortium, a group of 90 companies, reviewed the anatomy of data access and identified the latency and processing time of each component. The reason why NVMe outperforms all other protocols and interfaces is due to the following three main factors:

- Scalable Hardware Interface
- Shorter Hardware Data Path
- Simplified Software Stack

The key point is that NVMe is a controller interface that directly operates over a PCIe device interface. The storage controller or host bus adapter integrates with the device. Compare this with SATA, where the SATA device connects to the host system via a separate HBA that itself is attached to the host via a PCIe interface. NVMe reduces the signal path length, bringing the non-volatile memory closer to the CPU.

But a streamlined protocol that is free of legacy overhead is the key to unleash the performance of the PCIe bus and non-volatile memory devices. NAND and the recently introduced 3D XPoint are physically different from any traditional media. It does not rotate. It is a solid-state device. There is no variance in media speed, data can be accessed in parallel, and thus it does not need to have the same command set as a traditional drive. The NVMe command set contains only thirteen commands! Ten of these commands are administrative commands such as create I/O queue, three of them are I/O commands; Read, Write and Flush. In comparison, SCSI has over 160 commands, SATA has seven different write command sets alone. It is necessary for NVMe to shed legacy baggage to have the software stack to keep up with the hardware performance. The reduced complexity leads to a CPU cost reduction of each layer that is present in the storage stack.

The overall software footprint of the NVMe protocol is smaller than the HDD-era protocols. By reducing the number of layers, fewer CPU cycles are necessary to process the I/O. CPU cost removal means more CPU cycles for application workloads, thus improving overall utilization of the host and potentially better performance of even non-I/O bound workloads. Fewer CPU cycles result in more consistent behavior as it is less dependent of the fairness paradigm of the VMkernel. An AHCI connected device roughly consumes 27.000 CPU cycles to process one I/O, SAS is a bit more efficient and gobbles up 19.500 CPU cycles. NVMe uses 9100 cycles to complete a task. For fun, let's use one of the holy grails of storage land, one million IOPS. Let's say you want to obtain this with one server. Using an Intel Xeon 2630 v4, ten cores run at 2.20 GHz each. 2.20 GHz equals 2.2 billion cycles per second. Divide this number by 27,000 and you know you can potentially run 81,482 IOPS on a core. That means to obtain 1 million IOPS you need **12.42 cores** to generate one million IOPS with an AHCI connected device. That is one complete CPU package exhausted, leaving the other CPU package to deal with VM CPU cycles. By comparison, with NVMe it only takes **4.13 cores**.

Visualizing the NVMe storage stack and comparing this to the SAS storage stack reveals a less complex stack.

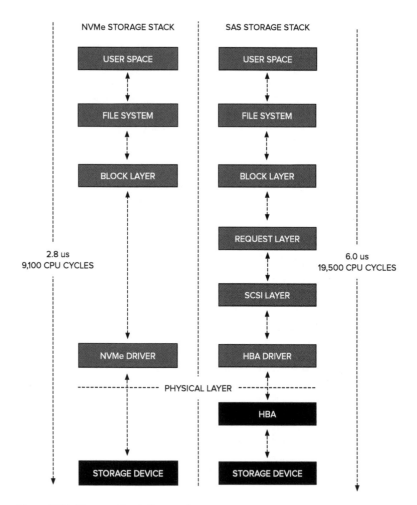

Figure 177: Storage Stack Comparison

The latency of non-volatile memory devices is substantially lower than traditional spinning media devices. With spinning media in mind, it does not matter that an extra layer adds a few microseconds latency when you measure the overall response time in milliseconds. When dealing with non-volatile memory devices such as NAND, it does matter. Popular NVMe devices such as the Samsung PM1725a and Intel P3700 are specifying a latency of 20 microseconds. Adding 4 microseconds of latency is an increase of 20%!

Scalable Queuing Interface

The queue mechanism of NVMe focuses on using the available CPU power of multi-core systems. The NVMe mechanism is entirely different from the traditional spinning media protocols. It allows for parallel operations by using queue pairs. Two kinds of queues exist that handle workload I/O: *Submission Queue* (SQ) and *Completion Queue* (CQ). These queues process the I/O commands; Read, Write, and Flush only. A separate management queue is used to create and delete additional SQ and CQ queues. Up to 64,000 queues can exist. By default, a core will run a SQ and CQ pair, but it is possible that the management queue spawns many SQs on a single core. These SQs can use the same CQ. Each queue can contain up to 64,000 commands. Compare this to SAS, which uses a single queue capable of holding 254 commands.

	MAXIMUM # OF QUEUES	MAXIMUM QUEUE DEPTH
AHCI	1	32
SAS	1	254
NVMe	65,535	64,000

Table 41: Storage Protocol Queue Comparison

By using message queues instead of command queues, a tremendous amount of CPU cycles are saved. The main advantage of this design is the asynchronous nature of the handshake. Traditional queues spend a lot of time synchronizing to determine progress. This architecture allows the host and NVMe controller to determine the status independently from each other.

Form Factor

NVM devices are available in multiple form factors. Common form factors for NVM devices are: 2.5-inch disk drive form factor or an Add-In Card (AIC) variant.

The AIC form factor contains many variations. They are available in *Half-Height, Half-Length* (HHHL) or the bigger form factor, *Full-Height, Half-Length* (FHHL).
As these don't fit blade servers; some vendors create *PCI mezzanine format* (PMC) devices to cater the need of blade architecture users. The M.2 form factor is available for both blade and rack server architecture.

Selection Criteria

Although the server form factor, blade versus rack, plays a significant role in the selection of the form factor, serviceability and compatibility are also important elements.

Serviceability

Many organizations prefer hot-pluggable components. It allows for adding more devices or replacing failed components without powering down the server. 2.5-inch disk drive format devices are suitable for such a strategy. Please note that not every 2.5-inch NVMe device is certified for hot plug operations, please verify before obtaining these devices.

> **Some PCIe NVMe devices support hot plug removal. The device needs to be logically removed prior to the physical hot removal of the device.**

Compatibility

Before the advent of host-local storage platforms, many vendors focused on removing components or reducing functionality within the server platform. Some servers are available without any storage controllers while others contain a simple storage controller aimed at connecting a boot device to the system. These simplified storage controllers are not able to process the magnitude of IOs a modern flash and 3D XPoint devices can drive. In this scenario, we recommend obtaining a PCIe NVMe device as this provides the best possible performance while minimizing components and overall complexity.

NVMe does not have a minimum supported CPU microarchitecture. NVMe is managed by the OS driver and as a result you can extend the life of your platform by expanding your system with NVMe.

Data-Path Length

Often 2.5-inch NVMe devices are connected to the system through a PCIe switch. It can have a marginal effect on bandwidth capacity if it needs to manage multiple NVMe devices. If your aim is to get the uncompromised performance, using an add-in card minimizes any form of overhead.

SATADOM

Two form factors that are gaining popularity are M.2 and *SATA Disk on Module* (SATADOM). Both form factors are designed to insert into an onboard connector directly. Depending on the version, an M.2 device can either use SATA or PCIe. SATADOM is only compatible wth SATA connectors.

These devices are attractive when drive slots are at a premium. Many customers building a host-local storage platform, such as vSAN, use their drive slots to contain large capacity storage devices. Assigning one or two drive slots for boot devices is costly. An alternative is to use either a SATADOM device or a M.2 SSD device as a boot device.

SATADOM uses NAND flash as the storage medium and usually equips a single flash chip due to their dimension restrictions. This single-chip design impacts the throughput of the device. It is still enough performance for servicing the boot process and normal OS operations. Yet, too low for participating in a host-local storage platform. The single NAND chip might have a challenge on maintaining reliability. If the chip fails, you need to replace the device.

Different chip types with higher levels of endurance are available to minimize the risk of failure. Although ESXi itself runs in memory, logging operations can affect the device endurance. We recommend storing ESXi logs, traces and core dumps in a centralized repository such as a syslog server to minimize write operations on the SLC SATADOM device. Please refer to *VMware KB article 2145210* for more details.

M.2

Using the same form factor for interfaces expedited the transition from spinning media to solid-state. SATA allowed for a broad adoption of flash. However, the industry is running into performance limitations of the interface. To maintain the adoption rate, a new form factor was developed that supports multiple physical storage and transport interfaces. M.2 supports the following standards:

INTERFACE	INTERFACE	BANDWIDTH
SATA	AHCI	600 MB/s
PCIe	AHCI	3930 MB/s
PCIe	NVMe	3930 MB/s

Table 42: M.2 Interface Specifications

One of the more distinct features is the case-less design, and it looks more like a memory DIMM than a flash drive. It shares the same kind of connector as memory as M.2 devices flush-mount into M.2 sockets on the system boards. A benefit of this design is that it does not require any power or data cables. Be aware that M.2 is not intended to be hot pluggable. The system needs to be powered off if you want to add or remove M.2 devices.

M.2 devices are available in different dimensions. A four-number code denotes the various sizes. The first two digits define the width of the device. The last two digits represent the length. The most popular types are type M.2 2260 and type M.2 2280. The M2 2280 is 22 mm wide and 80 mm long. The reason why different sizes exist is capacity. The longer the PCB, the more chips can be mounted on it. Typically, a type M.2 2280 supports up to eight NAND chips. As a result, an M.2 device can provide a capacity up to 1 TB.

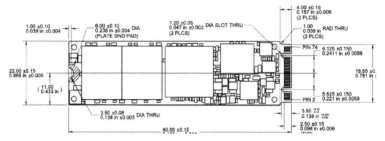

Figure 178: M.2 Form Factor Dimensions

M.2 PCIe AHCI versus NVMe

The PCIe version of the M.2 device demonstrates the importance of a transport interface purposely built for NVM devices. It's available with an AHCI and an NVMe transfer interface. The bandwidth is both the same as they use the same physical interconnect to connect the device to the system. When testing both devices against each other, the NVMe device is a clear winner. Multiple tests done by different online computer magazines show the benefit of the NVMe interface. The NVMe device outperforms the AHCI drive consistently, sometimes exceeding it by 30%. The diagram shows a workload test done by hardware.info.

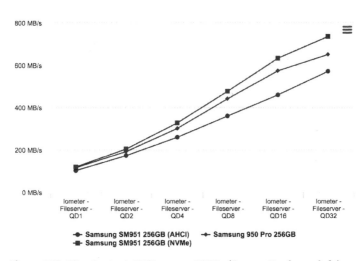

Figure 179: IOmeter test AHCI versus NVMe (Source Hardware.info)

Driver

A hardware component is only as good as the software controlling it. The device driver is a program that operates and controls the I/O device connected to the host. The driver communicates with the device through the computer bus or a communications subsystem to which the hardware device connects. ESXi operates with inbox drivers and partner async drivers. VMware creates the inbox driver while third-party vendors supply the async driver. Chapter *Host Network Architecture* covers the driver subsystem in great detail..

NVMe introduced a paradigm shift in the world of peripherals. NVMe defines both the transport interface and the method the device and storage controller are presented to the system. This design allows for a single, universal device driver for all NVMe devices. One driver to rule them all! As a comparison, the driver model of SAS does not define how the storage controller is presented to the system. This means that every vendor is required to develop a driver for every single device to support proprietary functionality. It has to update the driver for every software and hardware version.

The NVMe specification allows for the vendor to develop, test, and support his or her own driver. Intel is one of those vendors that provides an async driver for ESXi. Interestingly enough, the first inbox NVMe driver created for ESXi is based on the Intel driver. Async drivers often offer better performance than the native driver, but consider the management impact. Are you willing to absorb the management overhead of dealing with a nonstandard driver baseline for gaining extra performance?

Sometimes an async driver aligns better with a proprietary function of the device. In 2016 Frank published an article highlighting the difference of performance between the VMware NVMe Inbox driver and the Intel async driver and it clearly shows that the average latency is reduced when using the Intel async driver. For customers who depend on low-latency performance, the benefits outweigh the inconvenience. But if low-latency is not a requirement, async drivers may not be desired from a support and manageability perspective.

Verify Driver

ESXi does not remove the inbox driver when an async driver is installed. Executing the command: `esxcli software vib list | grep nvme` generates a list of all available *vSphere installation bundles* (VIB) on the system.

```
[root@esxi03:~] esxcli software vib list | egrep nvme
intel-nvme                     1.0e.1.1-1OEM.550.0.0.1391871 Intel  VMwareCertified  2017-05-13
nvme                           1.2.0.32-2vmw.650.0.0.4564106 VMW    VMwareCertified  2016-12-27
vmware-esx-esxcli-nvme-plugin  1.2.0.10-0.0.4564106                 VMware VMwareCertified  2016-12-27
```

Figure 180: Show Available NVMe VIBs

It does not narrow down which VIB is loaded. To verify the VIB in use execute the command: *esxcli system module list:*

```
[root@esxi03:~] esxcli system module list
Name                                Is Loaded  Is Enabled
----------------------------------  ---------  ----------
vmkernel                              true        true
chardevs                              true        true
user                                  true        true
crypto                                true        true
vsanapi                               true        true
vsanbase                              true        true
vprobe                                true        true
vmkapi_mgmt                           true        true
dma_mapper_iommu                      true        true
procfs                                true        true
vmkapi_v2_3_0_0_mgmt_shim             true        true
vmkapi_v2_2_0_0_mgmt_shim             true        true
iodm                                  true        true
vmkapi_v2_2_0_0_vmkernel_shim         true        true
vmkapi_v2_3_0_0_vmkernel_shim         true        true
vmkapi_v2_1_0_0_vmkernel_shim         true        true
intel-nvme                            true        true
```

Figure 181: Intel Driver Loaded and Enabled

The command esxcli system module get -m intel-nvme provides detailed insight on the version of the driver and if it is certified. Running certified drivers are important for security hardening. ESXi Secure Boot only works with certified drivers.

```
[root@esxi03:~] esxcli system module get -m intel-nvme
   Module: intel-nvme
   Module File: /usr/lib/vmware/vmkmod/intel-nvme
   License: BSD
   Version: 1.0e.1.1-1OEM.550.0.0.1391871
   Build Type:
   Provided Namespaces:
   Required Namespaces: com.vmware.vmkapi@v2_2_0_0
   Containing VIB: intel-nvme
   VIB Acceptance Level: certified
[root@esxi03:~]
```

Figure 182: Module Details

14

NON-VOLATILE MEMORY ARCHITECTURE

Data wants to be close to CPU, and the industry is moving towards that direction. The use of NVM devices inside the system allows for creating systems that provide extremely high IOPS to GB density. This paradigm shift transforms traditionally compute -centric hosts into compute and storage building blocks. It allows us to make scalable architectures that were plainly unimaginable a decade ago.

The difference in performance between NAND flash and memory are staggering. It seems we should not expect any drastic change from CPU microarchitectures in the foreseeable future. Processing speed has been hovering between 2 GHz and 3 GHz for the last five years, and the scaling is achieved by adding more cores. Memory advancements are slowly creeping forward. The industry is making up his mind if it is going to pursue the DDR5 standard. As a result, a deeper memory hierarchy is expected. Different forms of memory will exist in the system, and the necessity of clever data staging will be critical.

The introduction of 3D XPoint memory by Micron and Intel mid 2015 follows this paradigm. 3D XPoint fits between DRAM and NAND flash for the near-foreseeable future. It won't replace NAND flash as the capacity layer. Not because of technology reasons but it will be a challenge for the memory foundries to satisfy the demand for the next few years, the roadmap of device sizes seems to support this.

Memory architectures become deeper as 3D XPoint fills in the gap between DRAM and NAND. NAND flash provides us a high number of IOPS per GB and has a tremendous sequential access performance at high queue depths. However, its data management operations make it less suitable for low queue depth random access I/O operations. 3D XPoint is an entirely different architecture, providing byte-level addressable memory similar to DRAM. Exactly catering to the need that NAND flash fails to satisfy.

Understanding how NAND flash and 3D XPoint architectures operate, and how they differ from each other, provides insight that allows you to make the right choice for your host-local storage architecture.

Flash Technology Architecture

We are long past the days of 25,000 US Dollars NAND flash devices. NAND flash technology is omnipresent in both the consumer space and the enterprise space. PCIe devices, historically aimed at enterprise workloads, are becoming more popular amongst PC enthusiasts. Devices such as the Samsung M.2 960 PRO and the Intel 750 offer tremendous performance that is even sufficient for most SMB and small enterprise environments. However, performance should not be the only factor used when acquiring flash storage. Power loss data protection features and endurance should rank equally in the decision matrix. Enterprise devices have a larger pool of spare memory cells to maintain consistent performance while executing data management process. Power loss data protection allows your in-flight data to safely reach the non-volatile memory cell during a power outage, reducing the risk of data loss or corruption. Let's take a closer look at the internals of a modern NAND flash device architecture and operations.

NAND Flash Memory Cell Types

Spinning media use magnetism to store data, NAND flash memory cells apply a voltage to a cell to read, write and erase data. NAND Flash uses floating gate transistors to store data.

Floating gate transistors are generally referred to as a cell, and a threshold determines the data value. The number of thresholds and their respective value depend on which types of cells are used. Three cell types exist:

1. *Single level cell* (SLC)
2. *Multi-level cell* (MLC) (2-bit)
3. *Triple level cell* (TLC) (3-bit)

Simplified, an SLC cell has a threshold hovering around the 50% mark. If the amount of charge in the cell exceeds the 50% mark, the cell resembles the value 0. If it is below 50%, the logical value is 1. Interestingly enough, a 0 indicates that there is data stored in the cell, the opposite of how we normally use the 0 value in computer science. With triple cells, a threshold indicates the logical value of 3 bits. Seven thresholds are used representing eight different states. For example, if the cell holds a current close to the 62,5% mark, it reads as the logical value 011.

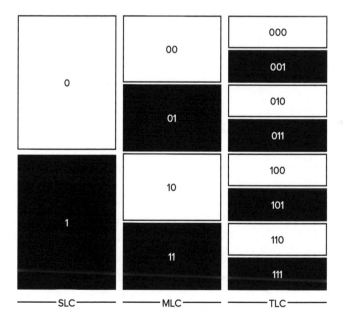

Figure 183: Cell Type Thresholds and Logical Values

The reason why this matters is that cell types can have an impact on the device endurance and I/O latency. NAND flash cells wear out. The write process stores electrons, while the erase process drains the charge in the transistor. To accurately fill the cell to a threshold to resemble the required logical value, the cell is drained first. This process is called the *Program and Erase* (P/E) cycle.

A NAND cell contains insulators. These insulators are there to help retain the proper voltage in the cell. The problem is that each and every time a P/E cycle occurs the insulator is damaged. Just a small amount, but this damage builds up over time making them lose their insulating capabilities. If this continues long enough, the insulators lose their purpose, leak voltage and may cause the cell to change the voltage state. Therefore, a cell has limited number P/E operations it can handle. After reaching the limit of P/E cycles, the cell is tagged as defective and is no longer used by the storage controller.

With the increased number of thresholds, the margins for successful detection of the bit value between these thresholds decrease. Similar to pouring a drink into a tiny glass, you won't mimic a fire hose, you gently pour the drink in. Elegantly. A similar approach is used fill the flash cell; the cell is filled to the correct threshold in a fluid manner. This resulted in slower programming in the past, but the industry made progress in this area.

The current enterprise NAND flash devices are equipped with MLC flash cells. Every major NAND flash vendor moved away from SLC as MLC performance and endurance increased. The reason is quite simple, SLC could not provide the capacity needed in today's world. The endurance and performance of MLC improved throughout the years, and there is a limit on how much NAND Flash cells you can store in a single device.

Mainstream vendors use MLC (2-bit) NAND flash cells. Because endurance of current MLC is adequate for most enterprise use cases.

Similar to CPU and DRAM, NAND flash is fighting the density war. More density equals more capacity. But density requires a more precise production process to fit more transistors on a single chip die.

Physics limits the size of the chip die. Therefore, the industry came up with another solution. Traditional NAND-flash scales in a 2-D way. The precision of the fabrication process and the dimension of the chip on the Y- and X-axis determine the number of transistors. The industry was aiming to move from a 20-nm manufacturing process to a 15-nm process until bright minds introduced another dimension to the NAND flash world. Similar to stacking multiple thresholds in a cell vertically, multiple cells can be stacked vertically.

Today, NAND scales in 3 dimensions: X, Y, and Z. As a result, the industry moved back from 20 nm to 40 nm. This increases the space between the cells and the cell size, allowing the cell to hold more electrons, and thus provide a higher tolerance for thresholds. This move increases cell endurance and reduces production cost. Samsung has been using 3D-NAND prominently since 2014, Intel's new NAND flash products in 2017 are all 3D-NAND. Intel is in the process of phasing out planar NAND (2D-NAND).

Internal Flash Device Architecture

Enterprise grade NAND flash devices are developed to provide fast read and write access to multiple threads. Writing in parallel and interleaving between internal components results in a stunning performance for sequential write I/O. Let's have a closer look at the NAND flash architecture.

The anatomy of a modern flash device is as follows: Bits are stored in a cell. Cells are organized in pages. Pages are grouped in blocks. Blocks are united in a plane, and a die contains multiple planes. Multiple dies exist inside a package.

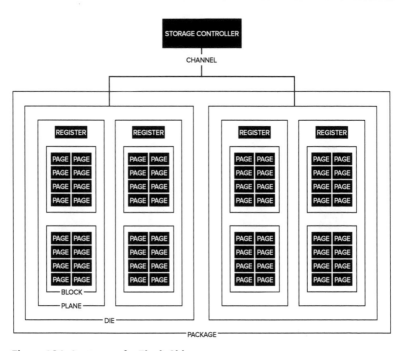

Figure 184: Anatomy of a Flash Chip

In general, a page is a unit of read and write operations and is eight or sixteen kilobytes in size. This is an interesting data point for people who want to run synthetic benchmarks. Sub-Page sized I/O generates a lot of overhead and reduce performance. Usually, a block contains between 128 and 256 pages, resulting in a block size between one and two MB. NAND flash can only be erased at block size. Typically, that results in migrating valid data to other blocks to make room for new incoming data. A later paragraph expands on this behavior in detail. A package contains four to eight dies.

Each plane incorporates a register that is used for transferring data in and out of the plane. Each package is connected to the storage controller via a channel. A full-duplex serial interface is used to communicate with NAND flash chips. This is the primary bottleneck for performance. Using multiple channels overcomes this bottleneck. Enterprise level storage controllers, such as the one on the Intel P3700 is equipped with 18 channels.

This allows the storage controller to access the NAND flash chips in parallel and interleave I/O operations across these chips. In total four levels of parallelisms are available:

- Channel level
- Chip level
- Die level
- Plane level

NAND flash can perform read and write operations as a unit of a clustered page. NAND flash is ordered in pages which are written and read as a unit as NAND flash cannot perform read and write operations simultaneously on the same NAND flash chips. Issuing read and write operations in parallel to different planes, or dies overcomes this limitation.

Pages across multiple planes and chips can be engaged at the same time. It can engage with flash packages in parallel or independently. Similarly, it can engage with the multiple chips inside a package or write to multiple planes on the same die. It's because of this behavior that flash devices with a higher number of flash chips (that is more capacity) perform better. The limitation of the storage controller bandwidth is solved by issuing commands in parallel against as many components as possible. However, writing data remains an expensive operation.

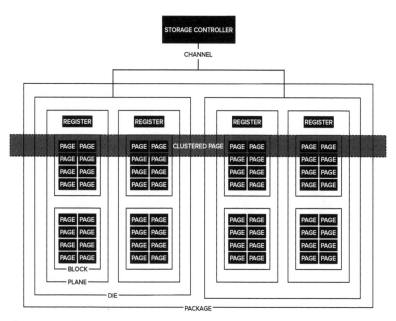

Figure 185: Clustered Page

> The performance of higher capacity devices is better due to the ability to parallelize I/O operations across a larger number of NAND flash chips then smaller capacity NAND flash devices.

I/O Operations

A NAND flash device uses a *Flash Translation Layer* (FTL) to map *Logical Block Addresses* (LBA) to *Physical Page Numbers* (PPN). The FTL is emulating a HDD and hiding the complex internals of NAND flash so that it can support the block device interface. The entirety of the software and physical stack is optimized for spinning media. Block device performance modeling focuses on the assumption that sequential access is much faster than random access. Complete systems are designed on that assumption. However, NAND flash has different performance characteristics. One distinctive behavior is that performance of NAND flash varies over time based on the number of I/O operations. This behavior stems from the four major constraints NAND flash has:

1. Asymmetric read and write latency
2. Erase before write requirement
3. Erase at block level operation
4. Write-impact on NAND flash cell durability

It all boils down to the point that NAND flash cannot do an in-place write operation. Blocks have to be erased first to accept new data. The goal of the FTL is to hide these constraints and works with the data management operations wear leveling and garbage collection to cover up the device internal operations. However, the NAND flash structure dictates how the flash device handles read and write operations.

Read Operations

It is not possible to read a single cell individually. Read operations align on the native page size of the device. Consequently, it is not possible to read less than one page at once. If you want to read 4 KB of data and the page size is 16 KB, the storage controller will fetch the full 16 KB. A useful data-point if you plan a synthetic benchmark! If your company develops its own applications, make the development team aware of the minimum efficient block size for read operations.

Write Operations

Writes follow the same structure as read operations, write operations align on a page and occur by page size. If 20 KB of data is written, two full 16 KB pages are used. The pages must be written out sequentially within a block, from low to high addresses. To write data to a page, the page must be in an erased state.

During the break-in period of a NAND flash device, the performance is optimal, but after a while, the performance starts to regress. This level of performance regression, and when this happens in the lifecycle, depends on the degree of additional flash cells and the intelligence of the storage controller. To write data to a full NAND flash device, the storage controller must apply an erase state to a block. The erase command is a NAND flash-native command. Applications and operating systems only issue read and write commands.

Each plane contains a page and cache register for swiftly moving data in and out. During a write operation, the storage controller does not write directly to a block inside a plane but instead writes it to the register. A separate process moves the data from the register to a block inside the plane. This hides the latency of the definitive write operation.

Read-Modify-Write

A typical I/O operation is the read-modify-write operation. Data is read from disk, modified and stored. Usually, the data is written by the application or OS to the same LBA. However, NAND flash does not allow in-place writes. As a result, the modified data is written to a different location, and the previous version of data is marked as stale. It is not immediately erased, as this requires the whole block to be evicted, but the storage controller depends on the garbage collection process to clean this mess up.

For example, the VM generates data A, B, C, and D. The FTL maps this data to four free pages. In step 1, the VM generates data A, B, and C. The FTL maps this data to three free pages. The application inside the VM generates some new data, D, and E, and read-modify-writes A, B, C. The FTL maps three new pages for the new data as it cannot overwrite the old data. Three free pages are now consumed by A1, B1, and C1. The old pages are now marked as stale. In step 3, the data management operations of the device move the current pages, D, E, A1, B1 and C1 to a new block and erase block 1 to get rid of stale data.

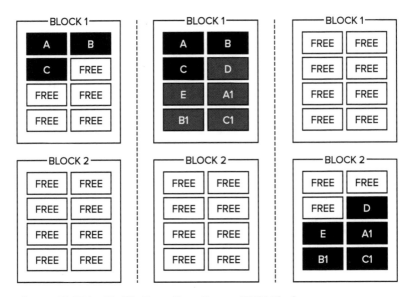

Figure 186: Write-Modify-Erase Operation on NAND Flash

Data Management Operations

Due to the lack of in-place writes and the coarse level of erase, NAND flash storage controllers utilize several data management operations.

Wear-Levelling

The wear-leveling operation is designed to lengthen the overall device lifespan by distributing data evenly across all pages. The wear-leveling process informs the FTL during a read-modify-write process to remap the LBA to point to the new block. Wear-leveling marks the old data as stale. Pointing to a new block avoids additional latency because the current block does not have to be erased. It also avoids hot-spots on the NAND flash device. Some applications like to update particular LBAs more frequently than others. If the same block is used over and over again, the insulators of this cell will wear out more quickly. The trick of pointing the FTL to a new block is to find a block with the highest amount of stale data inside. This avoids write-amplification, it is the task of the garbage collection process to identify these pages.

Write Amplification

Write amplification is not a data management operation but more a side effect of data management activities. Write amplification is the act of writing more data than necessary. A typical block size is 2 MB. You can imagine that valid pages are often on the move. After some hours of operation, blocks contain valid and invalid data. Invalid data is erased to make room for the new data. However, the valid data needs to be moved before the block can be erased. The migration of valid data is described as write amplification. The difference between the host writes and the NAND flash writes is called the *Write Amplification Factor* (WAF). Some devices expose SMART attributes to calculate the WAF. Most commonly, these metrics are referred as host program page count and background program page count or FTL program page count.

Garbage Collection

The efficiency of the garbage collection depends on how much write amplification occurs within a device. Enterprise devices employ intelligent garbage collection algorithms to keep write amplification to a minimum by selecting the correct block. If every block contains valid and invalid data, where is this valid data stored temporarily? To make this process possible, NAND flash devices have extra cell capacity that is not directly visible as consumable size. This is called overprovisioning.

Overprovisioning

The storage controller reserves additional capacity for internal operation. Typically, this is not a static area located at the end of the disk but more a dynamic range. The FTL has a maximum number of LBAs to provision. The overall LBA pool of the device is much larger, by migrating LBAs between the consumable space and internal processing space, a dynamic range of LBA's emerges. Imagine it as a sliding window of capacity that moves across the disk. This approach differs from formatting the device with a smaller partition size. Enterprise class devices usually have a 25% oversubscription space, but some exceptions exist such as the P3700 2TB NAND flash device, which has 40%.

Bad Block Management

After a flash cell has been erased beyond its limit, it cannot be programmed or erased anymore. From that point on, the cell is considered to be a bad block. However, pages in the block may contain valid data. If a page is detected that cannot be programmed and erased anymore, valid data existing in the block is copied over to a new block, and the bad block table is updated.

Bad-block Management (BBM) keeps track of bad blocks and manages read disturb errors. If a cell is continuously read without being rewritten, it can impact nearby cells. These cells could be modified as a result of the constant I/O of the neighbouring cell.

The error does not appear when reading the original cell but becomes apparent when reading one of the surrounding cells. Read disturb errors emerge when a particular cell is read more than 100,000 times without a program and erase cycle. To avoid read disturb, a threshold of reads is used. When the count exceeds the threshold, data in the block is copied over to a new block, and the original block is erased.

TRIM

A TRIM command allows the OS to mark which blocks of data should be deleted and, therefore, erased at the flash device layer. When deleting a file, operating systems, such as MS Windows do not physically erase the data on the disk but changes the status of the page from used to free. With rotating media, the OS does not have to inform the hard disk as it can just overwrite data into that same page in the future. With NAND flash devices, it is different due to the no in-place overwrite capabilities. A flash device only becomes aware when data is stale when the OS wants to write data to the same LBA. Only then, garbage collection recognizes deleted data as invalid data. If no writes are made to that same LBA, garbage collection moves the data to a new block in case the block needs to be erased.

With TRIM, the flash device is informed that data existing on that particular LBA is invalid. This improves garbage collection performance as the storage controller avoids copying over that stale data to a new block. It reduces write amplification, as wear leveling will not move the invalid data throughout the device anymore.

TRIM is a great addition to the flash management feature stack. Unfortunately, the majority of storage controllers do not pass TRIM commands to their connected SSD devices. TRIM can be seen as complementary to over-provisioning as the actual benefit of TRIM depends on the free user space on the NAND flash device and the timing of the OS trim command. TRIM initiates an erase command and, as described throughout this chapter, incur a lot of overhead. TRIM commands are triggered the moment the OS informs the storage controller, therefore impacting performance severely. The TRIM command will only work if the SSD controller, the operating system, and the file system are supporting it.

Most Linux operating systems support unmapping of blocks however, they do not generate UNMAP commands on virtual disks in ESXi 6.x. ESXi leverages SCSI-2 for SCSI support of virtual disks, while Linux expects a higher SPC-4 standard. This limitation prevents generation of UNMAP commands until the virtual disks can claim support for at least SPC-4 SCSI commands. The *vSphere APIs for Array Integration* (VAAI) contains the command UNMAP. TRIM gets converted by the VMkernel to the UNMAP command. vSAN (6.6 and older) does not support the UNMAP command.

Device Endurance

Hardware vendors put in a lot of effort to maximize the device endurance. Enterprise devices can write petabytes of data without impacting performance or losing data. Some architects incorporate cost-vs-wear trade-off during their selection process as they have found that some systems do not need these high device endurance specifications.

There are three metrics used to describe NAND flash endurance: *Drive Writes Per Day* (DWPD), *Terabytes Written* (TBW) or *GB written per day* (GB/day). All express the same thing. How do you compare these metrics?

It's good to note that the DWPD metric only spans the warranty period. And the TBW specification does not specify the years the device lasts. As a result, DWPD reports how many times you can overwrite the full capacity of the device on a daily basis during the warranty period. For example, A DWPD value of 3 for a 400 GB NAND flash device, shows that the device can withstand 1200 GB of data written to it every single day throughout its warranty period. TBW indicates the total amount of data that can be written to the NAND device before it is likely to fail. GBW per day is similar but on a more granular basis of 24 hours.

The trick is to understand that the warranty period is the key to understanding the real endurance. For example, if you shorten the warranty period, the DWPD value increases. For example, a DWPD value of 3 for the 400 GB for five years equals 1200 GB x 1825 days = 2,190,000 GB for the next five years, after that, the device might fail. But a DWPD value of 6 sounds twice as good as 3, but if the warranty period is two years that means the drive can endure 2400 GB x 730 days equals 1,752,000 GB for the next two years. You just lost 438,000 GB by selecting a device solely on DWPD value.

The TBW specification provides the raw number. The specified warranty period is irrelevant for this value. There is still a warranty period specified for reasons that you might not hit that value, and a component of the device fails.

The JEDEC Solid State Technology Association's standards subcommittee published the two standards JESD218 Solid-State Drive Requirements and Endurance Test Method and JESD219 Solid-State Drive Endurance Workloads to help consumers and vendors to determine endurance correctly. But let's be realistic. An Intel Development Forum presentation contained the statistic that the top 1% of users perform 50 GB writes per day.

As a result, the device processes 17,8 terabytes of writes in one year. The Intel P3700 specification lists 62.05 petabytes written, that would mean that the device could last 348 years. We expect the drive is replaced before it hits that number.

But if you are considering using consumer-grade NAND flash devices the numbers become interesting. Most of these NAND flash devices provide a decent to good enough performance baseline for virtualized workload. Let's compare the P3700 with the Intel 750 1.2 TB, 1/2 Height PCIe 3.0 device. It uses PCIe 3.0, therefore best-in-class bandwidth levels.

INTERFACE	INTEL 750	SAMSUNG 960 PRO	INTEL P3700
Capacity	1200 GB	1024 GB	1600 GB
Sequential Read (up to)	2,400 MB/s	3,500 MB/s	2,800 MB/s
Sequential Write (up to)	1200 MB/s	2100 MB/s	1900 MB/s
Random Read (up to)	440,000 IOPS	440,000 IOPS	450,000 IOPS
Random Write (up to)	290,000 IOPS	360,000 IOPS	150,000 IOPS
Endurance Rating	70 GB per day	800 TBW	43.8 PBW / 15 DWPD
Warranty Period	5 Years	5 Years	5 Years

Table 43: Technical Specification Consumer and Enterprise Devices

The performance of the 750 NAND flash device would be satisfactory for many enterprise workloads. The endurance could be considered to be risky. The P3700 is guaranteed to write 24,000 GB per day (1,600 x 15) for 1,825 consecutive days. The 750 is allowed to 70 GB per day, during its guaranteed lifetime it is allowed to write 127,750 GB, similar to one work week for the P3700. The Samsung 960 PRO can write 438 GB per day! Still not near the level of the Intel P3700, but it way beyond the average of writes that the top 1% generate.

Micron's 5100 Enterprise SSD product line caters to this need. It differentiates on Write IOPS and DWPD. Depending on your requirement you can take the cost versus wear into account.

DEVICE	CAPACITY	READ	WRITE	DWPD
ECO	480 GB – 8TB	93,000	31,000	1
PRO	240 GB – 4TB	93,000	43,000	2.5 - 3
MAX	240 GB – 2TB	93,000	74,000	5

Table 44: Micron 5100 Enterprise SSD

Investigating endurance of these devices is important. Our recommendation is not to search for the biggest number, but rather understand which device meets your needs.

Power Loss Data Protection Features

To reduce latency as much as possible storage controllers store data temporarily in the onboard DRAM cache memory. During a normal power-off operation, the system signals the storage controller to prepare for a shutdown and flush the data from the DRAM cache buffers to the NAND flash chips and update the latest metadata.

This flushing process is not triggered if the device unexpectedly loses power. If the storage controller is unable to write the data to the NAND flash chips on time, it can lead to data corruption or loss due to incomplete or partial writes. If a partially written sector is detected, the disk performs error recovery on that sector. Error recovery is a time-consuming process and can lead to overall performance reduction of the disk

To protect against power loss enterprise NVM devices contain capacitors. The capacitors are designed to store enough power to ensure the storage controller can write in-flight I/O and data in the temporary buffers to the NAND flash chips. In essences, these capacitors act as a UPS for the device.

3D XPoint

The upcoming range of NVM devices uses 3D XPoint technology (Intel Optane and Micron Quantx). What makes this technology so unique is that it provides byte-level addressable memory similar to DRAM. It can write in-place eliminating the four major constraints NAND possess. It does not require block-level erasing, reducing write amplification and thereby increasing endurance due to less wear and tear.

3D XPoint Memory Structure

3D XPoint architecture follows a similar design as NAND. An NVMe storage controller communicates across channels to the packages. Inside multiple dies exist that contain 3D XPoint memory cells. The memory cell structure is sliced up in columns, each comprising a memory cell and a selector. A cross point structure of wires connects the columns. The cross point architecture enables individual addressing of memory cells by selecting one wire on top and another at the bottom as demonstrated in the diagram below.

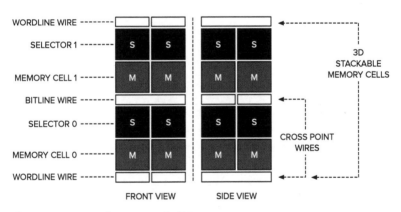

Figure 187: 3D XPoint Memory Cell Structure

Using selectors removes the needs for transistors. Transistors take up valuable space and reducing them in size is getting more difficult due to the laws of physics.

By completely getting rid of transistors in the memory cell, it allows for an increase in density, and it seems that it is cheaper too. Eventually, we will reap the benefits of this cost reduction once the technology is produced at large scale.

The controller can directly read the output of the cell. There are no blocks of pages. It's just a bit-addressable array. In addition, the bit does not have to be erased. New data can be placed inside the cell.

As a result, no erase or clear cycles is applied before writing. This solves two major problems faced by NAND flash.

- Non-uniform performance over time
- Asymmetric read and write latency

Non-Uniform Performance Over Time

As data can be written in-place and without the need of an erase cycle it does not matter whether this device is brand new or is filled completely. The I/O process is the same, providing it a uniform performance over time.

Asymmetric Read and Write Latency

Fewer operations used in a single I/O operation results in a reduction of latency and increased performance. The write performance of 3D XPoint devices is close to the read performance of the device.

Device Endurance

The absence of write amplification due to erase cycles provides better endurance due to less wear and tear on the memory cells. Wear leveling is still necessary on 3D XPoint memory cells. However, the device is not equipped with the same amount of overprovisioning space as NAND flash devices. The device contains spare capacity reserved for bad block management, translation layer for logical to physical addresses mapping and overhead for error correction processes.

Endurance metrics such as the TWD with NAND flash indicates the number of total writes the device can endure. These are the device writes, i.e. the host writes + write amplification. TBW on 3D XPoint is mainly host writes, plus some minor wear-leveling activities. Therefore, comparing TBW or other endurance ratings between NAND flash and 3D XPoint is similar to comparing apples to oranges.

Performance

What makes this architecture so useful is the ability to perform at a low queue depth. To get the best performance out of a NAND flash device, you must drive a high number of concurrent requests at a time to leverage the inherent parallelism of the device. Typically, this means *Queue Depths* (QD) of 128 or even higher. Also, a lot of vendor tests show a 100% read performance as this generates the best number.

Many enterprise applications require responsiveness. Low latency performance even if the application generates just a couple of I/Os. Interestingly enough, a lot of enterprise applications do not make enough concurrent requests that warrant a QD of 16. Granted, we need to take the I/O blending effect of ESXi into account, processing the workloads of many different VMs instead of a single enterprise application. But even ESXi hosts with a high consolidation ratio have a shallow IO stream occasionally.

> **Intel is the only vendor that has 3D XPoint devices available. Unfortunately, they cannot meet the demand of devices at the time of writing this book, and thus we were unable to obtain a device for testing. Therefore, we can only illustrate our point by using statistics provided by Intel. Time will tell whether the claims made are valid.**

An interesting chart is the difference in 4K 70/30 read-write performance at a low queue depth. The top line is the new Intel Optane SSD DC P4800X device. (Optane is the brand name of the Intel 3D XPoint technology). The bottom line is an Intel P3700 NAND flash device.

Interestingly the capacity of the P4800 is 375 GB, while the P3700 holds 1.6 TB. Typically, high capacity devices smoke low capacity devices due to the number of NAND chips and channels. In this comparison, the P4800 drive outperforms the NAND flash device eight times at a QD of 1. It reaches a stable state at a QD of 13. The graph nicely shows the increase of performance due to an increase of the QD for the NAND flash device. For us, It is mind blowing to see 500,000 IOPs or ~2 GB/s at a queue depth of 11.

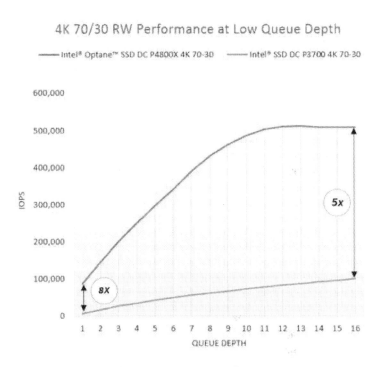

Figure 188: NAND Flash versus 3D XPoint Performance

The next chart *Read QOS in Mixed Workload* shows the benefit of in-place write operations on performance consistency. The dark, thick bar at the bottom indicates the response time of the P4800. It provides a consistent low response time for a mixed read and write workload. It is interesting to see that the range wherein the P4800 performs is below the fastest response time of the P3700.

If you look closely, you can still see a white gap between the worst case P4800 performance and the best case P3700.

Be aware that this chart looks like the P3700 performs inconsistently, but this chart more or less proves that every performance test is relative. Yes, compared to the P4800 is provides inconsistent behavior. Compare it to most enterprise NAND devices, and It is one of the most stable devices you have ever seen. Anandtech.com has plenty of material available raving about the consistent behavior of the P3700.

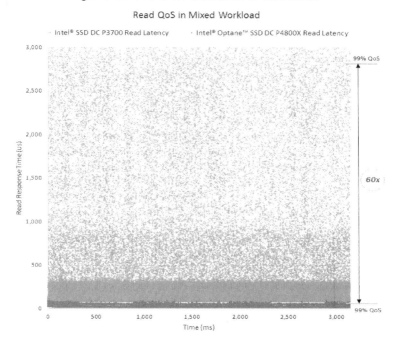

Figure 189: Performance Consistency NAND Flash versus 3D XPoint

NAND flash has a hard time dealing with random writes because of the need for many data management operations in this workload. If you continually push a high level of random I/O to a flash device you can see the impact of this background activity in the latency response.

Intel ran a test where they deploy new VMs at a rapid pace that issues user requests against a database. The right axis, in the figure *Average Read Latency under Random Write Workload,* which represents the performance of an offending write workload. It shows that the test is generating random write workloads, starting at 100MB/s and increasing this workload to over 700MB/s. This is drawn as the top gray stair-step line.

The left axis of the chart shows the read response time from a single thread random read workload. The ticker line somewhat mimicking the gray stair step line is the performance of reading response time from a single thread random read workload running on the P3700 NAND flash device. The read response time increases when more and more noisy neighbors show up.

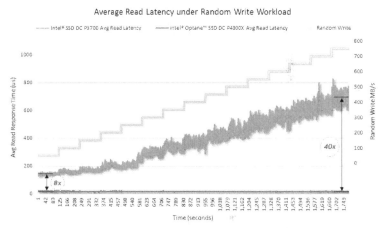

Figure 190: Impact of Noisy Neighbor Random Write Workloads

The P4800 as shown above has the behavior that we are looking for in the virtual datacenter. Clean, consistent performance that appears to be isolated from any other workload active on the system. Due to the isolation, the P4800 seems to be able to obtain a higher random write workload. Intel quoted that the NAND flash devices capped at 700 MB/s, while the 3D XPoint pushed to 2 GB/s.

3D XPoint vSAN Use Case

High peak performance at a low queue depth and the ability to absorb random writes make it a technology that can move the host-local storage platforms to the next level. The roadmap of the 3D XPoint device shows relatively low capacity drives for the foreseeable future. We think this is not a big deal because the capacity should be enough for the role this device should fulfill; the vSAN caching tier.

vSAN NVM Hierarchy

The I/O stream that hits the caching tier within vSAN is predominantly random in nature. The number of I/Os hitting the cache tier depends on the local workload, but regardless of the number or the type, it can be satisfied consistently and swiftly. Exactly what we need for providing the best user experience.

Destaging data from the caching layer to the capacity layer is done asynchronously in a sequential method. Leveraging the inherent parallelism by issuing sequential writes at a high queue depth ensures the fastest destaging possible. For this workload, a NAND flash device is the perfect fit. High capacity devices built for the sequential workload. This architecture creates a deeper NVM hierarchy, leveraging the correct device type for the predominant workload at a particular vSAN layer.

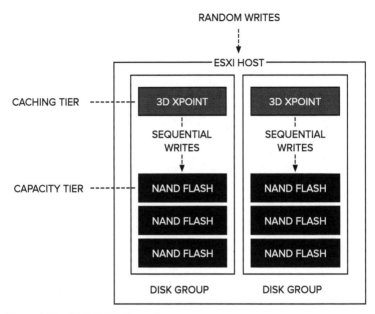

Figure 191: vSAN NVM Hierarchy

Near-Future NVM Solutions

With 3D XPoint we reached the point that the PCIe bus is becoming the bottleneck of the hardware layer of local storage technology. The 3D XPoint can provide better performance using a different bus.

Intel and Micron presented this chart to indicate how much latency they have reduced with the 3D XPoint architecture. 'Future NVM' is the 3D XPoint - as the name was not announced yet when they released this chart. The chart lists the following components:

COMPONENTS	DESCRIPTION
NVM Tread	Read time of cell
NVM xfer	Time to transfer data to the interface I/O pins
Misc SSD	Time for Data Management Operations such as address translation or garbage collection
Link xfer	Time to transfer data across Interface
Platform + adapter	Time to transfer data from host PCIe port to CPU pins
Software	Time to process I/O operation by OS.

Table 45: Component Description

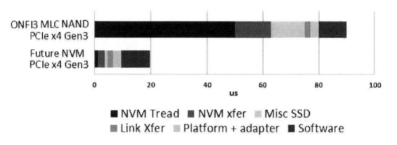

Figure 192: NAND Flash versus 3D XPoint Component Latency

NVDIMM

The latency of the first three components are considerably smaller, that is accomplished by changing the hardware architecture. The last three components have not changed when comparing both technologies to each other. Link xfer, platform + adapter and software are now the three major contributors to latency with 3D XPoint. The hardware vendors have no control over the storage stack of the multiple operating systems using the device, but the thing they can control is the adapter choice. It's expected to see 3D XPoint appear in a DIMM format by maybe the end of 2017. By moving directly on the memory bus, the PCIe bus is bypassed, and memory bus speeds are leveraged.

Moving NVM to the memory bus is not new. Today NVDIMM-N solutions are available. HPE NVDIMM-N provides 8 GB of persistent storage available through the memory bus and offers 17 GB/s bandwidth.

If multiple modules are used and NVDIMM-N memory interleaving is enabled the following bandwidth is available:

MAXIMUM BANDWIDTH	1 NVDIMM	2 NVDIMM	3 DIMM	4 DIMM
Maximum bandwidth for one thread on the local NUMA node	17 GB/s	34 GB/s	51 GB/s	68 GB/s
Maximum aggregate bandwidth for multiple threads on the local NUMA node	17 GB/s	34 GB/s	51 GB/s	68 GB/s
Maximum bandwidth for one thread on the remote NUMA node	17 GB/s	19 GB/s	19 GB/s	19 GB/s
Maximum aggregate bandwidth for multiple threads on the remote NUMA node	17 GB/s	19 GB/s	19 GB/s	19 GB/s

Table 46: NVDIMM-N Interleaving Bandwidth

NVDIMM-N memory interleaving is different from Node Interleaving described in detail in part 1. Node Interleaving is not supported if NVDIMM-N is present in DIMM slots. The remote threads hit the maximum QPI bandwidth, which is 19.2 GB/s. The recommendation is to equip both NUMA nodes with an equal number of NVDIMM-N modules.

It seems that NVDIMM will be a top priority for most memory and storage vendors. NVDIMMs provide exponentially better performance (bandwidth and latency) than other forms of host local storage components. JEDEC defined three different classes of NVDIMMs:

CLASS	MEMORY MAPPED	CAPACITY	LATENCY
NVDIMM-N	DRAM	1-10 GB	DRAM (ns)
NVDIMM-F	NAND	> 100 GB	NAND (us)
NVDIMM-P	DRAM+NAND	> 100 GB	NVM (high ns)

Table 47: JEDEC NVDIMM Taxonomy

NVDIMM-N exposes DRAM. The on-board NAND flash is not system mapped. The access method is a direct byte- or block-oriented access to DRAM. With NVDIMM-F the NAND flash is exposed, and the on-board DRAM is not system mapped. Therefore, the access method is block-oriented access through a shared command buffer which is often a mounted drive. This is interesting from a latency perspective since software is the primary culprit of latency. NVDIMM-P maps both the NAND flash and the DRAM. The access method can be persistent DRAM (NVDIMM-N) or block-oriented drive access.

At the time of writing the book, NVDIMM devices are only supported by Windows 2016, RedHat RHEL 7.3 and SUSE SLES 12 SP2.

Intel Xeon Skylake and NVDIMM

The new expected Intel Xeon Skylake (E5-2600 v5/2P) is reported to move away from the quad channel 3 DPC memory architecture and to a six-channel 2 DPC memory structure. The same number of DIMM slots is available, but it resolves the performance degradation constraint by distributing four DIMM slots across two new channels.

This architectural change is more than welcome for ESXi host servers as it drives higher memory capacities while retaining large amounts of bandwidth.

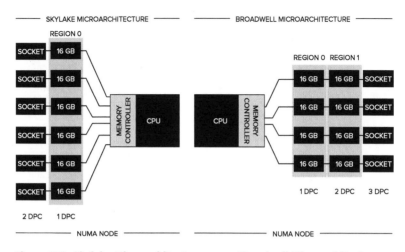

Figure 193: Skylake Microarchitecture versus Broadwell Microarchitecture

Designating the second DIMM slot to NVDIMM that maps as NAND affects the capacity requirement for the DIMM modules inserted into slot 1. Only six DIMM slots remain to provide memory capacity to the system. High capacity DRAM modules are required to provide similar capacity levels. Skylake will impact DRAM capacity configuration, to leverage six-channel, memory configurations as 96, 192 and 384 GB per NUMA node will become mainstream.

Data is interleaved across the six DIMMs in the same region. With high core count systems, this memory bandwidth is shared amongst all cores. The reduced number of slots available for DRAM and the increase in core count impacts the overall system design. As a result, faster DRAM speeds are required to cope with all the memory requests that are interleaved across a single region. As we discussed in the memory part of the book when memory speeds increase, true latency decreases, resulting in higher rates and overall better performance.

Intel Apache Pass

Intel Apache Pass is the codename for 3D XPoint in DIMM format. It could be NVDIMM it could be something else. We don't know yet. The question on everyone's mind is how will it impact memory operations. The key is to deliver an additional level of memory hierarchy, increasing capacity while abstracting the behavior of the new media.

It's key to understand that memory is accessed after an LLC miss. It can spend a lot of time waiting on DRAM. A number often heard is that it can spend 19 out of every 20 instruction slots waiting on data from memory. This figure seems accurate as the latency of an instruction inside a CPU register is 1 ns while memory latency is close to 15 ns. Each core requires memory bandwidth, and this impacts the average memory bandwidth per core. Introducing a media that is magnitudes slower than DRAM can negatively affect the overall system performance. More cycles are wasted on waiting on memory media.

Please remember that not every workload is storage I/O bound. Great system design is not only about making I/O faster. It's about removing bottlenecks in a balanced matter. It's essential that the storage I/O should not interrupt DRAM traffic.

An analogy would be a car that can go 65MPH. The car in front of it drives 55 MPH. By selecting another lane, the slower car does not interfere anymore, and it can drive the speed it wants. The problem is in this lane cars typically drive 200 MPHs.

The key point for both NVDIMM and Intel Apache Pass is that adding storage on the memory bus to improve I/O latency should not interfere with DRAM operations.

If the media access of 3D XPoint is abstracted and retains a similar load and store latency as DRAM, then this technology can be exciting. Introducing capacities of multiple 100s GB per module could get us to the holy grail of double-digit TB memory configurations.

15

vSAN STORAGE ARCHITECTURE

The majority of performance challenges originate from the storage layer. Data originating from a centralized storage resource has to fight physics (distance). After finally arriving in the host it has to make its ways through various layers of hardware and software before reaching the CPU. Moving data sources closer to resource providers is the common theme of this book. As a result, the focus of this chapter will be on vSAN.

vSAN is the storage component of the *Hyper-Converged Infrastructure* (HCI) solution of VMware. vSAN integrates with the vSphere stack to create a common virtualized platform, that provides compute and storage functionality using x86 server infrastructure. This architecture provides resource scalability and full integration with *Storage Policy-Based Management* (SPBM) to satisfy the resource requirement of each and every VM. A unique quality of vSAN is the increase of functionality with every software release. Features such as encryption, dedupe and compression are added, it is like a Tesla for datacenters. One morning you wake up, and you have new functionality ready to go. In general, traditional arrays do not offer this feature. From the day you buy it, to the day it retires, it usually offers the same feature-set.

What are the design challenges when leveraging a centralized storage solution? What benefits would the integration of storage core services into the hypervisor provide?

Scaling Storage Platforms

vSAN runs in the correct place within the hypervisor, the VMkernel layer. Operating at VMkernel level allows vSAN to scale out natively at host and cluster level. It reduces management overhead, minimizes CPU consumption and provides operational simplicity.

The VMkernel is a context-rich environment, allowing the hypervisor to apply core storage services to a VM and its components at a granular level. Being able to tag objects of the VM allows for smart placement as well as compliance checking decisions. Traditionally the logical design of the infrastructure dictates the quality and type of storage services for a VM. For example, if a VM needs to be highly available, the VM is placed on a datastore that is replicated synchronously between two storage arrays. VMs that don't need that level of availability are stored on datastores that are not replicated. Coupling capacity with storage service capabilities often results in unbalanced and error prone consumption of resources, especially when static sized LUNs are used.

For example, if you have an unbalanced number of VMs requiring replication, you can end up wasting a lot of capacity that has been allocated to non-replicated datastores. As VM growth is usually organic, moving VMs around, and reallocation of storage capacity to provide the appropriate data service is common. This often leads to increased complexity of VM placement. Mixing and matching storage services with VM requirements is tough to do at scale.

Policy-driven storage management used by vSAN leverages the context the VMkernel provides and applies storage services on a per-VM and VMDK basis when that VM is deployed on a vSAN datastore. Multiple VMs can reside on the same vSAN datastore while each VM has a different availability policy. This significantly simplifies VM provisioning while maximizing usage of storage resources.

Adopting Emerging Technology Rapidly

The use of commodity x86 server and storage hardware allows for agile and scalable infrastructure. This approach offers choice when it comes to hardware. By moving the core data services in software, it can run on most of the preferred hardware underneath. This framework leads to rapid adoption of emerging storage technologies in the datacenter. A good example is the upcoming 3D XPoint technology. During the launch of 3D XPoint VMware announced vSAN support for the future devices. Riding the hardware innovation curve is a difficult thing to do for centralized storage architectures.

Scale Storage Controller Resources

Integrating storage with compute allows for a modular design, i.e. building blocks. Centralized storage systems are mostly bottlenecked at the storage controller level, simple dual CPU systems trying to cope with the onslaught of high numbers of IOs while dealing with a lot of data management activities outside the normal data movement and data integrity operations. When expanding the clusters with more ESXi hosts, the storage demand increases, yet the storage controller resource pool in most cases remains the same. This creates a dilution of CPU resources at the storage controller per workload. By integrating storage core services in the kernel, all processes responsible for vSAN are scaled by the VMkernel. On average modern server systems have between 20 to 40 cores per host, and that number will grow with the new Intel Skylake platform. This number is per host and adding each host increases the available CPU resources immediately for the integrated storage platform.

This allows the architect to grow the storage platform more gradually. Graduated scalability does not necessarily mean ad-hoc design; it allows the architecture to adapt to the expected workload. It allows architects to expand in levels of granularity required. By aligning the storage performance management domain with the compute management domain, a better performance isolation model can be created.

Data Path

Integrating storage devices into the compute platform keeps the length of the I/O path a short as possible. Shortening the path is a common theme in the industry; similar to what NVMe is doing in the software stack. Reducing the path-length reduces latency and possible inconsistencies. Moving the data-flow pattern from the traditional north-south path to east-west helps to increase consistent performance.

When talking about north-south data paths, it refers to the data flowing from a server to a centralized storage platform such as a storage array. It's the most common design in today's datacenter. The storage area network design often follows the core-to-edge topology. This architecture contains edge switches that connect the ESXi hosts to a few high-capacity core switches. An inter-switch link connects the edge switch to the core switch. The same designs apply to storage arrays, it is either connected directly to the core switch or an edge switch. This network topology allows scaling out easily from a network perspective. Edge switches (sometimes called distribution switches) are used to extend the port count. Placement of ESXi hosts begins to matter in this design as multiple hops increase latency.

More edge ports appear when the vSphere clusters scale out. One of the drawbacks is that Edge-to-Core topologies introduce oversubscription ratios. And this leads to bandwidth availability issues. Most storage controllers don't allow scaling the network ports. This design stems from the era where storage arrays were connected to a small number of hosts running a single application. On top of that, it took the non-concurrent activity into account. Not every application is active at the same time and with the same intensity. Conventional mid-range storage arrays do not allow an expansion of uplinks within the storage controllers, creating a possible bottleneck. But one of the biggest challenges with using a shared network is performance isolation.

Providing Performance Isolation

Performance isolation is one of the most difficult challenges in the datacenter, whether they are on-premises or in-cloud. Ideally, workloads should not interfere with each other, but this is difficult to achieve when using shared storage infrastructure. A workload can be so storage resource intensive that it creates a ripple effect throughout the shared infrastructure. It can impact or interrupt workloads that don't even run on the same compute platform.

Interestingly enough, data paths are not managed as a clustered resource. There are features, both at cluster level and data-path level that can take workload activity and resource utilization into account, but not in a holistic, integrated manner. DRS can balance compute resources, but It is difficult to integrate a storage I/O balancer with current centralized storage platforms. With IP-based storage networks, multiple options exist to balance the workload across the outgoing ports. For example, the binding of multiple VMkernel NICs can be used to distribute workload; some storage vendors prefer a configuration using multiple VLANS to load balance across storage ports. When using NFS *Load Based Teaming* (LBT) can be used to load balance data across multiple NICs.

Unfortunately, all these solutions don't take the path behind the first switch port into consideration. How can you ensure that the available paths to the array are load-balanced based on VM demand and importance? Unfortunately for us today's virtual datacenter lacks load-balancing functionality that clusters these different layers, reduces hotspots and optimally distributes workloads. Let's focus on the existing available algorithms that are possibly present in virtual datacenters around the world.

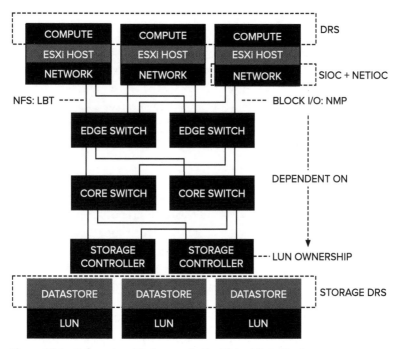

Figure 194: vSphere Load Balancers in the Virtual Data Center

Clustered Load Balancers

The only cluster-wide load balancing tools are DRS and Storage DRS. Both group resources into seamless pools and distribute workload according to their demand and their priority. When the current host cannot provide the resources a VM demands, the VM migrates to another host or datastore. DRS aggregates CPU and memory resources. Storage DRS tries to mix and match the VM I/O and capacity demand with the datastore I/O and capacity availability.

The layers between compute and datastores are equally important, yet network bandwidth and data paths are not managed as a clustered resource. Load balancing occurs within the boundaries of the host; specifically, they focus on outgoing data streams.

Although the existing workload is distributed across the available uplinks as efficiently as possible, no solution exists that pools the connected paths of the hosts in the cluster and distribute the workloads across the hosts accordingly.

Distributed I/O Control

Storage I/O Control (SIOC) is a datastore-wide scheduler, allowing distributing of queue priority amongst the VMs located on various hosts that are connected to that datastore. SIOC is designed to deal with situations where contention occurs. If necessary, it divides the available queue slots across the hosts to satisfy the I/O requirements based on the VM priority. SIOC measures the latency from the (datastore) device inside the kernel to disk inside the array. It is not designed to migrate VMs to other hosts into the cluster to reduce latency or bandwidth limitations incurred by the data path. In vSphere 6.5 SIOC has been redesigned and is now leveraging the VAIO framework and works in conjunction with SPBM. Describing SIOC in detail is unfortunately out of the scope of this book.

Network IO Control (NetIOC or NIOC) is based on a similar framework. It allocates and distributes bandwidth across the VMs that are using the NICs of that particular host. It has no ability to migrate VMs by taking lower utilized links of other hosts in the cluster into account.

Multipathing Software

VMware *Pluggable Storage Architecture* (PSA) allows third party vendors to provide their *Native MultiPathing* software (NMP). Within the PSA, *Path Selection Plugins* (PSPs) are active that are responsible for choosing a physical path for I/O requests. Three types of PSPs exist; *Most Recently Used* (MRU), Fixed and Round Robin. The *Storage Array Type Plugins* (SATP) run in conjunction with NMP and manages array specific operations. SATPs are aware of storage array details, such as whether It is an active/active array or active/passive array. For example, when the array uses ALUA (*Asymmetric LUN Unit Access*) it determines which paths lead to the ports of the managing controllers.

The Round Robin PSP distributes I/O for a datastore down all active paths to the managing controller and uses a single path for a given number of I/O operations. Although it distributes workload across all (optimized) paths, it does not guarantee that throughput will be constant. There is no optimization of the I/O profile of the host. Its load balance algorithm is based purely on equal numbers of I/O down a given path. Without regard to what the block size of I/O type is. RR will not balance on application workload characteristics or the current bandwidth utilization of the particular path. Similar to SIOC and NetIOC, NMP is not designed to treat data paths as clustered resource and has no ability to distribute workloads across all available uplinks in the cluster.

EMC PowerPath is a third party NMP and has multiple algorithms that consider current bandwidth consumption of the paths and the pending types of I/O. It integrates particular storage controller statistics avoiding negative effects by continuously switching paths. PowerPath increases the performance (and resilience) of storage paths because it can probe the link from the host to the back-end of a supported array and make decisions about active links accordingly. However, PowerPath hosts do not communicate with each other but balances I/O load on a host-by-host basis. Unfortunately. EMC PowerPath is only supported on a short list of storage vendors other than EMC own products.

Quality of Services On Data Paths

An end-to-end *Quality of Services* (QoS) on data paths would be an attractive solution; i.e. from VM to datastore. The hypervisor is a context-rich environment, allowing kernel services to understand which I/O belongs to which VM. However, when I/O exits the host and hits the network, the remaining identification is the address of the transmitting device of the host. There is no differentiation of priority possible other than at host level. Not all applications are equally important to the business therefore end-to-end QoS is necessary to guarantee that important applications gets the resources they deserve.

Storage Array Layer

Storage DRS can migrate VM files based on their resource demand. Storage DRS monitors the VMobserved latency; this includes the kernel and data path latency. Storage DRS incorporates the latency to calculate the benefit a migration has on the overall change in latency at source and destination datastore. It does not use the different latencies of kernel and data path to initiate a migration at compute level. Storage DRS starts a self-vMotion to load the new VMX file as it has a different location after the storage vMotion, the VM remains on the same hosts. In other words; Storage DRS is not designed to migrate VMs at the compute layer or datastore layer to solve bandwidth imbalance.

Most popular arrays provide asymmetric LUN unit access. Distributing LUNs across controllers is crucial as an imbalance of CPU utilization or port use of the storage controllers can be quickly introduced. LUNs can be manually transferred to improve CPU utilization. Unfortunately, this is not done dynamically. Manual detection and management are as good as people watching it, and not many organizations look at the environment at that scrutiny level all the time. Some might argue that arrays transfer the LUNs automatically, but that's when a certain number of 'proxy reads' are detected. This means that the I/O's are transmitted across the non-optimized paths, and likely either the PSP is not doing a great job, or all your active optimized paths are dead. Both not hallmarks of a healthy – or –properly architected environment.

Is Oversizing a Solution?

Oversizing bandwidth can help you so far, as its difficult to predict workload increase and intensity variation. The introduction of a radically new application landscape impacts current designs tremendously. When looking at the industry developments, it is almost certain that most datacenters will be forced to absorb these new application designs. Are the current solutions able to provide and guarantee the services they require and are they able to scale to provide the resources necessary?

Non-Holistic Load Balancer Available

In essence, the data-path between the compute layer and datastore layer is not treated as a clustered resource. Virtual machine host placement is based on compute resource availability and entitlement, disregarding the data path towards storage layer. This can potentially lead to hotspots inside the cluster, where some hosts saturate their data paths, while data paths of other hosts are underutilized. Data path saturation impacts application performance.

This is not a stab at the current solutions. It shows that it is a tough problem to solve, especially for an industry that relies on various components from different vendors, expecting everything to integrate and perform optimally. And think about moving forward and attempt to incorporate new technology advancements from all different vendors when they are available. And don't forget about backward compatibility, world peace might be easier to solve.

With this problem in mind, the existence of uncontrollable data paths, oversubscribed inter-switch links and its inability to be application aware, many solutions nowadays move away from the traditional storage architecture paradigm. Deterministic performance delivery and policy-driven management are the future.

vSAN Network Design Paradigm

vSAN moves away from the storage network topology described above and relies on point-to-point network architectures of the crossbar switch architecture to provide consistent and non-blocking network performance to cater its storage performance and storage service resiliency needs.

Leveraging point-to-point connections and being able to leverage the context-aware hypervisor allows you not only to scale easily, it allows you to create environments that provide consistent and deterministic performance levels.

vSAN 6.6 Requirements

vSAN is a flexible solution and allows you to select from a vast list of hardware options. Alternatively, vSAN ready nodes exist that consists of tested and certified hardware. vSAN ready nodes are a great alternative to manually selecting the components. If you design your server platform yourself, please ensure hosts have the following components:

Storage Requirements
- For Caching:
    - At least 1 SAS/SATA Solid State Drive, or a PCIe flash disk.
- For VM data storage:
    - Hosts running in a hybrid cluster configuration must have at least 1 SAS, NL-SAS or SATA magnetic Hard Disk (HDD).
    - Hosts running in an all-flash disk group cluster configuration must have at least 1 SAS/SATA Solid State Drive, or a PCIe flash disk.

- A SAS or SATA HBA, or RAID controller that is set up in non-RAID (pass through) or RAID 0 mode.
- Flash Boot Devices: See paragraph ESXi Boot requirements.

Memory Requirements
- Each host should contain a minimum of 32 GB of memory to accommodate for the maximum number of 5 disk groups and maximum number of 7 capacity devices per disk group.

Software Requirements
- ESXi hosts participating in a vSAN 6.6 cluster must be running ESXi version 6.5.0d.
- vCenter must be running vCenter version 6.5.0d.

Networking Requirements

- For hybrid configurations, each host must have a minimum of a single physical 1 GB Ethernet NIC available solely for vSAN use.
- For all flash configurations, each host must have a minimum of a single physical 10 GB Ethernet NIC available for vSAN use. This NIC can be shared with other traffic.
- In vSAN 6.6 and later releases, multicast is not required on the physical switches that support the vSAN cluster. If some hosts in your vSAN cluster are running earlier versions of software, a multicast network is still required.
- Each ESXi host in the cluster must have a VMkernel port, regardless of whether it contributes to storage. For more information, see the Set Up a VMkernel Network for vSAN section in the VMware vSAN documentation.
- vSAN 6.6 support vSAN deployments over layer 2 and layer 3 networking configurations.

Cluster Requirements

- A minimum of three ESXi hosts contributing local storage.
- For ROBO deployments, a minimum of two ESXi hosts is required with an additional vSAN Witness Appliance.
- All ESXi hosts must be managed by vCenter Server and configured as a vSAN cluster member.
- ESXi hosts in a vSAN cluster may not participate in any other cluster.

Notes

- vSAN requires exclusive access to the local disks in the ESXi host. vSAN disks cannot be shared with another file system, such as *Virtual Flash File System* (VFFS), VMFS partitions, or an ESXi boot partition.
- Do not format storage devices with VMFS or any other file system.
- Ensure flash storage is not claimed by vSphere Flash Read Cache.

ESXi Boot Requirements

ESXi boots from disk, but runs in-memory (RAM disk). Besides storing the bits to load the operating system, it provides storage capacity to store logs, traces, and dumps. Depending on the boot media, these files can be either captured in a RAM disk or stored on the device.

If you are running vSAN, you transformed your ESXi host in a system that is part of a storage platform. Almost everything can fail in the architecture, ESXi hosts, network switches, etc. If these devices fail it is just a matter of a reboot and the service is continued. However, when dealing with storage, we are talking a whole different ballgame here. If components fail, data corruption or data loss can occur. For that reason, it is important to keep track of the operations of the storage components.

And as a result, the responsibilities of an ESXi boot disk go beyond storing the files for the OS. A scratch partition is used for storing the following log files: tracing, logging, and the coredump. If a host is configured to boot from an SD card or a USB stick, ESXi stores the scratch partition on RAM disk. This means that they are not persisted if the host if rebooted.

DEVICE	MIN. SIZE	STORING LOGS	STORING TRACES	STORING CORE DUMPS
USB/SD	4 GB	No	RAM disk	Yes [1]
NVM SSD [2]	30 GB	Yes	Yes	Yes
HDD	30 GB	Yes	Yes	Yes
SATADOM	30 GB	Yes	Yes	Yes

Table 48: Boot Device Type Storing Log Files

1: If a host is equipped with more than 512 GB of memory, the core dump partition must be extended.
2: M.2 SSD devices are supported for boot disks.

Persisting VMkernel.log Files

If an ESXi host is equipped with an SD or USB disk as a boot device, the VMkernel log files are stored in the RAM disk. This means that these files are not persisted when a host reboots or PSODs.

The VMkernel log files are stored on persistent storage if HDD, SATADOM or SSDs are used as boot device. It is recommended to use a NAND flash device that has an endurance of 384 TBW.

It's our recommendation to store these files in a centralized location such as a syslog server or vRealize log insight. Because vSAN is a distributed platform, troubleshooting often requires analyzing logs of multiple ESXi hosts. It makes sense to store these log files centrally. Please note that storing log files and traces on the vSAN datastore is not supported as of writing.

> **Did you know each vCenter server customer is entitled to receive a 25-OSI pack of vRealize Log Insight 3.3 at no charge? Download the appliance from the vSphere download page.**

Persisting vSAN Traces

To provide the best support vSAN is configured to store trace files. These traces help VMware support to investigate failures and understand what's going on inside vSAN. Because of their importance, the traces are not stored in the RAM disk but on a permanent location in the system. Another thing you need to be aware of is that the full traces are not sent to a syslog server even if you have configured the system to use one. Since 6.2 the so-called urgent traces are redirected through the VMkernel to the syslog server, if a syslog server is defined of course. You can retrieve information about the vsantraces with the command: `esxcli vsan trace get`

```
[root@esxi01:~] esxcli vsan trace get
VSAN Traces Directory: /vsantraces
Number Of Files To Rotate: 8
Maximum Trace File Size: 45 MB
Log Urgent Traces To Syslog: true
[root@esxi01:~]
```

Figure 195: vSAN Traces Directory

The command esxcli system visorfs ramdlisk list provides an overview of the mount point and whether its included in coredumps. Please note the screenshot includes a subset of columns.

```
[root@esxi00:~] esxcli system  visorfs ramdisk list
Ramdisk Name  System  Include in Coredumps   Reserved  Mount Point
------------  ------  --------------------   --------  ------------------------
root          true                     tr   32768 KiB  /
etc           true                   true   28672 KiB  /etc
opt           true                   true       0 KiB  /opt
var           true                   true    5120 KiB  /var
tmp           false                 false    2048 KiB  /tmp
iofilters     false                 false       0 KiB  /var/run/iofilters
hostdstats    false                 false       0 KiB  /var/lib/vmware/hostd/stats
vsantraces    false                  true       0 KiB  /vsantraces
```

Figure 196: Mount Point vSAN Traces

If an ESXi host is equipped with an SD\USB disk as a boot device, the vSAN traces are stored in RAM disk and are only persisted during shutdown or panic.

> **The vSAN urgent traces provide critical information for VMware support to get a better idea of the situation. One of the best things about vSAN urgent traces is that they are in a human readable format instead of tons of binary data. That means you can dump them in a syslog or vRealize log insight.**

Capture Coredumps During System Halt

A core dump records the state of the VMkernel at the time of a *Purple Screen of Death* (PSOD). During install, the ESXi installer creates a coredump partition of 2.5 GB on the boot device.

The default size is adequate for ESXi hosts equipped with up to 1 TB of memory. If vSAN is enabled on the hosts, the default coredump partition size is adequate for hosts with 512 GB of memory and 250 GB of NVM in the caching tier.

Using the default core partition for larger systems results in truncated or partial core dumps as it cannot accommodate the complete core dump. To calculate an adequate size for the core dump partition, two factors need to be taken into account. The requirement of the core dump size based on disk group calculation and the size of the core dump based on the memory size. (Coredump = sizeOfCoredumpBasedOnDG + sizeOfCoredumpBasedOnDRAM)

Calculating the sizeOfCoredumpBasedOnDG factor, the following information is required:
- Number of disk groups inside the ESXi host.
- Size of Caching Device of each disk group.

The following metrics are used to calculate the DG factor:
RequirementOnSSDSize = (((size of SSD in GB)/100 GB) * 0.181) + 1.32

- For every 100GB cache tier, 0.181GB of space is required.
- Every disk group needs a base requirement of 1.32 GB.
- Data will be compressed by 75%.

For example, a 1.2 TB cache device results in the following calculation:
(((1200)/100 GB) * 0.181) + 1.32 = 3.492 GB

Calculate this for each disk group and combine the results. vSAN has a base requirement of 3.981 GB and add this number to the total result of the cache tier requirement. In this example, we are using two disk groups that are identical: 3.981 GB + 3.492GB + 3.492GB = 10.965 GB.

Apply the compression rate of 75%: 10.965 GB * 0.25 = 2.74125 GB

sizeOfCoredumpBasedOnDG = 2.74 GB

To calculate the `sizeOfCoredumpBasedOnDRAM` multiple the default core dump size per TB of memory. The system is equipped with 2 TB of memory, thus two times the default core size is required to contain a full core dump: `sizeOfCoredumpBasedOnDRAM = 2.56GB * 2 TB: 5.12 GB`

```
Coredump = sizeOfCoredumpBasedOnDG + sizeOfCoredumpBasedOnDRAM
Coredump = 2.74 GB + 5.12 GB = 7.86 GB
```

> **VMware KB article 2147881 contains a downloadable script that automatically computes the correct size of a core dump partition. The script uses the remaining free space on the boot drive and applies the new configuration. In addition, the script will resize the coredump slot size.**

You might ask yourself, why did they have me go to this calculation exercise while the script does this for me? Well, it might be possible that your local boot device is not big enough to contain the adequately sized core dump partition. By calculating it yourself, you can spare yourself the hassle of downloading the script, enabling SSH on your host and SCP'ing the script to your host. If the boot device does not have enough capacity, you are left with three other options:

- Obtain a bigger boot device.
- Use a VMFS volume to configure ESXi core dumps to file instead of a partition.
- Use Network Dump Collector Service integrated in the VCSA.

VMFS Datastore as Core Dump Repository
The *VMware KB article 2077516* provides the necessary steps to have the ESXi host to output the core dump directory to a VMFS datastore. Please be aware that datastores connected via Software iSCSI and Software FCoE are not supported for coredump locations.

Network Dump Collector Service
The VCSA contains the ESXi Network Dump Collector service. It is disabled by default, but easily configurable. For information, see the Configure ESXi Dump Collector with ESXCLI section in the vSphere Installation and Setup guide.

Please be aware that if the ESXi host cannot reach the Dump Collector server during a crash, the dump fails and cannot be retried. In addition, it uses UDP to transfer data to the vCenter server. If you want to ensure that core dumps are safely stored, increasing the boot device is the safest method for core dump retrieval after an ESXi host has halted.

> **Unfortunately, there is little known about the upcoming generation Dell PowerEdge (Gen 14) or HP Proliant (Gen 10). Hopefully these systems support M2 connectors. This might be the perfect boot device. Use a M2 NVMe SSD as boot device and retain all hot-pluggable disk slots at the front of the server for U.2 NVMe cache and U.2 NVMe capacity devices.**

vSAN Hardware Compatibility List

There are two ways to build a vSAN cluster yourself. Using a vSAN Ready Node or build your own vSAN node. vSAN ready nodes are preconfigured servers that are ready to use vSAN. Go to vsanreadynode.vmware.com and start the selection process. The online wizard provides a variety of commonly used profiles or allows you to fine tune your configuration by selecting compute and storage attributes. It's a great way to build a vSAN cluster that provides predictable and consistent performance.

If you like to customize your server platform more, vSAN allows building your own based on certified components. Select only the parts that are on the vSAN *Hardware Compatibility List* (HCL).

> **Please note, that the vSAN HCL can be different than the standard VMware Compatibility Guide. Make sure that you select the storage components from the vSAN HCL. This difference cannot be stressed enough! Go to vmwa.re/vsanhcl then click Build Your Own based on Certified Components.**

There are so many examples of community members who bought vSphere supported storage controllers to find out that the firmware or driver is not compatible with certain vSAN operations.
It is possible that the device just does not possess the functionality required for an error free and adequate vSAN performance.

Consumer-focused hardware components are providing adequate performance for small clusters or home-labs. This might provide the false impression that you can throw anything at vSAN. As one community member found out, the word Pro for consumer-grade components is short for Pro-Gamer, not for professional enterprise-grade functionality. Make sure you select enterprise grade parts. They have a higher endurance level, they contain power loss data protection features, and they consistently provide a high degree of performance. All align with a strategy ensuring reliable and consistent performance.

Storage Controllers and vSAN

Realistically, for many years local storage controllers did not play any significant role in host design. The performance of local storage controllers was not important. It provided sufficient throughput for the boot disks to service the OS. The importance of the part changed when NVM became the building for state-of-the-art distributed storage platform.

Over the last few years, we learned that performance differs between storage controllers. It differs between different vendors but also between controllers in the same product family. We learned that the firmware and the driver have a great impact. Although the component capabilities mostly determine the queue depth, it is the driver that dictates the actual setting. With vSAN you can use PCIe, SAS and SATA NVMe devices. NVM on a PCIe device has a dedicated controller. In most cases, multiple SAS or SATA drives share a system on-board or external HBA storage controller.

Adapter Queue Depth

The adapter queue depth can play a significant role for a particular workload. If a PCIe NVM device acts as a caching device then the adapter queue depth defines the overall queue depth for recent IOs. If multiple SAS devices connected to a single SAS controller provide the capacity layer, then the adapter queue depth defines the overall queue depth for 'cold' read IO.

To use the NVMe devices to their full potential a high queue depth in the storage stack is necessary. The vSAN HCL lists the queue depth of the certified device driver. In general, SATA disks have a QD of 32, while SAS devices have close to 256. Let's use a SAS controller as an example. According to the vSAN HCL, a common QD is 1024. That means that four devices could connect to the storage controller without being exposed to any form of bottlenecks. Most controllers have eight ports available. If you would connect eight devices, then it could be possible that performance could suffer.

One thing to note is the data management operations of vSAN. In the case of a rebuild, vSAN focuses on resolving the problem as quickly as possible. All to reduce the time window that exposes components to new failures. As a result, vSAN operates with a minimum rebuild rate to retain a minimum progress. Using a low QD storage controller or adding too many storage devices to the storage controller can impact the rebuild times and the overall protection of data.

You can check the controller queue depth by using the queue stats in esxtop. Open esxtop, go to disk adapter view (d), select add field (f) Queue stats (d). The storage controller queue depth is listed under AQLEN (Adapter Queue Length).

```
3:08:05pm up 23:25, 724 worlds, 0 VMs, 0 vCPUs; CPU

ADAPTR PATH  NPTH AQLEN    CMDS/s   READS/s  WRITES/s
vmhba0  -       2    31      5.27      3.51      0.00
vmhba1  -       0  2939      0.00      0.00      0.00
vmhba2  -       1  1023  23387.58  10529.05  12858.53
vmhba3  -       1  1024      0.00      0.00      0.00
vmhba64 -      14  1024     51.09     31.59     12.87
```

Figure 197: Adapter Queue Length

Esxtop output indicates that the adapter queue length of the storage adapters, but which adapter is mapped to what vmhba designation? The command esxcli storage core adapter list provides more insight.

```
[root@esxi00:~] esxcli storage core adapter list
HBA Name  Driver      Description
--------  ----------  -----------
vmhba0    vmw_ahci    (0000:00:1f.2) Intel Corporation Patsburg 6 Port SATA AHCI Controller
vmhba1    lsi_msgpt2  (0000:03:00.0) LSI Logic / Symbios Logic LSI2308_1
vmhba2    intel-nvme  (0000:02:00.0) Intel Corporation DC P3700 AIC
vmhba3    nvme        (0000:04:00.0) Micron <class> Non-Volatile memory controller
vmhba64   iscsi_vmk   iSCSI Software Adapter
[root@esxi00:~]
```

Figure 198: VMHBA Mapping

This system contains a SAS controller (vmhba1) with an adapter queue of 2939. What about the devices connected to the controller? The command esxcli vsan storage list provides the devices that are used by vSAN. The retrieved device names act as an identifier for the output of the command esxcli storage core device list -d devicename (Selective output of command is shown).

```
[root@esxcomp-03a:~] esxcli storage core device list -d naa.5000c5006250056f
naa.5000c5006250056f
   Display Name: Seagate Enterprise Capacity SAS Disk (naa.5000c5006250056f)
   Has Settable Display Name: true
   Size: 3815447
   Device Type: Direct-Access
   Multipath Plugin: NMP
   Devfs Path: /vmfs/devices/disks/naa.5000c5006250056f
   Vendor: SEAGATE
   Model: ST4000NM0023
   Revision: 0004
   SCSI Level: 6
   Is Local SAS Device: true
   Is SAS: true
   Device Max Queue Depth: 254
   Is Local: true
```

Figure 199: SAS Device Max Queue Depth

From a QD perspective this SAS controller is adequate enough to drive 11 devices (2939/254). In this scenario, the I/O operations can flow freely through the system. The quality of the driver impacts how fast the I/O gets on the device itself. To verify the driver and firmware version, use the command `esxcli storage san sas list`

```
[root@esxi00:~] esxcli storage san sas list
    Device Name: vmhba1
    SAS Address: 50:03:04:80:14:3d:89:00
    Physical ID: 0
    Minimum Link Rate: 1500 Mbps
    Maximum Link Rate: 6000 Mbps
    Negotiated Link Rate: 0 Mbps
    Model Description:
    Hardware Version:
    OptionROM Version:
    Firmware Version: 14.00.00.00
    Driver Name: lsi_msgpt2
    Driver Version: 20.00.01.00
[root@esxi00:~] 
```

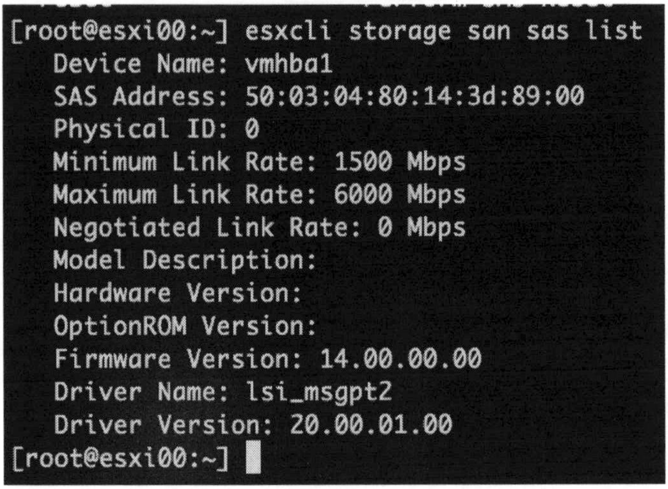

Figure 200: SAS Controller Information

Pass-Through Mode

The pass-through mode (pass-tru) of a storage adapter allows vSAN to consume the storage devices natively. Pass-through allows the I/O to flow through the minimum number of software layers. Some certified storage controllers do not offer the pass-thru functionality. In that case you need to configure each device as its own RAID-0 volume. Please note that RAID-0 is not preferred because of the operational overhead it brings. When RAID-0 is used and a device fails you cannot simply remove and add a device. You will need to create a new RAID-0 volume for that disk first before adding it to vSAN. The vSAN HCL lists the appropriate setting:

Brand Name	Model	Type	Feature	Product Description	Queue Depth	Supported Releases
DELL	HBA330	All Flash Hybrid	Pass-Through	Device Type: SAS VID: 1000 SVID: 1028 DID: 0097 SSID: 1f45	600,8316	vSAN 6.6 ESXi 6.5 ESXi 6.0 U3 ESXi 6.0 U2 ESXi 6.0 U1 ESXi 6.0
DELL	HBA330 Mini	All Flash Hybrid	Pass-Through	Device Type: SAS VID: 1000 SVID: 1028 DID: 0097 SSID: 1f53	600,8316	vSAN 6.6 ESXi 6.5 ESXi 6.0 U3 ESXi 6.0 U2 ESXi 6.0 U1 ESXi 6.0

Figure 201: HCL Feature Listing

Controller Cache

Storage controller cache can become a bottleneck for hypervisor I/O. It's recommended by VMware to disable the controller cache. If the cache cannot be fully disabled, attempt to configure the controller cache to read only. This ensures the writes are not hitting the controller cache first before hitting the device. Disabling write cache provides a clean path to the device and to vSAN.

vSAN Storage Policies

The vSAN storage policies define the storage requirements for the VMs.
They determine how VMs are provisioned and allocated within the vSAN
cluster to satisfy the requirements. vSAN is an object storage system
and manages data as objects, as opposed to VMFS, which manages data
as a file hierarchy. In vSAN, a VM is split into multiple objects. A VM can
consist of four different types of objects:

- VM home directory
- VMDK file
- Swap file
- Snapshot delta file

Each object in the vSAN cluster has its own RAID tree. This can be seen
as a tree of component configuration subject to the configuration of the
storage policy. In turn, this specifies a distribution specification for
vSAN. The placement of these components depends on the number of
storage devices, vSAN disk groups, and fault domains inside the vSAN
cluster.

> Covering all vSAN extensively is beyond the scope of the book. We
> recommend picking up the Essential Virtual SAN book by Cormac
> Hogan and Duncan Epping. Visit their sites for up to date info about
> the latest vSAN version; cormachogan.com and yellow-bricks.com.
> Visit storagehub.vmware.com. It's full with lots of technical
> documentation, and it provides access to the always-excellent
> Virtually Speaking Podcast.

The following table lists the available storage policies. vSAN 6.6
introduced a few rule changes to provide additional protection or
flexibility for stretched cluster scenarios. Please refer to the item *Per Site
Policies for vSAN 6.6 Stretched Clusters* on storagehub.vmware.com for
more details about stretched cluster policy behavior. Please note that the
only upgrade requirement for vSAN 6.5 customers when they use the
new rules in vSAN 6.6, is the requirement to upgrade the On-Disk format
from version 3 to version 5.

CAPABILITY	DEFAULT	MAXIMUM	DESCRIPTION[1]
Number of disk stripes per object	1	12	Minimum number of capacity devices the object is striped
Flash read cache reservation [2]	0%	100%	Flash capacity reserved for read cache for VMDK object. % VMDK size
Primary failures to tolerate	1	3	Defines the # of hosts & devices an object can tolerate. 1: Enables protection across sites. 0: Protection in a single site
Force provisioning	No	Yes	Object is provisioned regardless of policy satisfaction
Object space reservation	0	100%	% VMDK size that must be reserved
Disable object checksum	No	Yes	If option is set to no, the integrity of its data is ensured
Failure tolerance method	Performance	Capacity	Specifies data replication is configured for performance or capacity purposes.
IOPS limit for object	0	User-specified	Defines the IOPS limit

Table 49: vSAN Storage Policies

[1]: Please check storagehub.vmware.com or the vSAN 6.5 administration guide (en-002286-01).

[2]: Not available for vSAN AFA.

For example, if a VM is configured with the *primary failures to tolerate* (Failure tolerate) set to one, then a VMDK object of that VM is replicated to two storage devices across of separate ESXi hosts (RAID-1). If the *number of disk stripes per object* (Stripe width) is set to two, each replica is split into two equal portions and distributed across several storage devices (RAID-0).

vSAN applies a default storage policy if no custom policy is assigned to the VM. By default a failure to tolerate of 1 is applied to all objects belonging to the VM. The command `esxcli vsan policy getdefault` retrieves the default policy.

```
[root@esxi00:~] esxcli vsan policy getdefault
Policy Class  Policy Value
------------  ---------------------------------------------------------------
cluster       (("hostFailuresToTolerate" i1))
vdisk         (("hostFailuresToTolerate" i1))
vmnamespace   (("hostFailuresToTolerate" i1))
vmswap        (("hostFailuresToTolerate" i1) ("forceProvisioning" i1))
vmem          (("hostFailuresToTolerate" i1) ("forceProvisioning" i1))
[root@esxi00:~]
```

Figure 202: Default vSAN Policy

A vSAN component associated with the VM is the witness. This is necessary to determine quorum during failure handling and split-brain determination. If the VM contains enough objects that are distributed across multiple hosts, then vSAN may replace the functionality of the witness objects with votes per object. More than 50% of the components need to be available to achieve quorum. By removing the need of witness components, vSAN reduces the number of objects to manage and the number of I/O operations required to provide fault tolerance methods.

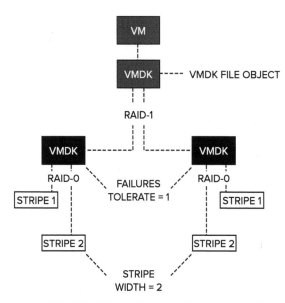

Figure 203: VMDK Object Tree Distributed Across Two ESXi Hosts

The components require storage devices. Some components are allowed to be stored on the same host or fault domain while others are not. Moving storage services from the infrastructure layer (replicated LUNs) to the VM level increases flexibility. However, it does require you to think about the cluster and host structure carefully.

vSAN Design Considerations

The ESXi host design of a vSAN cluster is the product of multiple finer-grained decisions and requirements. It should follow a top-down approach. The premise of a vSAN design should always be clustered based. How does the cluster satisfy the VM requirement defined by the storage policies? For example, what is the highest number of the failures to tolerate policy setting present in the cluster? The answer to that question results in the minimum number of hosts in the cluster.

The stripe width policy determines how many unique capacity devices the cluster requires that can contain an object, and components to satisfy the failure policy.

RAID-5 and RAID-6 erasure codes allow for a far better space efficiency than replication for the same level of data protection. However, it comes at a price, which is the amplification of I/O operations. Amplification of I/O operations can impact your overall performance. By selecting the correct cache and capacity device type can alleviate this problem a bit. The interesting thing is that traditionally these operations are contained within a host. But since vSAN is a distributed system, these occur across the cluster. This means that network plays a significant role in vSAN design. Networking is covered extensively in the next part.

The number of hosts in the cluster divided by the number of capacity devices results in a host design. Depending on the level of risk avoidance, multiple disk groups can be used to reduce the risk factor within the hosts. It can improve performance by leveraging parallelism. The following maximums have to be kept in mind when designing a vSAN cluster.

ITEM	MAXIMUM
Disk groups per host	5
Cache device per disk group	1
Capacity devices per disk group	7
Components per vSAN host	9000
Number of vSAN hosts in a cluster	64
VMs per host	200
VMs per cluster	6000
VMDK size	62 TB
Disk stripes per object	12

Table 50: vSAN 6.6 Configurations Maximums

All-Flash versus Hybrid Configuration

This design consideration boils down to cost versus consistent performance. A vSAN cluster equips magnetic drives for capacity is considered a hybrid configuration, a vSAN with flash capacity for both the cache as the capacity is an all-flash configuration.

The guideline for the capacity of the cache device for a hybrid configuration is 10%. If a cache miss occurs, vSAN retrieves the data from the magnetic disks. This results in inconsistent performance. Sometimes your data is provided in microseconds while other times your data is supplied in milliseconds. For example, on a good day that read is retrieved in 80 microseconds from flash. According to our 1-second scale that is 22 hours according, magnetic takes up eight milliseconds equaling to 92.59 days! Imagine if Amazon had a term of service like this.

Hybrid configurations used to provide more capacity per host, but with the advent of 4 TB NVM devices, this eradicates that motivation. And that brings the reason for the choice for all flash versus hybrid configurations back to cost.

Typically the cost of a storage platform is calculated by the capacity ratio it provides. This is similar to an Olympic sprinter only training on his right leg. Storage in the virtual datacenter is a major source of performance. Thus costs for a storage platform should be calculated with three axes in mind. So there goes our Olympic sprinter analogy. Capacity, latency and IOPS key metrics to determine if the storage system is the right tool for the job at hand.

With magnetic disks, the cost capacity per currency is fantastic, while the IOPS per currency is horrible. For example, the Intel P3700 2.0 TB serves up 450,000 IOPS and costs 3300 EUR. That is 0,007 EUR per IOPS. A Hewlett Packard Enterprise 1,2 TB 12G SAS cost roughly 400 EUR and provides 180 IOPS. That results in 2,22 EUR per IOPS. 2.The same goes for latency cost factor. With performance in mind, an AFA configuration makes sense.

We left out two other relevant metrics, heat dispensation and physical reliability in hostile environments. We've seen some vSAN AFA deployments in locations that could not be equipped with a hybrid configuration due to the involvement of mechanical parts.

> **Considering that the central theme of the book is designing a host configuration that provides consistent performance for modern platforms, we focus mostly on all-flash configurations for the remainder of the chapter.**

Balanced Cluster

A vSAN cluster can consist of ESXi hosts that contribute capacity to the vSAN cluster and non-contributing ESXi hosts. These hosts offer compute resources to the cluster, but consume capacity from the vSAN cluster. vSAN has no strict data locality policies for the capacity due to the failure tolerates and stripe width policies. Latency increases if the VM continuously reads and writes to and from a remote location. It may lead to longer paths and inconsistent storage performance compared to balanced vSAN cluster design.

> **We recommend using identically configured ESXi hosts per vSAN cluster. Each host contributes capacity to the vSAN cluster. This design provides the most balanced workload performance.**

vSAN Disk Group Architecture

A host that contributes capacity to the vSAN cluster equips local storage devices. vSAN teams the local storage devices into a disk group. A disk group contains one device for cache. It can contain multiple devices for capacity. One device acts as a cache device to the capacity devices within a disk group. The remaining disks in the disk group provide the raw capacity.

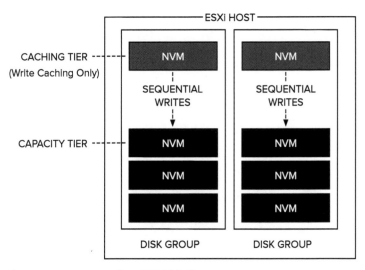

Figure 204: Anatomy of a vSAN Disk Group

Cache Tier & Capacity Tier Devices

In the all-flash configuration, Flash or 3D XPoint devices are used for both the flash tier as well as the capacity tier. The cache tier is responsible for processing writes. The capacity tier processes the incoming VM read operations while dealing with the incoming stream of data pushed (destaged) by the cache tier.

The **cache tier** is tasked to process writes as quickly as possible. They will be provided in a random pattern. As a result, the new 3D XPoint NVM devices look promising. It appears that they are perfect with their high-performance characteristics at a low queue depth and the ability to do in-place writes. No more delays caused by write-amplification will occur. The previous chapter contains in-depth information about 3D XPoint technology.

vSAN cache recommendations up to vSAN 6.6 were 10% of used capacity. Today, guidelines that are more workload focused. Buying a device with the largest capacity might be overkill. VMware published the following all flash cache ratio guidelines.

READ/WRITE PROFILE	WORKLOAD TYPES	AF-8 SYSTEMS*	AF-6 SYSTEMS	AF-4 SYSTEMS
70/30 Read/Write; Random	Read Intensive	800 GB	400 GB	200 GB
>30% Write; Random	Medium Writes	1.2 TB	800 GB	400 GB
100% Write; Sequential	Heavy Writes, sequential	1.6 TB	1.2 TB	600 GB

Table 51: Total Write Cache Per Host

* VMware created vSAN Node Profiles for large (AF-8), medium (AF-6) and small (AF-4) systems. Specifications about vSAN Node profiles can be found in the *vSAN Hardware Quick Reference Guide* online.

Please note that the recommendation is the total write cache per host. The 1.6 TB example uses a 2 x 800 GB configuration. This is mainly because of the vSAN write buffer limit. The write buffer limit is set to 600 GB. This buffer is used to hold the data that has not yet been destaged to the capacity tier. vSAN will apply a back-pressure mechanism if the write-buffer is nearing capacity. Depending on the number of writes (100% sequential writes), it can be advantageous to select larger devices. If the workload is predominantly read focused (70/30 Read/Write; Random), then vSAN will have ample time to destage the writes to the capacity tier.

If you obtain an 800 GB disk, 600 GB is used by vSAN for buffering writes. The remaining capacity is available for device-native data management operations such as wear leveling. As described in detail in the previous chapter, over-provisioning allows for consistent performance. The FTL has plenty of free space to map empty flash pages for valid data during write-amplification. vSAN is designed to never perform an in-place re-write of an existing SSD page. Block allocation is performed in a round-robin fashion keeping wear leveling in mind while avoiding inconsistent write −behavior.

> **Although vSAN is designed to reduce overhead as much as possible, It is recommended to obtain a NVM device with a high endurance rating for the caching tier.**

The write buffer limit of 600 GB gently nudges the architect in the right direction. Instead of using one gigantic device, design for a system that deploys multiple smaller cache devices. Parallelization of multiple devices helps to improve performance while reducing the size of the disk groups (Intra ESXi Host fault domain). However, flash drives are rapidly increasing in capacity. Please keep track of a number of capacity drives per disk group if you design allows to scale up the disk groups. The ratio cache-to-capacity can quickly become unbalanced.

> **Please be aware that there is no permanent read cache tier in the cache layer. Because vSAN destages write data asynchronously to the capacity tier it can happen that valid data is residing in the cache tier. As a result, most recent data access, particularly useful for read-after-write operations, are done in the cache tier. Nevertheless, for the majority of workloads the read-operations are served directly from the capacity tier. Due to write-bias of the cache tier, ensure you select NVM devices that perform well on write operations.**

The **capacity tier** experiences a mixed stream of I/O. Destaging data from the caching layer to the capacity layer is done asynchronously in a sequential method. Leveraging the inherent parallelism by issuing sequential writes at a high queue depth ensures the fastest destaging possible. For this workload, a NAND flash device is the perfect fit. However, read operations will appear randomly. Since NAND Flash chips cannot process read and writes simultaneously, the best-suited NAND flash devices are the ones that are equipped with a high number of channels. It is tough to discover the channels in a NAND flash device, but the rule of thumb is, the greater number of NAND flash chips the more channels it contains. In short, higher capacity drives provide better alternating I/O pattern performance.

Last, but certainly not least, try to match the endurance rating of both the cache devices and the capacity devices. vSAN introduces an additional level of write-amplification due to the logging to vSAN's metadata. vSAN optimizes metadata operations as much as possible, but be aware that there is a small overhead is present.

As described in detail in the previous chapter, ensure you compare the correct endurance value when reviewing multiple devices.

> High capacity NAND flash devices are equipped with a high number of channels. This improves parallelism and allows the capacity tier to process both reads and writes in a consistent manner.

Disk Group Sizing

The availability- and stripe width requirements of each VM determine the required storage space that the vSAN cluster should provide. A disk group is an intra-ESXi fault domain and a placement designation. Both are inherently connected to each other. If the cache device of disk group fails, vSAN evaluates the accessibility of the objects stored in the disk group and rebuilds them on another host if enough free space is available.

> Please note that the policy 'Number of failures to tolerate' does not have the word host in it. Any failure, whether It is the full host or just a device failure, counts as a failure. And as a result, a capacity device failure triggers rebuild and re-protect operations.

The design decision of the number of capacity devices is important. It impacts availability and performance. If selecting a high number of devices, it can expose you to an increased risk of device failure. To be honest, it is a tough act to balance. And with everything in life, going to the extreme typically exposes you to significant risk. To put it more popularly; *just because you can doesn't mean you should*. And with this in mind, the sweet spot should be slightly less than the maximum of seven disks.

> A quick survey showed that a great number of vSAN customers are deploying five capacity devices per disk group. A two-disk group design per host is common.

Moving away from the 'all eggs in one basket' paradigm is smart. From an availability – and performance perspective. Distributing the objects across multiple devices in the disk group helps to increase the read operation performance. Don't forget that the cache device needs to write the data to the capacity devices. This process is called destaging. NAND flash cannot perform read and write operations simultaneous on the same NAND flash chips. Issuing read and write operations in parallel to different planes, or dies overcomes this limitation. By using multiple capacity devices, you work around this constraint even further.

> By increasing the number of capacity devices, it leverages multiple PCIe channels to various devices in parallel.

vSAN 6.6 Memory Requirement

The caching and capacity tier configuration impacts the memory consumption of vSAN. Understanding this impact allows you to adjust your consolidation ratio calculation and VM-sizing, as vSAN eats into the available memory per NUMA node. The follow equation is used:

```
BaseConsumption + (NumDiskGroups x (DiskGroupBaseConsumption +
(SSDMemOverheadPerGB x SSDSize)) + (NumCapacityDisks *
CapacityDiskBaseConsumption))
```

COMPONENT	DESCRIPTION
BaseConsumption[1]	Fixed amount of memory consumed by vSAN per ESXi host
NumDiskGroups	Number of disk groups in the host, should range from 1 to 5
DiskGroupBaseConsumption[2]	Fixed amount of memory consumed by each disk group in the host
SSDMemOverheadPerGB[3]	Fixed amount of memory vSAN allocates for each GB of SSD capacity of cache tier
SSDSize	The size of the SSD in GB
numCapacityDisks	Number of capacity devices in disk group
CapactityDiskBaseConsumption	Fixed amount of memory consumed by capacity device in disk group

Table 52: vSAN Memory Consumption Calculation Components

1: BaseConsumption: is currently 5 GB. This memory is mostly used to house the vSAN directory, per host metadata, and memory caches. Please note that each all-flash node has a 1GB read cache located in-memory. vSAN 6.2 introduced Client Cache, a mechanism that allocates 0.4% of host memory, up to 1GB, as an additional read cache tier.

2: DiskGroupBaseConsumption: This is currently 636 MB. This is mainly used to allocate resources used to support inflight operations on a per disk group level.

3: SSDMemOverheadPerGB is currently 2 MB in hybrid systems and is 7 MB for all flash systems. Most of this memory is used for keeping track of blocks in the SSD used for write buffer and read cache.

Let's use an AF-6 series ready node from the *vSAN Hardware Quick Reference Guide* as a guideline for our calculation. This system has 2 x 200 GB flash, 8 x 1 TB capacity devices in a two-disk group disk configuration. This results in an overhead of:

```
5120 MB (2 x (636 MB + (14MBx200)) + (4 x 70)
5120 MB (2 x (636 MB + (2800) + (280)
5120 MB (2 x (3716 MB)
5120 MB + 7432 MB  = 12552 MB
```

VMware KB article 2113954 provides the vSAN memory consumption equation for 6.0 to 6.5, as demonstrated the memory requirements for vSAN 6.6 changed slightly.

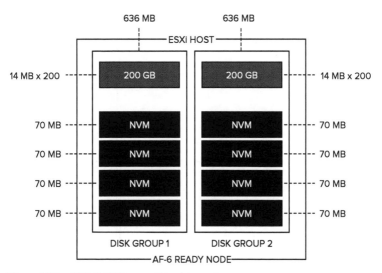

Figure 205: vSAN 6.6 Memory Requirement

Fault Tolerance Method

vSAN 6.2 introduced Fault Tolerance Method (FTM) and extends the available data protection methods. If the vSAN cluster contains enough ESXi hosts, you can choose between mirroring (RAID-1), and erasure coding (RAID-5 or RAID-6) data placement and parity pattern.

> **Please note that erasure coding is only available for all-flash configurations. The RAID-5 configuration requires a minimum number of hosts of four. Six ESXi hosts are necessary to configure a VM with a RAID-6 configuration.**

Using RAID erasure coding allows vSAN to deploy the objects across the storage on each ESXi host inside the vSAN cluster in a more space-efficient manner. The choice between RAID-5 and RAID-6 is determined by selecting the number of number of failures to tolerate. If one failure is selected vSAN applies RAID-5. If two failures are selected, vSAN applied RAID-6. The maximum number of failures vSAN can tolerate is three. If this number is selected, vSAN automatically selects mirroring.

FAULT TOLERANCE METHOD (FTM)				
Failures to Tolerate	RAID-1		RAID-5/6	
	Required Hosts	Recommended Hosts	Required Hosts	Recommended Hosts
1	3	4	4	5
2	5	6	6	7
3	7	8		

Table 53: Fault Tolerance Method Host Count for Object Distribution

Please note that recommended hosts specify the number of ESXi hosts to allow in-place rebuilds. If resilience is more important than capacity savings, then mirroring might be a valid option for fault tolerance. When comparing in-place rebuild functionality requirements, you need five hosts to tolerate two failures with mirroring. RAID-5 only tolerates one failure when using 5 hosts.

> If fault-domains are used, the fault domain number is the restricting number for FTT. When fault domains are not configured hosts behave as individual fault domains.

In-place Rebuilt Operations

An important aspect of the vSAN cluster is the ability to recover from a failure while still servicing I/O operations of the VMs. vSAN can rebuild components during a failure. Whether that will be in-place or after the replacement of the failed component depends on the number of cluster fault domains or ESXi hosts that can provide free capacity.

During a device or host failure, vSAN engages with the available object replicas and continue to process I/O operations for all VMs. Keep in mind that data is never replicated between disk groups inside the same ESXi host. Increasing the number of ESXi hosts in the cluster provides more possibilities for in-place rebuild operations than opting to scale up by increasing capacity devices inside the disk group or add another disk group to the same host.

Cache Device Failure

During a cache device failure, vSAN stops the I/O operations to that disk group for five to seven seconds and re-evaluates whether these objects are available anywhere else in the cluster. It's easy to ignore this number, but we are constantly focusing on driving down the latency. We want to move towards the ultimate goal of near-nanoseconds latency. We should not ignore that such a failure can cause a 7-second delay. 189,000 CPU cycles are wasted if the VM was scheduled continuously waiting on an I/O response. The operation stored in the register of the CPU just experienced a delay of 221.96 years here. To put this in perspective; George Washington was president of the United States or if we look to the future it isn't long before Kirk feels the wrath of Kahn. It makes sense to expose such an impact to the smallest number of VMs as possible.

If the VM is configured with the failures to tolerate policy that is equal or greater than one then objects are available on other hosts in the cluster. vSAN redirects all I/O operations of these failed objects to the replicas. In the meantime, vSAN attempts to re-protect the object by rebuilding the objects on the remaining hosts.

> **To reduce the impact of such an event, you should consider using multiple devices instead of one large device. If a device fails, it affects a lower number of objects (VMs).**

Please keep in mind that there is a break-even point on the number of devices to use for fault-domain reduction. At one point the impact level flattens out while the number of devices used simply increases complexity. Typically, most servers are equipped with a number of disk slots that prohibits the architect to explore the thresholds of the break-even point. Most customers create two disk groups within an ESXi host with a number of capacity devices satisfying their operational capacity, performance, and failure recovery needs.

Maintenance Mode Operations Impact

Designing the vSAN cluster should involve the impact of maintenance activities. When an ESXi host is placed into maintenance mode, the host does not contribute capacity to the cluster. As a result, the cluster capacity is automatically reduced. vSAN allows to select from three options when you place an ESXi host into maintenance mode:

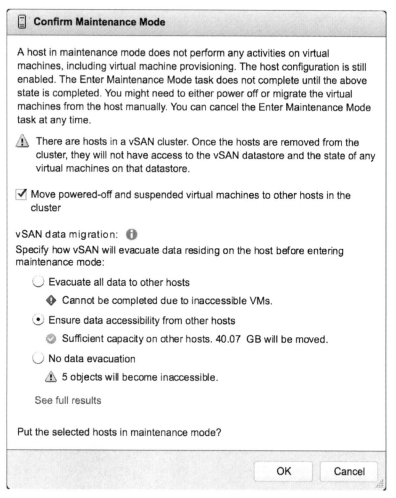

Figure 206: vSAN Data Migration Options

No data migration is quite self-explanatory. It can impact the availability of active VMs. Be aware that an ESXi host can play a significant role in the availability of a VM active on another ESXi host. This ESXi host can retain a replica object or a witness object. If one of the ESXi hosts is put into maintenance mode and contains either the replica or the witness object, recoverability might be at risk. This depends on the selected data migration option. When selecting the ensure accessibility option, only the objects of the VMs that are active are migrated. Replicas and witness objects of VMs running somewhere else are ignored.

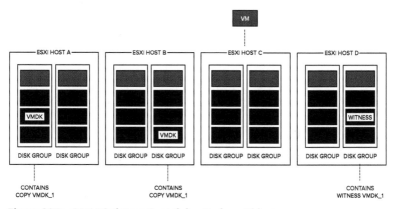

Figure 207: vSAN ESXi Host Containing Various Objects

For this reason, the ensure accessibility option is recommended for host patching and quick maintenance. If a host is decommissioned or disks in the disk groups are removed, it is recommended to select the option full data migration. This leads to a full redistribution of all types of objects across the available storage capacity devices inside the vSAN cluster.

> **Keep in mind that replica objects and witness objects cannot share a device that contains the original object. As a result, additional hosts are required to continue accessibility of VMs during maintenance mode.**

Stripe Width and All Flash vSAN

The stripe width policy splits the object into the number of specified components. If the policy is set to two, each VMDK object is divided into two components. These components are stored onto separate capacity devices. vSAN follows a vertical first, then horizontal placement. That means that by design vSAN attempts to place the stripes within the storage devices in the disk group first.

However, it is possible that the stripes will be placed in multiple disk groups. If data is requested, that resides partially in stripe 1 and partially in stripe 2; utilization will go through both disk groups. These disk groups can be on the same ESXi host, but be in other ESXi hosts in the cluster.

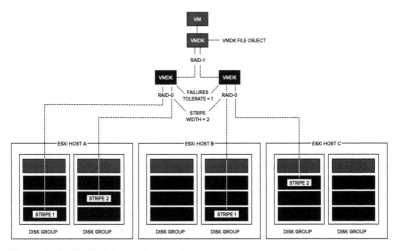

Figure 208: vSAN Objects Distribution

Interestingly enough in this scenario, since vSAN 6.0, it does not require a witness. It will weigh the voting according to the distribution of the stripe components. In the scenario depicted above, the stripe located on the same ESXi host will receive each one vote. One of the other stripes will receive two votes. Therefore, if ESXi host A fails, the remaining stripes still hold the quorum. By just using a record mechanism, vSAN removed the need to create another object (witness) that can interfere with obtaining an optimal distribution of objects.

The maximum component size of vSAN is 255 GB. That means that a 1500 GB VMDK is split up into six stripe components. vSAN 6.6 uses a capacity threshold of 80% on the capacity devices. If it reaches the threshold, components are split up sooner. This helps environments with large VMDK objects and relatively small capacity devices. It avoids slack space and fragmentation. It's even possible for vSAN to migrate data to get the overall consumed capacity below the threshold.

Please keep in mind that VDMK objects are deployed as thin disks by default. vSAN uses a 1 MB stripe size and round-robins across the available devices. If the stripes are distributed across multiple hosts, it writes to each of the capacity devices for equal consumption of capacity.

> **Be aware that if vSAN is equipped with small capacity devices while servicing a high number of VMs, or large footprint VMDKs, striping occurs automatically. This can lead to an increase in network traffic due to read operations and synchronous writes to the caching devices.**

Stripes are particularly useful for vSAN hybrid configurations. By using multiple stripes, you are using as many capacity devices as possible. Distributing load and increasing the total number of available IOPS to that VMDK object. Stripes in All-flash vSAN will increase parallelism, but you need to weigh the performance improvement against the growing complexity of placement and in network traffic.

> **Considering the performance of AFA devices and the induced complexity on maintenance and availability operations. Stripe Width of more than one should only be used to squeeze the last bit of performance from the system if the network can maintain a consistent throughput and latency performance.**

High stripe width count in an All-Flash vSAN can be interesting if the vSAN cluster is comprised of a vast number of hosts. If the cluster consists more than 24 hosts (approximately, not an absolute threshold), high stripe width counts can help to reduce rebuilt time during a device failure. Multiple hosts are engaged in the rebuilding process.

The density of stripes in a small cluster would end up nullifying any well-intended distribution effort. Each host would be swamped with rebuilding a high number of stripes.

CPU Interoperability

With each release of a new CPU microarchitecture, Intel is announcing improved or new CPU features. Exciting news for some, for most, It is always a question which application or OS will use that new interesting feature. vSAN design is focused on leveraging native CPU functionality as much as possible. With this in mind, new CPU microarchitecture becomes more interesting besides the core and cache count.

AVX Interoperability for vSAN RAID Parity Calculations

Advanced Vector Extensions (AVX) is a 256-bit instruction set extension to Intel SSE. Intel SSE is a 128-bit instruction set, and as a result, AVX is doubling the size instruction set registers available. Intel E5-2600 v3 (Haswell) introduced AVX2. AVX-512 is expected to be introduced by the upcoming Skylake microarchitecture (E5-2600 v5). AVX allows you to perform the same operation on multiple data points simultaneously without the need to overwrite the data in the same CPU register. This increases parallelism and throughput of floating point calculations.

AVX's ability to execute complex calculations without the need to overwrite the same data over and over again is extremely useful for RAID parity calculations. RAID erasure coding (scheme for encoding and partitioning data into fragments) extends a data value with a new value and allows recovery if any (RAID-5) or two values (RAID-6) are missing. In essence, these parity calculations use large regions of bytes. Larger CPU registers and the ability to retain those bits without overwriting them in place speeds these calculations.

Christos Karamanolis published the following findings:

> *In fact, we observed that performing Reed-Solomon calculations (Galois Field Arithmetic) using AVX2 is *faster* than performing simple XOR calculations without using AVX2! When we leverage AVX2 for both XOR and Reed-Solomon, the difference in cost (CPU cycles) between the two is under 10%. Virtual SAN 6.2 implements RAID-5 and Reed-Solomon-based RAID-6. It leverages SSSE3, which are present in all CPUs supported by vSphere, and AVX2 (present in Intel Haswell or newer).*

End-to-End Checksum

vSAN implements and end-to-end software checksum. The checksum allows vSAN to avoid data integrity issues due to failures happening at the physical device level. By default, It is enabled for every object. However, it can be disabled if the application applies check summing as well.

vSAN implements Common cyclic redundancy check CRC-32C method developed by G.Castagnoli, S.Brauer, M.Herrmann. For more information, read the paper: *Optimization of cyclic-redundancy-check codes with 24 and 32 parity bits*. vSAN leverages the Intel SSE4.2 instruction set. This allows the CPU to run three CRC instructions efficiently in parallel on a single core compared to the software version, which is optimized to process eight bytes at a time.

Intel AES for vSAN Encryption

vSAN provides the ability to encrypt data at rest. It can encrypt every object on the vSAN datastore. vSAN Encryption runs in the hypervisor and does not rely on *Self-Encrypting Drives* (SEDs) but leverages commodity CPU cycles. Encryption is performed using an XTS AES 256 cipher, in both the cache and capacity tiers of the vSAN datastore.

Intel started to support the *Advanced Encryption Standard* (AES) standard in their chipset back in 2008.

Every release AES calculations improve and reduce overhead. Intel E5-2600 v3 (Haswell) introduced support for AEX-XTS, which improves *AES-New Instruction* (AES-NI) set performance by 14%. Skylake is expected to improve this performance by another 17%. Both the software and hardware engineers are focused on reducing encryption overhead down to the absolute minimum. Having the most recent hardware support helps to drive down this overhead.

The technical paper *VMware vSphere Virtual Machine Encryption Performance VMware vSphere 6.5* contains performance tests result that show most operations are slightly affected by encryption. Whether this increase is acceptable for your workload is easily confirmed. And that is the beauty of storage profiles. Just enable the profile, test your workload and if this is not acceptable, turn it off. No need for additional investments in hardware. It's just a flip of a switch!

Use vSAN Observer to Monitor vSAN

vSAN Observer dashboard provides all the relevant information to monitor the behavior of the vSAN cluster. It is a part of the Ruby vSphere Console (RVC). RVC is an interactive command line shell for vSphere management. RVC is available on all vCenter types. Although it is not automatically enabled, it is embedded in the VCSA and quite easy to run.

1. Enable SSH access on the VCSA and log into the VCSA.
2. Enter the command `username@VCSA address` for example: `administrator@vsphere.local`
3. Enter the command `vsan.observer ~computers/<cluster name>/ --run-webserver –force`
4. Open a webbrower and go the the url: `http://<VCVA IP or FQDN>:8010/`

Please note that sometimes the system interprets the ~ character incorrectly. The workaround is to use the full path. In our lab this is: `vsan.observer /172.16.15.12/LAB/computers/IVY-BRIDGE/ --run-webserver –force`. To cover all the features is outside the scope of this chapter, we recommend you log on and take a tour!

16

CORE STORAGE

This chapter will dig into how the VMkernel layer interpreters the physical storage layer. The VMkernel has to manage storage I/O's from various storage subsystems like local storage devices, bundled together and utilized by for instance VMware vSAN, or central storage systems connected by a SAN.

Depending on the storage backend solution, the ESXi VMkernel storage paths connects the application all the way to the storage layer, that consists of either flash or disk devices. Various VMkernel and storage components are touched along the way. Every step of the way impacts performance because each step hits a queue of buffer.

Storage I/O Queues

What is a storage queue? To understand how the end-to-end storage data path works in the VMkernel, we should understand what storage queues are and where it live.

First of all, understand that there are two types of storage I/O's; Outstanding I/Os and IOPS. When an I/O is issued by a VM, the demand for that I/O is called an *Outstanding I/O* (OIO). From the storage backend perspective, where the VM data lives, the supply of that I/O is measured as *I/O Per Second* (IOPS). But are often referred to as 'commands'.

A storage queue is a mechanism that allows a storage I/O wait in line for its turn to be processed. Depending on the queue depth size, a specific number of I/O's can be processed in parallel. Using queues enables ESXi to share storage resources with multiple VMs. It also allows workloads to have their I/O's processed at the same time. Compare it with people waiting on the bus. When the bus arrives, it has capacity for an *x* amount of people. Once the capacity is reached, the bus will drive off. People that did not fit in that bus must wait for the next one. The same goes for storage I/O's. The remaining I/O's must wait in line to be processed. It would be beneficial to have a bus that can transport all the people waiting in line. Similar behavior is found in every queue along the data path.

Looking at the various queues, each with its own queue depth, we see a different picture depending on the chosen storage solution.

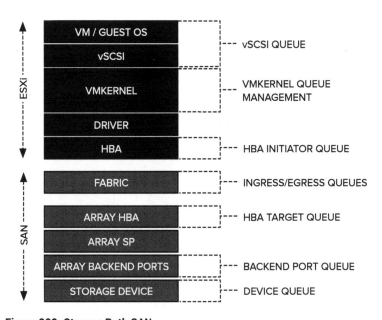

Figure 209: Storage Path SAN

This diagram shows the queues in the path from a guest OS to a storage device in a SAN array. It traverses the ESXi stack and connects to the *Storage Processors* (SP) over a fabric. The fabric itself incorporates switch port buffers (ingress and egress) that have a similar behavior to queues.

When a VM is accessing data stored on server-side resources (like with vSAN), the storage path is notable shorter in comparison to SAN storage resources. As explained in previous chapters, the key is to keep the data as close to the application as possible, to fully utilize the performance characteristics of a storage device. That resembles with the fewer queues that are used to reach the server-side storage resource. The lesser queues, the better because each queue will introduce additional latency.

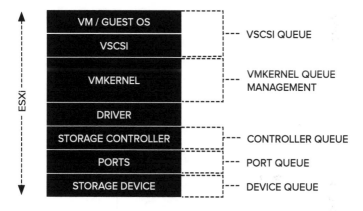

Figure 210: Storage Path Server-Side Storage

Obviously, the storage path stays within the ESXi host when it accesses local storage devices. After the VMkernel queue management, the storage controller is next in line. Depending on the chosen storage controller, it might have separate storage controller port queues before reaching the storage device.

The VMkernel storage framework consist of queues that correlate with some of the metrics that are seen in esxtop. These metrics provide insights on how your storage environment is setup in terms of queue depths.

QUEUE	DESCRIPTION
WQLEN	World Queue Length
AQLEN	Adapter Queue Length
DQLEN	Device Queue Length

Table 54: Storage I/O Queues

The *World Queue* (WQLEN) detemermines the maximum number of VMkernel active I/O's that the world is allowed to contain simultaneously. The storage *Adapter Queue* (AQLEN) detemermines the maximum of active I/O's in the VMkernel for the driver of a storage controller. As pointed out earlier, the queue depth is configured at driver level. This means that a newer driver version for the storage adapter can have a great impact on storage performance. The *Storage Device* (DQLEN) is the maximum number of active I/O for a specific storage device. Looking in esxtop, these metrics are seen in the disk adapter, disk device and disk VM views.

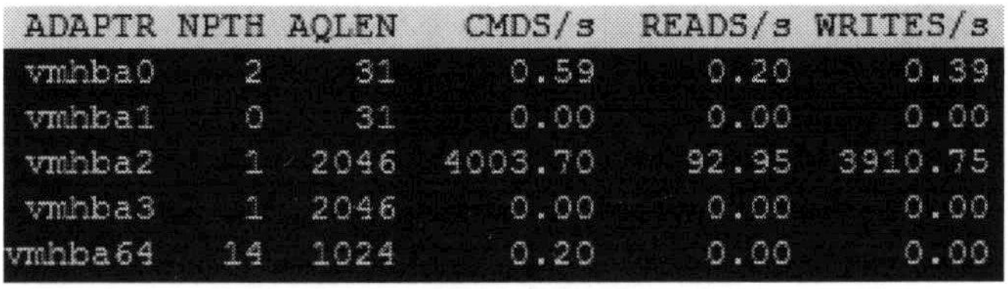

```
ADAPTR  NPTH  AQLEN    CMDS/s   READS/s  WRITES/s
vmhba0    2     31      0.59     0.20      0.39
vmhba1    0     31      0.00     0.00      0.00
vmhba2    1   2046    4003.70   92.95   3910.75
vmhba3    1   2046      0.00     0.00      0.00
vmhba64  14   1024      0.20     0.00      0.00
```

Figure 211: Esxtop Disk Adapter View

The *Adapter Queue* (AQLEN) is found in the disk adapter view. It lists the queue depth of the storage controllers. This way you can verify the queue depth of storage controllers that are already in production and match it to the HCL numbers. The adapter identifiers are somewhat abstract; you will only see the listed vmhbas. Using the `esxcli storage core adapter list` command shows what storage adapter and drivers are used. In this example, we would like to see what device is underneath the vmhba2.

```
[root@esxi03:~] esxcli storage core adapter list
HBA Name  Driver      Link State  UID             Description
--------- ----------  ----------  --------------  --------------------------------------------------
vmhba0    vmw_ahci    link-n/a    sata.vmhba0     (0000:00:11.4) Intel Corporation Wellsburg AHCI Controller
vmhba1    vmw_ahci    link-n/a    sata.vmhba1     (0000:00:1f.2) Intel Corporation Wellsburg AHCI Controller
vmhba2    intel-nvme  link-n/a    pscsi.vmhba2    (0000:02:00.0) Intel Corporation NVM-Express PCIe SSD
vmhba3    intel-nvme  link-n/a    pscsi.vmhba3    (0000:81:00.0) Intel Corporation NVM-Express PCIe SSD
```

Figure 212: Esxcli Adapter List

The storage adapter seems to be an Intel NVMe PCIe SSD. If we look at the storage device view in esxtop, we stumble upon the *Device Queue* (DQLEN) and the *World Queue* (WQLEN).

```
DEVICE                                          DQLEN  WQLEN  ACTV  QUED %
naa.600140512d8a962d0065d4682dbdf5d6            128      -     0     0
naa.60014051755a42cd7526d4f3fda8a7d4            128      -     0     0
naa.6001405241af0a3dd8d6d474cd85f8d4            128      -     0     0
naa.60014055fb71fc6db733d4e97db003d8            128      -     0     0
naa.6001405815a1e71deb1cd46e5d8d9ada            128      -     0     0
naa.600140587543643da3e1d414ed88b2d9            128      -     0     0
naa.6001405b8203ac0daff4d4e9ad8ba8d2            128      -     0     0
naa.65fdfe4035313633303044523434303001         2046     -     0     0
naa.65fdfe4036333730303034434331503201         2046     -     5     0
t10.ATA____INTEL_SSDSC2BA100G300000              31      -     0     0
t10.ATA____KINGSTON_SE100S3200G                  31      -     0     0
```

Figure 213: Esxtop Disk Device View

Checking what device or LUN is behind the storage device queue may require some research. The `esxcli storage core device list` command will present detailed information and capabilities for the storage device.

```
naa.65fdfe40363337303030434431503201
    Display Name: Local NVMe Disk (naa.65fdfe403633
    Has Settable Display Name: true
    Size: 1144691
    Device Type: Direct-Access
    Multipath Plugin: NMP
    Devfs Path: /vmfs/devices/disks/naa.65fdfe403633
    Vendor: NVMe
    Model: INTEL SSDPEDMW01
    Revision: 0171
    SCSI Level: 6
    Is Pseudo: false
    Status: on
    Is RDM Capable: false
    Is Local: true
    Is Removable: false
    Is SSD: true
    Is VVOL PE: false
    Is Offline: false
    Is Perennially Reserved: false
    Queue Full Sample Size: 0
    Queue Full Threshold: 0
    Thin Provisioning Status: unknown
    Attached Filters:
    VAAI Status: unknown
    Other UIDs: vml.010000000004356435136333730303043
    Is Shared Clusterwide: false
    Is Local SAS Device: false
    Is SAS: false
    Is USB: false
    Is Boot USB Device: false
    Is Boot Device: false
    Device Max Queue Depth: 2046
    No of outstanding IOs with competing worlds: 32
    Drive Type: unknown
    RAID Level: unknown
    Number of Physical Drives: unknown
    Protection Enabled: false
    PI Activated: false
    PI Type: 0
    PI Protection Mask: NO PROTECTION
    Supported Guard Types: NO GUARD SUPPORT
    DIX Enabled: false
    DIX Guard Type: NO GUARD SUPPORT
    Emulated DIX/DIF Enabled: false
```

Figure 214: Esxtop Disk Device View

The esxcfg-scsidevs command will provide similar information.

Now that we have looked into the various aspects of storage queues in the VMkernel layer, we can look into what we as an architect or administrator can do to optimize this part. For the majority of workloads, the default queue depth values will not require adjustment. But to create virtual datacenters that provides a high level of consolidation and consistent level of storage performance, fine-tuning of the storage queues may be necessary.

Integrated platforms such as vSAN are designed to operate and manage the storage devices autonomously. Complex operations such as dynamic queue management are automatically handled. vSAN is aware of device characteristics and active workload demand and adjusts parameters automatically if needed. Most customers tend to configure a static queue depth once and accept if these settings provide an adequate performance on average. Typically, this median approach does not handle peak loads well, while the system could handle this if other systems are adjusted dynamically. Highly scalable compute and platforms increase the need for cluster-level control mechanisms like (Storage) DRS and Storage I/O Control (SIOC). More information can be found on storagehub.vmware.com.

It is possible for each queue to have a different queue depth. This phenomenon can lead to a possible saturation in storage I/O processing. For example, you have an ESXi host with six local storage devices with a queue depth of 32 each. That will make for a theoretical queue depth total of 192. If these storage devices are connected to a storage controller using a queue depth of 128, it could result in 64 I/O's that will be held back by the VMkernel.

It will be beneficial for these kinds of scenarios to verify that your storage controller queue depth aligns with the sum of the queue depths of the connected storage devices. Therefore, an overall recommendation is to check the queue depth for your physical storage components in both the vendor documentation and the VMware HCL. Please determine the queue depth overcommit level, keep the number of queue depths for all storage constructs in the stack aligned as much as possible.

VMware vSAN has a distributed congestion control mechanism that would create back pressure if required. We do however prefer the least amount of congestion. And for that reason, VMware states a storage controller should adhere to a minimum queue depth of 256. A large as possible storage controller queue depth is desirable. The higher, the better!

William Lam's blog contains a community maintained list about queue depths for common storage devices and controllers. Link: **http://www.virtuallyghetto.com/2014/06/community-vsan-storage-controller-queue-depth-list.html**.

Storage Performance Metrics

Next to queue related metrics, the most typical metrics in esxtop to troubleshoot any storage performance issues are listed below. Please note that vSAN has its own esxtop view.

METRIC	DESCRIPTION
CMDS/s	Total number of commands per second and includes IOPS
DAVG/cmd	Average response time in milliseconds per command being sent to the storage device.
KAVG/cmd	Amount of time the command spends in the VMkernel.
GAVG/cmd	Response time as it is perceived by the guest OS.

Table 55: Esxtop Storage Metrics

The CMDS/s metric gives a view on the number of IOPS issued from a VM disk, storage controller or storage device depending on the esxtop view. Besides showing the IOPS, it also includes various SCSI commands such as SCSI reservations, locks, vendor string requests and unit attention commands that are sent to or received from the monitored VM or device.

CMDS/s	READS/s	WRITES/s	MBREAD/s	MBWRTN/s	DAVG/cmd	KAVG/cmd	GAVG/cmd	QAVG/cmd
0.00	0.00	0.00	0.00	0.00	0.00	0.00	0.00	0.00
37.40	0.78	31.97	0.02	3.44	17.22	0.01	17.23	0.00
0.00	0.00	0.00	0.00	0.00	0.00	0.00	0.00	0.00
0.00	0.00	0.00	0.00	0.00	0.00	0.00	0.00	0.00
0.00	0.00	0.00	0.00	0.00	0.00	0.00	0.00	0.00
0.00	0.00	0.00	0.00	0.00	0.00	0.00	0.00	0.00
0.00	0.00	0.00	0.00	0.00	0.00	0.00	0.00	0.00
44320.05	44252.81	67.24	1382.56	0.34	0.31	0.04	0.34	0.00
0.00	0.00	0.00	0.00	0.00	0.00	0.00	0.00	0.00
0.58	0.19	0.39	0.00	0.00	0.04	0.03	0.07	0.00

Figure 215: Esxtop Disk Device Metrics

The *Device Average* (DAVG) metric is the latency experienced at the storage device driver level. When a central storage solution is used, it includes the *Round-Trip Time* (RTT) between the HBA and the storage array. The DAVG metric is a good indicator for storage backend performance. Compare its value to the storage backend to see whether they match up. If they do, it can mean the storage array configuration and/or storage devices may not be up to the task and needs attention.

Looking at the *Kernel Average* (KAVG) latency counter, it tracks the latency of the VMkernel IOPS processing. It should be a small number when compared to the DAVG value, ideally close to zero. If this metric is high, it could indicate issues with a storage queue.

KAVG is closely followed by QAVG, which is the average queue latency. It is the sum of the time spent in queues in the storage stack and the service time spend by each resource in processing the request. Typically, this value is zero or is near to zero. Higher values can indicate storage queue issues.

The following additional metrics in the esxtop disk device view can help you even further troubleshooting storage performance.

ACTV	QUED	%USD	LOAD	CMDS/s
0	0	0	0.00	0.00
0	0	0	0.00	0.39
0	0	0	0.00	0.00
0	0	0	0.00	0.00
0	0	0	0.00	0.00
0	0	0	0.00	0.00
0	0	0	0.00	0.00
0	0	0	0.00	0.00
16	0	0	0.01	45616.53
0	0	0	0.00	0.00
0	0	0	0.00	0.58

Figure 216: Additional Esxtop Disk Device Metrics

ACTV represents the number of I/O's in the ESXi VMkernel layer that is currently active. This metric is applicable to worlds and LUNs.

QUED is the number of I/O's that are currently queued in the VMkernel. Queued I/O's are waiting for an open slot in the storage queue to be processed. A high value of QUED indicates saturated storage queues and signals a storage bottleneck. Investigation of various storage queues and increasing the correct queue depth should resolve this. If this situation occurs and is solved, it will result in improved storage performance in terms of higher IOPS (CMDS/s).

The **%USD** metric is the percentage of queue depth used by the VMkernel for active I/O's. Like QUED, it is a clear way to gain insights on queue depth usage for WQLEN. It is calculated using the following formula: %USD = ACTV / QLEN * 100%. It measures the number of available I/O queue slots that are in use.

The **LOAD** metric indicates the ratio of the sum of VMkernel active I/O's and queued I/O's to the queue depth of the world of LUN. This sum shows the total number OIO issued by the VM. If the LOAD counts value larger than one, be sure to check the QUED metric.

All in all, time spent on the operational effort to perform in-depth storage performance management can quickly get out of hand. Because we are adopting highly scalable compute and storage platforms, we find ourselves in need for solid monitoring tooling and cluster-level control mechanisms like (Storage) DRS and SIOC. These are tools and features that will help you get a better grip on your virtual datacenter and its storage backend. However, it is good to know how to read the esxtop storage metrics to swiftly cut down any storage performance related issue on a host-level.

Pluggable Storage Architecture

ESX 3.5 introduced *Pluggable Storage Architecture* (PSA). PSA allows third party vendors to provide their own *Native MultiPathing* (NMP) software. Within the PSA, three *Path Selection Plugins* (PSPs) are active that are responsible for choosing a physical path for I/O requests. NMP supports three types of PSPs; Most Recently Used (MRU), Fixed and Round Robin.

```
[root@esxi00:~] esxcli storage nmp psp list
Name               Description
-----------------  ------------------------------------------
VMW_PSP_MRU        Most Recently Used Path Selection
VMW_PSP_RR         Round Robin Path Selection
VMW_PSP_FIXED      Fixed Path Selection
```

Figure 217: Esxcli NMP PSP List

The *Storage Array Type Plugins* (SATP) run in conjunction with NMP and manages array specific operations. SATPs are aware of storage array specifics, such as whether it is an active/active array or active/passive array. For example, when the array uses *Asymmetric LUN Unit Access* (ALUA), it determines which paths lead to the ports of the managing controllers.

The Round Robin PSP distributes I/O for a datastore down all active paths to the managing controller and uses a single path for a number of I/O operations. Although it distributes workload across all (optimized) paths, it does not guarantee that throughput will be constant. There is no optimization on the I/O profile of the host. Its load balance algorithm is based purely on equal numbers of I/O down a specific path, without regards to the I/O block size. It will not be balanced on application workload characteristics or the current bandwidth utilization of the particular path. Similar to *Storage I/O Control* (SIOC) and *Network I/O Control* (NIOC), NMP is not designed to treat data paths as clustered resources and has no ability to distribute workloads across all available uplinks in the cluster.

Using the correct settings is crucial for your central storage array. An overall recommendation with the PSA is to align with the vendor recommendations. Each vendor or storage array model has its own suggested and supported PSP configuration.

For more detailed information about the PSA and related components we would like to refer to the '*Storage Design and Implementation*' book series by Mostafa Khalil.

VMFS

ESXi stores virtual disks in datastores. Datastores are logical containers abstracted from the physical storage that provide a monolithic model to store VMs files on. Datastores that reside on block-based storage often use the *Virtual Machine File System* (VMFS). Upcoming options for storing VM data are *Virtual Volumes* (VVol) or vSAN, which we described, extensively in earlier chapters. VMFS has been around since the introduction of ESX Server version 1. It was and still is widely adopted in virtual datacenters running vSphere. There are interesting considerations and features we would like to highlight.

First of all, we would like to emphasize the latest version of the file system, VMFS-6, introduced in ESXi 6.5. It includes some nifty new features like the support for 4K native drives in 512e mode. With the current capacity of disk media growing, the adoption of 4 KB sector, instead of the 512-byte sectors. This means metadata is aligned at the disk sector size. Even if the sector size is smaller than 4 KB, it is still aligned at 4 KB. The main advantage is that it provides better media error handling for large capacity disks.

Automatic Space Reclamation, also introduced with VMFS-6, is a long-anticipated feature that allows thin provisioned LUNs to be much more space efficient because it now has the ability to reclaim blocks that contain deleted data. It automatically uses the UNMAP primitive to do so.

UNMAP

ESXi 5.5 already introduced the new `esxcli storage vmfs unmap` command allowing deleted blocks to be reclaimed on thin provisioned LUNs that support the VAAI UNMAP primitive. This used to be a manual task that is now automated and included in the vCenter UI.

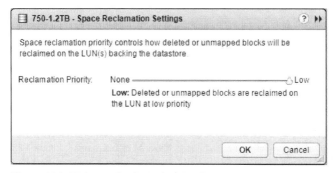

Figure 218: UI Space Reclamation Settings

Notice that the UNMAP reclamation policy can be set to either 'none' or 'low'. The policy can be set to 'high' using the esxcli commandlets, but this setting doesn't have any effect in the ESXi 6.5 release. The low setting indicates how long the blocks needs to be marked reclaimable before actually be processed which is around 12 hours. If you want immediate effect, you can still issue the esxcli command manually: `esxcli storage vmfs unmap -l <datastore>`.

More information about this command can be found in the *VMware KB 2057513*. To list and configure the UNMAP reclamation policy, the following esxcli command can be used: `esxcli storage vmfs reclaim config get/set -l <datastore>`.

```
Reclaim Granularity: 1048576 Bytes
Reclaim Priority: low
```

Figure 219: Esxcli UNMAP Reclamation Policy

VMFS uses the SCSI UNMAP command to indicate to the array that the storage blocks contain deleted data, so that the array can un-allocate these blocks. A cool detailed overview that shows the number of reclaimed blocks can be found in the VSI shell.

Command `cat /vmkModules/vmfs3/auto_unmap/volumes/ESXi03-SWAP/properties` provides details about the number of UNMAP I/Os and blocks per volume.

```
Volume specific unmap information {
    Volume Name                 :ESXi03-SWAP
    FS Major Version            :24
    Metadata Alignment          :4096
    Allocation Unit/Blocksize   :1048576
    Unmap granularity in File   :1048576
    Volume: Unmap IOs           :2
    Volume: Unmapped blocks     :110
    Volume: Num wait cycles     :0
    Volume: Num from scanning   :89
    Volume: Num from heap pool  :1
    Volume: Total num cycles    :866
}
```

Figure 220: Vsish UNMAP Reclamation Details

VMFS Locking

Shared block storage environments require specific locking mechanisms because multiple ESXi hosts access the same VMFS datastore. Data corruption is avoided because locking ensures that multiple hosts are not allowed to concurrently write meta-data. The locking mechanism of choice depends on the configuration of the storage backend. VMFS datastores can use the *Atomic Test and Set* (ATS) locking mechanism or use it in combination with SCSI reservations (ATS+SCSI).

Since VMFS-5, the ATS-only method is preferred given the storage backend supports the VAAI ATS primitive. This allows for hardware accelerated locking. If the storage backend does not support VAAI, or the datastore is upgraded from VMFS-3, the locking falls back to SCSI-2 reservations for locking. That could lead to storage performance degradation because of immense number of SCSI-2 reservations. To verify what type of locking is used for your VMFS datastore, you can issue the command `esxcli storage vmfs lockmode list`. It displays all the information about the datastores and support for ATS.

Type	Locking Mode	ATS Compatible	ATS Upgrade Modes	ATS Incompatibility Reason
VMFS-5	ATS	true	No upgrade needed	
VMFS-5	ATS	true	No upgrade needed	
VMFS-5	ATS	true	No upgrade needed	
VMFS-5	ATS	true	No upgrade needed	
VMFS-5	ATS	true	No upgrade needed	
VMFS-5	ATS	true	No upgrade needed	
VMFS-5	ATS	true	No upgrade needed	
VMFS-5	ATS+SCSI	false	None	Device does not support ATS
VMFS-6	ATS+SCSI	false	None	Device does not support ATS
VMFS-6	ATS+SCSI	false	None	Device does not support ATS
Non-VMFS	ATS+SCSI	false	None	Device does not support ATS

Figure 221: Esxcli VMFS Lockmode List

Interestingly to see in this screenshot, not all available VMFS-6 datastores support ATS and are therefore reverted to ATS+SCSI locking, possible impacting performance. Luckily, the majority of shared storage solutions nowadays support the full set of VAAI primitives. But from a migration point of view, you will see that VMFS datastores are often upgraded instead of newly created and migrated to.

> **It is good practice to not upgrade VMFS datastores, but create new ones and migrate your VMs using Storage vMotion. This will increase operational effort during migration, but it allows for the best performance and support of new features!**

Sizing and Scalability

Using VMFS datastores, right-sizing the LUN and datastore remains a difficult task. VMFS datastore sizing is all about capacity and performance versus contention trade-offs. An important factor is the number of ESXi hosts that are connected to the VMFS datastore. We reviewed the locking mechanisms and what you can do to make locking as efficient as possible while keeping impact on performance to a minimum. But from a storage capacity perspective, what is the right choice? Back in the days, 500 GB was often referred to as being the sweet spot for datastore sizing. But with today's requirements for giant workload datasets, as large as possible datastore looks to be the obvious choice.

When your environment only allows for a central storage array solution, you are presented with specific designing challenges. When you are deciding on LUN size and the number of hosts connecting to the VMFS datastore, you are trying to harmonize and balance across variables. Performance, resource utilization and configuration flexibility are important factors in making a decision.

Obviously, a one VMDK to one VMFS datastore relation will get you the best performance and zero interference from other VMs. Evidently, this is not the preferred option as it leads to an immense sprawl of LUNs and the configuration and operational overhead that comes with it. And the ESXi supported maximum configurations will likely come into play. The other extreme opposite is that one enormous VMFS will host all VMDK's. This will present you with inevitable locking issues, possibly resulting in performance degradation.

For a large part, it all comes down to locking. We already discussed hardware assisted locking which helps, but we would like to have insight if locking is causing any harm. Esxtop to the rescue once more! There are several metrics that provide understanding in the area of VMFS locking.

VMFS-6 introduces lock contention improvements and improved re-signaturing and scanning. Some of the lock mechanisms on VMFS were largely responsible for some of the biggest delays in parallel device scanning and file system probing on ESXi. Since ESXi 6.5 has higher limits on number of devices and paths, a big factor in enabling this support was to redesign device discovery and file system probing to be highly parallel. Source: https://storagehub.vmware.com/#!/vsphere-core-storage/vsphere-6-5-storage/vmfs-6/1

The ATS stats can be checked in esxtop if the storage array supports VAAI. In the disk adapter view, you can add the VAAI metrics that will include the ATS and ATSF metrics. The ATS metric is the number of ATS commands that are successfully completed. The ATS operation checks the on-disk sector and compares it to a given buffer. If identical, it will write new data into the on-disk sector.

The ATSF metrics identifies the number of ATS VAAI commands that are failed. This can be a result of a mismatch between in data trying to be written and the data on disk. This situation is mostly seen in the event of another ESXi host that is interested in the same lock. An additional reason could be that another ESXi host is applying a SCSI reservation to the underlying LUN. Ideally, the ATSF metric should be close to zero. The metrics are found in esxtop using the disk device view. The additional option 'VAAI stats' must be selected using the 'field' command using the 'f' key.

DEVICE	ATS	ATSF
naa.600140512d8a962d0065d4692dbdf5d6	676	0
naa.60014051755a42cd7526d4f3fda8a7d4	685	0
naa.6001405241af0a3dd8d6d474cd85f8d4	1234	0
naa.60014055fb71fc6db733d4e97db003d8	678	0
naa.6001405815a1e71deb1cd46e5d8d9ada	595	0
naa.600140587543643da3e1d414ed88b2d9	598	0
naa.6001405b8203ac0daff4d4e9ad8ba8d2	592	0
naa.65fdfe40343231353030375334303001	0	0

Figure 222: Esxtop ATS Metrics

If VAAI is not supported and SCSI reservations are being used, you can investigate the RESV/s and the CONS/s metrics in the esxtop disk adapter view using the 'resvstats' field. RESV/s provides information about the number of SCSI reservations per second while CONS/s shows the number of SCSI reservation conflicts per second.

ADAPTR	NPTH	RESV/s	CONS/s
vmhba0	1	0.00	0.00
vmhba1	0	0.00	0.00
vmhba2	1	0.00	0.00
vmhba3	1	0.00	0.00
vmhba64	14	0.00	0.00

Figure 223: Esxtop SCSI Reservation Metrics

A high number of ATSF or CON/s, depending on the locking mechanism, could indicate that too many ESXi hosts access a VMFS datastore. These metrics can provide insight on how many ESXi hosts should access the datastore. When we bring this information back to the initial question, how large should my VMFS datastore be? With too many locking errors, you should probably cut down on the number of ESXi hosts connecting to it. It still is a difficult exercise to size this correctly upfront.

So, should you start small and end big, capacity-wise? You can extend VMFS datastores. Extending a VMFS datastore allows you to pool storage and provides flexibility in creating a datastore large enough to support your workloads. But larger, extended VMFS datastores beholds additional risks.

In terms of availability and performance, it could be argued that spanning a VMFS datastore over multiple LUNs will impact the overall behaviour. Think about the performance consistency when using multiple storage back-ends to extend your VMFS datastore. Using different storage arrays to extend the datastore could lead to inconsistent behaviour. In terms of availability, spanning the datastore over multiple LUNs could introduce a higher risk of an underlying LUN not being available. When using VMFS extends, you could issue this esxcli command to check how many extends are in place per datastore: `esxcli storage vmfs extent list`. The following example shows no extents are used at this time.

```
[root@esxi02:~] esxcli storage vmfs extent list
Volume Name      VMFS UUID                                  Extent Number
------------     --------------------------------------     -------------
Glacier01        571b644f-e235b1ac-0646-001517bc8aca                    0
Glacier02        5725f85e-fa9a78b0-366b-001517bc8aca                    0
Glacier03        5746a9b1-ce2e76cf-a0e8-002590e371f8                    0
Glacier04        5746ab3c-ec567909-a42f-002590e371f8                    0
AFA01            57700953-26a9accf-07e7-002590e371f8                    0
AFA02            5770ed6a-d0ff820c-c7da-002590e371f8                    0
AFA03            5770f697-393b608c-3cd6-002590e371f8                    0
```

Figure 224: Esxcli Extend Number

If you start out small and are planning to extend VMFS datastores in the future, be sure to think about all the above. In addition we recommend you to review features like storage DRS. This can also be of great help to ensure an efficient distribution of for VMDK's from both a capacity and performance perspective.

Virtual Volumes

There are innovations that can help you with the burden of complex storage configurations and overall storage related operational overhead. We quickly want to highlight *Virtual Volumes* (VVol) as it helps architects and administrators to cope with the challenges introduced by a traditional storage approach. All obstacles when using conventional VMFS datastores are no longer applicable when adopting VVols.

The *VMware APIs for Storage Awareness* (VASA) provider, also referred to as the *Vendor Provider* (VP), is the software part that acts like a middleware layer between the storage array, vCenter and ESXi. The latter two connect to the storage array using the VASA provider to obtain information about its storage capabilities, status and topology. These capabilities are translated and connected to VMDKs using storage profiles.

When using a central storage array, be sure to check its ability to support VASA 3.0 to be able to make full use of the VVol benefits. VVols 2.0 was introduced with ESXi 6.5 expanding the already rich feature set. Find out more about VVol at storagehub.vmware.com.

17

VIRTUAL MACHINE STORAGE

Regardless of the underlying storage layer, the VM needs one or multiple virtual disks to present storage components to the guest OS. It doesn't matter whether local storage is used in combination with vSAN or traditional SAN and NAS solutions running various mediums and protocols. The abstraction layer of the storage foundation will be translated to the VM through different types of virtual storage controllers and disk types. In this chapter, we will explore various interesting aspects of storage components from a VM perspective.

Virtual Storage Adapters

Virtual storage controllers handle communication between the VM and its virtual disks, that are stored on the physical storage layer.
The storage adapters are abstracted from the hardware layer but are similar in function when compared with their hardware equivalents. There are several options to choose from when creating VMs with regards to their virtual devices. Let's take a look at some of the compatibility and limitations of the various storage controllers.

TYPE	DESCRIPTION
BusLogic Parallel	Virtual BusLogic Parallel SCSI adapter
IDE	Virtual IDE adapter for ATA disks
LSI Logic Parallel	Virtual LSI Logic Parallel SCSI adapter
LSI Logic SAS	Virtual LSI SAS adapter
VMware Paravirtual	VMware Paravirtual SCSI (PVSCSI) adapter
AHCI SATA	Virtual SATA adapter
vNVMe	Virtual NVM Express adapter

Table 56: Virtual Storage Controllers

While creating a VM, a default storage controller is chosen based on the used guest OS. For instance, when you create a Windows Server 2016 VM, the LSI Logic SAS virtual storage controller will be selected as it is optimized for that guest OS. The virtual storage adapters all have their own dependencies. For example, the vNVMe controller is only available as of VM hardware version 13. Another example is the BusLogic Parallel controller that does not support VMs with disks larger than 2TB.

A total of four SCSI controllers and four SATA controllers can be assigned to each VM. Each SCSI controller can contain up to 15 disks, making for a total of 60 virtual disks. The SATA controllers can contain up to 30 devices per adapter, although are primarily used to connect CD-ROM drives. All in all, these options allow for a lot of virtual disks per VM. But what is really necessary from a performance point-of-view when choosing your virtual disk layout? From a performance perspective, only SCSI of NVMe controllers are recommended. In the early days of ESXi we were confronted with an I/O limit of 256 per virtual storage adapter. Let's take a closer look at the paravirtual SCSI controller option and the newly introduced vNVMe controller.

PVSCSI

VMware commonly emulated storage adapters in ESXi. The obvious advantage being that the drivers are shipped in almost every modern guest OS. The drawback is that all performance limitations are also inherited. One example is the LSI logic controller where, to correctly emulate it, ESXi needs to tap into the virtual device emulation each time the guest OS submits an I/O.

The additional CPU cycles required to emulate storage controllers for storage I/O and CPU intensive workloads like many database environments can quickly become a challenge. It would be very beneficial if CPU utilization is kept as low as possible to use for workloads running in the VMs. The *VMware Paravirtual SCSI* (PVSCSI) was introduced by ESX(i) 4.0 (VM hardware version 7) to have no form of hardware dependency whatsoever. It is a lightweight virtual adapter with no hardware emulation. The primary objective for it is to send SCSI commands down to the VMkernel I/O stack as swiftly as possible. The PVSCSI adapter allows for lower CPU utilization without making concessions on storage performance. In fact, some official VMware test results show a slight storage performance improvement, especially with smaller block size I/Os.

The default virtual SCSI controllers in ESXi are compatible with all common guest OS systems without the requirement for additional drivers. If we look at the landscape of common IT applications, these vSCSI controllers will do a good job. However, if you have applications running a more than average CPU storage I/O load you could benefit from implementing PVSCSI controllers in your VMs. Think about *Online Transaction Processing* (OLTP) or other database and real-time workloads. Aside from a potential upswing in performance, the lower CPU utilization can make it worth your while to opt for the PVSCSI controller. Even though < 5-10% CPU utilization per VM is saved, this can still add up to a lot of CPU time saved when you take all the VMs in your virtual datacenter into account. CPU time that is best used for other purposes!

The usage of PVSCSI can have an impact on how you create VM and the need for additional drivers to present the disks to the guest OS. That operational 'overhead' is easily mitigated when using decent VM templates. When you manually create a new VM, it is required to attach a 'floppy drive' ISO file that contains the drivers if you wish to boot from the virtual disks bound to PVSCSI controller.

If you use a default vSCSI controller that used the guest OS built-in drivers to boot from and only use the PVSCSI controller(s) for data disks, the driver is included in the VM tools.

That brings us to an interesting point. How to decide how many virtual storage controllers and virtual disks to use for your VM? If you take a look at a typical database environment, it will contain an OS disk and separate disks for data files and log files.

By default, the PVSCI controller has a controller queue depth of 64. If you look at this from a theoretical side, it means only 32 I/O's can be processed at once per disk if you connect two VMDKs to the controller. That is because all VMDK's on a single vSCSI controller share the queue depth of that controller. It looks like it makes more sense to create two PVSCSI (max four) controllers, each connected to one VMDK. That way the full queue depth can be consumed by one VMDK. Another option can be to increase the queue depth of the PVSCSI controller. The max supported queue depth value for a PVSCSI adapter is 1024, but results may vary as described in *VMware KB article 2053145*. This article also elaborates on how to configure the queue depth of the PVSCSI adapter in Windows and Linux guest OS. An important take-away is that its queue depth is tunable, which is another plus for the PVSCSI adapter as the LSI Logic adapters allow for a static queue depth of 128.

In the end, it all comes down to knowing what your workload requires and what the I/O stress is per VM or even VMDK. Be sure to consider how your vSCSI controller and VMDK layout is setup and how it aligns with the physical storage components and the constraints on queue depths.

Virtual NVMe

We do have other options next to PVSCSI to reduce CPU overhead as ESXi 6.5 introduced the *virtual NVMe* (vNVMe) storage controller. vNVMe is a virtual storage controller that helps performance scalability for VMs, following the philosophy behind the NVMe interface for storage devices.

The primary benefits of using the vNVMe controller are the increased storage performance and lowered storage latency. Both accomplished by allowing multiple queues to process storage I/O in parallel. The performance of the vNVMe controller scales equally to the vCPUs configured for the VM making a perfect fit for transactional/database platforms of latency sensitive workloads. vNVMe allows for up to 64 queues and a queue depth of 64K per queue!

The SCSI overhead in the VMkernel storage stack is reduced and the excess of the in-guest SCSI execution overhead is avoided. This results in the possibility to save up a lot of guest OS CPU overhead compared to any of the other virtual SCSI controllers.

vNVMe is available as of VM hardware version 13 and is configurable via the UI. Up to 4 vNVMe virtual storage adapter, each capable of 15 vNVMe targets.

Figure 225: Virtual NVMe VM Hardware

> Although the vNVMe storage adapter is relatively new, we will see a lot of further improvements and new functionality in future releases of ESXi. It could make sense to use NVMe adapters now when deploying VMs, that are running latency sensitive workloads, and benefit from future enhancements automatically once you upgrade to a new ESXi release.

Virtual Disk Types

When adding virtual disks to your VM, you are presented with disk format options. When a *Virtual Machine Disk* (VMDK) is created, it can be allocated as a thin or thick disk. The following virtual disk types are supported in ESXi 6.5:

TYPE	DESCRIPTION	ZEROING
Zero Thick	Pre-allocated but not zeroed until write occurs in the regions.	Run-time
Eager Zero Thick	Pre-allocated and completely zeroed at creation.	Create-time
Thin	Not pre-allocated and not zeroed out until run-time.	Run-time
RDM	Virtual compatibility mode raw disk mapping.	-
RDMP	Physical compatibility mode (pass-through) raw disk mapping.	-

Table 57: Supported Virtual Disk Types

Zero Thick

Zero thick disk format, also referred to as Thick Provisioned Lazy Zeroed disks, is the default choice in ESXi when creating a VMDK. The disk space required for the virtual disk is allocated during creation. This means that if you create a virtual disk of 100 GB, that same amount is allocated on the storage backend. Any data remaining on the physical device is not erased during creation, but is zeroed out on demand on first write from the VM. The VM does not read stale data from disk.

Eager Zero Thick

The disk space required for the virtual disk is allocated at creation time. Contrary to the zeroed thick format, the data remaining on the physical device is zeroed out during creation. It can take longer to create disks in this format than to create other types of disks as all blocks needs to be zeroed before using the virtual disk.

Thin

Thin-provisioned virtual disk will only allocate disk space that is actually used. Unlike with the thick format, space required for the virtual disk is not allocated during creation, but is supplied, zeroed out, on demand. When using new (non-upgraded) VMFS6 datastores, space reclamation is possible in an automated way. This is a new feature since ESXi 6.5.

Thin or Thick?

Over the years, VMware engineers worked hard to reduce the performance difference between thin disks and thick disks. Many white papers have been written by performance engineers to explain the improvements made on thin-provisioned disks. Therefore, the question whether to use thin-provisioned disks or eager zero thick is not about the difference in performance, but about the difference in management.

When using thin-provisioned VMDKs you need to have a clear defined process. What to do when your datastore which stores the thin provisioned disks is running out of storage capacity? You need to define a consolidation ratio; It is important to understand what operational process might be dangerous to your environment (think 'patch Tuesday') and what space utilization threshold you need to define, before migrating thin-provisioned disks to other datastores.

Storage DRS can help you with many of the mentioned challenges. If Storage DRS is not used, thin-provisioned disks can require a seamless collaboration between virtualization teams (provisioning and architecture) and storage administrators. When this is not possible due to organizational cultural differences, thin provisioning is rather a risk than bliss.

Eager zero thick on the other hand might provide in some cases a marginal performance increase; the costs involved could outweigh the perceived benefits. First of all, eager zero thick disks need to be zeroed out during creation. When your array doesn't support the VAAI initiatives, this can take a hit on performance and the time to provision is extended.

With large sized disks being a common sight in the datacenters these days, this impacts provisioning time immensely.

Most virtualized environments use VMs, often configured with oversized guest OS disks and data disks, resulting in wasted space full of zeros. Thin-provisioned disks only occupy the space used for storing data, not zeros.

Storage vMotion goes out of its way to migrate every little bit of a virtual disk, this means it needs to copy over every zeroed-out block. Combined with the oversized disks, you are creating unnecessary overhead on your hosts and storage subsystem copying and verifying the integrity of zeroed out blocks. Migrating thin disks only requires migrating the 'user-data', resulting in faster migration times, lesser overhead on hosts and storage subsystem.

The introduction of VAAI in storage architectures several years ago helped a great deal to dispel thin-provisioning as forming a big challenge from a performance perspective. All flash storage architectures made the performance trade-off between thin and thick disks disappear completely.

> **VMware *vSphere Storage APIs – Array Integration* (VAAI), also referred to as hardware acceleration or hardware offload APIs, are a set of APIs to enable communication between VMware vSphere ESXi hosts and storage devices. The APIs define a set of 'storage primitives' that enable the ESXi host to offload certain storage operations to the array, which reduces resource overhead on the ESXi hosts and can significantly improve performance for storage-intensive operations such as storage cloning, zeroing, and so on. The goal of VAAI is to help storage vendors provide hardware assistance to speed up VMware I/O operations that are more efficiently accomplished in the storage hardware.**
> Source: vmware-vsphere-storage-api-array-integration-white-paper.pdf

In essence, thin-provisioned disks versus eager zero thick is all about resource and/or timesaving versus risk avoidance. Choose wisely!

P4

NETWORK RESOURCES

PROLOGUE

Virtual networking has gone from being a buzzword to being a staple of datacenter architecture over the last 15 years. While much has changed and many new features and concepts have been added, the basic premise has remained: leverage the hypervisor as a layer of indirection to implement networking features and resource allocation in a secure, flexible and manageable way.

We now have virtual switches, routers, firewalls, load balancers, and any number of other elements such that we can build any arbitrary topology possible in traditional networking, as well as many new ones. These virtual topology elements all have one thing in common: they tend to begin as a centralized appliance running in a VM emulating the traditional physical counterpart but over time are subsumed by distributed implementations living in the hypervisor.

Only by distributing these functionalities across the hypervisor hosts can we achieve the scalability and elasticity demanded by today's virtualized datacenters. Overlays and controllers like NSX allow the administrator to easily provision and consume logical networking topologies without much thought as to the physical infrastructure.

However, the performance and reliability of those logical topologies when it comes to actually moving packets is, of course, entirely a function of the performance and reliability of the underlying host networking resources.

Andrew Lambeth

Andrew Lambeth joined VMware in 2001 and worked primarily on the ESX networking stack, from pNIC driver to vSwitch to paravirtual guest drivers and most things between at one time or another. He led the vDS project to its release in vSphere 4 before leaving to join Nicira and work on the NVP controller project. Since returning to VMware with the Nicira acquisition he has been working on helping to define the long term architecture for the NSBU platform.

18

HOST NETWORK ARCHITECTURE

Today's innovation on network overlays and the demand for network I/O by network intensive workloads lead to an increased focus on the network infrastructure. Being an important fundament of today's virtual datacenter, the network layer must provide a solid foundation for the increased demand for network performance and stability.

From a network perspective, we are faced with the challenge of creating a stable, high performing and low latency networking stack.

Think about innovations like *Hyper Converged Infrastructures* (HCI) and *Software Defined Storage* (SDS), such as VMware vSAN. *Software Defined Networking* (SDN) like VMware NSX and *Network Functions Virtualization* (NFV) workloads. These are all examples of solutions or workloads that are highly dependent on the network layer within your virtual datacenter.

Part of the network infrastructure within your virtual datacenter is the host physical networking and the virtual networking components running within the ESXi host. In this part, we will discuss specific ESXi host network focus points that can help you create the infrastructure that is able to deliver increased availability, stability and performance.

Physical NIC

The physical part of the virtual network components in a ESXi host consist mainly of the *Network Interface Card* (NIC). This is the component that provides layer-1 connectivity to your physical network switches.

When looking at options for your host hardware configuration, the bandwidth of the interfaces (1/10/25/40/50 or even 100GbE), the number of interfaces, the type of connectors and the form factor are important considerations for choosing certain *physical Network Interface Cards* (pNIC).

In specific situations, the pNIC is already chosen by the physical host vendor of choice. Think about HCI solutions where you could be bound to predefined hardware appliances. These appliances are built out of specific building blocks including a fixed pNIC layout.

> **If your HCI solution uses hardware appliances with a fixed pNIC layout, you must be aware of the capabilities of the pNIC features. For example, if they match the performance enhancement requirements for virtual overlay networks.**

Next to the number of interfaces and the bandwidth of a pNIC, there is a collection of interesting features in modern pNICs that can severely decrease ESXi host CPU utilization or decrease network I/O latency. It is important to understand the impact of these features and when to apply them in your virtual datacenter. Common considerations when choosing your ESXi host pNIC layout are:

- What is the required bandwidth per host? Typical bandwidth greedy network loads are:
  - IP storage
  - NFV workloads
  - vSphere (Storage) vMotion
  - vSphere *Fault Tolerance* (FT)
- How many interfaces do I need for resilient connections to the physical datacenter switches?

- Are there any networks segments required to be physically separated from each other?
- Do I need multiple pNIC vendors for driver redundancy to avoid a *Single Point of Failure* (SPOF)?
- Is the correct form factor slot available in my ESXi host to support the pNICs theoretical throughput?

All are viable questions to correctly design an ESXi host pNIC layout. However, looking deeper into pNIC supported feature sets with network virtualization innovations in mind, you might want to extend the pNIC considerations with the likes of:

- What network virtualization offloading techniques are supported?
- Are multiple *Receive Data* (Rx) threads features such as *Device queues* (VMDq) or *Receive Side Scaling* (RSS) supported?
- Does the pNIC support *Single Root I/O Virtualization* (SR-IOV)?

Form Factor

When considering the type of pNIC you want to utilize, it is important to know what form factor your ESXi host hardware supports and has available. We define the following modern NIC form factors:

- PCIe extension card (half or full bracket height)
- *LAN on motherboard* (LoM)
- *PCI Mezzanine Card* (PMC)

When we talk about rack servers, we will likely need PCIe extension cards for additional NIC interfaces. Blade chassis' and its host blades typically support mezzanine cards. Mezzanine cards use the PCIe bus, but in a smaller package than normal PCIe extension cards making it a perfect fit for blade systems. Both compute architectures, blade- and rack servers, usually contain LoM interfaces by default.

PCI Express

All the modern form factors connect to the motherboard of your ESXi host using the *PCI Express* (PCIe) bus. The PCIe bus is a high-speed serial replacement of the older PCI/PCI-X bus architecture. The key difference between the PCIe and the older PCI architecture is the bus topology. The PCI architecture uses a shared parallel bus architecture, in which the PCI host and all devices share a common set of address, data and control lines. The PCIe architecture is based on a point-to-point topology, with separate serial links connecting every device to host.

A connection between any two PCIe devices is known as a link, and is built up from a collection of one or more lanes. All devices must minimally support single-lane (x1) link. PCIe devices may optionally support wider links fabricated of 2, 4, 8, 12 or 16 lanes. A PCIe card physically fits and operates correctly in any slot that has the same or more lanes that the actual card has. In example; an x1-sized card will work in any sized slot. In all cases, PCIe negotiates the highest mutually supported number of lanes. So, if you place a x4 card in a x16 slot, it would logically still work as x4 card.

The PCIe bus architecture has evolved over the years to support the increasing data rates of modern I/O devices.

> **With increased network bandwidth comes an increased need for PCIe bus speed. Ensure that you have the minimum number of PCIe x8 or x16 slots if you required high consolidation ratios or driver workloads with above average bandwidth requirements.**

The following table will give you an idea on what the theoretical maximum bus throughputs are for modern PCIe slots.

PCIe VERSION	BASE TRANSFER RATE	ENCODED DATA RATE			
		PCIe x1	PCIe x4	PCIe x8	PCIe x16
1.x	2.5 GT/s	4 Gb/s	8 Gb/s	16 Gb/s	32 Gb/s
2.x	5 GT/s	8 Gb/s	16 Gb/s	32 Gb/s	64 Gb/s
3.0	8 GT/s	7.9 Gb/s	31.5 Gb/s	63 Gb/s	126.4 Gb/s
4.0	16 GT/s	15.6 Gb/s	63 Gb/s	126 Gb/s	252 Gb/s
5.0 (future)	25 or 32 GT/s	24.6 or 31.2 Gb/s	98.4 or 126.4 Gb/s	196.8 or 252 Gb/s	393.6 or 504 Gb/s

Table 58: Maximum PCIe Bus Throughputs

This table deserves some explanation. What is GT/s and how does that relate to the Gb/s, or Gigabits per second, data rate?

The metric GT/s stands for gigatransfers per second. The relation with Gb/s can be explained by the encoding of the data that is traversing the PCIe bus.

Because PCIe is a serial bus with the clock embedded in the data, it needs to ensure that the adequate level of transitions (0 to 1 and 1 to 0) occur for the receiver to decode the clock. To increase the level of transitions, PCIe version 1.x and 2.x use the so-called 8b/10b line code, where every 8-bits are encoded into a 10-bit symbol that is then decoded at the receiver. So, the bus needs to transfer 10-bits to send 8-bits of encoded data. That results in an overhead of 20%.

With the introduction of PCIe 3.0 and future versions, the encoding scheme is upgraded from 8b/10b to 128b/130b encoding, meaning that the bus needs to send 130-bits to send 128-bits of encoded data. That reduces the data rate overhead to approximately 1.538%.

Let's look at a practical example of how to relate GT/s to Gb/s;
- PCIe 2.0 x4 card capable of 20 GT/s
  - 20 GT/s * (8b/10b) = 16 Gb/s

- PCIe 3.0 x4 card capable 32 GT/s
  - 32 GT/s * (128b/130b) = 31.5 Gb/s

To bring all this together, the point is that the data rate supported on the used PCIe bus should meet the pNIC interface(s) bandwidth.

For instance, the Cisco UCS VIC 1387 is a converged network adapter capable of processing 80 Gb/s. However, it uses the PCIe 3.0 x8 LOM form factor that is only capable of 63 Gb/s. This is one example where you would never be able to fully utilize the bandwidth of the pNIC because you are constrained by the PCIe bus bandwidth.

Converged Network Adapters

Next to 'normal' pNIC PCIe cards for Ethernet, there is something called a *Converged Network Adapter* (CNA). Using CNA allows you to combine the functionality of a *Host Bus Adapter* (HBA) and a NIC making it possible to connect to a *Fibre Channel* (FC) SAN network as well as an Ethernet network using the same physical adapter.

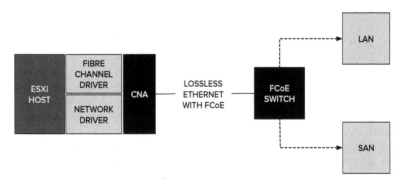

Figure 226: Converged Network Adapter

Depending on the hardware vendor and model, a CNA may extend the functionality of a traditional CNA by allowing you to virtualize storage and Ethernet network adapters. For example, the Cisco UCS solutions use the Cisco VIC interfaces. These interface cards will allow you to create up to 256 virtual HBAs or NICs per VIC.

pNIC Layout

When determining the network adapter type and form factor, other considerations come into play. Is a multi-vendor strategy important to have full software and hardware redundancy, or will it create unnecessary complexity?

For instance, think about the following scenario when using a rackserver:

- 2x LOM NIC 10 GbE interfaces
- 2x PCIe NIC 10 GbE interfaces
- Requirement for two separate vSwitches or DvSwitches
- Each (D)vSwitch must have two uplinks

Does it make sense to create each (D)vSwitch with one uplink using a LOM interface and one uplink using the PCIe NIC for a total of two uplinks?

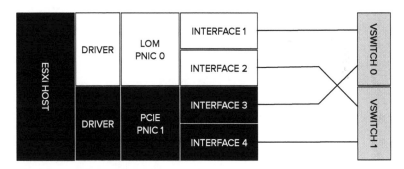

Figure 227: Esxcli pNIC Layout

This will provide an additional level of redundancy at hardware level as well as redundancy at driver level. But this only occurs if different NIC chipsets are used. However, what you want to achieve is predictable performance and stability on every level. An unwanted scenario is that your NICs from different vendors/models behave differently. If you introduce this level of resiliency, be sure to test both NICs and match them on bandwidth, as well as on supported features related to NIC offloading and the ability to have multiple network I/O threads.

List pNIC Layout

Listing you pNIC, also known as a vmnic, in a ESXi host can be done via the user interface, but the esxcli command will give you more detail of driver module versions and extended options: `esxcli network nic list`

This command will produce output of all pNICs including the used driver module, link status, MTU size and more.

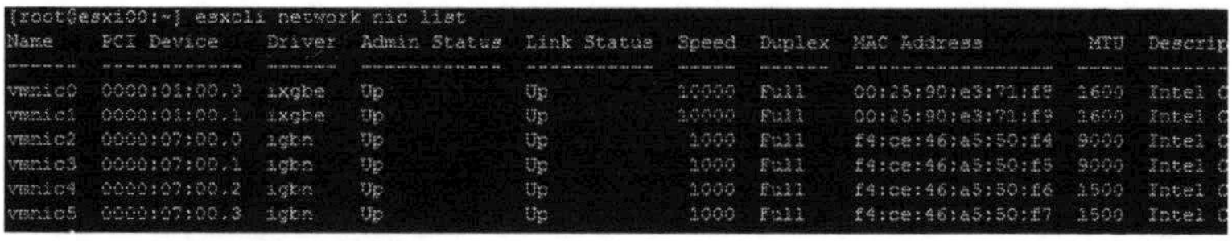

```
[root@esxi00:~] esxcli network nic list
Name    PCI Device    Driver  Admin Status  Link Status  Speed  Duplex  MAC Address        MTU   Descrip
------  ------------  ------  ------------  -----------  -----  ------  -----------------  ----  -------
vmnic0  0000:01:00.0  ixgbe   Up            Up           10000  Full    00:25:90:e3:71:f8  1600  Intel C
vmnic1  0000:01:00.1  ixgbe   Up            Up           10000  Full    00:25:90:e3:71:f9  1600  Intel C
vmnic2  0000:07:00.0  igbn    Up            Up            1000  Full    f4:ce:46:a5:50:f4  9000  Intel C
vmnic3  0000:07:00.1  igbn    Up            Up            1000  Full    f4:ce:46:a5:50:f5  9000  Intel C
vmnic4  0000:07:00.2  igbn    Up            Up            1000  Full    f4:ce:46:a5:50:f6  1500  Intel C
vmnic5  0000:07:00.3  igbn    Up            Up            1000  Full    f4:ce:46:a5:50:f7  1500  Intel C
```

Figure 228: Esxcli NIC Overview

To zoom in on even more detail about a specific pNIC, use the following esxcli command: `esxcli network nic get -n vmnic0`

The given information is important when investigating the pNIC and driver module feature capabilities that we will discuss in the upcoming chapters.

```
[root@esxi00:~] esxcli network nic get -n vmnic0
   Advertised Auto Negotiation: true
   Advertised Link Modes: 100BaseT/Full, 1000BaseT/Full, 10000BaseT/Full
   Auto Negotiation: true
   Cable Type: Twisted Pair
   Current Message Level: 7
   Driver Info:
         Bus Info: 0000:01:00.0
         Driver: ixgbe
         Firmware Version: 0x80000260
         Version: 3.7.13.7.14iov-NAPI
   Link Detected: true
   Link Status: Up
   Name: vmnic0
   PHYAddress: 0
   Pause Autonegotiate: true
   Pause RX: false
   Pause TX: false
   Supported Ports: TP
   Supports Auto Negotiation: true
   Supports Pause: true
   Supports Wakeon: false
   Transceiver: external
   Virtual Address: 00:50:56:52:89:65
   Wakeon: None
```

Figure 229: Esxcli NIC Details

Driver info will be displayed in full detail, including the bus info, actual used driver module and its firmware alongside the version.

Drivers

A hardware component is only as good as the software controlling it. The device driver is a program that operates and controls the I/O device connected to the host. The driver communicates with the device through the computer bus or a communication subsystem to which the hardware device connects. Looking at an ESXi host, we have the following driver constructs:

Driver types:
   - Partner async
   - VMware inbox

Driver models:
   - Native
   - Vmklinux

Driver Types

Looking at the driver types we distinguish the async and the inbox driver. The difference between them is that the async driver is like a 3rd party driver. It is made available by the hardware vendor for the specific I/O device and must be installed on the ESXi host. The inbox driver is the driver for I/O devices which is packaged within ESXi.

Because not every driver is written the same, the choice of device driver can make a big difference in terms of stability and performance for your pNIC. If you use specific building blocks for your IT infrastructure, it is good practice to have a driver baseline to ensure consistency and equal performance across your ESXi hosts.

The following command can be issued to install an async driver once you have downloaded and copied the package to a datastore, as described in the *VMware KB article 2137853* article: `esxcli software vib install -d /path/offline-bundle.zip`

You must use the absolute path to the offline bundle file. For example: `esxcli software vib install -d /vmfs/volumes/datastore01/offline-bundle.zip`

To check the current drivers or other vib's on a ESXi host the following command can be used: `esxcli software vib list`.

This will give you an output similar to this:

```
[root@esxi00:~] esxcli software vib list
Name                          Version                                    Vendor
----------------------------  -----------------------------------------  ------
ata-libata-92                 3.00.9.2-16vmw.650.0.0.4564106             VMW
ata-pata-amd                  0.3.10-3vmw.650.0.0.4564106               VMW
ata-pata-atiixp               0.4.6-4vmw.650.0.0.4564106                VMW
ata-pata-cmd64x               0.2.5-3vmw.650.0.0.4564106                VMW
ata-pata-hpt3x2n              0.3.4-3vmw.650.0.0.4564106                VMW
ata-pata-pdc2027x             1.0-3vmw.650.0.0.4564106                  VMW
ata-pata-serverworks          0.4.3-3vmw.650.0.0.4564106                VMW
ata-pata-sil680               0.4.8-3vmw.650.0.0.4564106                VMW
ata-pata-via                  0.3.3-2vmw.650.0.0.4564106                VMW
block-cciss                   3.6.14-10vmw.650.0.0.4564106              VMW
char-random                   1.0-3vmw.650.0.0.4564106                  VMW
ehci-ehci-hcd                 1.0-3vmw.650.0.0.4564106                  VMW
elxnet                        11.1.91.0-1vmw.650.0.0.4564106            VMW
hid-hid                       1.0-3vmw.650.0.0.4564106                  VMW
i40en                         1.1.0-1vmw.650.0.0.4564106                VMW
igbn                          0.1.0.0-12vmw.650.0.0.4564106             VMW
ima-qla4xxx                   2.02.18-1vmw.650.0.0.4564106              VMW
ipmi-ipmi-devintf             39.1-4vmw.650.0.0.4564106                 VMW
ipmi-ipmi-msghandler          39.1-4vmw.650.0.0.4564106                 VMW
ipmi-ipmi-si-drv              39.1-4vmw.650.0.0.4564106                 VMW
ixgben                        1.0.0.0-8vmw.650.0.0.4564106              VMW
lpfc                          11.1.0.6-1vmw.650.0.0.4564106             VMW
lsi-mr3                       6.910.18.00-1vmw.650.0.0.4564106          VMW
lsi-msgpt2                    20.00.01.00-3vmw.650.0.0.4564106          VMW
lsi-msgpt3                    12.00.02.00-11vmw.650.0.0.4564106         VMW
misc-cnic-register            1.78.75.v60.7-1vmw.650.0.0.4564106        VMW
misc-drivers                  6.5.0-0.0.4564106                         VMW
mtip32xx-native               3.9.5-1vmw.650.0.0.4564106                VMW
```

Figure 230: Esxcli VIB Module Overview

To find a specific driver or vib in this list you can use 'grep'. For example:

```
esxcli software vib list | grep ixgbe
```

The output of this command looks like this:

```
[root@esxi00:~] esxcli software vib list | grep ixgbe
ixgben                        1.0.0.0-8vmw.650.0.0.4564106              VMW
net-ixgbe                     3.7.13.7.14iov-20vmw.650.0.0.4564106      VMW
```

Figure 231: Esxcli ixgbe VIB Module Overview

A depreciated way of listing the used driver module version for a pNIC is the ethtool command. However, since ESXi 5.5, this command will not support native mode drivers. So, you should use the esxcli software vib list command instead.

Driver Models

With the release of ESXi 5.5, the native device driver architecture was introduced. Prior to vSphere 5.5, the device drivers supported were Linux-based (called vmklinux drivers) with an open source API interacting between the driver and the platform. William Lam (@lamw) did a great write up why this new driver architecture was released.

If we look back at the early days of ESX, VMware made the decision to use Linux derived drivers to provide the widest variety of support for storage, network and other hardware devices for ESX. Since ESX and specifically the VMkernel is not Linux, to accomplish this VMware built a translation (shim) layer module called vmklinux that sits in between the VMkernel and drivers. This vmklinux module is what enables ESX to function with the Linux derived drivers and provides an API which can speak directly to the VMkernel.

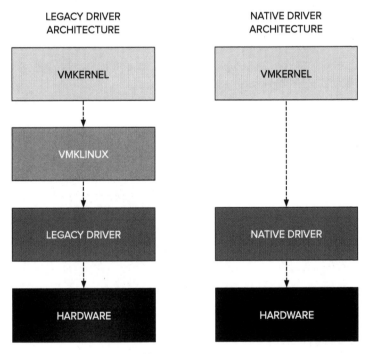

Figure 232: ESXi Driver Architectures

Why the change in driver architecture? Since the stability, reliability and performance of these device drivers are critically important to ESXi second to the VMkernel itself. There is a variety of challenges with this architecture in addition to the overhead that is introduced with the translation layer. The vmklinux driver module must be tied to a specific Linux kernel version and the continued maintenance of vmklinux to provide backwards compatibility across both new and old drivers is quite challenging. From a functionality perspective, there are also limitations by the capabilities of the Linux drivers as they are not built specifically for the VMkernel and cannot support features such as hot-plug. To solve this problem, VMware developed a new native device driver model interface that allows a driver to speak directly to the VMkernel and removing the need for the 'legacy' vmklinux interface.

These are the main benefits of the native device driver model:

- A more efficient and flexible device driver model compared to the legacy vmklinux model
- Standardized information for debugging/troubleshooting
- Improved performance, as we no longer have a translation layer. Using native drivers can save about 5%- 10% of CPU depending on packed rates and packet sizes
- Support for new capabilities such as PCIe hot-plug

The native device driver architecture was developed with backward compatibility in mind, because we all know it is not possible for the entire hardware ecosystem to port their current drivers in one release. To that extent, ESXi 5.5 can run a hybrid of both 'legacy' vmklinux drivers as well as the new native device driver. Going forward up till ESXi 6.5, VMware will be primarily investing in the native device driver architecture and encouraging new device drivers to be developed using the new architecture.

Now let's take a closer look at how the native device driver model works in ESXi. A new concept of driver priority loading is introduced with the native device driver model and the diagram below provides the current ordering of how device drivers are loaded.

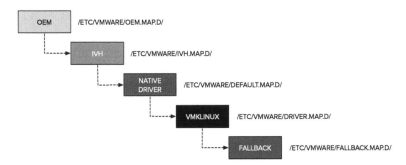

Figure 233: ESXi Device Driver Order

As you can see, the OEM drivers will have the highest priority and by default the native drivers will be loaded before the 'legacy' vmklinux drivers. On a clean installation of ESXi 6.5, you should see at least the /etc/vmware/default.map.d/ and the /etc/vmware/driver.map.d/ directories. These directories contain driver map files pertaining to native device and vmklinux drivers. Here is a screenshot of the map files for both directories on an ESXi 6.5 host:

```
[root@ESXi06:~] ls /etc/vmware/default.map.d/
elxnet.map            lsi_msgpt2.map        nmlx5_core.map        qflge.map
fakepmem.map          lsi_msgpt3.map        nrdma.map             qlnativefc.map
i40en.map             mtip32xx_native.map   ntg3.map              rste.map
igbn.map              ne1000.map            nvdroot.map           vmkata.map
intelnvdimm.map       nenic.map             nvme.map              vmkusb.map
iscsi_vmk.map         nhpsa.map             nvmxnet3.map          vmw_ahci_acpi.map
ixgben.map            nmlx4_core.map        pvscsi.map            vmw_ahci_pci.map
lpfc.map              nmlx4_en.map          qedentv.map
lsi_mr3.map           nmlx4_rdma.map        qfle3.map
```

Figure 234: Default.map.d Contents

```
[root@ESXi06:~] ls /etc/vmware/driver.map.d/
aacraid.map           forcedeth.map         mpt2sas.map           random.map
adp94xx.map           hid.map               mptsas.map            sata_nv.map
ahci.map              hpsa.map              mptspi.map            sata_promise.map
aic79xx.map           igb.map               nx_nic.map            sata_sil.map
ata_piix.map          ipmi_devintf.map      pata_amd.map          sata_sil24.map
bnx2.map              ipmi_msghandler.map   pata_atiixp.map       sata_svw.map
bnx2x.map             ipmi_si_drv.map       pata_cmd64x.map       tg3.map
cciss.map             ips.map               pata_hpt3x2n.map      usb-ohci.map
e1000.map             ixgbe.map             pata_pdc2027x.map     usb-storage.map
e1000e.map            megaraid2.map         pata_serverworks.map  usb-uhci.map
ehci-hcd.map          megaraid_mbox.map     pata_sil680.map       usb.map
enic.map              megaraid_sas.map      pata_via.map          vmxnet3.map
fnic.map              mlx4_core.map         qla4xxx.map           xhci.map
```

Figure 235: Default driver.map.d Contents

As mentioned earlier, native drivers will always load before vmklinux drivers by default. However, if you need to perform some troubleshooting, it is an option to disable the specific driver in question by using an esxcli command which is applicable to both native drivers as well as the vmklinux drivers. To do so, run the following esxcli command:

```
esxcli system module set --enabled=false --module=[DRIVER-NAME]
```

Driver Parameter Configuration

A driver module is typically a component that not always gets the attention it deserves. When you look at the parameters in the driver modules, you will see a lot of possibilities to fine-tune network devices to your needs. The number of parameters that can be configured depend strongly on the driver type and model. For example, it is perfectly possible that the *ixgbe* (Intel 10GbE) inbox driver has another parameter set than the *ixgbe* async driver version.

The parameters of a specific driver can be displayed using the `vmkload_mod -s <driver module>` command. However, the more modern esxcli command is preferred as it gives a cleaner output layout.

```
esxcli system module parameters list -m <driver module>
```

If we take the *elxnet* (Emulex 10GbE) driver module as an example we can see various interesting parameters like RSS, Dynamic NetQueue and VXLAN. We will discuss these features in the upcoming chapters.

```
[root@esxi00:~] esxcli system module parameters list -m elxnet
Name           Type          Value    Description
-------------  ------------  -----    -----------------------------------------------
DRSS           array of int           Number of RSS Queues to create on the Defaul
RSS            array of int           Number of RSS Queues to create, 0 = disable
debugMask      uint                   Enabled debug mask (default: DRIVER, UPLINK,
dyn_netq       bool                   Enable / Disable Dynamic Netqueue, 1 = enabl
emi_canceller  bool                   Enable / Disable EMI Canceller, 0 = disable
max_vfs        array of int           Number of PCI VFs to initialize, 0 = disable
msix           bool                   Enable / Disable MSI-X, 1 = enable (default)
vxlan_offload  bool                   Enable / Disable vxlan offload, 1 = enable (
```

Figure 236: Esxcli Elxnet Module Parameters

All listed parameters within a driver module are configurable. The following example shows how to disable the *vxlan_offload* parameter for the *elxnet* driver module for troubleshooting reasons.

```
esxcli system module parameters set -p vxlan_offload=0 -m elxnet
```

Be sure to check if the value has been reprogrammed by using the *list* command; `esxcli system module parameters list -m elxnet`. It will display the output for the *elxnet* driver with the *vxlan_offload* parameter with a value of '0'.

```
[root@esxi00:~] esxcli system module parameters list -m elxnet
Name            Type          Value  Description
--------------  ------------  -----  --------------------------------------------
DRSS            array of int         Number of RSS Queues to create on the Defaul
RSS             array of int         Number of RSS Queues to create, 0 = disable
debugMask       uint                 Enabled debug mask (default: DRIVER, UPLINK,
dyn_netq        bool                 Enable / Disable Dynamic Netqueue, 1 = enabl
emi_canceller   bool                 Enable / Disable EMI Canceller, 0 = disable
max_vfs         array of int         Number of PCI VFs to initialize, 0 = disable
msix            bool                 Enable / Disable MSI-X, 1 = enable (default)
vxlan_offload   bool             0   Enable / Disable vxlan_offload,1 = enable (d
```

Figure 237: Elxnet Module Vxlan Offload Disabled

Note that the value column will only show content if a parameter is configured manually. When at its default configuration, the parameter description column contains detailed information on what the current setting is.

Offloading

Offloading technologies were introduced to offload network or protocol specific processing to the network controller on the pNIC.
These techniques allow for lower CPU utilization by freeing up CPU cycles that are otherwise consumed for network I/O and less stress on the I/O subsystem within the host. Because some network I/O operations can be handled by the NIC controller, you will have more CPU resources to be consumed by the virtual workloads.

A generally accepted rule of thumb is that 1 Hertz of CPU processing is required to send or receive 1 bit/s of TCP/IP. For example, 5 Gbit/s (625 MB/s) of network traffic requires 5 GHz of CPU processing. This implies that 2 entire cores of a 2.5 GHz multi-core processor will be required to handle the TCP/IP processing associated with 5 Gbit/s of TCP/IP traffic. Since Ethernet (10GbE in this example) is bidirectional it is possible to send and receive 10 Gbit/s (for an aggregate throughput of 20 Gbit/s). Using the 1 Hz/(bit/s) rule this equates to eight 2.5 GHz cores. Source: https://en.wikipedia.org/wiki/TCP_offload_engine

However, offloading doesn't change what is sent over the network. In other words, offloading to the NIC can produce performance gains inside your ESXi host, but not across the network. The question that comes to mind is if the modern NIC, including its offloading technologies, is dimensioned for virtual networking? Is it still necessary to offload to the NIC with the current CPU capabilities and capacities, keeping Moore's law in mind?

Or is it more important than ever because of the increasing demand for network performance and bandwidth (10/40/100GbE) and considering the introduction of new network virtualization functionalities running in today's and tomorrow's virtual datacenters?

Multiple NIC offloading technologies exist, although the support for these features is strongly depending on the pNIC vendor, model and VMkernel configurations. Let's take a closer look at the most interesting offloading mechanisms available on modern NICs.

TCP Segmentation Offload

TCP Segmentation Offload (TSO) is the equivalent to *TCP/IP Offload Engine* (TOE) but more modeled on virtual environment, where TOE is the actual NIC vendor hardware enhancement. It is also known as *Large Segment Offload* (LSO). But what does it do?

When a ESXi host or a VM needs to transmit a large data packet to the network, the packet must be broken down to smaller segments that can pass all the physical switches and possible routers in the network along the way to the packet's destination. TSO allows a TCP/IP stack to emit larger frames, even up to 64 KB, when the *Maximum Transmission Unit* (MTU) of the interface is configured for smaller frames. The NIC then divides the large frame into MTU-sized frames and prepends an adjusted copy of the initial TCP/IP headers.

This process is referred to as segmentation. When the NIC supports TSO, it will handle the segmentation instead of the host OS itself. The advantage being that the CPU can present up to 64 KB of data to the NIC in a single transmit-request, resulting in less cycles being burned to segment the network packet using the host CPU.

To fully benefit from the performance enhancement, you must enable TSO along the complete data path on an ESXi host. If TSO is supported on the NIC it is enabled by default. The same goes for TSO in the VMkernel layer and for the VMXNET3 VM adapter but not per se for the TSO configuration within the guest OS.

To verify that your pNIC supports TSO and if it is enabled on your ESXi host, use the following command: `esxcli network nic tso get`.

The output will look similar the following screenshot, where TSO is enabled for all available pNICs or vmnics.

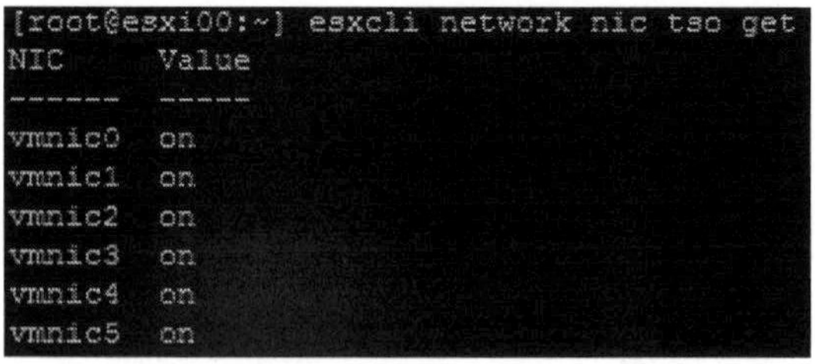

```
[root@esxi00:~] esxcli network nic tso get
NIC      Value
------   -----
vmnic0   on
vmnic1   on
vmnic2   on
vmnic3   on
vmnic4   on
vmnic5   on
```

Figure 238: Esxcli NIC TSO

In this case, TSO is supported by the NIC and therefore enabled by default. The next step is to verify whether TSO is active within the VMkernel layer. You can check that using the following command:

```
esxcli system settings advanced list -o /Net/UseHwTSO
```

The output will tell you the current configuration values for TSO within the VMkernel layer.

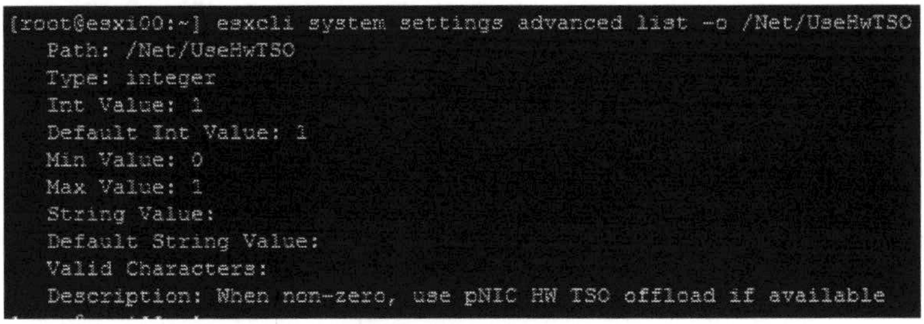

```
[root@esxi00:~] esxcli system settings advanced list -o /Net/UseHwTSO
  Path: /Net/UseHwTSO
  Type: integer
  Int Value: 1
  Default Int Value: 1
  Min Value: 0
  Max Value: 1
  String Value:
  Default String Value:
  Valid Characters:
  Description: When non-zero, use pNIC HW TSO offload if available
```

Figure 239: Esxcli NIC TSO Advanced Settings

As expected, the default value is set to '1', meaning that TSO will be active within the VMkernel if it is available on the pNIC.

If you do experience issues that could be related to TSO or situations where TSO would not be beneficial, it is possible to disable it. The easiest way to change is in the VMkernel layer. Since the VMkernel differentiates TSO for the IPv4 and IPv6 stack, you can disable TSO for either one using the following commands for specific pNICs:

```
esxcli network nic software set --ipv4tso=0 -n vmnicX
```

```
esxcli network nic software set --ipv6tso=0 -n vmnicX
```

Just change the '0' value to '1' to enable it,. Another way to disable TSO is to adjust the advanced system setting value /Net/UseHwTSO to '0'.

Even though TSO is supported and enabled on the NIC, enabled within the VMkernel and a VMXNET3 virtual adapter is used for the VM, you should also check the guest OS setting. Typically, all common Windows versions and Linux distributions support TSO.

To enable or disable TSO in a Linux operating system, use the command ethtool: `ethtool -K ethX tso on/off`. Where *X* is the correct interface number with in the Linux OS.

Looking at the latest Windows OS versions, TSO is enabled by default looking at the IPv4 TSO Offload setting. You are even able to enable or disable TSO for both IPv4 and IPv6 in the network and sharing center on the Windows control panel. Just select the properties of the correct network adapter and click configure and browse to the advanced tab.

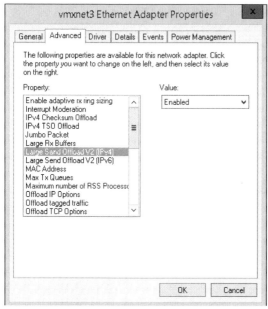

Figure 240: Windows VMXNET3 LSO Settings

Large Receive Offload

Large Receive Offload (LRO) can be seen as the exact opposite feature to TSO/LSO. It is a technique that aggregates multiple inbound network packets from a single stream into larger packets and transfers the resulting larger, but fewer packets to the network stack of the host or VM guest OS TCP stack. This process results in less CPU overhead because the CPU has fewer packets to process compared to LRO being disabled.

> **The important trade-off with LRO is that it lowers CPU overhead and potentially improves network throughput, but adds latency to the network stack.**

The potential higher latency introduced by LRO is a result of the time spent aggregating smaller TCP segments into a larger segment. Disabling LRO within the VMkernel, the VMXNET3 virtual adapter, and in the guest OS could be considered if the applications running on the ESXi host are latency-sensitive and highly relying on the TCP stack.

As with TSO/LSO, to fully utilize LRO functionality, it must be enabled across the complete data path. To check the LRO configuration for the default TCP/IP stack on the ESXi host, execute the following command to display the current LRO configuration values: `esxcli system settings advanced list -o /Net/TcpipDefLROEnabled`.

```
[root@esxi00:~] esxcli system settings advanced list -o /Net/TcpipDefLROEnabled
   Path: /Net/TcpipDefLROEnabled
   Type: integer
   Int Value: 1
   Default Int Value: 1
   Min Value: 0
   Max Value: 1
   String Value:
   Default String Value:
   Valid Characters:
   Description: LRO enabled for TCP/IP
```

Figure 241: Esxcli NIC LRO Advanced Settings

To disable LRO, change the advanced setting value `/Net/TcpipDefLROEnabled` to '0' using either the vSphere Web Client or esxcli.

Next to enabling or disabling LRO, it contains another configurable option. You are able to configure the length of the LRO buffer by using the following esxcli command: `esxcli system settings advanced list -o /Net/VmxnetLROMaxLength`.

You will notice that the default value is configured at 32000 bytes and is configurable up till 65535 bytes or 64 KB, which is equivalent to the absolute maximum size for a TCP packet.

```
[root@esxi00:~] esxcli system settings advanced list -o /Net/VmxnetLROMaxLength
  Path: /Net/VmxnetLROMaxLength
  Type: integer
  Int Value: 32000
  Default Int Value: 32000
  Min Value: 1
  Max Value: 65535
  String Value:
  Default String Value:
  Valid Characters:
  Description: LRO default max length for TCP/IP
```

Figure 242: Esxcli NIC LRO Max Length Settings

Adjusting the LRO buffer length could mean you can align it as good as possible to the network segment sizes used by your application workloads. Lowering the LRO buffer length could lead to a situation that provides you with the ability to potentially minimize the increased latency due to LRO, while keeping the LRO functionality enabled. However, because it is difficult to analyze your incoming network segments and determine how the LRO buffer length should be configured, it will probably be easier to make the decision whether to enable or disable LRO.

The LRO features are functional for the guest OS when the VMXNET3 virtual adapter is used. To check the VMXNET3 settings in relation to LRO, the following commands can be issued:

```
esxcli system settings advanced list -o /Net/Vmxnet3HwLRO
```

The output will show you if the hardware LRO is enabled for VMXNET3 virtual adapters:

```
[root@esxi00:~] esxcli system settings advanced list -o /Net/Vmxnet3HwLRO
  Path: /Net/Vmxnet3HwLRO
  Type: integer
  Int Value: 1
  Default Int Value: 1
  Min Value: 0
  Max Value: 1
  String Value:
  Default String Value:
  Valid Characters:
  Description: Whether to enable HW LRO on pkts going to a LPD capable vmxnet3
```

Figure 243: Esxcli NIC Hardware LRO Advanced Settings

```
esxcli system settings advanced list -o /Net/Vmxnet3SwLRO
```

The output will show you if the software LRO is enabled for VMXNET3 virtual adapters:

```
[root@esxi00:~] esxcli system settings advanced list -o /Net/Vmxnet3SwLRO
  Path: /Net/Vmxnet3SwLRO
  Type: integer
  Int Value: 1
  Default Int Value: 1
  Min Value: 0
  Max Value: 1
  String Value:
  Default String Value:
  Valid Characters:
  Description: Whether to perform SW LRO on pkts going to a LPD capable vmxnet3
```

Figure 244: Esxcli NIC Software LRO Advanced Settings

So, if the VMXNET3 virtual adapter is enabled or disabled to use LRO, the guest OS running within the VM must be configured accordingly. Modern Linux distributions support LRO since kernel 2.6.24 and when a VMXNET3 virtual adapter is used. You can either enable or disable LRO using the following command in the shell of the Linux guest OS, where X represents the number of the NIC in the guest OS: ethtool -K ethX lro on/off.

Looking at Windows, LRO can be enabled or disabled in a Windows Server 2012, Windows 8 or later. The LRO technology is listed as *Receive Side Coalescing* (RSC) in Windows. To check the status of the global state for LRO/RSC in Windows the *netsh* command should be issued using command prompt. After checking the global state, the LRO setting can be enabled or disabled using the VMXNET3 virtual adapter. The global state for LRO/RSC can be checked using this command: netsh int tcp show global. Output will look similar to this:

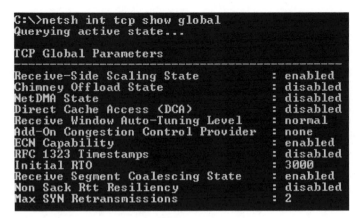

Figure 245: Windows RSC Parameter

If the RSC state is disabled, you can configure it to enabled. `netsh int tcp set global rsc=enabled`. Next up should be verifying if the LRO/RSC setting on the Ethernet adapter within Windows. Remember, this feature is only available using VMXNET3 virtual Ethernet adapters.

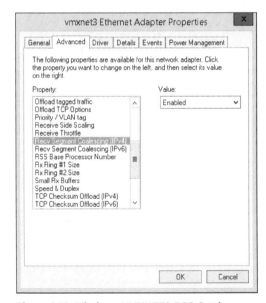

Figure 246: Windows VMXNET3 RSC Settings

You are able to configure Receive Segment Coalescing for both the IPv4 and IPv6 stack. As shown in the screenshot above, it is enabled by default when using VMXNET3.

Checksum Offload

Checksum Offload (CSO) or *TCP Checksum Offloading* (TCO) eliminates the host overhead introduced by check-summing for TCP packets.

> **The TCP header contains a 16-bit checksum field, which is used to verify the integrity of the header and data. For performance reasons the checksum calculation on the transmit side and verification on the receive side may be offloaded from the OS to the network adapter.** Source: https://kb.vmware.com/kb/2052904

With checksum offloading enabled, checksum calculations are allowed on the NIC chipset. That allows for saving cycles on the CPU and importantly cuts down on the bus communications to/from the NIC in the process. Differences are made for Rx and Tx checksums and where the checksum calculation is performed. Depending on the traffic flow and the CSO capabilities and configuration of all components involved, the checksum calculation will be executed on different level within the communication chain. A component can be the guest OS, the vNIC or the pNIC.

For instance; if a VM is communicating with another VM on another ESXi host, the transmit (Tx) checksum calculation is performed at both the pNIC and on the vNIC, granted both have CSO enabled. If CSO is not enabled on the vNIC, the checksum calculation will always be performed by the guest OS. However, if the pNIC has CSO disabled but it is enabled on the vNIC, checksum calculation will be performed in the VM kernel. The receive (Rx) checksum ideally will be handled by the pNIC on the ESXi host where the receiving VM resides if it is enabled. Because this will free up ESXi host CPU cycles, it makes sense to always enable CSO on the pNIC if supported.

The following command provides information about the checksum offload settings on your ESXi host: esxcli network nic cso get.

This will show you output on how checksum offload is configured for all the ESXi hosts pNICs. It will be enabled by default if the pNIC supports it.

```
[root@esxi00:~] esxcli network nic cso get
NIC         RX Checksum Offload   TX Checksum Offload
-------     -------------------   -------------------
vmnic0      on                    on
vmnic1      on                    on
vmnic2      on                    on
vmnic3      on                    on
vmnic4      on                    on
vmnic5      on                    on
```

Figure 247: Esxcli NIC CSO Settings

For troubleshooting purposes, you can disable checksum offload for a pNIC. One scenario that could benefit from CSO being disabled is when TCP packet dumps are made for troubleshooting. If the checksum calculation is offloaded to the pNIC, checksum mismatches could be seen in the packet dumps.

The following command can be used for disabling CSO for a specific pNIC: esxcli network nic cso set -n vmnicX.

Examining the guest OS, Windows in this case, reveals that CSO is also configurable for Tx and Rx using the VMXNET3 adapter.

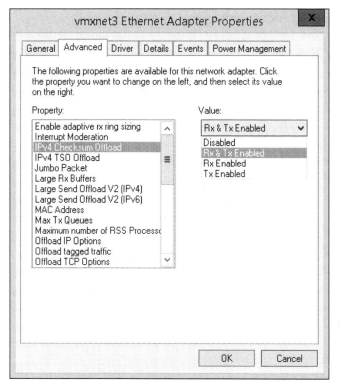

Figure 248: Windows CSO Settings

Be sure to enable or disable CSO on the entire network path in order for CSO to be fully effective.

Network Overlay

Current innovations on software defined virtual network solutions are gaining traction fast. In the advent of network virtualization and its constant evolution, we are now faced with an increase of new protocols that are introduced. These protocols all have the common purpose to create an overlay virtual network on top of the physical network constructs. They differ in the way they accomplish that. However, the basic functionality is often based on tunneling.

Current network overlay techniques are:

NAME	ABBREVIATION
Generic Network Virtualization Encapsulation	Geneve
Network Virtualization using Generic Routing Encapsulation	NVGRE
Network Virtualization Overlays 3	NVO3
Stateless Transport Tunneling	STT
Virtual Extensible LAN	VXLAN

Table 59: Network Overlay Technique Overview

VXLAN

Looking at the VMware SDN offering, VMware NSX, you will notice that it currently leverages the VXLAN virtual network overlay technique, which is probably the best-known network overlay protocol today. VMware NSX allows for distribution of additional services next to overlay networks. It provides a complete set of distributed services including logical switching, routing, firewalling, load balancing and more.

> **Increased bandwidth per host is a driver for distributed services like firewalls to prevent large scale north-south traffic.**

In the upcoming chapters, we will focus on VXLAN and discuss pNIC considerations when using VMware NSX.

> **VXLAN is a framework for overlaying virtualized layer-2 networks over layer-3 networks.** Source: https://tools.ietf.org/html/rfc7348

Adopting VXLAN overlay networks in your virtual datacenter will introduce a new CPU resource consumer on your ESXi hosts. VXLAN comes with the cost of CPU overhead because network packets need to be encapsulated and de-capsulated. That means protocol headers are added on the sender side and removed on the receiver side.

A VXLAN encapsulated packet looks like this:

Figure 249: VXLAN Packet

It is the added protocol headers that lead to a requirement for a minimal MTU size of 1600 bytes for the *Virtual Tunnel End Point* (VTEP) transport network used for VXLAN. Depending on the usage of the optional inner 802.1Q VLAN tags, the overhead can be up to 54 bytes in addition of the original 1500 bytes packet.

Unit	Size
Original header	1500 bytes
VXLAN header	8 bytes
Outer UDP header	8 bytes
Outer IP header	20 bytes
Outer MAC header	14 bytes
Optional 801.1Q tag	4 bytes

Table 60: VXLAN Header Size Overview

Added together that is a total of 1554 bytes that simply won't fit in a default MTU size of 1500 bytes. Therefore, a minimum MTU of 1600 bytes is required.

Next to the additional CPU cycles for the encapsulation and de-capsulation process some of the TCP pNIC offload capabilities, like TSO and TCO, are not available by default because VXLAN leverages UDP packets to encapsulate the Ethernet frames. As a result, this potentially leads to a substantial increase of CPU consumption, especially when running high packet rate workloads using NSX.

VMware NSX adoption is accelerating fast, but improper hardware choices could seriously reduce consolidation ratios in your virtual datacenter because the CPU cycles are used for VXLAN rather than for your application workloads.

> **VXLAN performance may vary based on the hardware components used in the ESXi host.**

Luckily, several vendors introduced VXLAN offloading on their pNIC offerings. Offloading VXLAN encapsulation and de-capsulation allows the pNIC to 'see' the inner Ethernet frame in the VXLAN packet. Because of this, it is now possible to apply TSO and CSO for the encapsulated Ethernet frames.

Depending on the used pNIC and the supported offloading feature set, VXLAN enabled networks can now achieve a near line-rate performance. Be sure to check what your pNIC and your driver module support regarding VXLAN offload. We will look closer on how to properly do so in chapter *What does my pNIC support?*

Geneve

Next to the VXLAN protocol, the *Generic Network Virtualization Encapsulation* (Geneve) will be a supported network overlay technology in future releases of VMware NSX. In 2014, the authors published an *Internet Engineering Task Force* (IETF) draft on Geneve. The authors include Intel, Microsoft, Red Hat and VMware.

> **The aim from the beginning was to make this a multivendor effort (similar to VXLAN) with broad support from partners and the ecosystem. The hardware ecosystem can benefit from an industry consensus on a single encapsulation for the long term, removing the need to support multiple encapsulations in their silicon.**
> Source: https://cto.vmware.com/geneve-vxlan-network-virtualization-encapsulations/

Current network overlay protocols, like VXLAN, will not be decommissioned with the arrival of Geneve. Instead, the Geneve approach provides common, collective instructions among them. That will result in other software components being able to hook into Geneve only, rather than having to comply to multiple network encapsulation 'standards'.

So it is more like a framework for tunneling virtual networks rather than being a prescriptive protocol (like VXLAN). This approach was taken to tackle limitations that will obstruct future virtual network implementations and innovation.

> **The Geneve frame format consists of a compact tunnel header encapsulated in UDP over either IPv4 or IPv6. A small fixed tunnel header provides control information plus a base level of functionality and interoperability with a focus on simplicity. This header is then followed by a set of variable options to allow for future innovation. Finally, the payload consists of a protocol data unit of the indicated type, such as an Ethernet frame.**
> Source: https://datatracker.ietf.org/doc/draft-gross-geneve/

The most common limitation of current overlay protocols is that they lack flexibility. Specifically, the lack of scalability of the *Virtual Network Identifier* (VNI) field. This metadata field is fixed in size and is used to pass network virtualization parameters.
Geneve solves this by using an extensible *Type Length Value* (TLV) format to encode metadata in. The TLV tunnel header structure has a variable length and allows for flexible parameter usage. It can be used for VNI data or for various other purposes.

Although the Geneve encapsulation protocol is relatively new, it makes sense that you consider opting for a pNIC that already supports Geneve offloading, like the Intel X710 NIC, when choosing the pNIC vendor and model for your ESXi hosts. Geneve offloading means that the pNIC is able to de-capsulate the Geneve packet to perform CSO or even TSO and LRO for the inner payload. Having a pNIC that supports Geneve offloading allows you to be flexible when new network overlay innovations are introduced in the near future.

pNIC Features

Besides offloading capabilities, it is interesting to recognize the additional features your pNIC of choice supports. The feature set of a pNIC can greatly impact your virtual network performance and ability to consume the maximum amount of bandwidth per ESXi host.
Even more interesting is the application of these features when you introduce overlay network techniques like VXLAN in your virtual datacenters.

Virtual Machine Device Queues

Intel's *Virtual Machine Device queues* (VMDq) is the hardware component used by VMware's NetQueue software feature since ESX 3.5. Dynamic NetQueue was introduced with the release of ESXi 5.5.

> **VMDq is a silicon-level technology that can offload network I/O management burden from ESXi. Multiple queues and sorting intelligence in the chipset support enhanced network traffic flow in the virtual environment and by doing so freeing processor cycles for application workloads. This improves efficiency in data transactions toward the destined VM, and increases overall system performance.**
> Source: intelligent-queueing-technologies-for-virtualization-dell-paper.pdf

The VMDq feature, in collaboration with NetQueue, allows network packets to be distributed over different queues. Each queue gets its own ESXi thread for packet processing. One ESXi thread represents a CPU core.

When data packets are received on the network adapter, a layer-2 classifier in the VMDq enabled network controller sorts and determines which VM each packet is destined for. After setting the classifier it places the packet in the receive queue assigned to that VM. ESXi is now only responsible for transferring the packets to the respective VM rather than doing the heavy lifting of sorting the packets on the incoming network streams. That is how VMDq and NetQueue manage to deliver efficiency for CPU utilization in your ESXi host.

It is important to understand that VMDq and NetQueue are only a necessity when utilizing modern pNICs with10GbE bandwidth or higher in your ESXi host. One CPU core simply can't process those amounts of network packets involved with higher bandwidth capable pNICs. It is however not required for 1GbE interfaces because nowadays one ESXi thread, or one CPU core, is perfectly capable of processing up to 1GbE of network bandwidth. VMDq has actually been depreciated by Intel since vSphere 5.5 for the igb (Intel 1GbE) driver.

Modern pNICs that support NetQueue through VMDq are able to distribute packets based on filters. Those filters are made up by certain attributes, typically consisting of outer MAC addresses or VLAN IDs. You can check the filter capabilities on your pNIC inside your ESXi host.

```
esxcli network nic queue filterclass list
```

This esxcli command gives information about the filters supported per vmnic and used by NetQueue.

```
[root@esxi00:~] esxcli network nic queue filterclass list
NIC       MacOnly   VlanOnly   VlanMac   Vxlan   Geneve   GenericEncap
--------  --------  --------   -------   -----   ------   ------------
vmnic0    true      false      false     false   false          false
vmnic1    true      false      false     false   false          false
vmnic2    false     false      true      false   false          false
vmnic3    false     false      true      false   false          false
vmnic4    false     false      true      false   false          false
vmnic5    false     false      true      false   false          false
```

Figure 250: Esxcli NIC Queue Filterclass List

Note that in this example screenshot, you see two types of pNIC are shown, both supporting different filters. The *ixgbe* (vmnic0 and vmnic1) driver supports the NetQueue filter based on MacOnly, meaning only outer MAC addresses are supported, while the *igbn* (vmnic2 to vmnic5) driver supports the VlanMac filter.

Another detail shown in this screenshot is that NetQueue looks to be developed to support the likes of the VXLAN and Geneve overlay protocols as well as the traditionally supported filters.

> **NetQueue is enabled by default when supported by the underlying network adapter.**

Today, most common NICs support NetQueue filters based on MAC addresses. For common Ethernet networks that solves the problem of being constrained by only one queue, which equates to one CPU thread, for receiving network packets per pNIC. Packets with the same destination MAC address are processed by a single queue.
However, this could cause serious sprawl of queues where not every queue is required. Not every VM is the same when it comes to network I/O utilization, so why have queues for every one of them? It would be better to have incoming network I/O spread over multiple queues where it is really required.

Dynamic NetQueue

That is where Dynamic NetQueue, introduced in ESXi 5.5, comes into play. Dynamic NetQueue is more practical in the way it distributes filters over queues. It bundles filters on a single queue up to the point where the load reaches a certain threshold. Only then will it utilize the next queue. This will lead to more efficient utilization of CPU cores by only consuming more when required instead of gobbling each CPU core in sight.

Using Dynamic NetQueue could reduce CPU usage by 10-40%, obviously strongly depending on the number of VMs and network I/O pressure. Not every pNIC will support the same number of VMDq queues. The number of available hardware queues go from two up to the excess of sixteen. However, with Dynamic NetQueue being queue efficient, not all the hardware queues will be used. It is possible you will only utilize two to four queues. To check how many queues your pNIC supports, you can use the following command:

```
esxcli network nic queue count get
```

This will output the queues for all vmnics in your ESXi host. The output will look similar to the following screenshot.

```
[root@esxi00:~] esxcli network nic queue count get
NIC       Tx netqueue count  Rx netqueue count
--------  ------------------  ------------------
vmnic0             4                   4
vmnic1             4                   4
vmnic2             1                   1
vmnic3             1                   1
vmnic4             1                   1
vmnic5             1                   1
```

Figure 251: Esxcli NetQueue Count

Notice that multiple queues are only available on the 10GbE *ixgbe* adapters (vmnic0 and vmnic1). As stated before, VMDq/NetQueue typically is not available on 1GbE adapters. The vmnic2 till vmnic5 adapters are in fact *igbn* 1GbE adapters for which Intel depreciated the VMDq feature. Depending on the pNIC, it might even be possible to fine-tune the number of queues that could be spun up by NetQueue by configuring the driver parameters.

If required, for troubleshooting purposes for example, it is possible to disable NetQueue on a ESXi host level using the following command:

```
esxcli system settings kernel set --setting="netNetqueueEnabled" --value="false"
```

VXLAN and NetQueue

VXLAN and NetQueue are not the best of friends when it comes to distributing network I/O over multiple queues. That is because of the way VTEPs are setup. With a VMware NSX implementation each ESXi host in the cluster contains at least one VTEP, dependent upon the NIC load balancing mode chosen. The VTEP is the component that provides the encapsulation and de-capsulation for the VXLAN packets. That means all VXLAN network traffic from a VM perspective will traverse the VTEP and the receiving VTEP on another ESXi host.

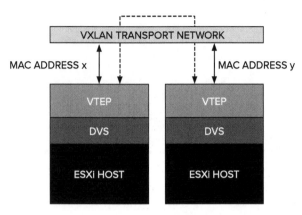

Figure 252: VXLAN VTEP Intra Host Communication

Therein lies the problem when it comes to NetQueue and the ability to distribute network I/O streams over multiple queues. This is because a VTEP will always have the same MAC address and the VTEP network will have a fixed VLAN tag. MAC address and VLAN tag are the filters most commonly supported by pNICs with VMDq and NetQueue enabled. It will seriously restrict the ability to have multiple queues and thereby will possibly restrict the network performance for your VXLAN networks.

VMware NSX now supports multi-VTEPs per ESXi host. This helps slightly as a result of the extra MAC addresses, because of the increased number of VTEPs per ESXi host. NetQueue can therefore have more combinations to filter on. Still, it is far from perfect when it comes to the desired network I/O parallelism handling using multiple queues and CPU cores. To overcome that challenge, there are some pNICs that support the distributing of queues by filtering on inner (encapsulated) MAC addresses. RSS can do that for you.

Receive Side Scaling

Receive Side Scaling (RSS) has the same basic functionality that (Dynamic) NetQueue supports, it provides load balancing in processing received network packets. RSS resolves the single-thread bottleneck by allowing the receive side network packets from a pNIC to be shared across multiple CPU cores.

Single VM receive performance was evaluated for Mellanox 40GbE NICs. Without RSS, the throughput is limited to only 15Gbps for large packets, but when RSS is turned on for the pNIC and the VM, the throughput increases by 40%. The configuration also helps in the small packet receive test case, and the throughput is increased by 30%.

RSS helps if VXLAN is used because traffic can be distributed among multiple hardware queues for VXLAN traffic. NICs that offer RSS have a throughput of 9.1Gbps for large packet test cases, but NICs that do not only have a throughput of around 6Gbps. The throughput improvement for the small packet test case is also similar to that of the large packet test case. Source: VMware performance blog.

The big difference between VMDq and RSS is that RSS uses more sophisticated filters to balance network I/O load over multiple threads. Depending on the pNIC and its RSS support, RSS can use up to a 5-tuple hash to determine the queues to create and distribute network IO's over.

A 5-tuple hash consists of the following data:

- Source IP
- Destination IP
- Source port
- Destination port
- Protocol

The ability by RSS to use hash calculations to determine and scale queues is key to achieve near line rate performance for VXLAN traffic. The behavior that a single MAC address can now use multiple queues is very beneficial for VXLAN traffic running over the VTEPs. Keep in mind RSS is not required for 1GbE pNICs, but it is a necessity for 10/25/40/50/100GbE pNICs for the same exact reason as it is for VMDq and NetQueue.

The pNIC chipset matters because of the way the RSS feature scales its queues. Depending on the vendor and model, there are differences in how RSS is supported and how queues are scaled.

Looking at the Intel NIC products for example, we noticed that the Intel X520/540 NIC chipsets scale RSS based on the VXLAN packet source port included in the outer UDP information. The Intel X710 NIC is able to scale RSS based on the *Virtual Network Identifier* (VNI) value in the VXLAN header. Being able to scale RSS based on inner VXLAN headers allows for a more granular way to distribute incoming network I/O over multiple queues that correlate to CPU cores. The various constructs of a VXLAN packet are shown in the following diagram.

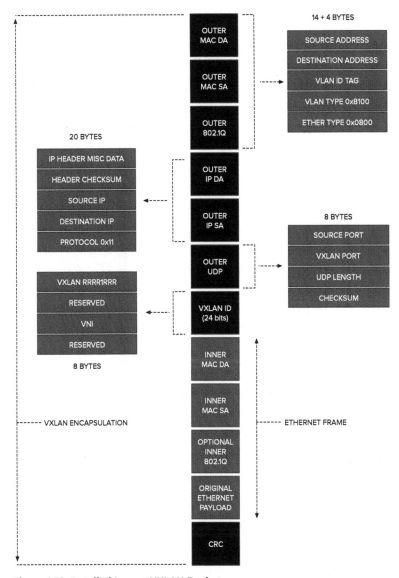

Figure 253: Detailed Layout VXLAN Packet

One of the interesting facts of RSS is that it is not able to direct the incoming network stream to the same CPU core on which the application process resides.

That means if an application workload is running on one core, the incoming network stream using RSS can very well be scheduled on another core. This could result in poor cache efficiency if the used cores are running within different NUMA nodes. However, you could argue the real impact of this 'limitation'.

RSS is not enabled by default like its semi-equivalent VMDq. It needs to be enabled in the driver module. It depends on the used driver module if the RSS parameters should be set to enable it.

The problem with the driver module settings is that it is not always clear on what values to use in the configuration. The description of the driver module parameters differs a lot among the various driver modules. That won't be a problem if the value of choice is either zero or one, but it is when you are expected to configure a certain number of queues.

The RSS driver module settings are a perfect example of this. Looking at the example of the *ixgbe* driver, the following description is given when executing the `esxcli system module parameters list -m ixgbe | grep "RSS"`. The description is quite ambiguous:

"Number of Receive-Side Scaling Descriptor Queues, default 1=number of cpus"

This implicates that you should configure RSS with a specific number of CPUs. But how can we determine what to configure? The same information about the *b2xnx* driver module is somewhat clearer:

"Control the number of queues in an RSS pool. Max 4."

The *b2xnx* example is more straightforward. You can configure up to four RSS queues per pNIC. However, how do you decide whether you need one, two or four queues?

The result of the number of queues configured determines how many CPU cycles can be consumed by incoming network traffic.

A higher number of queues will result in higher network throughput. But if that throughput is not required by your workloads, can configuring too many queues result in an inefficient way of consuming CPU cycles? That will depend strongly on how many cores you have available in your ESXi host. Obviously, the number of queues will have more impact on the CPU consumption with regards to the total CPU cycles available if you have eight CPU cores compared to an ESXi host that contains 36 cores.

In the end, It is hard to determine what to configure. Let's be realistic, there are too many variables when it comes to determining what settings to adopt for your (overlay) network utilization upfront.

More insights on how to fine-tune your environment after a *Proof-of-Concept* (PoC), or after you have taken the workload into production will be a more practical approach in most cases. That is because you will be able to monitor your workloads on (overlay) network performance and throughput. But it is important to understand that you can change the parameters when you are running into limits on network performance or throughput.

RSS in the Guest OS

To fully make use of the RSS mechanism, an end-to-end implementation is recommended. That means you will need to enable and configure RSS in the guest OS in addition to the VMkernel driver module. That allows the guest OS to distribute incoming traffic across its entitled vCPUs. This can help with processing received network packets, whether the traffic is originating from a conventional network or from a VXLAN network. The VXLAN traffic will already be de-capsulated when it arrives in the guest OS so no difference is made on that part.

RSS will be available to the guest OS when the VM hardware version is 7 or higher and the VMXNET3 virtual network adapter is used.

The interesting thing here is that in the following screenshot, which is a Windows 2012 R2 VM, RSS is enabled by default in the global TCP settings.

```
C:\>netsh int tcp show global
Querying active state...

TCP Global Parameters
----------------------------------------------------------------
Receive-Side Scaling State          : enabled
Chimney Offload State               : disabled
NetDMA State                        : disabled
Direct Cache Access (DCA)           : disabled
Receive Window Auto-Tuning Level    : normal
Add-On Congestion Control Provider  : none
ECN Capability                      : enabled
RFC 1323 Timestamps                 : disabled
Initial RTO                         : 3000
Receive Segment Coalescing State    : enabled
Non Sack Rtt Resiliency             : disabled
Max SYN Retransmissions             : 2
```

Figure 254: Windows RSS Parameter

However, if you check the advanced settings within the VMXNET3 virtual Ethernet adapter, RSS is disabled.

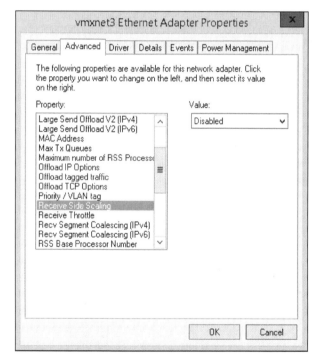

Figure 255: Windows RSS Configuration

In this case, that means you will need to manually enable RSS for the virtual Ethernet adapter. Be sure to check if RSS is supported by the guest OS and if it requires manual configuration.

Note that RSS was not functional for VMXNET3 on Windows 8 and Windows Server 2012 or later because an issue caused by an update in a release for the VMXNET3 driver. More specifically, this was seen in VMXNET3 driver version 1.6.6.0 to 1.7.3.0. Be sure to update to the latest VM tools (at least version 10.1.7).

Figure 256: Windows RSS Maximum Processors

The number of vCPUs used in the Windows guest OS running on your VM is configurable, but is set to *Not Present* by default. It is configurable to value 1, 2, 4 or 8 that is equivalent to the number of vCPUs used for RSS.

The Linux guest OS combined with the VMXNET3 virtual network adapter can also take advantage of RSS together with multi-queue in the in-guest driver. This allows the Linux OS to scale Tx and Rx queues over the vCPUs entitled to the VM. By default, a Linux OS has the same number of transmit and receive queues.

Multi-queuing is enabled by default in your Linux guest OS when the latest VMware tools version (version 1.0.24.0 or later) is installed or when the Linux VMXNET3 driver version 1.0.16.0-k or later is used. Prior to these versions, you were required to manually enable multi-queue or RSS support. Be sure to check the driver and version used to verify if your Linux OS has RSS support enabled by default.

pNIC Support

We talked about several offloading capabilities or features delivered by the pNIC. But what is actually supported by your pNIC?

When you are assembling a new ESXi host or configuring an existing one, you should first figure out what is required from a virtual networking perspective in your virtual datacenter. Are you planning for high network loads or are you looking to adopt overlay networking? It helps if you know what you are looking for in a pNIC.

It is recommended to follow these three steps to fully verify if the feature you are looking for is supported and enabled.

Step 1:   Check the support of the pNIC chipset
Step 2:   Check the support of the driver module
Step 3:   Check if the driver module needs configuration

The first step is to check the vendor information about the supported features on their NIC product. Let's take the combination of a 10GbE Broadcom QLogic 57810 NIC and the VXLAN offload feature as an example.

Looking at the datasheet of the QLogic 57810 NIC, it clearly states that VXLAN offloading is supported.

QLogic 57810S SFP+/DA

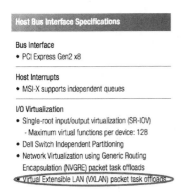

Figure 257: Qlogic 57810 Characteristics

Now that we know the hardware bit supports VXLAN offloading, it is time to check if the driver module does. An easy way to verify this is by retrieving the driver module details and check the support on the VMware *Hardware Compatibility List* (HCL).

Secondly, we should check what driver module is used for your pNICs. We can do so by listing the NICs within the ESXi host: `esxcli network nic list`.

That will give you the information, from which you can derive the driver used. In this case, the *bnx2x* driver module. To get the specific driver information, like the driver and firmware version, you can use the following command: `esxcli network nic get -n vmnicX`.

The output contains the driver information that allows you to look up the specific information on the VMware HCL.

```
# esxcli network nic get -n vmnic0
 Advertised Auto Negotiation: true
 Advertised Link Modes: 1000baseT/Full, 10000baseT/Full
 Auto Negotiation: true
 Cable Type: FIBRE
 Current Message Level: 0
 Driver Info:
        Bus Info: 0000:01:00.0
        Driver: bnx2x
        Firmware Version: FFV7.12.19 bc 7.12.5
        Version: 2.713.10.v55.4
 Link Detected: true
 Link Status: Up
 Name: vmnic0
 PHYAddress: 1
 Pause Autonegotiate: true
 Pause RX: true
 Pause TX: true
 Supported Ports: FIBRE
 Supports Auto Negotiation: true
 Supports Pause: true
 Supports Wakeon: true
 Transceiver: internal
 Wakeon: MagicPacket(tm)
```

Figure 258: Esxcli NIC bnx2x Driver Information

The information provided in this screenshot can be used to verify if the pNIC feature is supported in the used driver module. Using the HCL at **www.vmware.com/resources/compatibility**, we should be able to find the driver and what features it supports.

It may come in handy to have more information available about the pNIC and the driver used if the HCL has a lot of listings. In that case, you also need the hardware ID properties to make sure you are looking at the correct driver in the HCI:

- Vendor-ID (VID)
- Device-ID (DID)
- Sub-Vendor-ID (SVID)
- Sub-Device-ID (SDID)

To extract that information from your ESXi host, you can use the vmkchdev -l | grep vmnic command. This will list additional hardware ID information about the vmnics.

```
[root@esxi00:~] vmkchdev -l | grep vmnic
0000:01:00.0 8086:1528 15d9:1528 vmkernel vmnic0
0000:01:00.1 8086:1528 15d9:1528 vmkernel vmnic1
0000:07:00.0 8086:150e 103c:1780 vmkernel vmnic2
0000:07:00.1 8086:150e 103c:1780 vmkernel vmnic3
0000:07:00.2 8086:150e 103c:1780 vmkernel vmnic4
0000:07:00.3 8086:150e 103c:1780 vmkernel vmnic5
```

Figure 259: Vmnic Hardware ID Information

The output can be interpreted as follows:

0000:01:00.0   ***8086:1528 15d9:1528***   *vmkernel vmnic0*

The bold section shows the hardware device properties in the format
VID:DID SVID:SSID. When you are in doubt which VMware HCL entry you
should choose for your pNIC, this information allows you to identify the
unique HCL entry. The *bnx2x* driver entry in the HCL with the matching
driver version shows that VXLAN offloading is supported.

ESXi 6.5	bnx2x version 2.713.10.v55.4	7.13.xx

Feature Category	Features
IO Device	SR-IOV,VXLAN-Offload

Figure 260: VMware HCL bnx2x Driver Entry

So, why do we need the third step to verify the supported features? This
specific example will show you that. The interesting thing about the
bnx2x driver module is that certain settings are supported but not
enabled by default, in particular the VXLAN offload feature.

```
esxcli system module parameters list -m bnx2x
```
The parameters list command shows the driver module for the *bnx2x*
driver module.

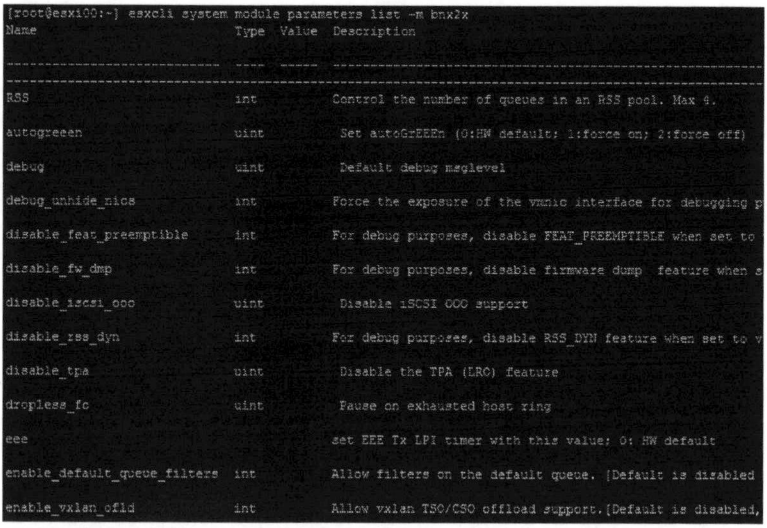

```
[root@esxi00:~] esxcli system module parameters list -m bnx2x
Name                           Type  Value  Description
-----------------------------  ----  -----  ------------------------------------------------------------
-----------------------------------------------------------------------------------------------------
RSS                            int          Control the number of queues in an RSS pool. Max 4.
autogreeen                     uint          Set autoGrEEEn (0:HW default; 1:force on; 2:force off)
debug                          uint          Default debug msglevel
debug_unhide_nics              int          Force the exposure of the vmnic interface for debugging p
disable_feat_preemptible       int          For debug purposes, disable FEAT_PREEMPTIBLE when set to
disable_fw_dmp                 int          For debug purposes, disable firmware dump  feature when s
disable_iscsi_ooo              uint          Disable iSCSI OOO support
disable_rss_dyn                int          For debug purposes, disable RSS_DYN feature when set to v
disable_tpa                    uint          Disable the TPA (LRO) feature
dropless_fc                    uint          Pause on exhausted host ring
eee                                         set EEE Tx LPI timer with this value; 0: HW default
enable_default_queue_filters   int          Allow filters on the default queue. [Default is disabled
enable_vxlan_ofld              int          Allow vxlan TSO/CSO offload support.[Default is disabled,
```

Figure 261: Bnx2x Driver Parameter List

The parameter *enable_vlxan_ofld* is stated to be disabled by default. This is the perfect example why you should always check if a manual configuration is required for a feature to be enabled. Do not automatically assume the driver feature is enabled when it is supported.

Jumbo Frames

The ability for the vSwitch to communicate using a larger frame size can be beneficial for network throughput and in turn have a positive effect on high network utilization workloads. The default MTU size for an Ethernet frame is 1500. When the MTU size is configured at 9000 bytes or larger, it is referred to as a jumbo frame.

Jumbo frames and their pros and cons are still a point of discussion in modern virtual datacenters. There are a lot of different opinions out there, so it is a good idea to elaborate on this topic and how you should weigh the performance gains and the possible risks involved with jumbo frames.

> **Jumbo frames or 9000-byte payload frames have the potential to reduce overheads and CPU cycles.**

Typically, jumbo frames are considered for IP storage networks or vMotion networks. The gain in performance comes from the fact that more bytes can be transported across the network in less packets, thus reducing the overhead from the host.

A lot of jumbo frame performance benchmarking is already described on the Internet. Looking at various tests by multiple virtualization professionals, you will see a variety of opinions whether to adopt jumbo frames or not. Adopting jumbo frames could result in higher network throughput at the cost of slightly increased latency. In the end, the discussion is always about if the possible performance gain outweighs the possible risks that are introduced when implementing jumbo frames.

MTU Mismatch

If we put the performance aspects aside, we can consider the possible risks involved when implementing jumbo frames. The most important thing about implementing jumbo frames is, to be effective, it must be enabled end-to-end in the network path to work.

The main risk when adopting jumbo frames is, that if one component in the network path is not properly configured for jumbo frames, a MTU mismatch may occur. The main concern should be if the network and storage components are correctly configured for jumbo frames. The scenario where your data-set is at risk, is the following one:

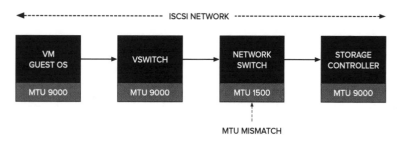

Figure 262: Jumbo Frames Test Network Switch MTU Mismatch

We simulated this scenario in a lab setup to capture the behavior of MTU mismatches in the IP storage (layer-2) network. The guest OS in this scenario is a Windows 2012R2 VM running with an in-guest iSCSI LUN connected to it. We captured the iSCSI (TCP 3260) frames on this VM on the dedicated iSCSI network adapter that is connected to the dedicated iSCSI VLAN.

The lab network switch is configured with a standard MTU size of 1500. So, this is where the MTU mismatch occurs. Looking at the captured data, we immediately see the black marked *TCP ACK unseen segments* when I/O's are written to the LUN. Not exactly what you want to see in your production environment. This can lead to serious issues for your dataset because of possible data corruption.
This behavior is expected though. Within a layer-2 network, the Ethernet switch simply drops frames bigger than the configured switch port MTU. This means that you are possibly silently black-holing traffic which exceeds the 1500 byte frame size.

> **It is important to understand that fragmentation will occur at layer-3, but not on layer-2 networks.**

This is a characteristic of a layer-2 Ethernet network. Typically, IP storage networks and vMotion networks are implemented as layer-2 networks, although vSphere vMotion supports layer-3 networks. The same outcome as the first scenario would occur if our storage interfaces on the storage controllers were mismatching in MTU. But the following scenario will not present us with a problem.

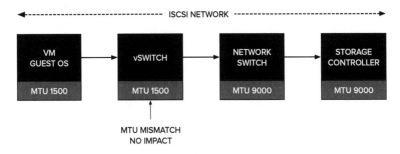

Figure 263: Jumbo Frames Test Source MTU Mismatch

The test above will cause your dataset no harm, because a frame of 1500 bytes simply fits very well in the 9000 byte port MTU of the switch. Once every component in the network path is configured with a MTU of 9000, the errors disappeared as the following capture shows:

```
Protocol  Length  Info
iSCSI      102  SCSI: Read(10) LUN: 0x00 (LBA: 0x005fdfe0, Len: 16)
iSCSI     1514  SCSI: Data In LUN: 0x00 (Read(10) Response Data) SCSI: Response LUN: 0x00 (Read(10)) (Good)
iSCSI      102  SCSI: Read(10) LUN: 0x00 (LBA: 0x005fdff0, Len: 16)
iSCSI      426  SCSI: Data In LUN: 0x00 (Read(10) Response Data) SCSI: Response LUN: 0x00 (Read(10)) (Good)
iSCSI      102  SCSI: Read(10) LUN: 0x00 (LBA: 0x005fe000, Len: 16)
iSCSI      102  SCSI: Read(10) LUN: 0x00 (LBA: 0x005fe010, Len: 16)
iSCSI     1230  SCSI: Data In LUN: 0x00 (Read(10) Response Data) SCSI: Response LUN: 0x00 (Read(10)) (Good)
iSCSI     8342  SCSI: Read(10) LUN: 0x00 (LBA: 0x005fe020, Len: 16)SCSI: Write(10) LUN: 0x00 (LBA: 0x0309f3a
iSCSI     8294  SCSI: Write(10) LUN: 0x00 (LBA: 0x00e63af0, Len: 16)SCSI: Data Out LUN: 0x00 (Write(10) Requ
iSCSI     8294  SCSI: Write(10) LUN: 0x00 (LBA: 0x013fd850, Len: 16)SCSI: Data Out LUN: 0x00 (Write(10) Requ
iSCSI     1230  SCSI: Data In LUN: 0x00 (Read(10) Response Data) SCSI: Response LUN: 0x00 (Read(10)) (Good)
iSCSI     8294  SCSI: Write(10) LUN: 0x00 (LBA: 0x00cb6e30, Len: 16)SCSI: Data Out LUN: 0x00 (Write(10) Requ
iSCSI      102  SCSI: Read(10) LUN: 0x00 (LBA: 0x005fe030, Len: 16)
iSCSI     1514  SCSI: Data In LUN: 0x00 (Read(10) Response Data) SCSI: Response LUN: 0x00 (Read(10)) (Good)
iSCSI      102  SCSI: Read(10) LUN: 0x00 (LBA: 0x005fe040, Len: 16)
iSCSI     1514  SCSI: Data In LUN: 0x00 (Read(10) Response Data) SCSI: Response LUN: 0x00 (Read(10)) (Good)
iSCSI      190  SCSI: Data In LUN: 0x00 (Read(10) Response Data) SCSI: Response LUN: 0x00 (Read(10)) (Good)
iSCSI      102  SCSI: Read(10) LUN: 0x00 (LBA: 0x005fe050, Len: 16)
iSCSI      102  SCSI: Read(10) LUN: 0x00 (LBA: 0x005fe060, Len: 16)
iSCSI      102  SCSI: Response LUN: 0x00 (Write(10)) (Good)
iSCSI      102  SCSI: Response LUN: 0x00 (Write(10)) (Good)
```

Figure 264: Jumbo Frames Wireshark Output

Whether to use jumbo frames is still a viable question. Depending on the situation, it could be a good fit to implement jumbo frames where it may be beneficial. For instance, a greenfield implementation of an infrastructure can be configured with jumbo frames if the tests show improved performance. The risk that (future) infrastructure components are mis-configured, MTU-wise, can be mitigated by introducing strict change and configuration management along with configuration compliance checks.

> **Changing the default MTU on your infrastructure components is no longer a question; it is a must because of network virtualization.**

The funny thing is, while we are adopting overlay services in our virtual datacenters, the MTU sizes must change accordingly. Think about your transport network(s) in your VMware NSX environment. Because of VXLAN encapsulation, you will be required to 'up' your MTU to a minimum of 1600 bytes.

Configure Jumbo Frames

To adopt jumbo frames in your virtual datacenter, be sure to have pNICs that support the use of jumbo frames. Even if most modern pNICs do, don't assume yours do. Verify it! To properly configure jumbo frames on your ESXi host, the applicable VMkernel interface must be configured with a value of 9000 bytes, which is the maximum value. In addition to the VMkernel interface, the vSwitch itself should be configured accordingly. Since ESXi 5.1, the MTU size may be configured using the UI. Prior to that, you were required to configure it using the shell.

Be sure to remember that all components in the network path must be configured with jumbo frames if you choose to adopt it. Ideally you are able to configure the network components with an even larger MTU size, like 9216 bytes. That allows for more headroom when transferring packets with a 9000 byte size with IP overhead in mind.
A quick way to verify the MTU settings using the ESXi shell are the following commands. This first command will list all vSwitches with their corresponding MTU settings: `esxcfg-vswitch -l`.

```
[root@esxi00:~] esxcfg-vswitch -l
Switch Name        Num Ports    Used Ports    Configured Ports    MTU
vSwitch0           2432         8             128                 9000

   PortGroup Name              VLAN ID    Used Ports    Uplinks
   vMotion-01-1GbE             12         1             vmnic2,vmnic3
   vMotion-00-1GbE             12         1             vmnic2,vmnic3
   Management Network          10         1             vmnic2,vmnic3
```

Figure 265: Esxcfg vSwitch Configuration

The following command will list the MTU settings among other settings for the VMkernel interfaces: `esxcfg-vmknic -l`.

```
[root@esxi00:~] esxcfg-vmknic -l
Interface   Port Group/DVPort/Opaque Network
 Broadcast          MAC Address          MTU
vmk0          Management Network
 172.16.10.255    f4:ce:46:a5:50:f4 1500
vmk1          vMotion-00-1GbE
 172.16.12.255    00:50:56:6d:d8:60 9000
vmk2          vMotion-01-1GbE
 172.16.12.255    00:50:56:65:62:87 9000
```

Figure 266: Esxcfg VMkernel Interfaces Configuration

The most important part of configuring jumbo frames, is to verify that the complete network path is correctly configured for jumbo frames.

The most reliable way test this, is to ping the other endpoint from the ESXi console with a large byte size and the *no defragment* bit set. That way you are sure the packet is not fragmented in your network. The following command can be used: `vmkping -s 8972 -d <ip address>`

Note that we are using a packet size of 8972 and not the full 9000 for the ping test. That is because of the IP header overhead of 20 bytes and the ICMP header of 8 bytes. If a ping using this command succeeds, you correctly verified that the entire path is jumbo frame 'enabled'.

It might even come in handy to perform the same tests on another TCP/IP netstack like VXLAN using the following commands:

`vmkping ++netstack=vxlan <ip address> -d -s <packet size>`

or

esxcli network diag ping --netstack=vxlan --host <ip> --df --size=<packet size>

19

VMKERNEL NETWORK

The virtual part of networking in the vSphere stack is handled in the ESXi VMkernel. This is the part where the physical network devices are tied to the virtual network components.

Looking at the ESXi VMkernel networking data path, you will see that the ESXi kernel uses specific threads for transmitting and receiving network I/O to and from the VMs. Differences are made between the transmit and the receive because these are handled by different threads within the kernel.

> **There is no fixed metric for the maximum performance of the vSphere (D)vSwitch. It is all about how much CPU time the VMkernel can consume for processing network I/O.**

The question about the overhead of virtualization and how this impacts networking performance is a rather hard one to answer. As always, it depends greatly on the components used and the configurations within the hypervisor and its networking components. In the context of vSphere, we talk about virtual network constructs like the pNIC, the vNIC and the (Distributed) vSwitch. The physical pNIC is the only construct that is clear on how much bandwidth it can handle, even though there are many variables as previously discussed in this book.

Looking at the virtual components, the actual figures are more abstract. So, if you are looking for fixed metrics on what the actual performance capability of a (Distributed) vSwitch or vNIC is, you are asking yourself the wrong question. The question should be; how much CPU resources can be used by the ESXi kernel for processing network I/O?

It is important to understand that both type of threads for receiving and transmitting network I/O consume CPU cycles. So how do we make sure these threads can consume the CPU cycles they require?
As shown in the following diagram, the transmit threads, called Tx thread, lives at the vNIC. It handles the network I/O transmitted from the vNIC as well as the virtual networking stack, including the vNIC emulation type; VMXNET3 and E1000E virtual network adapters. The vSwitch, the uplink layer and packet scheduling up to the pNIC driver are also accounted for by the Tx thread when transmitting network data from the VM to another host or VM.

The cycles consumed for receiving I/O streams are accounted for by the so-called Netpoll threads which reside on the pNIC side in the ESXi VMkernel. It handles the network I/O received on the pNICs and the transport to its destination vNIC. By default, only one Netpoll thread is available per pNIC.

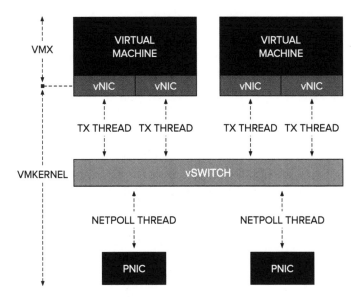

Figure 267: ESXi VMkernel Networking Data Path

The same goes for the transmit (Tx) thread, only one Tx thread is active per VM by default. The number of Tx threads is not automatically adjusted to the number of vNICs that are configured on the VM. So, no matter if the VM has one or ten (current maximum) vNICs, only one Tx thread is active

When a network data stream is set up between two VM's on the same host, the Tx thread handles the transmission of network I/O from the source VM as well as the delivery of the receiving VM that resides on the same ESXi host. This is logical as no interference of the pNIC is required.

The Tx and Netpoll threads are worldlets. Worldlets are high priority kernel contexts that are usually used for I/O processing. Each thread is mapped to a pCPU. The transmit (Tx) and receive (Netpoll) threads consume CPU cycles. If your workload(s) in your virtual datacenter has a large appetite for network I/O, like telco or NFV applications, you can become constrained by the number of threads, thus CPU cores, which the VMkernel is able to utilize for network I/O.

Luckily, it is possible to configure additional threads, creating more worldlets that allow for more network I/O. Each additional thread provides extra capacity for network I/O because more CPU cycles can be consumed. One extra worldlet or thread equals a CPU core worth of extra cycles.

Netpoll Thread Scaling

As stated before, each pNIC in your ESXi host is equipped with one Netpoll thread by default. However, when the pNIC supports the NetQueue or RSS feature, the Netpoll threads can be scaled.

When either one of these features is enabled and/or configured in the pNIC driver module, additional threads will be spun up depending on the feature used and based on the network I/O streams as discussed in the VMDq and RSS chapters.

The CPU cycles used for the Netpoll thread are accounted to the VMX world of the VM. In esxtop, the metric %SYS reflects the time being charged to the VM for processing received network packets by the Netpoll threads.

The following screenshot shows the esxtop output for CPU with the specific test VM GID (24868) expanded. We immediately see the %SYS metric for VMX running at around 214%. In this case, this VM was the receiving part of a packet-generator test. That explains the amount of time being charged to the VM for receiving network packets.

```
9:19:20pm up  5:23, 542 worlds, 1 VMs, 8 vCPUs; CPU load average: 1.78, 1.80,
PCPU USED(%):  46  51  91 8.2  44  52  97 4.5  27  77  19  83 AVG:  50
PCPU UTIL(%):  89  94  99  15  83  92 100 5.7  48 100  33 100 AVG:  71
CORE UTIL(%):  97      99      96     100     100     100     AVG:  98

      ID      GID NAME                            NWLD    %USED    %RUN    %SYS
   70441    24868 vmx                                1   214.96    0.00  214.96
   70443    24868 NetWorld-VM-70442                  1     0.00    0.00    0.00
   70444    24868 vmast.70442                        1     0.01    0.01    0.00
   70452    24868 vmx-vthread-12                     1     0.00    0.00    0.00
   70453    24868 vmx-vthread-13:DPDK-PKTGEN02       1     0.00    0.00    0.00
   70454    24868 vmx-mks:DPDK-PKTGEN02              1     0.01    0.02    0.00
   70455    24868 vmx-svga:DPDK-PKTGEN02             1     0.04    0.05    0.00
   70456    24868 vmx-vcpu-0:DPDK-PKTGEN02           1   102.94  100.27    0.00
   70458    24868 vmx-vcpu-1:DPDK-PKTGEN02           1    83.74  100.29    0.00
   70459    24868 vmx-vcpu-2:DPDK-PKTGEN02           1    88.45  100.28    0.00
   70460    24868 vmx-vcpu-3:DPDK-PKTGEN02           1    99.32  100.27    0.00
   70461    24868 vmx-vcpu-4:DPDK-PKTGEN02           1     0.11    0.18    0.00
   70462    24868 vmx-vcpu-5:DPDK-PKTGEN02           1     0.01    0.01    0.00
   70463    24868 vmx-vcpu-6:DPDK-PKTGEN02           1     0.05    0.07    0.00
   70464    24868 vmx-vcpu-7:DPDK-PKTGEN02           1     0.01    0.02    0.00
   70457    24868 LSI-70442:0                        1     0.00    0.00    0.00
```

Figure 268: Esxtop VM %SYS Consumption

The interesting thing about the %SYS metric is the fact that it is already using a lot more that 100%. There is a relation with CPU cores in your ESXi host and the, for instance, %SYS metric. You can state that one CPU core is able to produce 100%. So, by the looks of the screenshot, already three CPU cores are utilized for processing received network packets.

Using the *net-stats* command, you are able to really dig into the various worlds that are used within the ESXi network data path. The following command will output a lot of information including what worldlet ID's are used for the various virtual networking constructs: net-stats -A -t vW.

If we want to look at one of the vmnics that is used in this test, we can see what *sys* worldlets are used.

```
{"name": "vmnic1", "switch": "DvsPortset-0", "id": 67108868, "mac
   "txpps": 0, "txmbps": 0.0, "txsize": 0, "txeps": 0.00, "rxpps"
   "vmnic": {"devname": "vmnic1.ixgbe",
      "txpps": 0, "txmbps": 0.0, "txsize": 0, "txeps": 0.00, "rxpps
      "sys": [ "66076", "66243", "66244", "66245", "66246", "66247",
```

Figure 269: Net-stats vmnic1 Details

Using the VSI shell, we can check the description of the worldlets. Start the VSI shell by typing `vsish`. Here you can look up the names of the worlds by inserting command `cat /world/<world id>/name`.

`cat /world/66243/name` outputs the world name, in this case *"vmnic1-pollWorld-10"*. The given example is in fact a Netpoll thread for vmnic1. Checking the worldlets on the vmnics is a way to check how many Netpoll threads are in use and as a result proving that features like NetQueue or RSS are working correctly. That is because these features will enable the ability for more Netpoll threads to be spun up.

Tx Thread Scaling

Each VM is armed with only one Tx thread by default. As network packets are transmitted from the VM towards the pNIC layer via the VMkernel, ESXi consumes CPU cycles. These cycles, or CPU time, will also be accounted to the VM itself.

> **Because the CPU cycles used by the Tx thread or threads are accounted to the VM, you should be careful with applying CPU limits to the VM. CPU limits can seriously impact the network I/O performance capability for your VM. Although it seems that CPU limits are not widely adopted, think about the pay-as-you-go allocation model in vCloud Director. This allocation model will place a reservation as well as a limit on your VM. Just be aware of the possible implications that CPU limits may introduce on network performance.**

The difference between the Tx thread and the Netpoll thread is the fact that the Tx thread is not accounted for in the %SYS metric. This was the case in older ESXi versions, like 5.5. In ESXi 6.5, the Tx threads are identified in esxtop in the CPU view as *NetWorld-VM-XXX*. It is now much more clear on what the costs are of transmitting large numbers of networks packets from that specific VM. It allows you to have a better understanding if a VM is constrained by the amount of CPU time that is spent on transmission of data.

Again, only one Tx thread is spun up by default. That correlates with one CPU core. This is why the NetWorld will not trespass the ±100% of %USED.

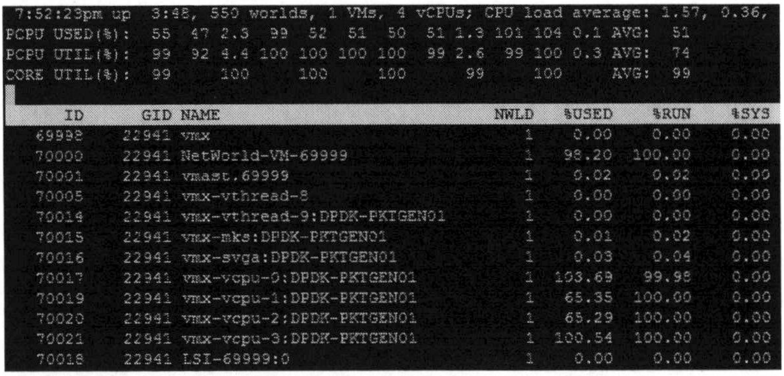

```
7:52:29pm up  3:48, 550 worlds, 1 VMs, 4 vCPUs; CPU load average: 1.57, 0.36,
PCPU USED(%):   55   47  2.3  99    52   51   50    51  1.3 101 104 0.1 AVG:  51
PCPU UTIL(%):   99   92  4.4 100   100  100  100    99  2.6  99 100 0.3 AVG:  74
CORE UTIL(%):   99       100       100       100        99      100     AVG:  99

      ID      GID NAME                              NWLD   %USED    %RUN    %SYS
   69998    22941 vmx                                  1    0.00    0.00    0.00
   70000    22941 NetWorld-VM-69999                    1   98.20  100.00    0.00
   70001    22941 vmast.69999                          1    0.02    0.02    0.00
   70005    22941 vmx-vthread-8                        1    0.00    0.00    0.00
   70014    22941 vmx-vthread-9:DPDK-PKTGEN01          1    0.00    0.00    0.00
   70015    22941 vmx-mks:DPDK-PKTGEN01                1    0.01    0.02    0.00
   70016    22941 vmx-svga:DPDK-PKTGEN01               1    0.03    0.04    0.00
   70017    22941 vmx-vcpu-0:DPDK-PKTGEN01             1  103.69   99.98    0.00
   70019    22941 vmx-vcpu-1:DPDK-PKTGEN01             1   65.35  100.00    0.00
   70020    22941 vmx-vcpu-2:DPDK-PKTGEN01             1   65.29  100.00    0.00
   70021    22941 vmx-vcpu-3:DPDK-PKTGEN01             1  100.54  100.00    0.00
   70018    22941 LSI-69999:0                          1    0.00    0.00    0.00
```

Figure 270: Esxtop VM NetWorld Consumption

In the screenshot above, the VM in question was running the transmit side of the packet-generator test. The *NetWorld-VM-69999* world was constantly running up to 100%. This is a clear example of a VM being constrained by only one Tx thread.

A relatively quick solution is to add an additional Tx thread. You can add more as needs require. Looking at the network view in esxtop, you will be able to see what vNIC is processing the largest amount of network I/O. In this specific case, we knew exactly what vNIC was in extra need of network processing power.

You can add an additional Tx thread per vNIC. This is configured as an advanced parameter in the VM configuration. The ethernetX.ctxPerDev = 1 advanced setting is used for this. The 'X' stands for the vNIC for which the parameter is set. You can configure each vNIC with a separate Tx thread. However, that will create unnecessary Tx threads in your VM and potentially consume CPU time in an inefficient way, because not every vNIC is likely to require its own Tx thread. It really is a setting that is driven by demand. If your workload running in the VMs has a large appetite for network I/O, take a closer look at what vNIC could benefit from additional Tx threads.

Once the additional Tx thread(s) are configured, you want to verify that it is activated. Additional Tx threads will appear in esxtop in the CPU view as *NetWorld-Dev-<id>-Tx*. By being added as a separate world, a clear overview can be generated on which NetWorld is processing the majority of network I/O as a result of the CPU usage associated with that thread.

```
9:14:43pm up   5:11, 555 worlds, 1 VMs, 4 vCPUs; CPU load average: 1.75, 0.54,
PCPU USED(%):  50   46   88   15   45   52   52   51   65   38   92   11 AVG:   50
PCPU UTIL(%):  86   82  100   28   78   83  100  100  100   78  100   22 AVG:   79
CORE UTIL(%):  96        100        95       100       100       100      AVG:   98

       ID      GID NAME                                      NWLD    %USED     %RUN    %SYS
    71931    34999 vmx                                          1     0.00     0.00    0.00
    71933    34999 NetWorld-VM-71932                            1    51.04    71.97    0.00
    71934    34999 vmast.71932                                  1     0.01     0.01    0.00
    71939    34999 vmx-vthread-8                                1     0.00     0.00    0.00
    71940    34999 vmx-vthread-9:DPDK-PKTGEN01                  1     0.00     0.00    0.00
    71941    34999 vmx-mks:DPDK-PKTGEN01                        1     0.02     0.03    0.00
    71942    34999 vmx-svga:DPDK-PKTGEN01                       1     0.04     0.05    0.00
    71943    34999 vmx-vcpu-0:DPDK-PKTGEN01                     1    93.19   100.08    0.00
    71945    34999 vmx-vcpu-1:DPDK-PKTGEN01                     1    62.91   100.08    0.00
    71946    34999 vmx-vcpu-2:DPDK-PKTGEN01                     1    71.98   100.03    0.00
    71947    34999 vmx-vcpu-3:DPDK-PKTGEN01                     1    71.16   100.08    0.00
    71944    34999 LSI-71932:0                                  1     0.00     0.00    0.00
    72101    34999 NetWorld-Dev-67108879-Tx                     1    52.80    77.85    0.00
```

Figure 271: Esxtop VM NetWorld-Dev Consumption

In this screenshot, you will notice that the additional Tx thread is active and processing network I/O. This is one way to determine if your advanced setting is working correctly. Another way of doing so is to use the command: `net-stats -A -t vW`.

Looking at the *net-stats* results, you will notice that by default only one *sys* entry is available that is associated with the default single Tx thread.

```
{"name": "DPDK-PKTGEN01.eth3", "switch": "DvsPortset-0",
 "txpps": 0, "txmbps": 0.0, "txsize": 0, "txeps": 0.00,
 "sys": [ "243724" ],
 "vcpu": [ "243733", "243735", "243736", "243737" ]},
```

Figure 272: Net-stats vNIC eth3 Details

The *sys* entry '243724' is the world ID. Using the VSI shell, we can check the description of the worldlets. When we look up this world ID using `cat /world/243724/name`, the name *NetWorld-VM-243723* is shown.

This is the default Tx thread handling all the outgoing network I/O for the VM and all its vNICs. When additional Tx threads are added to the VM vNIC(s), you will see multiple *sys* entries in the *net-stats* results for the specific vNIC.

```
{"name": "DPDK-PKTGEN01.eth3", "switch": "DvsPortset-0"
  "txpps": 0, "txmbps": 0.0, "txsize": 0, "txeps": 0.00
  "vnic": { "type": "vmxnet3", "ring1sz": 512, "ring2sz
    "lropct": 0.0, "lrotputpct": 0.0, "rxucastpct": 0.0
    "maxqueuelen": 0, "requeuecnt": 0.0, "agingdrpcnt":
    "txdisc": 0.0, "qstop": 0.0, "txallocerr": 0.0, "tx
  "rxqueue": { "count": 1},
  "txqueue": { "count": 1},
  "intr": { "count": 1 },
  "sys": [ "194786", "242681" ],
  "vcpu": [ "194830", "194832", "194833", "194834" ]},
```

Figure 273: Net-stats vNIC eth3 Additional Sys World

Next to the default NetWorld-VM-194785 entry, you will also spot the additional Tx thread with the world name '*NetWorld-Dev-67108880-Tx*'. The name of the world already states it is a NetWorld for a specific device or vNIC if you will. It is the same world as seen in esxtop.

Equipping more vNICs in a VM with their own Tx thread will lead to more vNIC entries with multiple *sys* entries in the *net-stats* output. In addition to the esxtop output, verifying the existence of the Tx threads could prove useful when you are implementing these for your network I/O sensitive workloads.

Tuning Considerations

It can be challenging to virtualize workloads that are network I/O and latency sensitive. We already discussed various offloading mechanisms, features and ways to claim more CPU time for the VMkernel to handle Rx and Tx network traffic to and from the VM. It might not be enough for your specific workload.

The following chapters will discuss various additional tuning considerations. These are usually adopted for telco, NFV or real-time data workloads that are typical latency sensitive or have specific characteristics for high packet rates.

Interrupt Coalescing

Adjusting interrupt coalescing, which is also referred to as NIC coalescing, can improve workloads with a large network I/O footprint.

> **Interrupt coalescing is a feature implemented in hardware under driver control on high-performance NICs, allowing the reception of a group of network frames to be notified to the OS kernel via a single hardware interrupt.**
> Source: https://www.vmware.com/support/ws55/doc/ws_performance_nicintc.html

The ability of interrupt coalescing to reduce the number of interrupts can lead to a potential decrease in CPU utilization because of the grouping of network frames in a single hardware interrupt. Since it cooperates with the hardware, a pNIC supporting interrupt coalescing is a requirement.

> **In system programming, an interrupt is a signal to the processor emitted by hardware or software indicating an event that needs immediate attention. An interrupt alerts the processor to a high-priority condition requiring the interruption of the current code the processor is executing. The processor responds by suspending its current activities, saving its state, and executing a function called an interrupt handler (or an interrupt service routine, ISR) to deal with the event. This interruption is temporary, and, after the interrupt handler finishes, the processor resumes normal activities. There are two types of interrupts: hardware interrupts and software interrupts.**
> Source: https://en.wikipedia.org/wiki/Interrupt

The mechanism of grouping network frames can however introduce additional latency. The question whether to disable or enable interrupt coalescing depends on your workload characteristics.

Will it benefit more by saving up CPU cycles for your applications on your ESXi host or does your workload require the lowest latency possible?

Interrupt coalescing is disabled by default if you set the VM latency sensitivity to 'high'. This is because of the introduced additional network latency, something you want to prevent when servicing a latency sensitive application.

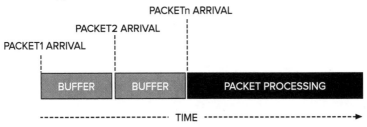

Figure 274: Packet Processing with Interrupt Coalescing

When we consider the additional latency that is introduced when interrupt coalescing is enabled, we are talking about the range of a few hundred microseconds up to milliseconds. Most workloads are not that submissive to extreme low latency. That is exactly why interrupt coalescing is enabled by default for the VMkernel layer if the pNIC supports it and for vNICs when the VMXNET3 virtual network adapter type is used.

There are parameters to further tune the use of coalescing. But first, let's check what parameters are active on your pNICs. You can gain insights on that using the following esxcli command: esxcli network nic coalesce get.

```
[root@esxi00:~] esxcli network nic coalesce get
NIC     RX microseconds  RX maximum frames  TX ms  TX Maximum frames  Adaptive RX  Adaptive TX
------  ---------------  -----------------  -----  -----------------  -----------  -----------
vmnic0  62               0                  0      0                  Off          Off
vmnic1  62               0                  0      0                  Off          Off
```

Figure 275: Esxcli pNIC Coalescing Configuration

The esxcli command will output information about coalescing support as well as the active status or configuration, Rx and Tx microseconds and frames. When applicable, the adaptive settings are also provided. ESXi even differentiates between high packet rate and low packet rates when it comes to interrupt coalescing. Information about the behavior of a pNIC, when it processes packets, will be available by expanding the following commands to view the status for high or low packet rate:

```
esxcli network nic coalesce high get
esxcli network nic coalesce low get
```

We have looked at these commands extensively. However, they do not seem to give a full picture just yet. It looks like these commands are already built-in but will be fully functional in future ESXi releases.

```
[root@esxi00:~] esxcli network nic coalesce low get -n vmnic0

  NIC: vmnic0
  Packet rate: 0 pps
  RX delay time: 0 microsecond
  RX delay packets: 0
  TX delay time: 0 microsecond
  TX delay packets: 0
```

Figure 276: Esxcli pNIC Coalescing Output

The introduced delay for both Rx and Tx can be pointers to help you understand how your workload is impacted by interrupt coalescing. Ideally, these commands could provide data points that help you make the decision to re-configure or disable interrupt coalescing.

Another way to get insights current interrupt coalescing and statistics on the posted and requested interrupts for a specific interface can be found using the VSI shell; cat /net/portsets/DvsPortset-0/ports/<port-id>/vmxnet3/rxqueues/0/rxCoalesce.

```
rx queue coalesce stats {
    current queue depth:64
    whether dynamic coalescing is enabled:1
    rx intr index used for this queue:0
    is tx/rx queue separated:0
    rx coalesce stats:coalesce2 rx stats {
        # total intrs posted to guest:996446
        # total intrs requested:1300583
        max rx queue length reached:64
        # rx intrs posted from haltCheck:0
        # (rx) intrs posted immediately because VM is halted:92
        # haltChecks:11046
    }
}
```

Figure 277: VSI Shell pNIC Rx Coalescing Output

The value of the number of packets used to queue before generating an interrupt can be configured in either a static or to an adaptive value for both Rx and Tx traffic flows. This can lead to a nice balance between CPU savings and latency values. Configuring interrupt coalescing on a virtual network adapter to a static value will force ESXi to queue a number of packets up to the configured value before interrupting the VM or transmitting the packets in the queue. When set to a static configuration, ESXi will queue up to 64 packets by default.

When set to dynamic mode, the pNIC will determine a fitting interrupt generation rate based on the network I/O load. The default static value ranges from 1 to 64. To change the default value for interrupt coalescing configure the VM advanced setting `ehernetX.coalescingParams`. To enable or disable interrupt coalescing, change the VM advanced setting `ethernetX.coalescingScheme` to '0' or '1'.

It is important to understand that regardless of the packets queued or the coalescing configuration, ESXi will not wait longer then 4 milliseconds before creating an interrupt. Situations like the VM being idle can also trigger VM interrupts or packet transmission.

Interrupt Throttling

Where interrupt coalescing focuses on the interrupts as send to the VM layer, interrupt throttling is a strict host feature. It will coalesce interrupts from the pNIC to the ESXi host. The goal is again to save CPU time being spend on interrupts during network I/O peaks.

However, the same goes for interrupt coalescing as it does for interrupt throttling. If your workload is latency sensitive, it might not be beneficial to use it. Creating a delay on the pNIC to deliver the received packets is introducing additional latency, and it is exactly what interrupt throttling does.

It is recommenced to see if the pNIC and its used driver allow you to disable interrupt throttling when running latency sensitive workloads. Looking at the driver module parameters by using `esxcli system module parameters list -m <driver module>` you can see how to disable interrupt throttling for your specific driver module. For the Intel 10GbE ixgbe driver this is done using the following command: `esxcli system module parameters set -m ixgbe -p "InterruptThrottleRate=0"`.

If you disable interrupt throttling, you can also trim down the benefits of LRO since some pNIC that support hardware LRO automatically disable it when interrupt moderation is disabled. As a result, ESXi its software LRO feature will have fewer packets to coalesce into larger packets for each interrupt.

Please note that not using interrupt throttling on your pNIC can be profitable for your latency sensitive applications, but not per se for your other workloads. Think about your ESXi cluster strategy so you are able to serve each workload characteristic to the fullest. Consolidate latency sensitive workloads on a separate cluster and do the same for your 'default' IT workloads.

Polling versus Interrupts

The previous tuning considerations focus on handling interrupts. The VMkernel is relying on the physical device, the pNIC in this case, to generate interrupts to process I/O. This traditional style of I/O processing incurs additional delays on the entire data path from the pNIC all the way up to within guest OS.

Using poll mode, the driver and the application running in the guest OS will constantly spin waiting for an I/O to be available. This way, an application can process the I/O almost instantly instead of waiting for an interrupt to occur. That will allow for lower latency and a higher *Packet Per Second* (PPS) rate.

The main drawback is that the poll mode approach consumes much more CPU time because of the constant polling for I/O. Basically, it consumes all the CPU you offer it. Therefore, it is primarily useful when the workloads running on your VMs are extremely latency sensitive. Obviously, it is a perfect fit for data plane telecom applications or real-time latency sensitive workloads.

Using the poll-mode approach, you will need a poll-mode driver in your application which polls a specific device queue for I/O. From a networking perspective, Intel's *Data Plane Development Kit* (DPDK) delivers just that. You could say that the DPDK framework is a set of libraries and drivers to allow for fast network packet processing.

> **Data Plane Development Kit (DPDK) greatly boosts packet processing performance and throughput, allowing more time for data plane applications. DPDK can improve packet processing performance by up to ten times. DPDK software running on current generation Intel® Xeon® Processor E5-2658 v4, achieves 233 Gbps (347 Mpps) of LLC forwarding at 64-byte packet sizes.**
> Source: http://www.intel.com/content/www/us/en/communications/data-plane-development-kit.html

DPDK in a VM

Using a VM with a VMXNET3 network adapter, you already have the default paravirtual network connectivity in place.

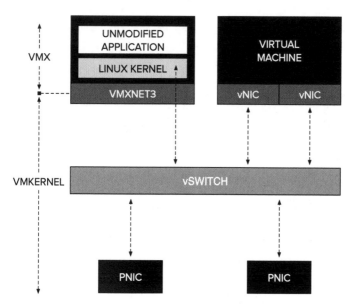

Figure 278: Default Paravirtual Device Connectivity

It is recommended to use the VMXNET3 virtual network adapter when you are using a DPKD enabled application. It helps if you have a pNIC that is also optimized for the use of DPDK. Since DPDK version 1.8 which was released in 2014, the VMXNET3 *Poll-Mode Drivers* (PMD) are included which contains features to increase packet rates.

> The VMXNET3 PMD handles all the packet buffer memory allocation
> and resides in guest address space and it is solely responsible to free
> that memory when not needed. The packet buffers and features to be
> supported are made available to hypervisor via VMXNET3 PCI
> configuration space *Base Address Registers* (BARs). During RX/TX, the
> packet buffers are exchanged by their *Guest Physical Address* (GPA),
> and the hypervisor loads the buffers with packets in the RX case and
> sends packets to vSwitch in the TX case.
> Source: http://dpdk.org/doc/guides/nics/vmxnet3.html

When investigating a VM running a DPDK enabled application, we see
that the DPDK enabled application is allowed to **directly** interact with the
virtual network adapter.

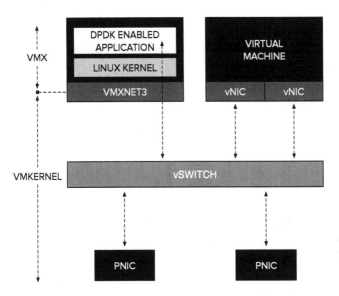

Figure 279: Intel DPDK Paravirtual Device Connectivity

Since Intel DPDK release 1.6, vSphere's paravirtual network adapter
VMXNET3 is supported. The emulated E1000 and E1000E virtual network
adapters are already supported since DPDK version 1.3, however are not
recommended. Using the DPDK enabled paravirtual network adapter will
still allow you to fully use all vSphere features like High Availability,
Distributed Resource Scheduling, Fault Tolerance and snapshots.

Ring Buffers

When the ESXi host receives a burst of incoming packets, the ring buffers come into play. This is especially the case when there is a slight delay in processing the packets because of the hardware interrupt handler that schedules the packet its software interrupts, also known as a soft *Interrupt Request* (IRQ).

The ring buffer sizes depend on what pNIC vendor and model is used. By increasing the Rx and/or Tx ring buffers size, you will decrease the chance of experiencing dropped packets during packet rate spikes. The current Rx buffer parameters for the pNIC can be obtained using the following esxcli command: `esxcli network nic ring current get -n vmnic0`.

```
[root@esxi00:~] esxcli network nic ring current get -n vmnic0
    RX: 344
    RX Mini: 0
    RX Jumbo: 0
    TX: 1024
```

Figure 280: Esxcli Output NIC Ring Buffer Settings

It is possible to adjust the current RX/TX ring buffer parameters of a pNIC using the same esxcli namespace. The following example changes the values for the Rx and Tx ring buffers. Obviously, the Rx Mini and Rx Jumbo parameters can also be re-configured.

```
esxcli network nic ring current set –n vmnic0 –r <value> -t <value>
```

The settings above apply to the pNIC. Equally, or even more, important are the ring buffer values in the guest OS.
A pre-requisite of tuning the in-guest buffer values is the usage of the VMXNET3 virtual network adapter. Looking at the Windows OS, the values are not present by default but are changeable using the pre-defined values.

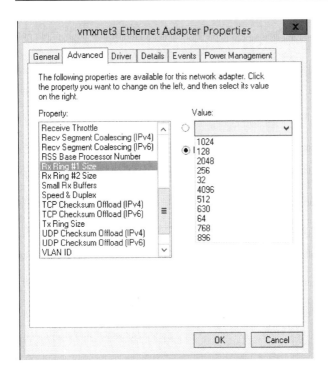

Figure 281: Windows VMXNET3 Ring Buffer Parameters

Within a Linux distribution, the current Rx and Tx can be viewed using this command where 'X' represents the NIC number: `ethtool -g ethX`.

Changing the current ring buffer values can be done using the following command: `ethtool -G eth1 rx <value> tx <value>`
So, now we know how to change the ring buffer values. But how do we determine what to configure?

That is the hard part. As always, it depends on the configuration of your ESXi host and the performance characteristics of the workload running in your VM. Luckily there is a way to verify if your VM is running out of ring buffers. That would provide insights on how to adjust the ring buffers within the guest OS and on your pNIC. First or all, we need to check which vNIC to focus on. In this specific case, the pktgen test VM that is receiving is used.

```
PORT-ID  UP  SPEED  FDUPLX  USED-BY                       TEAM-PNIC  DNAME
67108868  Y  10000     Y    vmnic1                             -     DvsPortset-0
67108866  Y  10000     Y    vmnic0                             -     DvsPortset-0
67108872  -     -      -   69432:DPDK-PKTGEN02.eth0         vmnic0   DvsPortset-0
67108871  -     -      -   69432:DPDK-PKTGEN02.eth2         vmnic1   DvsPortset-0
67108870  -     -      -   69432:DPDK-PKTGEN02.eth3         vmnic1   DvsPortset-0
```

Figure 282: Esxtop Network Port-IDs

Esxtop in the network view can be used to retrieve the Port-ID used by the vNIC that is the candidate for analysis. We will look into the Rx behavior of eth0 or vNIC0. Using the VSI shell, we can verify that the vNIC in question is indeed leveraging the VMXNET3 virtual network adapter. The following command shows the details of the Port-ID as retrieved using esxtop.

```
cd /net/portsets/DvsPortset-0/ports/67108872
cat status
```

```
/> cd /net/portsets/DvsPortset-0/ports/67108872
/net/portsets/DvsPortset-0/ports/67108872/> cat status
port {
   port index:8
   portCfg:
   dvPortId:7
   clientName:DPDK-PKTGEN02.eth0
   clientType:port types: 5 -> VMM Virtual NIC
   clientSubType:port types: 9 -> Vmxnet3 Client
   world leader:69432
   flags:port flags: 0x401d3 -> IN_USE ENABLED WORLD_AS
   Impl customized blocked flags:0x00000000
   Passthru status:: 0x20 -> DISABLED_BY_PG
   fixed Hw Id:00:50:56:b2:e4:a7:
   ethFRP:frame routing {
      requested:filter {
         flags:0x00000019
         unicastAddr:00:50:56:b2:e4:a7:
         numMulticastAddresses:0
         multicastAddresses:
         LADRF:[0]: 0x0
         [1]: 0x0
      }
      accepted:filter {
         flags:0x00000009
         unicastAddr:00:50:56:b2:e4:a7:
         numMulticastAddresses:0
         multicastAddresses:
         LADRF:[0]: 0x0
         [1]: 0x0
      }
   }
   filter supported features:features: 0 -> NONE
   filter properties:properties: 0 -> NONE
   rx mode:properties: 0 -> INLINE
   tune mode:Tuning mode: 0 -> default
}
```

Figure 283: VSI Shell Port-ID Details

In the previous screenshot, we see that we are looking at the correct vNIC as stated in the *'clientName'* value and that the *'clientSubType'* is using the VMXNET3 client as expected.

Looking at the statistics for this specific vNIC, we see Rx behavior that was not shown in esxtop. It can be disturbing thinking your network is not experiencing dropped packets where this might be the case when investigating on a deeper level.

> **If you are investigating the possibility of your VM experiencing dropped Rx or Tx packets, always look at the values in the VSI shell. The dropped packets in esxtop showed a %DRPTX and %DRPRX value of zero during tests where the VSI shell information stated otherwise. As always, a word of caution is in order when working with the VSI shell.**

The following command is used to extract the correct values for this vNIC and its associated Port-ID: `cd /net/portsets/DvsPortset-0/ports/67108872`
`cat stats`

```
/net/portsets/DvsPortset-0/ports/67108872/> cat stats
packet stats {
   pktsTx:248
   pktsTxMulticast:8
   pktsTxBroadcast:223
   pktsRx:10994483036
   pktsRxMulticast:2
   pktsRxBroadcast:847
   droppedTx:0
   droppedRx:82035
}
```

Figure 284: VSI Shell Port-ID Statistics

The output clearly shows a large sum of dropped Rx packets. Remember this vNIC is part of the receiving end of a pktgen VM. We can now examine the possible reason why we are experiencing dropped Rx packets. A good reason for this could be that the burst of incoming network packets ran out of ring buffers.

Let's first focus on the more detailed Rx information provided in the VSI shell. Because we verified earlier on that this vNIC is in fact using the VMXNET3 client, we should enter that level in the VSI shell. It is in that directory we can see the rxSummary information.

```
/net/portsets/DvsPortset-0/ports/67108872/vmxnet3/> cat rxSummary
stats of a vmxnet3 vNIC rx queue {
   LRO pkts rx ok:0
   LRO bytes rx ok:0
   pkts rx ok:1822821899
   bytes rx ok:109369313940
   unicast pkts rx ok:1822821834
   unicast bytes rx ok:109369310040
   multicast pkts rx ok:0
   multicast bytes rx ok:0
   broadcast pkts rx ok:65
   broadcast bytes rx ok:3900
   running out of buffers:44549
   pkts receive error:0
   1st ring size:512
   2nd ring size:512
   # of times the 1st ring is full:775
   # of times the 2nd ring is full:0
   fail to map a rx buffer:0
   request to page in a buffer:0
   # of times rx queue is stopped:0
   failed when copying into the guest buffer:0
   # of pkts dropped due to large hdrs:0
   # of pkts dropped due to max number of SG limits:0
   pkts rx via data ring ok:0
   bytes rx via data ring ok:0
   Whether rx burst queuing is enabled:0
   current backend burst queue length:0
   maximum backend burst queue length so far:0
   aggregate number of times packets are requeued:0
   aggregate number of times packets are dropped by PktAgingList:0
```

Figure 285: VSI Shell Port-ID VMXNET3 Rx Summary

A lot of information is presented in the output. The size of the 1st and 2nd ring buffer is good information, but the most critical information we want to focus on is the number of times both ring buffers are full. As exposed in the screenshot, the number of times the 1st ring is full has a value of 775! This is a clear indication that the ring buffer size should be increased. In line with the endless stream of information the VSI shell provides, we can even dig a little deeper. All Rx queues for this vNIC are presented in this directory.

The following command allows us to see inside the Rx queue and extract queue specific Rx information. cd /net/portsets/DvsPortset-0/ports/67108872/vmxnet3/0/cat stats

```
/net/portsets/DvsPortset-0/ports/67108872/vmxnet3/rxqueues/0/> cat stats
stats of a vmxnet3 vNIC rx queue {
   LRO pkts rx ok:0
   LRO bytes rx ok:0
   pkts rx ok:2724140898
   bytes rx ok:163448453880
   unicast pkts rx ok:2724140823
   unicast bytes rx ok:163448449380
   multicast pkts rx ok:0
   multicast bytes rx ok:0
   broadcast pkts rx ok:75
   broadcast bytes rx ok:4500
   running out of buffers:67013
   pkts receive error:0
   1st ring size:512
   2nd ring size:512
   # of times the 1st ring is full:1196
   # of times the 2nd ring is full:0
   fail to map a rx buffer:0
   request to page in a buffer:0
   # of times rx queue is stopped:0
   failed when copying into the guest buffer:0
   # of pkts dropped due to large hdrs:0
   # of pkts dropped due to max number of SG limits:0
   pkts rx via data ring ok:0
   bytes rx via data ring ok:0
   Whether rx burst queuing is enabled:0
   current backend burst queue length:0
   maximum backend burst queue length so far:0
   aggregate number of times packets are requeued:0
   aggregate number of times packets are dropped by PktAgingList:0
```

Figure 286: VSI Shell Port-ID VMXNET3 Rx Queue Information

In this case, we are looking at queue number zero. The cat stats command gives similar output with regards to the Rx summary information. We are again presented with numbers indicating the incoming packets are running out of buffer space. The 1st ring buffer is once more the limiting factor.

The directory /net/portsets/DvsPortset-0/ports/67108872/vmxnet3/ only contains one directory, that would indicate that only one Rx queue is active for this vNIC. Note that multiple Rx queues, or Netpoll threads, that are spun up by either NetQueue or RSS, are presented at the pNIC level.

A solution for the buffers being flooded can be solved by increasing the ring buffer values for the pNIC as well as in the guest OS running in your VM. Remember there is not one correct setting to use for your ring buffer configuration. It requires adjustment and testing to make sure your buffer sizes can handle the incoming packet streams. Be sure that, at all times, the correct driver for your pNIC is used as prescribed by its vendor.

Tx Buffers

In collaboration with the Tx threads living at the vNICs, a software Tx queue of packets queued for transmission exists in the VMkernel ESXi pNIC layer. This queue is depending on the Tx buffers for that specific vmnic. Next to this software queue, there also is the pNIC driver Tx queue to take into account.

The Tx worldlet is visible under the pNIC if you look at the `net-stats -A -t vW` output.

```
{"name": "vmnic1", "switch": "DvsPortset-0", "id": 67108868, "mac
   "txpps": 0, "txmbps": 0.0, "txsize": 0, "txeps": 0.00, "rxpps":
   "vmnic": {"devname": "vmnic1.ixgbe",
     "txpps": 0, "txmbps": 0.0, "txsize": 0, "txeps": 0.00, "rxpps
   "sys": [ "66076", "66243", "66244", "66245", "66246", "66247",
```

Figure 287: Net-stats Output pNIC Sys Worlds

If we look at the '*sys*' values and retrieve their name using the VSI shell, we can spot the '*vmnic1-0-tx*' worldlet proving this queue resides in the pNIC uplink layer.

It could be that if a workload is network I/O intensive with large bursts of transmit packets. A queue overflow would happen that leads to packets being dropped in the uplink layer. It is possible to configure the maximum length of the Tx queue for the pNIC software queue by reconfiguring the /Net/MaxNetifTxQueueLen advanced system setting. Remember this is a host setting. It applies for all workloads running on the ESXi host.

It can be increased up to 10,000 packets using the following command.

```
esxcli system settings advanced set -i 10000 -o
/Net/MaxNetifTxQueueLen
```

As with the Rx ring buffer parameters, the Tx buffers within the pNIC driver can also be retrieved using the following esxcli command:

```
esxcli network nic ring current get -n vmnic0
```

```
[root@esxi00:~] esxcli network nic ring current get -n vmnic0
  RX: 344
  RX Mini: 0
  RX Jumbo: 0
  TX: 1024
```

Figure 288: Esxcli Output NIC Tx Buffer Settings

The default Tx buffer size depends on the used pNIC. As seen in the screenshot above, this pNIC by default maintains a current Rx buffer size of 1024 packets. Like the software Tx queue, the pNIC driver transmit ring can also be the constraining factor under high transmit loads. You can adjust the Tx buffer ring size to your liking: `esxcli network nic ring current set -n vmnic0 –t <value>`

Using this esxcli command it is possible to increase the Tx buffer ring size to a maximum of 4096.

SplitRx Mode

SplitRx Mode is a technology that allows a VM to use multiple CPU cores to process incoming network packets that are handled by a single queue. The ability to leverage multiple CPU cores allows the VM to consume more CPU time and, by that, significantly improve incoming network performance. However, the improvement SplitRx Mode potentially brings only applies to specific workloads. It is primarily used in scenarios that involve multicast network traffic, like the example of multiple VMs that are running on the same ESXi host and all are receiving multicast traffic from the same source.

SplitRx Mode was introduced in ESXi 5.0 and enabled by default for the required VMXNET3 virtual network adapter since ESXi 5.1. It will kick in automatically when ESXi detects that a single network queue on a pNIC is excessively utilized and is handling more than 10,000 broadcast or multicast *Packets Per Second* (PPS).

You have the freedom of choice to disable SplitRx Mode for an entire ESXi host. You can do so by configuring the following advanced setting on the ESXi host level; `NetSplitRxMode = "0"`

If a workload could benefit from SplitRx Mode, it is possible to enable it for specific vNICs within a VM even though the ESXi host setting to use SplitRx Mode is disabled. All you need to do is add an advanced setting within the VM configuration that will enable SplitRx Mode for a specific vNIC: `ethernetX.emuRxMode = "1"`

The 'x' represents the virtual network adapter. Keep in mind that this setting will not take effect before you restart the VM or re-connect the vNIC.

NUMA Aware I/O

When running modern high bandwidth capable pNICs (25/40/50 or 100GbE) in a ESXi host, you want to be able to achieve the highest performance capable. An interesting part of this is being able to place your workload on the same NUMA node, which is also controlling the PCIe pNIC. That could lead to a significant increase of performance, up to 20% higher throughput. It also could lead to decreased CPU overhead because of CPU scheduler efficiency. The actual gains may vary depending on the pNIC used.

Since ESXi 6.0, it is possible to set an ESXi host advanced setting that makes ESXi strive to schedule all VMkernel networking threads on the same NUMA node that controls the PCIe pNIC. The next step is the CPU scheduler that tries to schedule the network I/O intensive VMs on the same host on the same NUMA node.

The setting is disabled by default because it can compromise the way the workloads are distributed across the ESXi host NUMA nodes. If you want to enable the option, set the host advanced setting `Net.NetNetqNumaIOCpuPinThreshold` to a value between 0 and 200. The configurable value represents a percentage.

If you set the value to 50, NUMA I/O will be applied up to the point where the network load trespasses 50%. When it does, the VMkernel will conduct default scheduling where VMs and Rx/Tx network threads are scheduled across other NUMA nodes.

Impact of Port Mirroring

Proper network monitoring and troubleshooting tools are essential in every IT environment, but even more so for NFV, telecom and real-time workloads. It allows the network administrators to gain overall insights on how the (virtual) network is behaving from a performance perspective or for profound troubleshooting. For advanced tracing tooling or packet analysers and security tools like intrusion detection solutions, it could be a requirement to configure a port mirroring session. It is possible to configure a port mirroring session on your distributed vSwitch.

For those not familiar with port mirroring, it is the capability on a (virtual) network switch to send exact copies of network packets as seen on a switch port to another switch port. This is also referred to as a *Switch Port Analyzer* (SPAN). That allows the tooling to analyse the traffic flows passing the original switch port. When looking at the virtual switch ports on the distributed vSwitch, network administrators are even able to capture packets between two VMs running on the same ESXi host by configuring a port mirroring session on the distributed vSwitch.

It is all a good game from an operations point-of-view. However, when you are running high packet rate workloads, the use of port mirroring can seriously impact your packet rate. Such applications, like telco payload applications, are interfered by the port mirroring mechanism. This is all due to the CPU time that is necessary to process the network packets and, when port mirroring sessions are active, the VMkernel is processing twice as much packets instead of only the primary packet stream.

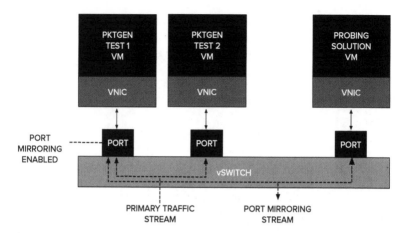

Figure 289: Port Mirroring Flows within One ESXi Host

So, we are fine-tuning our virtual datacenter to accommodate network sensitive workloads. We are looking for ways to increase network performance. With port mirroring, however, we risk that these settings are nullified.

Typical IT workloads won't be bothered by the additional packet processing pressure that port mirroring introduces, but the same cannot be said about NFV or other network performance sensitive workloads. A word of caution is applicable when combining such workloads with port mirroring.

20

VIRTUAL MACHINE NETWORK

The VM can be provided with different types of network connectivity. The basic functionality is not that different from physical networks. The VMs are connected to virtual switches, either a Standard vSwitch or a Distributed vSwitch, using virtual wires from the virtual network adapters that are configured in the VMs. In this chapter, we will explore the various aspects of VM network components.

Virtual Network Adapters

The vNIC is a virtual network adapter. Depending on the OS of choice, a default virtual network adapter is chosen. For example, when a Windows 2016 server is configured, the virtual network adapter type E1000E is used by default. Of course, you have the freedom of choice to configure the VM to use another supported network adapter. The following virtual network adapters are available in ESXi 6.5:

- E1000
- E1000E
- Flexible
- Vlance
- VMXNET
- VMXNET2 (Enhanced)
- VMXNET3
- SR-IOV pass-through
- PVRDMA

The types of network adapters that are available when deploying or re-configuring a VM depend strongly on the configured guest OS version within the VM and whether it is a 32 or 64-bit OS. The main difference between the various virtual network adapter types is whether it is an emulated or a paravirtual network adapter. Zooming in on the most common virtual network adapters, the E1000E and the VMXNET3 adapter, there are some interesting differences in their appearance in the guest OS and behaviour with respect to network performance.

An emulated adapter has the ability to mimic a hardware device while it assumes that it can make autonomous decisions regarding the control of the hardware. Examples of emulated virtual network adapters are the E1000 and the E1000E virtual devices. An E1000 adapter emulates an Intel 82545EM Gigabit Ethernet NIC. The E1000E adapter is the emulated version of the Intel 82574 Gigabit Ethernet NIC. That means that these emulated network adapters will present themselves to the guest OS as their emulated counterparts. Drivers for the emulated network adapters are available by default in most modern operating systems. Remember that an improved network driver for the E1000E network adapter is provided in hardware version 8, which was introduced with ESXi 5.0.

Paravirtual network adapters are more self-aware. It presents a software interface to VMs that is correlative, but not fully identical to that of the hardware fundament. The drivers for the paravirtual network adapters are written to run in a hypervisor and are not aware that it is fully autonomous. That means they have no hardware counterpart. The VMXNET, VMXNET2 (Enhanced) and VMXNET3 adapters are examples of paravirtual network adapters. The VMXNET and VMXNET2 virtual network adapters have been available since ESX/ESXi 3.5. VMXNET2, also known as VMXNET Enhanced, already provided high networking performance like support for jumbo frames and several hardware offload mechanisms. VMs running in ESXi 6.5 can contain up to 10 vNICs.

To configure a VM with a VMXNET3 virtual network adapter requires additional drivers to be installed within the guest OS because the OS vendors does not provide built-in drivers for it. The correct drivers are included in the VMware tools.

The 3rd generation of the VMXNET paravirtual network adapters is not related to the 'legacy' paravirtual network adapters VMXNET or VMXNET2. All the features that a VMXNET2 adapter supports, are included in a VMXNET3 adapter, next to new qualities like backing for IPv6 offload and multi queue support like RSS. Advanced network performance tuning mechanisms, like interrupt coalescing, LRO and the ability for a VM to have multiple vNIC Tx threads are also supported by the VMXNET3 virtual network adapter.

VMXNET3 has been available since VM virtual hardware version 7 that was introduced in ESX/ESXi 4.0. More information about the various para network adapters and their performance differences are included in the following VMware paper:
http://www.vmware.com/pdf/vsp_4_vmxnet3_perf.pdf. Although slightly out-dated, the information is still valid as it shows the performance gains over the VMXNET generations.

To give you an example of how the E1000E is presented in a Windows OS, we created a test VM with an E1000E vNIC. We can clearly see that it emulates an Intel 82575L Gigabit adapter as stated before.

Figure 290: E1000E Network Adapter in Windows

The fact that is presented as a Gigabit network adapter is interesting. We verified that the Windows OS actually sees it that way as shown in the following screenshot.

test E1000E Status

General

Connection

IPv4 Connectivity:	No Internet access
IPv6 Connectivity:	No Internet access
Media State:	Enabled
Duration:	00:13:38
Speed:	1.0 Gbps

Figure 291: E1000E Presented as a 1GbE Adapter

Does that mean that it can only handle up to 1GbE of network bandwidth? It does not. The fact that it is an emulated Intel 82575L Gigabit adapter says nothing about the possible throughput of the virtual network adapter, as we will show in upcoming network bandwidth test results.

The VMXNET3 virtual network adapter is depending on the driver that is packaged with the VMware tools and will present itself as a VMXNET3 Ethernet Adapter in the test VM.

test VMXNET3
Network
vmxnet3 Ethernet Adapter

Figure 292: VMXNET3 Network Adapter in Windows

In contrast to the E1000E adapter, the VMXNET3 adapter is seen as a 10GbE capable network adapter.

test VMXNET3 Status

General

Connection

IPv4 Connectivity:	Internet
IPv6 Connectivity:	No Internet access
Media State:	Enabled
Duration:	00:05:02
Speed:	10.0 Gbps

Figure 293: VMXNET3 Presented as a 10GbE Adapter

So, the newest versions of both the emulated and the paravirtual network adapters are different in how they are exposed in the guest OS. But what are the differences in base performance?

E1000E versus VMXNET3

To test the difference in performance between the E1000E and VMXNET3 virtual network adapters, we set up a test environment consisting of an Iperf server (receiver) and Iperf client (sender) both running on a default Windows 2012 R2 VM with 4 vCPUs entitled to it. Both VMs are running on the same ESXi host, so no pNICs are present in the network data path in this test. Iperf3 is set to run for 30 seconds in a single stream with default settings using a read or write TCP buffer length of 128 KB. Looking at the first test, using the E1000E adapter, we see the following results:

Figure 294: E1000E Adapter Iperf Test Results

The same test was run with the VMs both configured to run the VMXNET3 virtual network adapter.

```
[ ID] Interval          Transfer    Bandwidth
[  4]  0.00-30.00  sec  25.4 GBytes  7.28 Gbits/sec                sender
[  4]  0.00-30.00  sec  25.4 GBytes  7.28 Gbits/sec                receiver
iperf Done.
```

Figure 295: VMXNET3 Adapter Iperf Test Results

Interesting to see is that the bandwidth throughput test results are in favour of the E1000E adapter. That was not entirely anticipated, as the older E1000 was known to have a significant performance gap when compared to the paravirtual adapter family.

Perhaps even more interesting to see was the CPU utilization within the guest OS. This is where an important difference in both network adapters was revealed. The average guest OS CPU utilization for both the sender and receiver VM was captured.

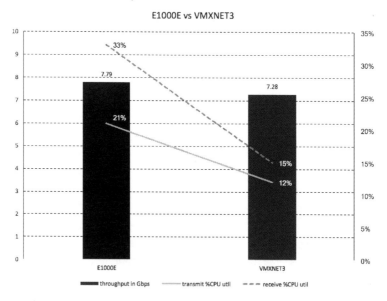

Figure 296: Iperf Test Results Combined Including CPU Utilization

Looking at this graph, you will notice that the guest OS CPU utilization within the server and client VM were considerably lower when using the paravirtual VMXNET3 adapter instead of using the emulated E1000E network adapter. That is an important difference. You will save a lot of guest OS CPU time when running a paravirtual network adapter if you are dealing with heavy network I/O pressure workloads.

It is because of the flexibility and freedom of choice that makes the VMXNET3 the highly recommended option for your VMs and templates. Think about all the configurable options and features, as mentioned in this chapter, that are not available on other types of network adapters but the VMXNET3 adapter. The VMXNET3 allows you to optimally tune your VM, the application for maximum network performance and the lowest latency possible along with the least possible CPU overhead. We encourage you to use the VMXNET3 virtual network adapter unless there is a clear reason why not to use it.

DirectPath I/O for Networking

Since ESX 4.0 the vSphere DirectPath I/O technology is supported. It is a hardware-assisted feature that requires *Intel Virtualization Technology for Directed I/O* (VT-d) when using an Intel CPU. Intel is supporting VT-d since the Nehalem CPU family.

Looking at the network stack, DirectPath I/O allows the VM to directly access the pNIC instead of using a virtual network device like using an emulated or paravirtual network adapter. Although the latter can sustain high network throughput, DirectPath I/O allows for even more CPU cycle savings in comparison to the use of paravirtual network adapters. That is because it bypasses the execution layer within the VMkernel. As DirectPath I/O pins a VM vNIC to a pNIC, you will get a guaranteed bandwidth for your workload. It is almost the only way to really enforce this type of guarantee, to have absolutely no over-commitment on your pNIC. The question is whether your workloads will ever demand this? With the innovation on high bandwidth speed networks, like 40 or 100 GbE, it is less likely that one VM will need exclusive access to a pNIC for guaranteed bandwidth. The CPU savings, and possible lower latency, could be a reason to configure a 'direct access to a pNIC' solution.

Having said that, DirectPath I/O comes with a lot of drawbacks. A lot of vSphere features like pNIC sharing, snapshots, vMotion, Fault Tolerance, *Network I/O Control* (NIOC) and memory overcommit are not compatible with DirectPath I/O.

That narrows down situations of when a virtual workload could benefit from using DirectPath I/O. As stated before, it enforces a one-to-one ratio with regards to pNIC, meaning one VM will claim an entire pNIC. Typically, DirectPath I/O is used for virtualized workloads with extraordinary high network packet rate characteristics, where the CPU overhead savings outweigh the incompatibility of the listed vSphere features while one pNIC is sacrificed because it cannot be used by another workload.

Single Root I/O Virtualization

Single Root I/O Virtualization (SR-IOV) and DirectPath I/O share the same basic functionality. They both bypass the VMkernel layer and provide direct access from the VM to the pNIC that could lead to a higher network performance, lower CPU utilization and lower latency because the hypervisor doesn't need to process the packets in the VMkernel layer. In other words, network packet processing does not rely on the network stack in the VMkernel layer. The main reason to choose SR-IOV over DirectPath I/O is the ability to share a pNIC over multiple VMs, making it the more obvious choice for pass-through pNIC access.

The functionality of SR-IOV was born out of the challenge to handle large sums of interrupts when dealing with high packet rate data plane traffic workloads. SR-IOV was released in 2007; with Intel being one of the main contributors in the PCI-SIG. SR-IOV is supported in ESXi since ESXi 5.1.

SR-IOV is a PCIe technology that divides a single PCIe hardware interface, or *Physical Function* (PF), in multiple virtual functions, also referred to as virtual ports. You could deem the PF as being your pNIC interface or port. The PF contains transmit and receive descriptors that tell the pNIC where to send data to and from.

The *Virtual Functions* (VF) have lightweight PCIe resources like registers and *Base Address Registers* (BAR) to inform the device of its address mapping and such. The VF only contains the absolute minimum to process data.

If we take a look at the SR-IOV data path for incoming packets, we see that it first comes across the pNIC that support the SR-IOV feature. An incoming packet will be placed in the pNIC its layer-2 sorter. Based on MAC address or VLAN id the packet is put into a specific queue, also referred to as pool. The SR-IOV driver will fill up the descriptors and begins to address the SR-IOV device. Next, the packet will be DMA-ed using the descriptor filled out by the SR-IOV driver. The VM is not aware where it resides in the physical memory. The location is, in fact, a virtual address filled out by the descriptor. So, the DMA process hits the pNIC chipset where Intel VT-d will need to remap the virtual DMA address to the actual address. Because of the VT-d re-mapper function the packet will find its way to and from the VM.

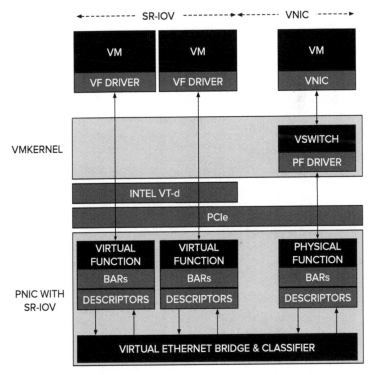

Figure 297: SR-IOV Constructs Overview

Important to know is that each VF will have a dedicated queue for resources. Each VM that uses a VF is assigned to a dedicated resource.

The VM will load the SR-IOV driver for the VF and ESXi will tell it what PF it maps to. To use SR-IOV for your VMs, you need hardware support. Intel VT-d and a pNIC that supports SR-IOV are both required.

Depending of the pNIC of choice and system configuration, a maximum number of VFs is supported. That number can vary between pNIC vendor and model. Also, the pNIC layout can be of influence if you adopted a multi-vendor pNIC layout. For instance, an Intel X710 10GbE adapter supports up to 128 VFs per device and an Intel X540 supports 63 per device. Be aware that if you use converged network adapters, FCoE and SR-IOV cannot be configured simultaneously on the same port.

Regardless of the number of VFs supported, you are always constrained by the bandwidth of the pNIC interface(s). You can still over-scribe the utilization of the pNIC. A common misconception is that if you use SR-IOV, you can have dedicated bandwidth entitled to your VM. That is certainly not the case. In most situations where SR-IOV is a good fit, like telco applications, oversubscription of resources is not advisable. Be sure you monitor for pNIC interface bandwidth and application latency to verify that some level of fairness is applied when it comes to bandwidth or packet rates per virtual function.

Using SR-IOV does, like DirectPath I/O, come with a lot of restrictions. The following vSphere features are not supported:

- vSphere vMotion
- Storage vMotion
- NetFlow
- VXLAN Virtual Wire
- vSphere High Availability
- vSphere Fault Tolerance
- vSphere DRS
- vSphere DPM
- VM Suspend and Resume
- VM snapshots
- MAC-based VLAN for pass-through virtual functions
- Hot addition and removal of virtual devices, memory, and vCPU

Looking at this long list, the adoption of SR-IOV for your workloads can be a big trade-off fest. Especially the disability to use vSphere HA can be of great impact on your availability strategy. Applications running on a SR-IOV enabled VM should incorporate resiliency on the application layer when you need to adhere to a SLA. In a lot of cases where you think you need SR-IOV, you could research how to tune your environment for higher network performance and lower latency, based on using the VMXNET3 adapter, together with the tuning considerations we discussed earlier in this book.

But, the cost of business can be that the use of SR-IOV is inevitable. Your workloads simply require the lowest possible latency, CPU overhead and need to have direct access to the hardware devices. To configure a VM to use SR-IOV, you first need to enable SR-IOV on the pNIC, also referred to as a vmnic, and configure the number of virtual functions on it.

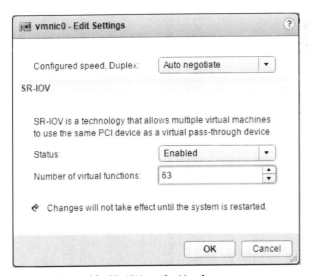

Figure 298: Enable SR-IOV on the Vmnic

As previously explained, the maximum number of VFs depends on the pNIC layout and support. The Intel X540 used for the screenshot above supports up to 63 VFs per device. After enabling SR-IOV with the number of VFs required and supported, a reboot of the host is required to apply the changes.

After the reboot, your VM can be equipped with a virtual network adapter of type 'SR-IOV pass-through'. Edit the VM settings and choose the PF and VF. Connect it to a port group and you are done.

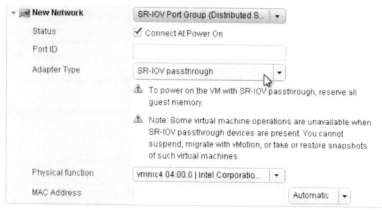

Figure 299: Configure a VM with a SR-IOV Network Adapter

Beware, the VM now requires a 100% memory reservation because of the guarantee that the pass-through device can access all of the VM its memory. The following screenshot will show that the VM is mapped to a VF running on the chosen PF.

- SR-IOV network adapter 1
Adapter Type	SR-IOV passthrough
MAC Address	00:50:56:b2:48:fe
DirectPath I/O	Not supported ⓘ
Network	SR-IOV-portgroup (connected)
Allow Guest MTU Change	Disallow
Physical Function	vmnic0 0000:01:00.0	Intel Corporation Ethernet Controller 10 Gigabit X540-AT2
Virtual Function	0000:01:10.0	Intel Corporation X540 Ethernet Controller Virtual Function

Figure 300: Verify the SR-IOV Adapter Settings

The SR-IOV pass-through network adapter will present itself in the guest OS as a *'pciPassthru'* device.

pciPassthru15
Unidentified network
Intel(R) X540 Virtual Function

Figure 301: SR-IOV Network Adapter in Windows

E1000E versus VMXNET3 versus SR-IOV

Once properly configured, we can take a look on how things are performing. SR-IOV seems to be the de facto default when it comes to high packet rate or low latency NFV workloads. But is it outperforming a network stack, using the VMkernel layer and a paravirtual network adapter by a significant difference that makes you accept the constraints and limitations introduced by SR-IOV?

The following bandwidth tests are performed on two Windows 2012 R2 VMs running Iperf3. The VMs are equipped with 4 vCPUs, 8 GB memory and one vNIC connected to an Intel X540 pNIC. Each VM is running on a separate ESXi host, running vSphere 6.5 and are connected via a 10GbE network. The entire test environment is not running any additional workloads. The ESXi and guest OS are running with default settings. We want to stress that the test results may vary when tested on other infrastructure components and their configuration, but it will provide some insights on how the various virtual network adapters compare when tested under the same conditions. The captured values are measured in the guest OS.

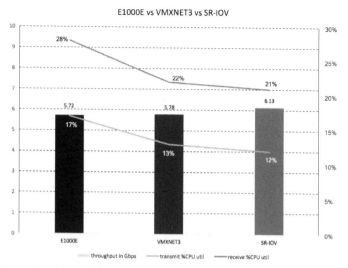

Figure 302: Virtual Network Adapter Test Results

When examining the test data, we quickly see that our expectations match the results. The bandwidth utilization is highest when running on a SR-IOV adapter. The CPU utilization is lowest using SR-IOV. What is interesting to see is the fractional difference between the paravirtual VMXNET3 adapter and the SR-IOV adapter.

Another thing that was noticeable during the test with a SR-IOV adapter, the vmx GID does not show a *NetWorld-VM* worldlet. That makes perfect sense because the VMkernel is not involved in the network data path when a pass-through device is used.

```
6:04:57pm up 1 day 20:12, 530 worlds, 1 VMs, 4 vCPUs: CPU load average: 0.10, 0.09, 0.03
PCPU USED(%): 2.3 2.9  18 1.2 0.3  1S  11 0.2 0.7 9.3 0.1 0.1 AVG: 5.2
PCPU UTIL(%): 2.7 3.1  21 1.8 0.4  14  11 0.3 0.8 9.2 0.1 0.1 AVG: 5.5
CORE UTIL(%): 5.7       22     15      11   9.9    0.2       AVG: 10

     ID      GID NAME              NWLD    %USED   %RUN    %SYS   %WAIT %VMWAIT   %RDY
  68973   18676 vmx                  1     0.01    0.01    0.00  100.00      -    0.00
  68976   18676 vmast.68974          1     0.00    0.00    0.00  100.00      -    0.00
  68980   18676 vmx-vthread-8        1     0.00    0.00    0.00  100.00      -    0.00
  68981   18676 vmx-mks:NGN2         1     1.03    1.14    0.00   99.10      -    0.00
  68982   18676 vmx-svga:NGN2        1     0.43    0.49    0.00   99.74      -    0.03
  68984   18676 vmx-vcpu-0:NGN2      1    17.24   18.35    0.00   81.89    0.00   0.01
  68986   18676 vmx-vcpu-1:NGN2      1    11.97   11.27    0.00   88.96    1.03   0.01
  68987   18676 vmx-vcpu-2:NGN2      1    15.22   14.55    0.00   85.68    0.00   0.01
  68988   18676 vmx-vcpu-3:NGN2      1    10.28   10.03    0.00   90.12    0.00   0.09
  68985   18676 LSI-68974:0          1     0.00    0.00    0.00  100.00      -    0.00
  68989   18676 vmx-vthread-9:NGN2   1     0.00    0.00    0.00  100.00      -    0.00
```

Figure 303: Esxtop Capture while Testing with SR-IOV

Whether to use SR-IOV or use an optimized VMXNET3 network adapter remains the question. Just be sure to test your workload against both options to see the impact on CPU utilization, bandwidth throughput and even extend the tests with packet-rate and latency. Based on that information you can make a well-founded decision whether to go for pass-through or paravirtual.

Virtual RDMA

Nowadays, we are presented with the need for high bandwidth at the lowest possible latency within our network stack for telecom or real-time trading workloads. This demand drives the adoption for solutions to directly access hardware. DirectPath I/O for networking and SR-IOV laid the path for VMs to be able to direct access a hardware device, but came with a lot of limitations. Virtual RDMA is an even more advanced approach to bypass the VMkernel and to directly access the pNIC device while maintaining support for essential vSphere features like vSphere FT and vMotion.

ESXi 6.5 introduces support for paravirtual *Remote Direct Memory Access* (RDMA) *Host Channel Adapters* (HCA) to VMs. This allows for communication between VMs using *Paravirtualized RDMA* (PVRDMA) network adapters. Since ESXi 6.5, this feature is available for VMs using a Linux guest OS (Linux kernel 4.6 and later). It is compliant to the *RDMA over Converged Ethernet* (RoCE) version 1.0.

> **RDMA allows direct memory access from the memory of one computer to the memory of another computer without involving the OS or CPU. The transfer of memory is offloaded to the RDMA-capable *Host Channel Adapters* (HCA). A PVRDMA network adapter provides remote direct memory access in a virtual environment.** Source: https://pubs.vmware.com/vsphere-65

As shown in the following logical overview of RDMA, you will see that the application is able to directly program the network device to perform DMA to and from memory, bypassing the VMkernel. It means that network processing is pushed onto the device that is responsible for performing protocol operations. The result is a significant decrease of CPU time being consumed for packet processing, and essentially lowering latency. That is why RDMA is popular in today's *High Performance Compute* (HPC) platforms.

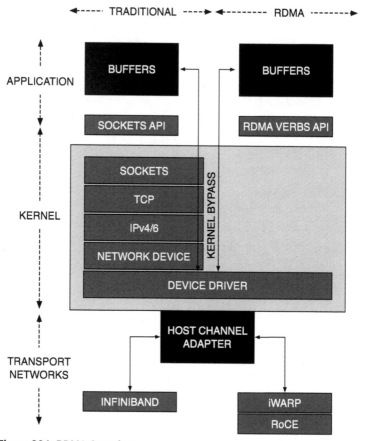

Figure 304: RDMA Overview

The developed paravirtual device driver, also referred to as *Virtual RMDA* (vRDMA), for RMDA capable fabrics is the most performance efficient way for VMs to directly control physical RDMA devices. The current maximum of ESXi 6.5 is one vRDMA adapter per VM. The vRDMA driver allow multiple VMs to access physical RDMA devices using a collection of industry standard interfaces practicing the Verbs API.

For VMs to be eligible to communicate over vRDMA adapters, they are required to run VM hardware level 13 and must be connected to a Distributed vSwitch. Command `esxcli rdma device list` will list the logical devices in your ESXi host eligible for RDMA use. A VMkernel adapter that is used as uplink on the Distributed vSwitch must be tagged to enable it for vRDMA communication. This is done using the host advanced setting `Net.PVRDMAVmknic` and configuring it with the correct adapter, i.e. vmk1. To check which VMkernel adapters are associated with vRDMA, the `rdma device vmknic list` command is used. It is important to understand that vRDMA doesn't support NIC teaming. When configuring the Distributed vSwitch, remember that the HCA should be the only uplink on it.

Once everything is in place, the vRDMA network adapter will automatically pick the correct method of communication between the VMs. If two VMs running on the same ESXi host want to communicate with each other using RDMA, the so-called *memcpy* RDMA function will be used without the interference of physical RDMA devices. If the VMs reside on different ESXi hosts, a HCA is required. The HCA is a pNIC that implements a RDMA engine and must be configured to be the uplink on the Distributed vSwitch.

Once the control path is established, the CPU is almost completely spared from spending CPU time while data is transferred between the VMs using RDMA because the data path will bypass the kernel, so there is no OS involvement.

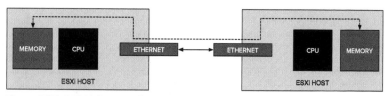

Figure 305: RDMA Data Path

When comparing TCP/IP and RDMA you will notice both transport networks have in common that they both serve a server-client model. Both rely on a connection for resilient transport. The big difference is that TCP/IP relies on an in-order sequence of bytes where RDMA uses an in-order sequence of messages using the Verbs API functions. RDMA further differentiates from TCP/IP by using the *zero-copy* principle. That means that data is transferred directly from virtual memory on one node to virtual memory on another node.

RDMA over Converged Ethernet

Typically, HPC platforms use high performance transport networks like InfiniBand, *Internet Wide Area RDMA Protocol* (iWARP) and RoCE for RDMA communication. For now, ESXi 6.5 supports RoCE version 1 and 2 and its associated I/O ecosystems. The beauty of RoCE is that it leverages Ethernet, making it relatively easy to adopt in datacenters.

The main difference between both RoCE versions is that RoCE version 1 is an Ethernet link protocol. So, it allows for communication between ESXi hosts that are connected to the same Ethernet broadcast domain (VLAN). RoCE version 2 is an internet layer protocol meaning its packets can be routed. A lot more information about RoCE and how it compares to InfiniBand and iWARP is found here:
https://en.wikipedia.org/wiki/RDMA_over_Converged_Ethernet.

21

vSWITCH UPLINKS

As the traffic flows to and from the ESXi hosts, it is transported onwards to other VMs or other physical network endpoints. The vSwitch uplink is a key component of a well functioning network architecture. Typically, you want to accomplish a redundant connection between the ESXi host and the physical network switches. Ideally, the network packets are distributed between the multiple uplinks to be as efficient as possible with the available bandwidth. That will lead to a vSwitch configuration that is using at least two pNIC interfaces to be configured as a team.

There are various vSwitch load balancing algorithms that regulate how traffic is distributed between multiple pNICs:

- Route based on originating virtual port
- Route based on source MAC hash
- Route based on IP hash
- Route based on physical NIC load
- Explicit failover order

We will look a bit further in the most common teaming configurations with a focus on using the Distributed vSwitch. The Distributed vSwitch is often the preferred choice over a Standard vSwitch from a configuration consistency and manageability point of view. VMware recommends it when adopting vSAN in your cluster(s) for those specific reasons. That is why Distributed vSwitch is included in the vSAN licensing meaning you will automatically get it when you embrace vSAN.

Looking at the teaming configurations, a distinction can be made between *Link Aggregation Group* (LAG) and Route based on physical load, also referred to as *Load Based Teaming* (LBT).

Link Aggregation Group

The generic term that is used to refer to any kind of bonding of NIC uplinks is a LAG. Within the options of a LAG, you will find the static EtherChannel and the *Link Aggregation Control Protocol* (LACP).

EtherChannel

An EtherChannel is a Cisco proprietary link aggregation technique. It can group two to eight physical links into one logical link, providing potential increased throughput and fault tolerant links. EtherChannel can provide incremental trunk speeds up to 8 GbE with gigabit adapters and up to 80 GbE using 10GbE adapters and so on.

The aggregation of the multiple interfaces can be done in a static way (mode on) or dynamically manner by using LACP or *Port Aggregation Protocol* (PAgP), which is also a Cisco proprietary solution to achieve the same functionality as LACP.

Link Aggregation Control Protocol

LACP is a standardized (802.3ad) way for automating LAG configurations. Components that are LACP capable will discover each other by sending LACP packets tot the '*slow_protocols_multicast*' address 01-80-c2-00-00-02. A negotiation will take place about how to realize the LAG. Dynamic configuration should be desirable as it avoids configuration issues and mismatching switch settings. LACP is supported since ESXi 5.0 and the enhanced LACP version is available as of ESXi 5.5.

Enhanced LACP support brings some additional features to the table. For instance, multiple LAGs can be created instead of just one LAG as supported in ESXi 5.1. Another enhanced LACP feature is that it supports an extensive set of LACP load balancing types as supposed to ESXi 5.1 that only supports the source/destination IP hash based load balancing option. You have the choice to set up the LACP load balancing by using the source or destination based on IP address, VLAN id, MAC address, TCP/UDP port and Source port ID or a combination. The chosen configuration should resemble the physical switch LACP configuration. A hash is created for LACP to determine what path within the LACP connection to use.

IP-HASH

When adopting EtherChannel, the load-balancing algorithm Route based on IP-hash option comes into play. Let's have a closer look how it works under the hood.

Based on the source and destination IP address, the VMkernel distributes the load across the available NICs in the vSwitch. The calculation of outbound NIC selection is described in *VMware KB article 1007371*. To calculate the IP-hash yourself you can convert both the source and destination IP-addresses to a Hex value and compute the modulo over the number of available uplinks in the team.

VIRTUAL MACHINE	IP ADRESS	HEX VALUE
VM1	164.18.1.84	A4120154
Backup Server	164.18.1.160	A41201A0
Application Server	164.18.1.195	A41201C3

Table 61: VM Hex Values

VM1 opens two connections, one connection to a backup server and one connection server to an application server. The vSwitch is configured with two uplinks.

Connection 1:
VM1 → Backup Server (A4120154 Xor A41201A0 = F4) % 2 = 0

Connection 2:
VM1 → Application Server (A4120154 Xor A41201C3 = 97) % 2 = 1

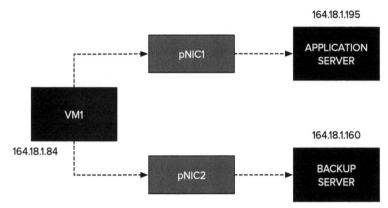

Figure 306: VM1 Connections

IP-hash treats each connection between a source and destination IP address as a unique route and the vSwitch will distribute each connection across the available uplinks in the vSwitch. However due to the pNIC to vNIC affiliation, any connection is on a per flow basis. A flow cannot overflow to another uplink; **this means that a connection is still limited to the speed of a single pNIC**. A real-world user case for IP-hash would be a backup server, which requires a lot of bandwidth across multiple connections.

IP-hash (or LACP for that matter) increases complexity. For IP-hash to function correctly, additional configuration at the physical network layer is required. IP-hash needs to be configured on the vSwitch if EtherChannel technology is used at the physical switch layer. Using EtherChannel, the switch will load balance connections over multiple ports in the EtherChannel. Without IP-hash, the VMkernel only expects to receive information on a specific MAC address on a single vNIC.

This results in some sessions to go through to the VM while other sessions will be dropped. When IP-hash is selected, the VMkernel will accept inbound MAC addresses on both active NICs.

For each connection, the VMkernel selects an appropriate uplink which introduces additional overhead. If a VM is running a front-end application and communicates 95% of its time to the backend database, the IP hash calculation is almost pointless. The VMkernel needs to perform the math for every connection and 95% of the connections will use the same uplink because the algorithm will always result in the same hash.

It is possible that a second VM is assigned to use the same uplink as the VM that is already saturating the link. Let's use the first example and introduce a new VM named VM3. VM3 connects to the backup server.

VIRTUAL MACHINE	IP ADRESS	HEX VALUE
VM3	164.18.1.86	A4120156

Table 62: VM HEX Value

Connection 3: *VM3 → Backup Server (A4120156 Xor A41201A0 = F6) % 2 = 0*

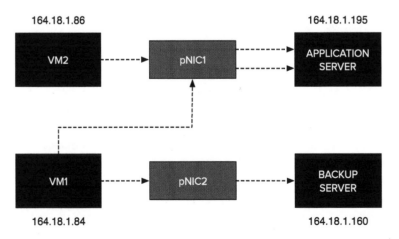

Figure 307: VM Connections

Due to IP-hash load balancing policy being unaware of utilization, it will not rebalance if the uplink is saturated or if VM are added or removed due to power-on or (DRS) migrations. DRS does not initiate a rebalance if a VM cannot send or receive packets due to pNIC saturation. In the worst-case scenario, DRS can migrate VMs to other ESX servers, leaving all the VMs that are saturating a NIC while the other VMs utilizing the other NICs are migrated. Admitted it is a little bit of a stretch, but being aware of this behaviour allows you to see the true beauty of the Load Based Teaming policy.

Due to the pNIC-to-vNIC affiliation per connection a misbehaving VM generating many connections can cause some sort of denial of service on all uplinks on the vSwitch. If this application would connect to a vSwitch with 'Port-ID' or 'based on physical load' only one uplink would be affected.

Beacon probing does not work correctly if EtherChannel is used, you should avoid using it. ESXi broadcasts beacon packets out of all uplinks in a team. The physical switch is expected to forward all packets to other ports. In EtherChannel mode, the physical switch will not send the packets because it is considered as one link. No beacon packets will be received and can interrupt network connections. Cisco switches will report flapping errors.

Load Based Teaming

LBT was introduced with ESX(i) 4.1 and is only available for the Distributed vSwitch. LBT takes the VM network I/O load into account and tries to avoid congestion by dynamically reassigning and balancing the virtual switch port to pNIC mappings.

LBT maps vNICs to pNICs and remaps the vNIC-to-pNIC affiliation if the load exceeds specific thresholds on an uplink. LBT uses the same initial port assignment as the 'originating port id' load balancing policy, resulting in the first vNIC being affiliated to the first pNIC, the second vNIC to the second pNIC, etc.

After initial placement, LBT examines both ingress and egress load of each uplink in the team and will adjust the vNIC to pNIC mapping if an uplink is congested. The NIC team load balancer flags a congestion condition if an uplink experiences a mean utilization of 75% or more over a 30-second period.

LBT requires standard access or trunk ports. It does not support EtherChannels. **The beauty of LBT is that no additional configuration on the physical switch side is required, thus reducing complexity.** Because LBT is moving flows among the available uplinks of the vSwitch, it may create packets re-ordering. The VMkernel will examine the congestion condition after each time window. This calculation creates a minor overhead opposed to using the static load-balancing policy 'originating port-id'.

LBT is utilization aware, vNIC to pNIC mappings will be adjusted if the VMkernel detects congestion on an uplink. In the previous example both VM1 and VM3 shared the same connection due to the IP hash calculation. Both connections can share the same pNIC as long as the utilization stays below the threshold. It is likely that both vNICs are mapped to separate pNICs. In the next example a third VM is powered up and is mapped to pNIC1. Utilization of pNIC1 exceeds the mean utilization of 70% over a period of more than 30 seconds. After identifying congestion LBT remaps VM2 to pNIC2 to decrease the utilization of pNIC1.

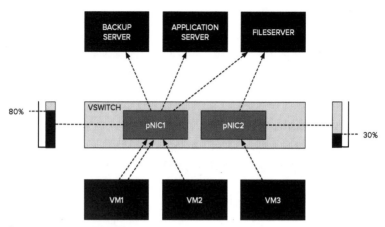

Figure 308: LBT Initial Placement

After identifying congestion, LBT remaps VM2 to pNIC2 to decrease the utilization of pNIC1.

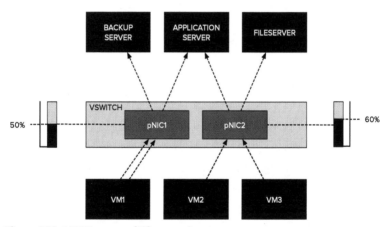

Figure 309: LBT Remapped Placement

Although LBT is not integrated in DRS it can be viewed as complimentary technology next to DRS. When DRS migrates VMs onto a host, it is possible that congestion is introduced on a particular pNIC. Due to vNIC to pNIC mapping based on actual load, LBT actively tries to avoid congestion at pNIC level and attempts to reallocate VMs.

By remapping vNICs to pNICs it will attempt to make as much bandwidth available to the VM, which ultimately benefits the overall performance of the VM.

When using a Distributed vSwitch it is recommended to use LBT instead of IP-hash or LACP. LBT has no additional requirements on the physical network layer, reduces complexity and is able to adjust to fluctuating workloads because it is more tied to the VMkernel. Due to the remapping of vNICs to pNICs based on actual load, LBT attempts to allocate as much bandwidth possible where IP hash or LACP just distributes connections across the available physical NICs.

> **While vSAN does initiate multiple connections, there is no deterministic balancing of traffic. However, additional vSphere traffic types sharing the same team could still leverage the aggregated bandwidth by distributing different types of traffic to different adapters within the team. VMware recommends: Use Load Based Teaming for load balancing.**
> Source: vmware-virtual-san-network-design-guide-white-paper.pdf

22

HOST EVICTION

The main theme of the book is to create an host infrastructure that provides consistent performance. By leveraging the newest technologies and configuring the systems correctly, we can drive high consolidation ratios. Hosts are getting larger and larger. We are coming across ESXi hosts with terabytes of memory. Providing consistent performance requires a focus beyond the host itself. You need to cater to the needs of daily operations and possible disaster avoidance activities to retain the necessary service levels.

DRS load balancing, maintenance mode, and other daily operations require ample bandwidth when using these large systems to their full potential. Rapid host eviction is crucial for disaster avoidance, and should not be ignored when calculating the bandwidth requirements. Multi-NIC vMotions allows the ESXi host to consume multiple uplinks to cater the bandwidth requirements of these activities.

Increased consolidation ratios and VM sizing require sufficient bandwidth for host eviction.

A valid question is whether multi-NIC vMotion is still necessary with the introduction of higher bandwidth pNICs (25/40GbE and higher). What is the bottleneck for the maximum number of vMotion operations per host?

When reviewing the ESXi 6.5 documentation, there is still a restriction of four concurrent vMotion operations per host when using 1GbE interfaces in your vMotion enabled network. Eight concurrent vMotion operations are possible when using 10GbE interfaces.

Designing your vMotion Network

Even though the limits are not yet raised to suit higher bandwidths, there are other measures you can take to accelerate host eviction. A well-designed vMotion network will be beneficial for achieving this in the shortest time possible. Before ESXi 5.x, designing a vMotion network was relative straightforward, select the fastest NIC and assign it to a vMotion vmknic. Multi-NIC introduces some configuration challenges. The combination of NICs, failover mode and load balancing policy need to be taken into consideration when configuring your vMotion network.

vMotion balances the vMotion operations across all available NICs. For a single vMotion operation as well as multiple concurrent vMotion operations. By using multiple NICs it reduces the duration of a vMotion operation and host eviction, but it also benefits the following activities:

Manual vMotion processes: Allocating more bandwidth to the vMotion process will result in faster migration times. The less time spend on monitoring a manual process means more time you can spend on other, more important, operations.

DRS load balancing: Based on the average time per migration and the number of concurrent vMotion process, DRS restrict the number of load balancing operations it can process between two load balancing runs. By providing more bandwidth to the vMotion network, DRS is able to run more load balancing operations in between runs, which in turn benefits the resource distribution within the cluster. Better resource distribution means better resource availability for the VMs, which in turn means better performance for your applications.

Maintenance mode: Faster migration times, means reducing the time a host enters maintenance mode. With the increase of consolidation ratio, the time it takes to migrate all the VMs off the host is increased as well. This can have impact on your SLA and the ability to service the host within the allowed maintenance time window.

Multi-NIC setup

The vMotion process leverages the vmknic instead of sending packets directly to a physical NIC. To use multiple NICs for vMotion, multiple vmknics are required. Review *VMware KB article 2007467* for an up-to-date instruction on how to configure a multi-NIC vMotion network.

Failover Order and Load Balancing policy

Each vmknic should only use one active pNIC, this results in only one valid load balancing policy and that is 'Route based on originating virtual port'. This setup inhibits physical NIC load balancing such as IP hash or the LBT load balancing policy. The reason why the active/standby failover order is the only valid and supported configuration is because of the way vMotion load balancing works. The vMotion process itself handles load balancing, based on its own algorithm, vMotion picks a vmknic for a specific network packet. As vMotion expects the vmknic to be backed by a single physical NIC, sending out data through a given vmknic ensures vMotion that the data traverses that dedicated physical NIC. If the pNICs were configured in a load-balancing mode, this could interfere with the vMotion level load balancing logic. vMotion would not be able to predict which physical NIC is used by the vmknic and possible sending all vMotion traffic over the same NIC, even if Motion sends the data to different vmknics.

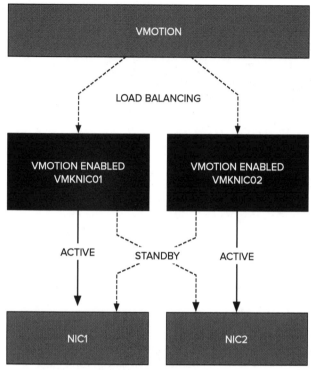

Figure 310: Multi-NIC vMotion Overview

Ensure that each pNIC is configured in a consistent and correct way across the vMotion network within the host and across all the hosts inside the cluster. VMware vCenter is very conservative and if it detects a mismatch it drops the number of concurrent vMotion operations on that host back to two regardless of the available bandwidth. Therefore, always check on each level if the link speed, MTU and duplex settings are identical, both on the pNIC side as well as the physical switch side.

As stated before, vCenter allows four concurrent vMotion operations on a host with a 1GbE vMotion network and eight concurrent vMotion operations on a host with a 10GbE vMotion network by default. Be aware that this is based on the detected link-speed. In other words, if the pNIC needs to report at least a 10GbE link speed to have vCenter allow eight vMotion operations.

If the pNIC reports less than 10GbE, vCenter allows a maximum of four concurrent vMotion operations on that host. To stress it again, the number of concurrent vMotions is based on the detected link speed.

For example, some converged network adapters allow setting a hard limit on the link speed. This results in a reported link speed of less than 10 GbE. We have seen many environments where the CNA were configured to provide between 2 to 8 GbE to the vMotion network. Although they will offer more bandwidth than 1 GbE per vMotion process, it will not result in in an increase in the number of concurrent vMotions, limiting the number of concurrent vMotion operations to four.

To emphasize, vCenter is very conservative; multi-NIC vMotion limits are currently determined by the slowest available vMotion NIC. This means that if you include a 1GbE NIC in your 10GbE vMotion network configuration, that host is restricted to maximum of four concurrent vMotion operations per host. Our advice is to never mix NIC speeds in your vMotion network.

23

DISTRIBUTED STORAGE NETWORK

Again, this may not fall directly under a host resource but is important enough to mention in our opinion. Without going into too much detail, we want to accentuate the need to follow the scalable distributed storage model when it comes to designing your Ethernet storage network.

To be honest, it is probably the other way around. The networking experts in this world introduced scalable network architectures while maintaining consistent and predictable latency for a long time now. The storage world is just catching up. Nowadays, we have the ability to create scalable distributed storage infrastructures, following HCI innovations. Because the storage layer is distributed across ESXi hosts, a lot of point-to-point connections between ESXi hosts will be utilized for storage I/O's.

Typically, when a distributed storage solution (like VMware vSAN) is adopted, we tend to create a pretty basic layer-2 network. Preferably using 10GbE or more, line-rate capable components in a non-blocking network architecture with enough ports to support our current hosts. But once we scale to an extensive number of ESXi hosts and clusters, we require more network interfaces to connect to our ESXi hosts. That is where the so-called spine and leaf network architecture comes into play.

Each leaf switch in a spine-leaf network architecture connects to every spine switch in the fabric. Using this method, the connection between two ESXi hosts will always traverse the same number of hops. Except for when the hosts are connected to the same leaf.

This methodology provides a predicable latency, thus consistent performance, while scaling your virtual datacenter. It is the consistency in performance that makes the spine/leaf network architecture so suitable for distributed storage solutions.

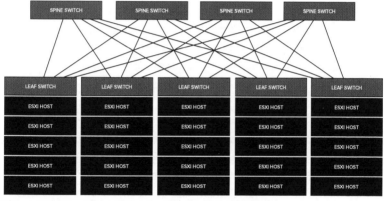

Figure 311: Exemplary Spine-Leaf Network Architecture

A spine-leaf topology can be a layer-2 or layer-3 network. The key is, when it is designed as a layer-2 network, to create a loop-free fabric. Also, you might want to consider bandwidth requirements. When using vSAN, the bandwidth utilization between the ESXi hosts depend strongly on the fault tolerance methods as defined in the VM Storage Policies and the configured fault domains. Depending on these factors, data is written and/or read from a certain number of ESXi hosts.

It can be a challenging exercise to predict bandwidth utilization between ESXi hosts when using a distributed storage platform. That is why it could be a good idea to thoroughly think about your VM storage policy designs together with the storage I/O characteristics of your workloads

Network architectures like spine/leaf networks are not fixed to distributed storage related services. Thinking about it, it is pretty much a perfect fit for every distributed service solution out there. Think about the distributed network services as provided by VMware NSX!

Make sure that when you are in the process of designing a scalable datacenter using distributed services, to design your network accordingly. It could make sense to introduce a spine/leaf network from starters if you anticipate substantial future growth for your virtual datacenter.

REFERENCES

P1: CPU Resources

C.A. Waldspurger, W.E. Weihl (1995). **Stride Scheduling: Deterministic Proportional-Share Resource Management.**

J.R. Goodman and H.H.J. HUM (2009). **MESIF A Two-Hop Cache Coherency Protocol for Point-to-Point Interconnects.**

M. Bhandaru and E. Dehaemer (2013). **Providing energy efficient turbo operation of a processor.** Patent App. PCT/US2012/028,865.

D. Molka, D. Hackenberg, R. Schöne and M.S. Müller (2009). **Memory Performance and Cache Coherency Effects on an Intel Nehalem Multiprocessor System.**

R. Schöne, D. Molka, M. Werner (2014). **Wake-up Latencies for Processor Idle States on Current x86 Processors.**

A.B. Skrenes (2016). **Experimental Evaluation of Speed Scaling Systems.**

R. Karedla (2014). **Intel Xeon E5-2600 v3 (Haswell) Architecture & Features.**

Q. Ali (2013). **Host Power Management in VMware vSphere 5.5.**

S. Kim (2016). **VMworld 2016 USA INF8089 Extreme Performance Series vSphere Compute and Memory.**

Intel (2012). **Intel Xeon Processor E5-2600 Product Family Uncore. Performance Monitoring.** Reference Number: 327043-001.

Intel (2014). **Optimizing Performance with Intel Advanced Vector Extensions.**

Intel (2016). **Intel® 64 and IA-32 Architectures Optimization Reference**

Manual. Order Number: 248966-033.

VMware KB Article 1017926 (2016). **Troubleshooting a virtual machine that has stopped responding: VMM and Guest CPU usage comparison**.

ACPI (2016). **Advanced Configuration and Power Interface Specification Version 6.1**.

P2: Memory Resources

VMware (2016). **Configuration Maximum vSphere 6.5** (EN-002346-01).

D. Lee, Y. Kim, V. Seshadri, J. Liu, L. Subramanian, O. Mutlu (2013). **Tiered-Latency DRAM: A Low Latency and Low Cost DRAM Architecture**.

U. Drepper (2007). **What Every Programmer Should Know About Memory**.

R. M. Kadri, S. F. Contreras (2012) **Method and system for reducing trace length and capacitance in a large memory footprint background**. Patent App. PCT/US2009/040997.

D. Malech (2014). **DDR4 LRDIMMs Unprecedented Memory Bandwidth on Samsung DDR4 LRDIMM Enabled by IDT's Register and Data Buffer**.

B. Jacob, D. Wang (2002). **DRAM: Architectures, Interfaces, and Systems**.

B. Schroeder, E. Pinheiro, W. Weber (2009). **DRAM Errors in the Wild: A Large-Scale Field Study**.

I. Bhati, M. Chang, Z. Chishti, S. Lu, B. Jacob (2016). **DRAM Refresh Mechanisms, Penalties, and Trade-Offs**.

Y. Kim, R. Daly, J. Kim, C. Fallin, J. Lee, D. Lee, C. Wilkerson, K. Lai, O. Mutlu1 (2014). **Flipping Bits in Memory Without Accessing Them: An Experimental Study of DRAM Disturbance Errors**.

Inhpi (2011). **Introducing LRDIMM – A New Class of Memory Modules**.

Dell (2012). **Memory Performance Guidelines for Dell PowerEdge 12th Generation Servers**.

Jedec (2014). **DDR4 SDRAM Registered DIMM Design Specification**. Rev 1.00.

JS Choi (2014). **Next Big Thing: DDR4 3DS**.

Jedec (2015). **DDR4 SDRAM UDIMM Design Specification**. Rev 1.10.

HPE (2015). **Overview of DDR4 memory in HPE ProLiant Gen9 Servers with Intel Xeon E5-2600 v3**.

Cisco (2017). **Cisco UCS B200 M4 Blade Server Spec Sheet**. Rev D.16

K. Adams, O. Agesen (2006). **A comparison of software and hardware techniques for x86 virtualization**.

S. Inabattini, A. Jagadeeshwaran (2017). **DRS Cluster Management with Reservation and Shares**.

C.A. Waldspurger (2002). **Memory Resource Management in VMware ESX Server**.

G. Irazoqui, M. Sinan Inci, T. Eisenbarth, B. Sunar (2014). **Wait a minute! A fast, Cross-VM attack on AES**.

T.Sneath (2010). **PDC10: Mysteries of Windows Memory Management Revealed: Part Two**.

VMware (2011). **Enterprise Java Applications on VMware Best Practices Guide.**

VMware (2008). **Performance Evaluation of Intel EPT Hardware Assist**

A. Mashtizadeh, Irfan Ahmad (2013). **Memory compression policies US 8484405 B**

P3: Storage Resources

Micron, (2006). **TN-29-19: NAND Flash 101 Introduction**

Intel, (2017). **Product Brief: Intel® Optane™ SSD DC P4800X Series**

HP, (2016). **HPE 8GB NVDIMM User Guide for HPE ProLiant Gen9 Servers**

VMware, (2015). **An overview of VMware Virtual SAN caching algorithms**

Cormac Hogan, (2015). **VMware Virtual SAN Diagnostics and Troubleshooting Reference Manual** (v.1.0)

VMware, (2016). **Configurations Maximums vSphere 6.5** (EN-002346-02)

Christos Karamanolis, (2016). **The Use of Erasure Coding in VMware Virtual SAN 6.2**

Intel, (2012). **Intel® Advanced Encryption Standard (AES) New Instructions Set**.

P4: Network Resources

VMware (2017). **VMware vSphere 6.5 Documentation Center**

VMware (2016). **Configuration Maximum vSphere 6.5** (EN-002346-01).

J. Heo, L. Singaravelu (2013). **Deploying Extremely Latency-Sensitive Applications in vSphere 5.5**.

VMware (2015). **Best Practices for Performance Tuning of Telco and NFV Workloads in vSphere**.

VMware (2013). **Best Practices for Performance Tuning of Latency-Sensitive Workloads in vSphere VMs** (EN-001169-02)

VMware (2011). **Network I/O Latency on VMware vSphere 5** (EN-000786-00).

VMware KB Article 1001805 (2015). **Choosing a network adapter for your virtual machine.**

J. Nicholson (2016). **VMware Virtual SAN 6.2 Network Design Guide.**

VMware KB Article 2055140 (2016). **Understanding TCP Segmentation Offload (TSO) and Large Receive Offload (LRO) in a VMware environment.**

Intel *(2016)*. **Advanced Settings for Intel Ethernet Adapters** (000005593).

Intel *(2017)*. **Tuning Throughput Performance for Intel Ethernet Adapters** (000005811).

R. Mehta (2015). **Leveraging NIC Technology to Improve Network Performance in VMware vSphere** (EN-001694-00).

Intel (2008). **VMDq Technology Overview.**

H. Ohara (2012). **X86 hardware for packet processing.**

B. Davie, T. Sridhar (2014). **Geneve, VXLAN, and Network Virtualization Encapsulations.**

W. Lam (2013). **ESXi 5.5 introduces a new Native Device Driver Architecture.**

D. Haryachyy (2015). **Understanding DPDK.**

Intel (2012). **PCI-SIG SR-IOV Primer.**

B. Davda, A. Ranadive (2012). **Toward a Paravirtual vRDMA Device for VMware ESXi Guests.**

INDEX

M

N

P

Q

R

Made in the USA
Lexington, KY
06 August 2018